Eternal Sovereigns

Eternal Sovereigns

INDIGENOUS ARTISTS, ACTIVISTS, AND TRAVELERS REFRAMING ROME

Gloria Jane Bell

Duke University Press · *Durham and London* · 2024

Printed in the United States of America on acid-free paper ∞
Project Editor: Livia Tenzer
Designed by Courtney Leigh Richardson
Typeset in Garamond Premier Pro by Westchester Publishing Services

Library of Congress Cataloging-in-Publication Data
Names: Bell, Gloria Jane, [date] author.
Title: Eternal sovereigns : Indigenous artists, activists, and travelers reframing Rome / Gloria Jane Bell.
Description: Durham : Duke University Press, 2024. | Includes bibliographical references and index.
Identifiers: LCCN 2023056173 (print)
LCCN 2023056174 (ebook)
ISBN 9781478030881 (paperback)
ISBN 9781478026617 (hardcover)
ISBN 9781478059844 (ebook)
Subjects: LCSH: Catholic Church—Missions—North America. | Esposizione missionaria vaticana (1924–1927 : Vatican City) | Indians of North America—Material culture. | Indian art—North America. | Museums—Acquisitions—Moral and ethical aspects. | Museums and Indigenous peoples. | Ethnological museums and collections—Vatican City. | Colonization—Religious aspects—Catholic Church.
Classification: LCC E98.M34 B45 2024 (print) | LCC E98.M34 (ebook) | DDC 708.008997—dc23/eng/20240412
LC record available at https://lccn.loc.gov/2023056173
LC ebook record available at https://lccn.loc.gov/2023056174

Cover art: Lakota Sioux, Sun Dance drawing, ca. 1875. Pigments on muslin, 83 × 138 cm. Ethnological Museum *Anima Mundi*, Vatican Museums, inv. no. 107323.

For my family in the now and hereafter

Contents

Illustrations

Figures

Plates

Acknowledgments

I have been lucky to travel to many places and meet many interesting people to complete this book. The research never ends! In 2022 I completed a Terra Foundation for American Art fellowship at the American Academy in Rome, conducting research and documentation for the book. During the process of writing and research, many librarians and archivists have shared information with me. In Rome, the Propaganda Fide Library was a great help and resource. The Jesuit Archives, Archivum Generale OMI Romae, and the Capuchin Archive also shared documents. The Vatican Apostolic Library and Vatican Secret Archive also provided access and research support.

Anthropologists, conservators, art historians, archivists, and artists have provided interesting stories along the way. In Italy, *grazie mille* to Christine, Anna, Elisabetta, Emanuela, and Jennifer for their moral support. The book would not have been complete without a viewing of Gian Lorenzo Bernini's *Ecstasy of Saint Teresa* and seemingly almost divine intervention. Friends at the American Academy in Rome provided coffee and encouragement at the right moments. *Cappelletti*, good conversations, and good wine, discussing art, museum practices, and the eternal wonder of Rome kept me going. In North America, thank you to Silver, Mae, and my mom, Jane.

In Chicago, I spent time at the Newberry Library as a Frances C. Allen fellow, studying the sketchbooks of Ferdinand Pettrich. Yale Divinity Library and Archive holds an important collection of Italian children's games. The Mill Hill Missionaries Archive in Liverpool, England, shared with me an important set of photographs of the exhibition. I have traveled also to London to conduct archival work: thank you to the staff at the British Film Institute. Social Sciences and Humanities Research Council of Canada (SSHRC) and a FRQSC (Fonds québecois de la recherche sur la sociéte et la culture) New Researchers Award supported my archival research in Italy, the United States, and Canada. During my doctoral studies, the Vanier Canada Graduate Scholarship program, the Joseph-Armand Bombardier Canada Graduate Scholarship (CGS), and the Cordula and Gunter Paetzold Fellowship at the University of British Columbia provided support. I completed a summer fellowship at the Terra Foundation for American Art in Giverny that was also an important moment to think through the work of Edmonia Lewis and the significance of world's fairs in the early twentieth century. Thank you to Ken and the editorial team at Duke University Press for their support in the production of the book.

Introduction

A NOMAD IN THE ROMAN ARCHIVES

Writing from the Margins

Journal: First Encounter with the Vatican Museums

APRIL 2016. *The sky gleamed a bright robin's-egg blue, and I felt excited, nervous, and jet-lagged as I headed toward the Vatican Museums. After months of preparing for this trip, I had finally arrived in Rome for my research. The city's mix of Renaissance and Baroque buildings casts long shadows. I perceived a different sense of space here, a more intimate impression of scale that I hadn't felt before in other cities. Walking by Gian Lorenzo Bernini's colonnade and the opulence of Saint Peter's on my way to Vatican City, I was filled with an overwhelming sense of excitement, as if I was floating through Rome.*

The Vatican Museums, with their thick stone walls and the entryway lined with security guards and their larger-than-life metal detectors, were an imposing, austere space to enter. I waited in a long line to be admitted to the museum collections. I walked up a ramp that curled around like a snake, while most visitors took the elevators. Halfway up the ramp, I found myself on the Cortile delle Corazze, standing in front of a small display that reminded me of a natural history museum (figure I.1). *Miniature models of canoes from the Americas and across the globe were on exhibit and, according to the wall text, intended to show the "respect of the Catholic universe toward non-European cultures." They were the very canoes that had been sent in for the Vatican Missionary Exposition of 1925, and they continued a strange afterlife here, in an out-of-the-way entry point, and also on display below in the basement as part of the Vatican Missionary Ethnological Museum. These belongings, literally and symbolically ostracized from the other collections, reinforced the patronizing perspective of pope Pius XI, who demanded Indigenous artworks from across the globe be sent in for the 1925 exposition to glorify missionaries as heroes.*[1] *Beside the vitrines were blown-up black-and-white photographs of unnamed Indigenous peoples, placed there without any contextual information, erasing any sense of their identities or the specificities of their cultures. The display reminded me of exhibitions of First Nations art in other European and North American museums, such as the Musée du Quai Branly in Paris, where the curatorial emphasis was placed on the "premodern and primitive" nature of Indigenous peoples; there was no acknowledgment of their modernity.*[2] *I was shocked that the Vatican Museums were repeating the same display strategy and colonial language of possession and propaganda the curators had used in the exposition's Halls of the Americas almost a century earlier. For me, however, the canoes were also a reminder of the multiple innovative technologies Indigenous peoples use for transport and the many ways that Indigenous peoples move across time and space.*

After photographing the collection of miniature canoes, I went to the Missionary Ethnological Museum, which the Vatican has situated in the basement beside the exits, restaurant, and bathrooms, and beneath the Pinacoteca. The Pinacoteca houses masterpieces of Italian art and is given a very prominent location in the Vatican Museums. The position of First Peoples art, situated directly below the Pinacoteca in a dark and out-of-the-way location, evoking the problematic hierarchies of art, is not a coincidence in my mind. I walked down the stairs into the basement. A rush of visitors hustled by as I peered through the glass. Although I had been denied curatorial access to the Vatican Missionary Ethnological Museum, I went to see what I could see regardless. Through the clear glass I could make out German artist Ferdinand Pettrich's busts and full-length figures in the center of the room (figure I.2). *I thought to myself how little had changed; in photographs from 1925, Pettrich's sculptures also stood front and center in the Hall of North America, while the reviewers ignored the Indigenous cultural belongings*

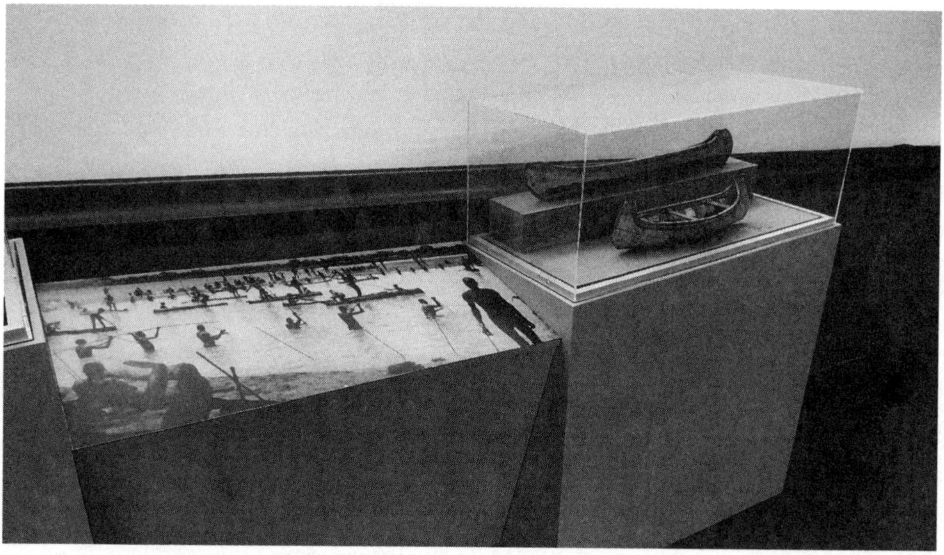

FIGURE I.1. Installation of miniature canoes from Turtle Island at the entrance of the Vatican Museums, Vatican City, May 2023. Photograph by the author.

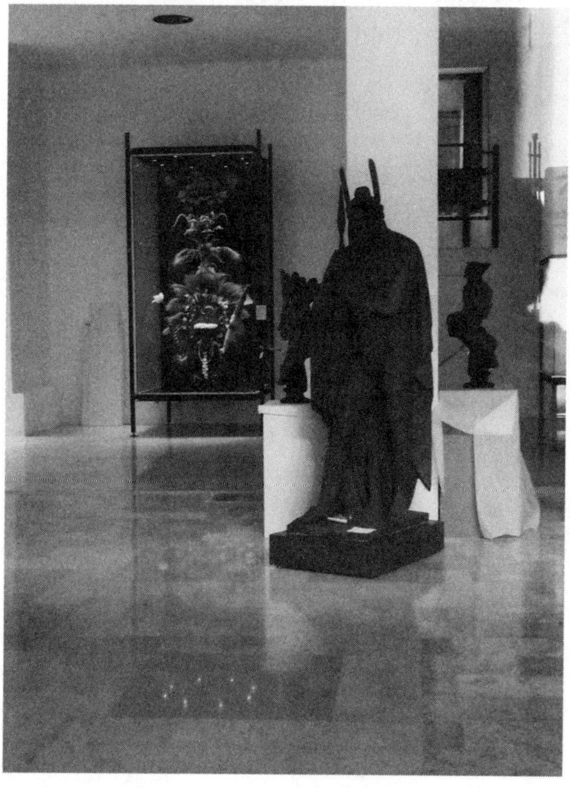

FIGURE I.2. Installation view, sculptures by Ferdinand Pettrich, Vatican Missionary Ethnological Museum, Vatican Museums, Vatican City, April 2016. Photograph by the author.

around them. The curatorial texts in the exhibition described the materials as "gifts" given to pope Pius XI, thus repeating the same colonial and missionary language of possession and ownership that denied the cultural belongings as signifiers of Indigenous peoples' cultural and intellectual sovereignty. The term "gift" also incorrectly denoted that they were freely given. I kept looking, and I saw pottery and other cultural belongings from across Turtle Island. The pottery appeared to be from the Acoma Pueblo, an Indigenous community of the Southwest.

Peering at the display through the glass and at the museum texts, I thought about the irony of it all. How could so little have changed in terms of curatorial methods in the twenty-first century? Feelings of annoyance and anger and dread rushed through me at the patronizing tone presented by the museum texts and display methods. I wanted to throw a rock into the glass cases and shatter the exhibition. I took note of my reaction and continued walking.

The Vatican Missionary Exposition

On Sunday, December 21, 1924, pope Pius XI solemnly ascended the Vatican staircase and opened the holy door to the Vatican Missionary Exposition (VME). Standing in one of the exhibition's central rooms, the Hall of North America, surrounded by stolen sacred and secular cultural belongings of the Indigenous peoples of North America, he welcomed tourists and pilgrims alike into the Vatican.[3] Pius XI proclaimed 1925 to be a "holy year," a church jubilee. The commemorative card shown in plate 1 emphasizes the year as a sacred event, and the VME was central to the celebrations. This unprecedented exhibition was held on the grounds of the Vatican, with specially designed pavilions showcasing the art and artifacts from missions across the continents, including the Americas, Asia, Oceania, and Africa. Pius XI declared that the materials sent in from afar shone light in the darkness to highlight missionary work. Upon the exposition's closing, he further professed that the objects displayed had a "silent eloquence."[4] By using these words he meant the objects functioned as hushed markers of missionary progress, rendering the Indigenous makers and their belongings as voiceless in a paternalistic and romanticizing framework that continues to this day in the exhibition spaces of the Vatican Museums (Musei Vaticani). This phrase also informs what I call "pope culture," an ethos of conquest and plunder that harkens back to the exploitation of Indigenous peoples since the Renaissance. After Pius XI closed the VME, he established the Missionary Ethnological Museum in 1926. In 2019 the Missionary Ethnological Museum changed its name to the Ethnological Museum *Anima Mundi*, a collection that imprisons more than ten thousand Indigenous American belongings.

In contrast to these colonial and missionary views, this book argues that the Indigenous materials displayed at the VME are cultural belongings and travelers that were sent to Rome but never returned home. By focusing on material culture, this project centers the ongoing importance of artworks for Indigenous communities and offers a multitude of new ways of thinking through Indigenous experiences during the period of the VME, as well as considering Indigenous artists and artistry in Rome in the late nineteenth and early twentieth centuries. In this book, I focus on Indigenous American artists and artworks and draw inspiration from the art and activism of Indigenous artists globally. A key aim of this study, which analyzes many archives and artists across Italy and Turtle Island (Canada and the United States), is to upset and unsettle the discourse of complacent Vatican missionary institutions.

Drawing inspiration from the broader methodological shift in the humanities on the part of scholars of Indigenous and settler descent toward telling stories that center Indigenous artists and artworks, this study rethinks art history and visual culture to destabilize the language and legacies of settler colonialism and emphasize Indigenous ways.[5] As an Indigenous scholar of Métis heritage, I have woven sketches of my personal experience into my archival research and theoretically inflected textual analysis. Presenting my journaling, correspondence, and photography creates a personal, embodied narrative that contrasts with the many sterile and colonial archival environments I have worked in across Italy, the United States, and Canada. My journal entries tilt the hierarchy of value that exists within the European and American archival structures and modes of history writing I have encountered, and thus diminish the understanding of archival documents as privileged forms of acceptable, dominant knowledge. By including my personal experience as part of the scholarly analysis, the work questions and expands what counts as art history.

Eternal Sovereigns focuses on the art histories of Indigenous activists, artists, missionaries, and travelers as well as cultural belongings that have engaged with Rome and the Vatican from 1830 to the present day. By concentrating on the Halls of the Americas at the VME and focusing on Indigenous experiences and histories in Canada and the United States, this project is the first to take up the history of Indigeneity as presented in exhibitions at the Vatican and in Rome.[6] To this day, the recognition of Indigenous presences at the Vatican remains largely unacknowledged, a situation that perpetuates the settler-colonial myth that Indigenous people have disappeared and furthers the structural violence of Catholicism. *Eternal Sovereigns* will change the conversation by bringing to light what has been deleted, ignored, and silenced to create a new story about Indigeneity and art at the Vatican. Pius XI celebrated the VME during what was also one of the most aggressive assimilative periods of the Indian Act in Canada (1876 to present). Thus, unpacking the VME allows us to expand our knowledge of collecting histories, analyze global exhibitions of art in the colonial era, consider ethical concerns around consent and stolen Indigenous cultural belongings, and come to a moment of reckoning with the legacy of residential schools. Whereas previous scholars have focused on the Catholic theological and anthropological aspects of the VME, this study centers and adds nuance to Indigenous American visual culture and insists on recognizing the multiple ways Indigenous and papal visual culture interact and are part of unfolding power displays.[7]

The book's title, *Eternal Sovereigns*, asserts that Indigenous nations retained, and continue to maintain, sovereignty over their representations—on their own terms—despite the impact of forced Catholic colonization as well as the obfuscating forces of the western canon of art history. Sovereignty is a term that references the reclamation of Indigenous power and agency across time, space, and scholarly disciplines.[8] In this context, I use it to reclaim, restore, and re-story Indigenous visual and material culture. The book also examines the competing sovereignties of settler, Indigenous, and papal visual culture. Through an analysis of a variety of images and objects—such as the statuary of Native American delegations; artworks including beaded moccasins, drawings, and sculptures by Native American artists; and children's games made by missionaries and missionary accounts—this book examines the mobility and global reception of Indigenous artists and artworks in Rome at a time when ethnography and Indigenous art were burgeoning in the global imagination and Rome was being transformed into a modern city. Art historian Hal Foster's ideas about archives remind me that projects like mine can be "retrieved in a gesture of alternative knowledge or countermemory."[9] Such a study is of great importance today, as the Vatican has yet to return these belongings to the people from whom they were stolen.

The Halls of the Americas section of the VME, the primary focus of this study, held over four thousand objects, including photographs, sculptures, textiles, and wax mannequin displays, organized by the anthropologist and Verbite priest Wilhelm Schmidt. Drawing on archival evidence, Indigenous methodologies of storytelling, and art historical analysis, I re-story the Halls of the Americas to reclaim and reanimate Indigenous visual culture that was displayed and remained in Pius XI's collection afterward. The book focuses on Indigenous peoples of Canada and the United States whose cultural belongings were featured at the VME, and it critically analyzes representations of Indigenous peoples in sculpture, drawing, and photography in the VME's illustrated journal, the *Rivista Illustrata della Esposizione Missionaria Vaticana* (Illustrated magazine of the Vatican Missionary Exposition).

Combining the tools of visual analysis from art history with interdisciplinary storytelling strategies, *Eternal Sovereigns* creates a research methodology that reframes Rome and develops new insights into global art exhibitions, international networks of Indigenous arts, and archival theories and methods. The title also suggests the holistic spiritual relationships that Indigenous artists had in the process of creating artworks displayed at the exhibition, and the nonlinear relationship between Indigenous souls and Indigenous travelers rather than the linear Christian one espoused at the VME and throughout the Vatican spaces today. The title also evokes the spirit and the everyday in which every Indigenous soul matters. This research works against the traumatic legacy of missionary labors at residential schools and throughout Indigenous communities across Turtle Island. Catholic missionaries operated the majority of residential schools and subjected Indigenous children to mental, physical, and spiritual abuse in an attempt to assimilate them into Canadian society. Over one hundred and fifty thousand First Nations, Métis, and Inuit children attended these horrific institutions and died as a result of these residential schools, and the trauma for survivors and their families continues.[10]

Terminology and Inspiration: *Indigenous*, *Indigeneity*, and *Worldbuilding*

By using the term *Indigenous* as an Indigenous scholar, I connect my initiative with the broader political project of affirming rights for Indigenous peoples and with the goal of recognition for Indigenous studies worldwide. Within the Canadian context, *Indigenous* includes the First Nations, Métis, and Inuit, and within the United States, it is a reference to Native Americans. Whenever possible, I refer to an artist's particular community and name the Indigenous individual, to push back against the legacy of colonialism and lack of naming that occurred at the VME. Missionaries did not record the names of Indigenous artists, nor were their belongings considered art in the majority of the VME record. The haphazard way in which no names were recorded gives a sense of the colonial fury and greed of pope Pius XI's coercive practices and his looting of sacred treasures from communities. Indigenous peoples' names did not matter, as if they were subhuman and without rights in the brutish collecting practices of papal greed. Today this dynamic of not naming continues in the Ethnological Museum *Anima Mundi* in a reiteration of the salvage paradigm and a reminder of the belongings as stolen treasures. The practice of naming more broadly in art history and the humanities is an ongoing research challenge since the archives often fail to acknowledge Indigenous and Black artists due to colonial methods of recordkeeping.

This book challenges several colonial assumptions prevalent in art historical literature on First Nations, Métis, Inuit, and Native Americans. For example, it exposes the false notion that Indigenous peoples and their cultural belongings had disappeared by the early twentieth century and that Indigenous people only lived outside modern metropolitan cultures and certainly not in Europe. This study contributes to the larger scholarship that examines the global mobility of Indigenous travelers and their belongings during the late nineteenth and early twentieth centuries by considering their agency, artistry, and audacity. By *audacity* I mean the perseverance of Indigenous artists to create artworks and live their lives under multiple forms of colonial duress.[11] This interdisciplinary method seeps into the archival cracks and contributes to archival studies, art history, and material culture studies, creating what I call "ancestral art history lessons." I hope the stories and images contribute to understanding Indigeneity, Rome, and the Vatican in new, entangled, and unsettling relationships with one another. Studying the artistry and audacity of Indigenous artists in tension with missionary ephemera and accounts through the lens of the VME offers insights into Rome's transformation into a modern city—one that is reliant on Indigenous arts and artists and permeated by the ongoing fraught dynamics of truth and reconciliation.[12]

Eternal Sovereigns builds on transnational Indigenous scholarship that emphasizes the mobility of Indigenous peoples and frames Indigenous arts within a global context. I align my thinking with Native scholars and activists such as Haida/Tsimshian art historian Marcia Crosby, who reminds us of the "Imaginary Indian" and the ways that settler-colonial identities have used Native representations as foils and projections for settler-colonial myths.[13] However, I am more interested in how Indigenous people have played active roles in shaping their own lives. As Gwichya Gwich'in scholar Crystal Fraser and Métis scholar Zoe Todd note, "If Indigenous people are present in historical records, they are often depicted as passive bystanders, rarely free agents in their own right and far removed from narratives that highlight agency or sophistication."[14] Building on Fraser and Todd's observation, *Eternal Sover-*

eigns emphasizes the entangled nature of Indigenous cultural belongings and the Catholic colonial archival record in the Eternal City, as Rome has long been called. My theoretical approach draws inspiration from thinkers such as Turtle Mountain Chippewa scholar Danika Medak-Saltzman, Anishinaabe literary scholar Gerald Vizenor, Apache curator and anthropologist Nancy Mithlo, Sioux historian Phillip Deloria, and Ho-Chunk museum scholar and historian Amy Lonetree, all of whom center their own experiences as Indigenous people working through complex colonial relations in the Americas.[15] Anthropologist Ann Laura Stoler's articulation of archives as spaces of incomplete and fraught dynamics of colonial power provides a useful point of orientation for the archival element of the research, which goes "against the grain."[16] Considering archives as repositories not only of colonial power, this book renders them as spaces that evidence the ways that Indigenous arts and peoples have influenced and intersected with colonizers on a global stage as actors and agents. It is a form of worldbuilding.

Journal: The Vatican Apostolic Library, Vatican City

DECEMBER 2016. *Pope Sixtus IV della Rovere founded the Vatican Apostolic Library in 1475. He initially donated pope Nicolas V's collection of 824 Latin manuscripts.*[17] *Since then, the papal collections have grown substantially. Yesterday, with a bit of trepidation in my chest, I walked toward the Vatican and Saint Peter's down the large avenue cleared by Mussolini during the rebuilding of Rome in the 1930s* (plate 2). *The Maltese crèche was up, and the sun was a burnt red, looming over Saint Peter's and the Castel Sant'Angelo. As I was walking out the door, I said a prayer to the divine to help me with my research and to stay calm. I had an anxious feeling, not overwhelming but there, and one that I had come to associate with the entire Vatican City, but perhaps it was more appropriately suited to just my experience dealing with the Vatican Museums. It was warm out despite it being December. I walked through the main square at Saint Peter's. There were a few armed police officers in black uniforms and some tourists taking photos with selfie sticks. I continued to Porta Sant'Anna, and just at that moment Beyoncé's "Halo" came on in my headphones, tuned to Italian radio, and I wondered about the song about halos and heroes there in Vatican City, a city steeped in Christian and Roman iconography. I had a foreboding sense in the back of my mind because, in talking with several archivists in Rome, I had been warned that the people at the Vatican can be quite nasty and not to expect much. Extreme bureaucracy. It was very quiet and calm as I passed by a Swiss Guard at the entrance to Vatican*

City. He smiled and directed me to the Vatican passport office, where I dropped off my Canadian passport and proceeded about one hundred meters straight ahead, then under a curved arch and past another guard. I flashed my Vatican Secret Archive library card and took a right, then entered the first door, where the Vatican Library secretary worked. After waiting for fifteen minutes, I was summoned into the secretary's private office. A little crèche with an angel holding the word "Gloria" watched me as I filled out my information in block letters on a green paper to attain access to the archives.

I wondered about the appropriateness as well as the fatalistic aspect of my research. Could my work make a difference with all the patriarchal customs and bureaucratic measures in Vatican City and across Rome that I had encountered and continued to work through?

The secretary welcomed me with a microchip card and told me it was for life, all in quick Italian. She explained that I needed to sign in electronically every time I entered and exited the library, and that the microchip card was also needed to open and close the cloakroom. She then handed me a stack of papers about library expectations to read through. I saw a monk in a white robe with a few lines on his face and a twirled mustache. "Arrivederci," the porter said as I exited back into the courtyard. The space was massive and imposing as the walls of the museum encircled me. I looked ahead of me and noticed the square windows far above on the opposite wall. They were set back into the wall like a garrison, a reminder of the Vatican as a space of violence in its missionary and colonial endeavors. Several floors below, the Vatican Missionary Ethnological Museum holding Indigenous cultural belongings from around the globe waited for me.

On Secrecy, Whispers, and Missing Documents: Theorizing the Gaps in Colonial Archives

When I first set out to do this research, I was not sure what I would find in the archives, although I imagined I might uncover missionary bulletins, including accounts written by missionaries about their experiences of fieldwork with Indigenous communities and their lives more broadly. I have looked through archives across Rome, including the Propaganda Fide Library and Archive, Societas Verbi Divini Archive, Archivum Romanum Societatis Iesu, Archivum Generale OMI Romae, Vatican Apostolic Library, Vatican Secret Archive, and the Vatican Fototeca Archive. I have also consulted the Oblate archives and Jesuit archives in Canada and made inquiries to archives in the United States, England, Ireland, and Mexico. I have perused the Edward E.

Ayer Special Collections of the Newberry Library in Chicago and the Yale Divinity Library Special Collections. The archives, collections, and materials I have consulted are representative of Catholic missionary history and more broadly of the western colonial archive. Even after conducting research for this book in Italy and Turtle Island for more than eight years, including secret meetings with archivists and curators, the process remains difficult—it is like a time warp in that it can go on without end if one lets it. The archives contain numerous objects, including photographs of the VME, a plethora of missionary bulletins from various religious orders, official papal decrees on the material to be sent in, and the *Rivista Illustrata*. These materials, although numerous, represent only one side of the story. They do not tell an Indigenous-focused narrative or include key Indigenous histories. The colonial and uneven nature of the documents in the archive provides a jumping off point, though. The stories I am telling are part of a creation of Indigenous art histories, of using fragmented evidence to establish new ways of understanding Indigenous American arts and lives through the lens of the exhibition in Vatican City.

Notes from Rome: "Indigenous People Need to Get Over Genocide," Unanswered Letters, and Archival Experiences

My journal reflections and more personal analyses in this book create a counternarrative to the static record of the official VME. The Vatican Museums' website describes it in this way: "In 1925 Pope Pius XI organised a major event: the Vatican Exposition, to make known the cultural, artistic and spiritual traditions of all peoples. The great success of the Exposition, which displayed more than 100,000 objects and works of art from all over the world to more than a million visitors, convinced the Pontiff to transform the temporary event into a permanent exhibition."[18] As anthropologist Johannes Fabian notes, "Reflexivity asks that we 'look back' and thereby let our experiences 'come back' to us."[19] My research process has not been linear or straightforward, and I have encountered many roadblocks, such as documents that went missing in archives after requesting them, reticent and reluctant curators, nasty conservators, whispers, and inaccessible archives. This is evidence of the structural violence of archival spaces, a pattern that has become more apparent as I study the archives further. By structural violence I mean the lack of access for scholars to some of the Vatican archives and holdings, including those of the Vatican Missionary Ethnological Museum (now *Anima Mundi*), for reasons never explained, and the ambivalence of curators and archivists about making material accessible.

This suppression of archival documents and indifference to research requests is unethical. I also refer here to the Vatican Museums' lack of response to requests to visit cultural belongings from myself and other Indigenous curators working in the field as well as emails and meetings with a conservator at the American Academy in Rome, during one of which she exclaimed to me over a cappuccino, "Indigenous people need to get over genocide."[20] This type of simplistic yet revealing colonial thinking is present also in the Vatican catalogs and the overall narrative presented in the Ethnological Museum *Anima Mundi*. I also raise here the historical and ongoing brutality caused by missionary labors and the structural programs of genocide enacted through things such as the 1493 papal bull *Inter caetera* (discussed below) and later the imposition of the Indian Act. The Ethnological Museum *Anima Mundi* is in essence a violation of human rights. In not acknowledging the impacts of Catholic colonialism, including the papal bulls, the colonial devastation of the 1925 Vatican Missionary Exposition, the ongoing legacy of residential schools, and the genocidal labor of missionaries in Indigenous communities, and in obscuring the narratives of looting and plunder which form the basis of the collection, the Vatican Museums perpetuate papal violence. In countering this violence, this project joins the work of researchers across disciplines who are recovering unacknowledged histories that have yet to be narrated and creating countermemories.[21]

It is important to note here that the Vatican's "ethnological collection" was closed for about a decade, but now it is open again, as the Ethnological Museum *Anima Mundi*, and visitors can visit some Indigenous belongings from the Americas. The belongings, stolen treasures, are displayed without Indigenous makers' names, community names, or any discussion of the devastation caused by the VME and pope Pius XI's greed.[22] Gaining entry to the Ethnological Museum *Anima Mundi* archive and collections held in storage is an ongoing research challenge, and its archive remains largely inaccessible due to its unethical practices of document suppression, exclusion of Indigenous researchers and community requests, and ambivalence regarding ethics. Over the past eight years, I have written several times to pope Francis; written to the current curator at the Ethnological Museum *Anima Mundi*, Father Mapelli; spoken and exchanged written correspondence with conservators and Vatican curators; spoken with Jesuit archivists and Capuchin archivists in Rome; and written to Prime Minister Justin Trudeau and former Minister of Aboriginal Affairs Carolyn Bennett of Canada regarding my research and the lack of access to the archive for researchers (two of my letters are included in the appendix of this book). As of this writing, no Indigenous researchers from Turtle Island, including myself, have been granted access.[23] This is part of the Vatican's ongoing structural violence and lack of willingness to enter into a conversation about decolonial practices. I also understand this lack of access as part of the rhetoric of decolonization.

This book's analysis of the VME, and with it an acknowledgment of colonial and Indigenous histories, is a way of moving beyond the rhetoric of truth and reconciliation into understanding and reckoning with the past as it unfolds in the present. The archival record requires a critical reinterpretation in order to center Indigenous perspectives and issues within the VME narrative and work against the structural violence and culture of conquest present at the Vatican. When I first encountered documents in the Vatican archives, I did not know how to "read" them; they presented me with an almost insurmountable hostility and the ambivalence of missionary oppression. I want to unpack this violence and look beyond the prejudiced surface readings that were offered in the VME. As South African historian Helena Pohlandt-McCormick wrote about her experiences working with archival documents in the context of apartheid, "Documents are never innocent."[24] Especially for Indigenous histories, it is crucial to critique archives that have enabled colonialism. Take, for example, the papal bull *Inter caetera*, issued in March 1493 by pope Alexander VI. Indigenous people, according to this decree, did not have souls and were considered subhuman, thereby legitimizing the Catholic Church's colonial project of expansion in the Americas by enslaving Indigenous people. This work included the genocide of Indigenous communities and the destruction of Indigenous artworks. This document is held at the Vatican archives, the very place where I conducted my fieldwork. During the genocide of Indigenous peoples of the Americas, this and other documents were used to justify colonialism and negate the livelihoods of Indigenous Americans, with devastating and profound impacts. By 1512, pope Julius II had adjusted papal attitudes toward Indigenous peoples and recognized them as people with souls, yet they were still seen as in need of Christian redemption.[25] Four hundred and thirty-two years later, the VME reiterated the same limited language and linear Christian concept of time found in the papal bulls regarding the redemption of the souls of "pagans." For example, it promised that the exhibition would "present to visitors the life, customs and habits of the most obscure tribes in the remotest regions of the earth."[26]

Scholars are deeply implicated in the archive on many levels. For example, historian Antoinette Burton writes that when the intellectual Durba Ghosh was doing archival work in India and London, "She was not only reading the archives, the archives were also reading her."[27] In many ways, I, too, was shaped by the processes of working in the archives, especially since I was conducting archival conversations in Italian and English with curators, Jesuit archivists, Native studies allies in Rome, and others. I have worked in Italian and English; written correspondence in Italian, French, and English; and read archival documents in Italian, English, and French. I have also encountered some Algonquin language dictionaries and other Indigenous language materials that were seized by missionaries for the library at the VME.[28] Thus, the project requires an engagement with multiple languages and much translation. All this, too, remains a partial process and presents a larger complexity than if I were working solely with English documents.

Thinkers in Indigenous studies must contend with an extra layer of accountability for our research processes and writing: we knowingly work with archival records that always remain partial. Todd and Fraser note that "for Indigenous peoples, access to state or church archives is complicated, given ongoing settler-colonial realities that frame and govern archives in Canada." They add that "to decolonise the archives requires an erasure or negation of the colonial realities of the archives themselves. Given the inherent colonial realities of the archives as institutions, any effort to decolonise or Indigenise the archives in Canada can therefore only ever be partial."[29] As a Métis person, I can attest to the mental, emotional, and physical struggles of working through archives. Knowing that Indigenous peoples have been subject to emotional, physical, and intellectual brutality that continues due to the ongoing legacies of settler colonialism, particularly the remnants of missionary-based programs, produces a weight and a sense of responsibility.

Throughout this process, I have had numerous phone calls with my mom, who supports my work. We remain engaged with the realities of Indigenous peoples and with challenging the systemic racism that Indigenous communities have faced and still do. We talk about youth suicide and the legacy of residential schools and how we can address these terrible realities. My mom inspires my work, and for that I am thankful. I do not take my position for granted as a scholar. The more research I do, the more I read, write, and teach, the more important I feel it is to be writing histories that engage Indigenous issues. The words of Indigenous curators Lee-Ann Martin and Gerald McMaster resonate with me: "To be an Aboriginal person, to identify with an indigenous heritage in these late colonial times, requires a life of reflection, critique, persistence and struggle."[30] In this spirit of persistence, I present this book.

Altered Photographs and Alternative Facts

In straddling the disciplines of art history and archival studies, I am pulled toward the importance of visual analysis and the politics of art, and also drawn into telling and creating Indigenous histories. This work aims to bring these two disciplines together and rethink them. The book draws on a variety of material culture, and I also include a series of altered photographs based on my archival and museum encounters (see figure 3.4 and plates 2, 10, and 16). Positioning neon lettering and emphatic phrases over photographs of sterile archival spaces unsettles both the archive and the image in ways that complement my scholarly analysis. I produce the altered images to put cracks into the archive on historical and ideological levels as well as to provide new ways of imagining colonial spaces that speaks to Indigenous ways of being and thinking and the loss encountered through missionary violence. I consider this project as a type of worldbuilding. In the various images, I have experimented with horizontal, vertical, and diagonal phrases in English and Cree and have used numbers drawn from the Vatican missionary archives to complicate the sterile facade of statistical data and facts present in the VME record.[31] These images also deploy a form of confusion and disorientation to unsettle the Vatican spaces. I hope the altered photographs and the re-storying of the Vatican exhibition create a way of honoring Indigenous lives and experiences that were never acknowledged within archival records.

Perhaps when I started this research, I imagined a complete record might have been available in the archives. Since then, I have amassed a large collection of missionary ephemera and documents about the VME, but they persist in telling only one side of the story and thus function in many ways as a trap.[32] Moreover, traces within the documents themselves suggest Indigenous alternatives. The documents are not objective truths, but crafted articulations. For example, the *Rivista Illustrata*, the illustrated journal of the VME, remains a critical source for my project, but I was overwhelmed when I first started flipping through it as it includes over eight hundred pages of writing by missionaries, complemented by photographs. Initially I focused on some photographs of Indigenous women and men in the southwest United States, and on closer inspection, I realized the captions and descriptions of the images had multiple errors. This presented an important moment to begin to question the entire structure of "truth" presented within the exhibition spaces and to understand the fallibility of the interpretations in the *Rivista Illustrata*. The curatorial arrangement of Indigenous arts and material culture within the exhibition space and the *Rivista Illustrata* served the VME's agenda to render Indigenous peoples as static, mute, and without agency.

The lure of the archives, the ever-present possibility that I might find something new, drew me further and further into them in an endless hunt. This search is a seductive one; I could keep exploring archives across the world in the hope that I might come across another trace of the VME, what philosopher Jacques Derrida alludes to as the possibility and lack of the archive.[33] Especially for Indigenous artists and scholars, a sustained engagement with colonial archives has been fruitful not only for understanding the legacies of colonialism but also for creating new spaces for Indigenous articulations. Certainly this project is about archival documents, but it is also about what is not in the archive, what is beyond the scope of papal understanding and missionary writing. In this way, Indigenous perspectives on art and history can be illuminating for understanding other histories not presented in the limited scope of the *Rivista Illustrata* or the Halls of the Americas. For Indigenous peoples, stories are theories that inform ways of being in the world, and appreciating this capacity provides another path of illuminating the significance of Indigenous cultural belongings.

Notes from Rome: Beyond the Time and Culture of Conquest

In 2016, Indigenous leaders from several First Nations across Turtle Island participated in the Long March to Rome, calling for the rescinding of these papal edicts. Their march pushed back against colonial time and space and the disastrous impacts articulated by the papal bulls legitimizing *terra nullius* (treating land as if it belonged to no one) and the accompanying Doctrine of Discovery (allowing the "discoverers" to take possession). In 2022, an Indigenous delegation from Turtle Island, including youth and elders from First Nations and Métis and Inuit communities, was brought into a corner of the Ethnological Museum *Anima Mundi*, which was not open to the public yet, and haphazardly shown stolen belongings from their communities. A few stolen belongings were brought out, with no information provided. The museum's curator Father Mapelli and the staff insisted they were stewards of the collection, and the delegation was not permitted to handle or hold their own community belongings. This colonial dynamic continues.

Looking at the photographs of staff in the Ethnological Museum *Anima Mundi* handling Indigenous American belongings is disturbing and informative.

In particular, the photographs show Vatican curator Father Mapelli and conservationists handling and pointing at Indigenous belongings, such as the Inuvialuit kayak seized by Catholic missionaries for the VME.[34] This special seal skin kayak, made with skill and care to transport and sustain Inuit communities, is an archive of Indigenous knowledge and arctic sovereignty. To me these photographs showing the conservators and curators wrongfully handling Indigenous belongings and the policing of touch by the Vatican Museums is a reminder of the ongoing violence of the Vatican Museums, a signifier of the abuse of Indigenous peoples and greedy seizure of sacred belongings by pope Pius XI. Thousands of Indigenous belongings remain as prisoners behind glass in the museum and in the subterranean vaults, bereft from their communities, makers, and Indigenous care. Indigenous conservation methods are not employed, and Indigenous curators and communities are not consulted. Indigenous communities have made some requests for repatriation of cultural belongings, but to date nothing has been returned, and the Vatican does not engage in restitution, consultation, or outreach.[35] Throughout *Eternal Sovereigns*, I consider the Roman archives in tension with the activism and presence of First Peoples, which work as a counternarrative to Vatican colonial policy.

Many Indigenous interpretations and orientations are beyond the space and time of colonial archives, and today more than ever these Indigenous spaces and narratives matter. In this story, many Indigenous cultural belongings and Indigenous American artists, such as Edmonia Lewis (1844–1907), ventured beyond familiar territories to Rome and the space of the Vatican, creating and occupying new places of potential for Indigenous peoples. The presence of Indigenous cultural belongings and Lewis's engagements within the city of Rome are expansive alternative conceptions to the limited linear narrative suggested by the VME. The research focuses on Indigenous experience in the nineteenth and twentieth centuries, but an engagement with Indigeneity at the Vatican also requires one to think expansively into previous centuries and into the future. I am interested here in honoring Indigenous lives, the artists who were once known but never named, the artists who were living in Rome such as Lewis, and the cultural belongings that never got the respect they deserved at the VME. I see this research as a gesture toward honoring the many unacknowledged lives of Indigenous makers, artists, missionaries, and scholars who traveled and slept and reside today in Rome.

Many, indeed, thousands, of Indigenous travelers reside today as prisoners in the strongholds of the Vatican, taken by missionaries to satisfy papal greed and lust over the centuries. The VME was one of the most profound examples of papal avarice in the early twentieth century and part of the salvage paradigm of colonial collecting and fascist colonial expansion. Its legacy and colonial influence continue. For example, there are many important early Latin American Indigenous belongings and documents held at the Ethnological Museum *Anima Mundi* and the Vatican Apostolic Library. This study is a historiography of Indigenous cultural belongings, reframing papal narratives of conquest and greed and unpacking the lack of consent in Vatican Museums' displays and archival practices. This project reframes histories of collecting and provides an alternative history of world exhibitions and the VME, questioning and decolonizing the "gift" language and legacy prevalent in the Vatican archives and museums. Many of the Indigenous cultural belongings and archives discussed in this book have never been adequately studied due to the Vatican Museums' suppression of their archival records and their gatekeeping. Not allowing Indigenous researchers and other scholars to access and research their precious community belongings is ongoing horrible violence. While museums across the globe are working with Indigenous communities to repatriate and rematriate their colonial-era collections, the Vatican Museums remain firm in their stance of papal greed with the ongoing incarceration of Indigenous life.

The dreadful legacy of missionary-cum-papal violence continues and is made tangible throughout by including my journal entries and analysis of material and visual culture. Thus, this book takes up a form of storytelling and worldbuilding by shifting the narrative to cultural belongings, travelers, and artists that were previously unacknowledged and ignored and by placing Indigenous travelers at the heart of the story to disrupt the Vatican's colonial purview. The dynamic of papal control suppressing Indigenous cultural belongings and spirituality at the VME continues to this day in the Ethnological Museum *Anima Mundi*. This book will unsettle ambivalent Vatican discourse, providing further material and impetus for study centering Indigenous artists, activists, and travelers by piercing the colonial heart of the Vatican and raising awareness of the precious Indigenous American heritage held captive in the Vatican vaults and the genocidal history of the Catholic church. The book is also about bringing back honor and respect for historical and contemporary Indigenous communities. The book is a new and an old story about Rome contributing to creative ways of decolonizing museum ethics and archives, Italian studies, and unsettling art history. It is imperative we understand Indigenous art and papal collections and come to a moment of reckoning with colonial church history in the broader discourse of truth and reconciliation across the globe.

Chapter Summaries

The larger historical sweep of the book begins with a prehistory of the Indian Museum (as it was first called) at the Vatican and then moves through an analysis of the 1925 exhibition that is interspersed with my recent archival encounters in the Vatican and throughout Rome. It concludes with Anthony Martin Fernando's protest at the VME, an account that underscores the timeliness of the book's exploration of Indigenous cultural sovereignty.

Chapter 1, "Unsettling the Indian Museum in Rome: Ferdinand Pettrich and Edmonia Wildfire Lewis," provides a historical precursor to the VME by placing the sculptures and life experiences of Ferdinand Pettrich, a white German artist, in productive comparison with those of Edmonia Lewis, an Ojibwe and Haitian American artist.[36] By assessing the two artists and visually analyzing their work, the chapter unsettles core colonial assumptions espoused in studies of neoclassical art: that Indigenous peoples belonged in the past, had no place in the future, and existed only on the margins of civilization. Comparing Pettrich's and Lewis's lives and artworks challenges the binaries of past/present, wild/civil, and Indigenous/settler within neoclassical art. Their relationship has not been documented in the colonial archive, and my consideration of the two artists together constitutes an intervention in art history. Staging a creative dialogue between the evidence of Lewis's artworks and life and Pettrich's "Indian Museum," which he displayed at the Vatican, extends conceptions of Indigeneity as a state of survival amid the violence of colonial rule. Both artists led international lives and traveled across the globe, circulating ideals and ideas of Indigeneity through their artworks and their personal encounters with collectors, the Vatican, admirers, and nemeses. Considering their efforts in tension provides new insights into the problem of agency in representing Indigenous nations in art, ways of thinking about Indigenous presence in Rome and at the Vatican Museums, and the limits of neoclassicism as an artistic genre and a colonial mindset.

The second chapter , "'The Most Exhaustive Record of the World's Progress Ever Displayed': Pope Pius XI's Culture of Conquest and Visitors' Experiences at the Vatican Missionary Exposition," contends that the arrangement and interpretation of Indigenous arts and material culture within the exhibition space of the VME and the pages of the *Rivista Illustrata* served the VME's goal by rendering Indigenous nations as static. It first provides a detailed discussion of the VME, showing how the vast number of materials from all over the globe overwhelmed missionary organizers and visitors to the exposition. In the

Halls of the Americas and within the *Rivista Illustrata*, the organizers at the Vatican portrayed Indigenous Americans as pagans who existed outside the time and space of western progress and Christian civilization, rather than as contemporary citizens of the world. By creating a visual regime to produce so-called knowledge, the VME used Indigenous American visual culture to form what pope Pius XI called "silent eloquence." He positioned Indigenous visual culture as trophies of his domain to glorify missionaries as heroes. The chapter further contextualizes the exhibition by imagining a visitor walking through the grandeur and cacophony of 1920s Rome and Saint Peter's and into the VME. To conclude, it considers a series of contemporary fairs and expositions to contextualize the VME as a competitive spectacle and a form of "pope culture" in the age of world's fairs.

The third chapter, "'A Window on the World' of Colonial Unknowing: Dioramas, Children's Games, and Missionary Perspectives at the Vatican Missionary Exposition," focuses on missionary viewpoints. Dioramas and board games for children that were included in the VME form part of the cultural archive and constitute the visual evidence of the exposition's attempt to present itself as a "window on the world." However, as I argue, the VME was replete with colonial unknowing and actively denied and disavowed Indigenous agency in the Americas.[37] The children's games displayed at the exhibition had bright colors, stereotypical imagery of Indigenous peoples, and instructions to baptize and pray for "heathens." They encouraged children and adults to understand Indigenous communities and their cultural practices as property of the Catholic Church and without agency. To counteract this elision, the second half of the chapter incorporates a discussion of the realities that Indigenous children of the Americas faced in residential schools run by Catholic missionaries in North America in the early twentieth century. The chapter argues that the VME must be understood within a larger global network of institutions that were part of the settler-colonial project to eradicate Indigenous lifeways. For readers in North America, residential schools are likely the most familiar and notorious of these institutions, and this chapter connects the role of vision and art making that these schools mobilized in "educating" Indigenous children to the VME. The games and the dioramas of the VME offer a "window on the world" into the attitudes of missionaries toward Indigenous children—evidence of how their seeing, looking, and understanding flowed one way. Missionary attitudes and practices perpetuated violence against Indigenous peoples in the Americas.

The fourth chapter, "Eternal Sovereigns and Ancestral Art: Ancient Archives, Relatives, and Travelers at the Vatican Missionary Exposition," works against the official Vatican narrative to consider how cultural belongings made using Indigenous methods and hands resonate beyond missionary anxiety and outside the colonial space of the Halls of the Americas. Although missionaries and pope Pius XI considered them as silent markers of missionary progress because of their removal from Indigenous communities, I contend that they endure in the present as markers of Indigenous cosmologies and understandings. The chapter focuses on five works by once-known Indigenous artists: an Anishinaabe, Nipissing, and Kanien'kehá:ka wampum belt, a Passamaquoddy Christ on the Cross, a Lakota Sun Dance drawing, Cree beaded moccasins, and a Kwakwaka'wakw ancestral sun mask (see figures 4.2–4.4 and plates 11–15). The artworks have a persuasive glory and power that the missionaries working for the VME and recent curators at the Vatican Museums failed to consider in their brief and problematic interpretations in the *Rivista Illustrata* and the catalog *The Americas: Collections from the Vatican Ethnological Museum* (2015).[38] Indigenous cultural belongings matter; as teachers, ancient archives, and evidence of self-sustaining practices, they create ancestral art history lessons that disrupt both pope Pius XI's and pope Francis's logic of "silent eloquence" and the pervasive but not all-encompassing views of missionaries and visitors.

The book closes with an epilogue about Anthony Martin Fernando (1864–1949), an Aboriginal activist who protested settler colonialism at the entrance to the 1925 exposition by giving political leaflets to visitors. Although Fernando may have thought of himself as a lone activist—and certainly the headline of his leaflet suggests that he thought of himself as one of a few—his actions may be considered more broadly as one of countless Indigenous acts of survival and resistance during the VME and beyond.[39] Fernando's narrative, like Lewis's story and those conveyed by Indigenous cultural belongings, present the experience of Indigenous peoples' engagements with Rome and the Vatican as makers of history and brings us into an Indigenous time and space beyond the culture of conquest.

1

UNSETTLING THE INDIAN MUSEUM IN ROME

Ferdinand Pettrich and Edmonia Wildfire Lewis

Journal: The Vatican Museums

MAY 2023. *I walked through the Pio Clementino Museum and galleries to the Cortile del Belvedere. My feet felt like they were going to fall off from all the strolling, but I was also excited thinking about Edmonia Lewis and Ferdinand Pettrich wandering around the Vatican galleries together. Edmonia Lewis, the first Indigenous and Black artist to become a sculpting celebrity and a celebrity who sculpted, was and is really inspiring for me and the overall ethos of my research. All the records I have sifted through at the Vatican without any mention or discussion of Indigenous artists were depressing, but when I found out about Lewis and her oeuvre in Rome, the whole dynamic shifted. In the cortile, I was confronted with a larger-than-life sculpture of an idealized male figure. The torso was chiseled out of smooth white marble. This was the Apollo Belvedere, an ancient Roman statue, rediscovered in the Renaissance. I thought about how the statue was praised by the American painter Benjamin West at the Vatican in 1760 when he exclaimed, "My God! How like it is to a young Mohawk warrior!"*[1] *American readers and artists following in West's stead then came to Rome, or read about it in his narratives, and studied ancient models in their search for inspiration. West identified Indigenous American nations with this ancient Roman heritage, seeing parallels with warrior cultures, and ideas of classical timelessness and male beauty. Although this identification is problematic for the denial of Americans' complicity in the removal of First Peoples from across Turtle Island and West's highly constructed tale, the equation inspired many readers and artists throughout the nineteenth century.*

I wondered about Pettrich and Lewis sketching the ancient Apollo Belvedere and visiting the works of Antonio Canova in their search for inspiration to create Indigenous American subjects.[2] *Americans including Lewis and international artists like Pettrich drew motivation from the Apollo in their aim to create idealized statuary of Indigenous peoples. Yet Lewis's presence is far from the "Imaginary Indian" that West fantasized about and projected onto the Apollo sculpture, and the evidence of her multiple studios and success in Rome also worked against the neoclassical tendency to view Indigenous peoples as dead or complacent in the wake of settlers. Like West and Pettrich, she also capitalized on the transnational desire and demand for Indigenous subjects on both sides of the Atlantic, resulting in commissions for sculptural busts and figures by such notables as the Marquess of Bute, Henry Wadsworth Longfellow, and Frederick Douglass.*[3]

The Roman *Carte de visite*: An Anishinaabe Artist in Rome

The only known Roman portrait of artist Edmonia Lewis (1844–1907) appears on a *carte de visite* made circa 1876, a decade after she had settled in the city (see plate 3).[4] Photographed at the prestigious Fratelli D'Allesandri studio in Rome (photographers to the pope), this rare image depicts Lewis in her prime at the age of thirty-two. Her hands crossed over her chest in a confident pose, a cravat tied around her neck in bohemian fashion, she projects an aura of confidence and cosmopolitan worldliness, at ease in the Eternal City. Her expression is relaxed, and she has a slight smile. She used these cards to advertise her vocation as a sculptor in Rome, giving them to potential patrons, artist friends, writers, critics, and admirers, and even to pope Pius IX.[5] The card bears the legend: "Flli D'Alessandri, Corso No 12, Roma." Journalists of the day remarked on her visible difference as an artist of color: one, writing in 1866, described her as an "interesting novelty" and a "lady of color."[6] Lewis drew upon elements of her Anishinaabe and Haitian background to emphasize the distinctiveness of her heritage compared with that of her white American colleagues, although her pose and dress echo those of her fellow bohemian artists of the time. Lewis wanted to advertise her prominence as a sculptor to gain support in the form of commissions. She was the youngest of her female colleagues, and her experiences in Boston and Rome evidence her drive and ambition in a field dominated by white men.[7] Lewis made calculated choices throughout her career starting from a young age.

During her teenage years, Lewis seized the opportunity to study first at New York Central College in McGrawville, an abolitionist school, and then at Oberlin College (from 1859 to 1863), the first interracial and coed college in the United States.[8] In the winter of 1862, while she was completing a liberal arts degree with a focus on sculpture, a mob of angry students accused her of poisoning two female colleagues.[9] The mob severely beat her before her trial. Defended by James Mercer Langston, a prominent Black lawyer, she was acquitted of the charges. Despite these hardships, she persevered. She then moved to Boston, where she joined a group of abolitionist activists headed by William Lloyd Garrison. Inspired by the artistic culture and civil rights movement in Boston, she met Edward Brackett, a neoclassical sculptor, and began to work directly with clay and create casts of hands.[10] A journalist described this training period of her life as the "spiritual epiphany of an unsophisticated Indian in the face of the civilized white man's 'stone image.'"[11] However, I would argue her talent with marble, determination, and artistic acumen allowed her to create sophisticated works that ventured beyond solely white men and honored and complicated Indigenous and Black lives. She completed the exercises Brackett gave her, showing aptitude and mastery, building her artistic skill and competence. Seizing the moment during the Civil War, she made busts of Robert Gould Shaw, an American hero who led a regiment of Black troops into battle. She sold one hundred plaster busts and, with the proceeds, she purchased her ticket to Rome and returned only sparingly to the United States.[12] With its ancient allure, sublime ruins, neoclassical community of artists and opportunity for freedom and cultural experiences, Rome was the perfect place for an emerging sculptor. Within ten years she had achieved much success and made a name for herself in the Eternal City as a sculptor of renown.

Lewis had the Roman *carte de visite* made to showcase her sophistication in preparation for the papal visit to her studio.[13] Lewis converted from Protestantism to Catholicism, and it is easy to imagine she felt more comfortable in

Italy than in the United States. Fluent in Italian, she spent most of her life in Italy (from 1866 to 1895), where she produced many sculptures based on Henry Wadsworth Longfellow's *The Song of Hiawatha*, including the marble bust *Minnehaha* (1868; see figure 1.2). She found respite in Italy outside the anti-Black and anti-Indigenous atmosphere of the United States. Her departure to Rome was indeed a matter of professional survival. In an interview with the *New York Times* in late 1878, she stated that "I was practically driven to Rome, to obtain the opportunities for art culture, and to find a social atmosphere where I was not constantly reminded of my color. The land of liberty had no room for a colored sculptor."[14]

Lewis often discussed her Anishinaabe (Ojibwe) heritage as well and crafted this as part of her artistic persona. Although she did not, for example, pose with any quillwork or beaded moccasins, or against a backdrop that might signal an overt Indigeneity in her *carte de visite*, she mentioned her First Nations ancestry with the media and in her artistic circles, and in this way drew attention to her unique heritage. This visiting card is exceptional in that Lewis actively chose to have it made, whereas photographers such as Charles Milton Bell often took photographs of Native American subjects for consumption by others. They were not usually collected or distributed by the subjects themselves.[15] The significance of Lewis's *carte de visite* should not be underestimated, as she was the first artist of Native American descent to gain international recognition.[16] She advertised her prominence as a sculptor not simply to attract commissions but also to announce and claim her place as an artist of international distinction.[17]

Lewis defied colonial expectations. Her biography is important for understanding her role as a participant in the artistic community of German artist Ferdinand Pettrich (1798–1872) and his contemporaries. In this context, we should acknowledge Lewis's subject position as she worked through neoclassicism, a dominant movement in art and architecture that had its epicenter in Rome, which drew international artists with its ancient allure, and that was imbued with a culture of denying Indigenous peoples' modernity. In their statuary, paintings, and other artistic forms, neoclassical artists placed Indigenous peoples in the past rather than in contemporary time. Famous examples include Thomas Crawford's *The Indian* (1856) and Pettrich's *Dying Tecumseh* (1856; see figure 1.1), a marble statue that glorified the death of a Shawnee leader and not inadvertently celebrated settler colonialism. Many of Lewis's white contemporaries remarked—sometimes favorably, sometimes not—on Lewis's extraordinary situation as an artist of color, a Native, an "aborigine," an Indian.[18] They expressed shock because they had conditioned themselves to a neoclassical statuary that only represented Native people as dying out in the wake of settler-colonial takeover across Turtle Island (as represented in the works by Pettrich, Crawford, and many others), not as making artworks or living a fulfilling life.[19]

Lewis's modernity and her ability to create art using the language of a largely white, colonial artistic milieu unsettled the codes and conventions of the art world. Her life and artworks present a much-needed alternative to the staid depictions of Indigenous peoples within the oeuvre of neoclassical production and a striking point of comparison with Pettrich. Lewis challenges both colonial racist assumptions regarding what Indigenous American people could do and did in a period of aggressive cultural erasure and genocide, and the binaries of neoclassical art. Her artworks, voice, and lifestyle choices remain a singular and inspiring narrative of creativity and international presence in the art world.

Creative Juxtapositions: Ferdinand Pettrich and Edmonia Wildfire Lewis

This chapter places into productive tension the statuary and life stories of Ferdinand Pettrich, a white German artist, and Edmonia Wildfire Lewis, an Ojibwe Haitian artist, both active in the nineteenth century. Through the tools of comparison and visual analysis, it challenges the colonial assumptions prevalent in the neoclassical art movement that Indigenous peoples had disappeared from history and that they existed only outside modern metropolitan cultures and certainly not in Europe.[20] Comparing their lives and sculptures challenges the neoclassical binaries of Indigenous subjects and artists, and opens up conceptions of Indigeneity as a state of survival amid the violence of colonial rule in the international contexts in which Lewis and Pettrich worked.

The chapter examines the sculpture *Dying Tecumseh*, part of the so-called Indian Museum created by Pettrich. Drawing inspiration from his sojourns in the Americas, including Washington, DC, and then Rio de Janeiro, he created his Indian Museum over a period of twenty years, from 1837 to 1857, to capitalize on popular interest in Native Americans and to make a record of his experiences and encounters with Indigenous peoples in Washington during treaty negotiations. He developed his museum, a series of sketches, lithographs, and plaster models, in Washington, DC (from 1835 to 1842) and then continued the work in Rio de Janeiro (from 1842 to 1857). Having received a papal commission, Pettrich donated his Indian Museum to the Vatican in 1858 and moved from South America to Rome. His museum, including *Dying Tecumseh*, formed a prominent visual anchor in the Hall of North America at the

1925 Vatican Missionary Exposition (VME).[21] The Pettrich sculptures continue to have a significant visual presence at the Vatican Museums in the Ethnological Museum *Anima Mundi*. Pettrich's statuary features several busts and larger-than-life sculptures of Indigenous American chiefs and medicine men as well as bas-relief battle scenes in a neoclassical style.

Artists across Europe, Britain, and the Americas from the late eighteenth through the nineteenth century worked in the neoclassical style, striving to create a new visual language based on the emulation of ancient Greek and Roman ideas of civilization and beauty, inspired by antiquity and archaeological discoveries of ruins in Pompeii that began in 1747. The Eternal City, brimming with antiquities, enticed European and American artists, who then brought the movement back to the United States.[22] Neoclassical artists praised the classical qualities of clarity, order, rationality, and didacticism. The artistic language emphasized emotional restraint and self-sacrifice, lack of ornamentation, the glorification of heroic death, and allusion to the mythologies and political histories of ancient Rome and Greece.[23]

Building on Enlightenment ideas of rationality, exploration, and scientific observation, artists were also influenced by the discovery and exploitation of Indigenous peoples in the Americas, a contradiction inherent in the idealistic values of neoclassicism, a term that in its birth in the eighteenth century conveyed the revival of the arts.[24] They discussed the moralizing power of sculpture and, in their colonizing mindset,[25] understood Indigenous peoples as epitomizing the ideal of the noble but doomed savage. Statuary by Pettrich, Thomas Crawford (1814–57), and others promoted the misperception that Indigenous people existed solely in the past. To make an intervention in the consideration of neoclassical depictions of Indigenous peoples, the second half of the chapter explores Lewis's art and life experience, focusing on her sculpture *Minnehaha*.

Studying Pettrich and Lewis together reveals the international demand for Indigenous art and artists in the cosmopolitan city of Rome. Both living in Rome in the 1860s, Lewis and Pettrich would have experienced the tumultuous period of the Risorgimento. This movement eventually resulted in the unification of Italy after a period of complex negotiations and battles between the Italian people and the papal states. Rome became the capital of unified Italy in 1871. Pettrich sculpted Native Americans as proud individuals, but his creation of the Indian Museum in the fragile medium of plaster for pope Pius IX firmly located Indigenous communities in the past. His sketches, created in an ephemeral medium, contrast with the permanence of Lewis's work in Carrara marble. Lewis drew on her lived experience in creating sculptures that celebrated Indigenous life and designed an artistic persona that centered on her Indigenous identity. Her sculptures invite complex readings for their layered meanings, and their permanence in the medium of marble also suggests the longevity of Indigenous peoples. Her works and her life experience defied colonial perspectives inherent in many neoclassical sculptures by her colleagues that Indigenous people had died out. These unresolved frictions emerge in response to the colonial archive and the complexity of being an Indigenous artist during the genocidal removal of Indigenous communities across Turtle Island. Contemplating the artists together unsettles presumptions about the mobility of First Peoples, and the permanence of Indigenous life in marble, beyond linear conceptions of art and settler fantasies of manifest destiny.

Rome—Washington—Rio—Rome: Pettrich Sculpting Indigenous Nations

Ferdinand Pettrich trained in Italy under prominent neoclassical sculptor Bertel Thorvaldsen (1770–1844), the successor to neoclassical sculptor Antonio Canova (1757–1822). Pettrich arrived in Rome in 1819 for an extended period of study. Eventually Thorvaldsen encouraged Pettrich to venture to America and depict a new and exotic subject matter: Native Americans.[26] Pettrich then moved to Washington, DC, in 1835 and also spent time in Philadelphia and Baltimore, leaving the United States in 1842.[27] During his time in Washington, he created busts of political figures, including Indigenous Americans who visited the capital to negotiate treaties with the federal government. One night at his Washington studio, near where the Corcoran Gallery of Art stands today, he was attacked and stabbed in an apparent assassination attempt.[28] Scholars suggest that anti-immigrant nationalists attacked Pettrich due to jealousy. They wanted the contract for the statue *Washington Resigning His Commission*, intended for Washington Square in Philadelphia, to go to the American artist Horatio Greenough, not to a foreigner.[29] After a heated debate in the House of Representatives, Pettrich lost the commission and received little compensation.[30] My interpretation is that xenophobic nationalists attacked Pettrich in an act of vandalism, and perhaps also because his works promoted American Indian visibility, not simply because of his status as a foreigner.

In 1830, just five years before Pettrich arrived in the United States, the Indian Removal Act had been passed by Congress at the urging of President Andrew Jackson, and during Pettrich's American career, President Martin Van Buren aggressively pursued Jackson's policies.[31] He forcibly relocated the Cherokee from the southeast to Oklahoma and removed almost all Indigenous nations east of the Mississippi.[32] The US government displaced over seventy thousand Indigenous people from their homelands during the Trail of Tears after they ceded their land to the government in exchange for land in "Indian Territory." Sauk leader Black Hawk returned to his homelands in Illinois in 1832 so that his people could grow corn and feed themselves, only to be violently pushed out by white settlers in the Black Hawk War.[33] A drawing of Black Hawk exists in Pettrich's sketchbook. From this, Pettrich made a bust and included it in his Indian Museum.[34]

Because Pettrich's sculptures, drawings, and lithographs of Indigenous Americans were markers of Indigenous visibility, specifically his depictions of the treaty delegations in which many Indigenous tribes from across Turtle Island participated between 1837 and 1842, they stood as reminders of Indigenous histories and peoples, perhaps threatening settler attitudes, and thus provided a motive for the vandals who attacked him in his studio in Washington. Yet the title Pettrich chose for his overall vision and project, Indian Museum, suggests that he too, like other artists of the time, including Crawford and Luigi Persico (1791–1860), believed in and created artworks that conformed to the myth of the vanishing Indian and westward expansion, thereby aiding the settler-colonial project of Indigenous elimination. The title also suggests his familiarity with and interest in the hardship of Native Americans depicted in such projects as George Catlin's popular Indian Gallery, a large collection of paintings and artifacts that Catlin (1796–1872) exhibited in London. Besides seriously wounding Pettrich, the vandals who attacked him also destroyed a dozen of his plaster sculptures of Indigenous Americans.[35] Before he left for Brazil in 1842, Pettrich made larger sketches on the walls of his studio based on the meetings he had witnessed in Washington between Native American leaders and the US government.[36] He later redrew these, in a series of sketchbooks now held at the Newberry Library in Chicago (see figures 2.8 and 2.9), and developed the drawings into a series of lithographs, a collectible, lower-cost medium. On October 18, 1842, the *United States Gazette* of Philadelphia advertised these works and Pettrich's upcoming departure for Brazil; the lithograph booklet was titled *Portraits of Distinguished Indians from Several Tribes, Who Visited Washington in 1837; also a Faithful Representation of the Indian War Dance, Which Took Place during Their Visit; Drawn on the Spot by Ferdinand Pettrich* (1842).[37]

Pettrich's inscription on one of the sketchbooks reads, "Fleeting sketches of Indian tribes according to Nature by Ferdinand Pettrich Artist, 10th August 1842, Washington City."[38] He changed the wording for the lithographs to appeal to collectors and a public interested in the veracity and documentary quality of his works, which complicate the generalizing tendencies of neoclassical artists such as Crawford. Yet Pettrich's use of the term "fleeting" also suggests his belief that Indigenous Americans would soon disappear and, in this way at least, conforms to settler-colonial ideas of the time. "Fleeting" could mean quickly done to give a sense of authenticity to the works, in that they were recorded in the moment. Yet the phrase "according to Nature" also suggests Pettrich's belief in the romantic vanishing Indian trope. The lithograph publication also gives details about the context of the works: "The above portraits were originally drawn from life, full-size, on the four walls of Pettrich's studio and now for the first time reduced and presented to the public by Ferdinand Pettrich. Lithographed by Edward Weber and Co, Baltimore, 1842."[39] The description emphasizes the veracity of the depictions and their documentary nature. Although still heavily influenced by ideals of classical antiquity, Pettrich drew inspiration from real people.

In 1843, to recuperate from the attempted assassination, Pettrich moved to Brazil, a warmer climate, and worked the sketches into plaster *bozzetti* (models) while employed at the court of Emperor Dom Pedro II in Rio de Janeiro, creating busts and sculptures. It was in Brazil that he continued his vision for an Indian Museum to memorialize Native American people. His mobility contrasts with the stasis of his statues and busts and his term for the project, Indian Museum, which implies the death and end of Indigenous life. Further, his removal from Indigenous subjects—he created the busts and statues on another continent and over a period of about twenty years—also highlights his lack of awareness of ongoing issues for First Peoples and the large role his imagination played in the creation of the works. His sketchbook remained a key source of fantasy and rumination for his statuary throughout his artistic production.

Pettrich's Settler Fantasy of Tecumseh

Missing from the sketchbook are any preparatory drawings for Pettrich's statue *Dying Tecumseh*. Unlike the other Indigenous leaders he rendered, he never saw Tecumseh; he worked from his imagination and his observations of other Indigenous delegations. *Dying Tecumseh* is perhaps Pettrich's best-known work, due at least in part to the prominence of the collections that hold it: the Vatican Museums (plaster) and the Smithsonian in Washington, DC (marble). Tracing the life story of this sculpture shows the strong international interest in Pettrich's work and in representations of Indigenous Americans at the time.

Pettrich completed *Dying Tecumseh* in marble in 1856 in Brazil to the praises of the royal family and the ambassador from Rome. Impressed with *Dying Tecumseh* and the busts of other Indigenous Americans that Pettrich created, the ambassador wrote to pope Pius IX, stating that he "was greatly surprised to find an artist of such extraordinary talent so far from Rome, the cradle of the fine arts."[40] Shortly after he asked Pettrich to return to Rome with his work, due to the pope's interest.[41] When Pettrich left Brazil in 1857, he shipped the marble statue of Tecumseh to Gurney's Art Gallery in New York City at 707 Broadway.[42] The US Capitol exhibited it in 1864, and it eventually landed in the Smithsonian American Art Museum, where it remains on display (see figure 1.1).[43] Pettrich had made a nearly identical version of *Dying Tecumseh* in terra-cotta-colored plaster while in Rio de Janeiro. This he donated to the Vatican, and it was featured in the Hall of North America at the VME.[44]

Tecumseh (1768–1813) led the Shawnee but envisioned a future not only for his community but also for Indigenous nations across Turtle Island. Persistent and persuasive, he devoted his life to fighting against the white settlement of Native American lands across the Great Lakes region and rallied hundreds of Indian soldiers in the pan-Indian resistance.[45] He lost his life at the Battle of the Thames in Ontario on October 5, 1813, allied with the British against

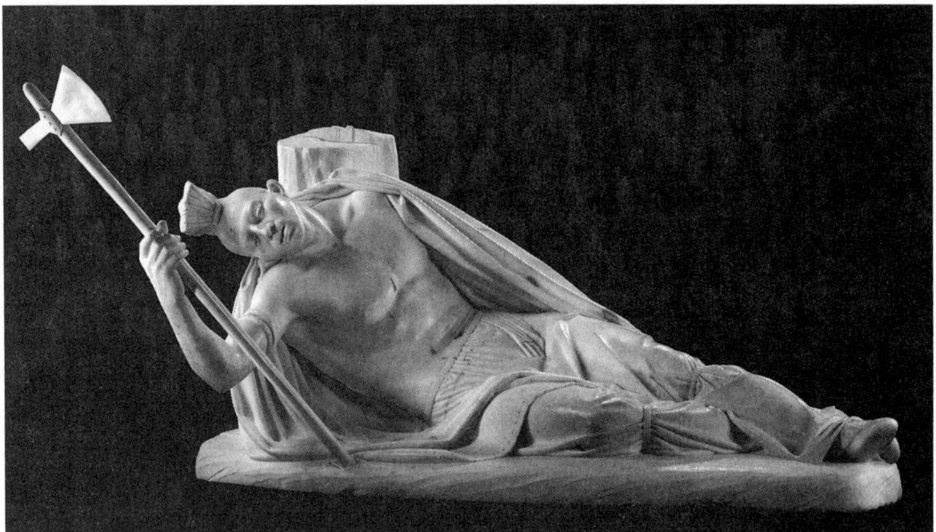

FIGURE 1.1. Ferdinand Pettrich, *Dying Tecumseh*, 1856. Marble with painted copper alloy tomahawk, 93.1 × 197.2 × 136.6 cm. Courtesy of Smithsonian American Art Museum, Washington, DC.

American invaders. Pettrich depicted him at a crucial moment: dying, he props himself up using his tomahawk to encourage his troops to keep fighting. Tecumseh's confederacy, a group of several thousand Indigenous warriors in the Northwest whom Tecumseh and his brother, Tenskwatawa, had inspired to fight with him, disbanded after his death. Through statuary such as Pettrich's, Tecumseh became part of popular myth as a doomed Native American hero.[46]

Tecumseh used gesture effectively in his practice as an orator. As historian John Sugden notes, "with fiery and expressive oratory he would excite Indian listeners across the frontier, antagonizing some, spellbinding others, unsettling most."[47] In an excerpt from a speech he gave days before his last battle, he scolded the British commander, General Henry Procter, for abandoning him and his warriors to fight against the American forces: "Father! You have got the arms and ammunition which our great father sent for his red children. If you have an idea of going away, give them to us, and you may go and welcome for us. Our lives are in the hands of the Great Spirit. We are determined to defend our lands, and if it be his will, we wish to leave our bones upon them."[48] From Tecumseh's words, it is easier to understand the moment Pettrich depicts. He wanted to memorialize a fallen hero, reminiscent of the figure depicted in the Dying Gaul, a famed Roman copy of a Greek bronze showing one of the defeated Gallic warriors who had attacked ancient Pergamon.[49] The bullet hole in Tecumseh's right temple and the wounds in his chest and abdomen ultimately defeat him. The fading Gaul, a brave warrior, also has an open wound carved into his chest, as he slumps down to succumb to death. Colonizing armies defeated the perishing Gaul just as they conquered Tecumseh. He never sat for a portrait, and American troops disfigured his body after his death.[50] Pettrich depicts him in a moribund moment, leaning back, with an idealized muscular body, parted lips, and half-closed eyes, as if he is speaking his last words of encouragement. Located in Rome and in Washington, Pettrich's *Dying Tecumseh*, largely a composite fantasy work, reinforced settler-colonial ideas that Indigenous Americans had run out of time and posed no physical threat to American settler advancement.[51]

Tecumseh leans against an axed tree stump, a symbol of the inevitable "progress" of white civilization, although the viewer might also interpret it as a memento mori, a symbol of Tecumseh's mortality. Nicolai Cikovsky notes that "the stump affirmed civilization's conquest of nature, [and] its connotations of death—of violent death—were a constant reminder that this conquest was brutal and final, and that the wilderness that civilization destroyed could never be restored."[52] Pettrich, with his use of the dead stump, no doubt referenced this settler fantasy. In the nineteenth century, American artists working at the

Capitol in Washington, and viewers of their works, recognized the equation between the tree stump and the end of Indigenous American life and lamented the loss of nature but paradoxically not the forced removal of Native Americans onto reservations and off their traditional lands.[53] Government policy, which artworks at the Capitol implicitly supported, as well as popular writers, insisted that Native people represented an earlier, uncivilized stage of human evolution and argued that they would inevitably die out due to their "savage" state. Pettrich, like other artists at the time, also worked in this vein, promoting the eradication of Indigenous peoples and drawing on the popularity of and interest in Indigenous figures.[54]

Slight differences distinguish the two versions of Pettrich's *Dying Tecumseh*. The plaster version bears two bullet holes, one at the temple and the other in the chest. In the marble version, Pettrich depicts only one bullet hole, placed at Tecumseh's temple. Both renditions have an incised tattoo of a snake on Tecumseh's chest. However, the Shawnee during Tecumseh's time did not decorate their bodies with tattoos in this manner and would not have used the snake symbol in this fashion.[55] Given that Pettrich spent some of his American sojourn (from 1835 to 1843) in Philadelphia working for the marble mason John Struthers, he likely had access to the library and natural history collections at the American Philosophical Society. Perhaps he saw illustrations there that inspired him and prompted him to take creative liberties with the tattoo design. While there, he may also have visited Charles Wilson Peale's Philadelphia Museum, where he could have informed himself about the diverse traditions of the Indigenous nations he depicted in sketches, lithographs, and sculpture, perhaps viewing Peale's lively portrait *Joseph Brant Thayendanegea* (ca. 1797).

The tattoo could also be a fantastical interpretation of body art that Pettrich saw when tribal delegations visited his studio during his time in Washington, or it could simply be a creative flourish.[56] It could also be a nod to the Mohawk warrior in Benjamin West's painting *The Death of General Wolfe* (1770), who sports snake and bear clan tattoos across his upper chest and arms, and thus a gesture also to West's neoclassical tendency to link the noble warriors of Native America with those of ancient Greece. Pettrich's work confirmed visitor's expectations in its reliance on classical Roman tropes of the noble dying warrior and its emphasis on the idea of a linear "progress" of civilization with the modern west at its apex.

Pettrich memorialized settler displacement and takeover of Indigenous lands during the mid-nineteenth century, and the Indian Museum, including *Dying Tecumseh*, is a stark reminder of settler-colonial violence. Tellingly, when the US Capitol placed the marble statue of Tecumseh in the House of Representatives between 1864 and 1868, they were also legislating a series of anti-Indian policies.[57] Tecumseh, a remarkable Native leader with vision, strength, and purpose, continues to be thought about and referenced in the American and European imaginations. Indeed, the Smithsonian recently unveiled the marble version of the sculpture again, at the National Portrait Gallery. The statue is a visual anchor in the American gallery. Surrounded by American landscape paintings, it is subsumed into a narrative of the triumphs of American settler colonialism over Indigenous lands. Looking at the sculptures of Tecumseh at the Smithsonian and Vatican Museums, there is no critical wall labeling, an absence that leaves unchallenged this idea of Indigenous people as out of time and as static museum objects. Other sculptures created around the same time that celebrated Indigenous death include Persico's commission for the Capitol, *The Discovery of America* (1844), and Horatio Greenough's *Rescue* (1850). These sculptures were later removed due to the racist depictions of the elimination of Indigenous life and the triumph of settler colonialism.[58]

Tecumseh surely rests uneasily in relation to the two statues of him in Washington and Rome. The paradox of inclusion would not have been lost on him; leading the resistance movement, he did everything he could to denounce and repel American settler colonialism.[59] He unified Indigenous groups and allied with the British because of their promises to protect Indigenous sovereignty against the encroaching American frontier.[60] Yet, the two versions of *Dying Tecumseh* by Pettrich perform two functions. First, they are reminders of the popularity of the image of Indigenous peoples as noble but doomed that was prevalent in Europe, America, and Oceania. Second, neoclassical statuary located in prominent metropolitan imperial spaces such as Washington, Rio de Janeiro, and Rome functioned as visual signifiers of settler colonialism and Indigenous displacement.

Pettrich's Indian Museum

In August 1857, Pettrich traveled to London and exhibited "the bold and classic forms of the Red Indian races" at an exhibition of the New Society of Painters in Watercolours at the Pall Mall Gallery, capitalizing on popular interest in Indigeneity across the Atlantic.[61] Visitors saw Pettrich's works at the Egyptian Hall, where American painters such as George Catlin had displayed a collection of 474 paintings and artifacts of Indigenous peoples from across Turtle Island in 1839.[62] In May 1858, Pettrich moved back to Rome to present the Indian Museum to pope Pius IX, after which he was granted a papal pension. His works became the visual authority on Indigeneity in Europe. He remained in Rome for the next two decades, the period during which Edmonia Lewis lived there.

For the Indian Museum, he created thirty-three pieces, including life-size sculptures, bas-relief works, sixteen busts, and nine *bozzetti* (plaster casts) painted in a terra-cotta color to replicate neoclassical admiration for antiquity as well as a nod to Indigenous skin tones. The Indian Museum attracted the attention of both scholars and tourists who visited the collection, and it held pride of place in the Lateran Palace of the Vatican Museums, as tourist guidebooks noted.[63] The organizers of the 1925 VME moved it to the Hall of North America, where it featured prominently.

Until the exhibition *Portrayals of Native Americans in Times of Treaties and Removal* in Dresden in 2013, the Indian Museum remained in near obscurity.[64] Pettrich's statuary collection is the first and only body of work to depict Indigenous Americans in the Vatican Museums. Scholars and church representatives used it to create racist theories about Native American presence.[65] In an article by the Jesuit Father Bresciani, the author centers Pettrich's Indian Museum within a discussion of the origins of Indigenous Americans. He posits a relationship to ancient Egypt, as well as to the ancient Phoenicians, a connection that other scholars and artists at the time, such as Benjamin West, also asserted.[66] The comparison between Indigenous Americans and ancient Greeks and Egyptians strongly influenced neoclassical thinking.[67] Pettrich is part of the long legacy of European artists depicting Indigenous Americans for a largely European and American audience, thereby contributing to the colonial archive of Native American representations, a problematic legacy that includes historical reenactments.[68] He created the Indian Museum to show off his skill in sculpture and to ensure a pension to support himself and his family for the rest of his career.[69]

Yet these works display a significant tension. On the one hand, he depicted Indigenous Americans as proud individuals with distinctive personalities at a moment when they were engaged in peace talks with the US government and petitioning for their land rights. Pettrich's renderings of Indigenous people with individual details in the busts and the sketchbook give a sense of their gravitas and dignity as human beings. On the other hand, the placement of them in his Indian Museum firmly located Indigenous people in the past, emphasizing their status as anachronisms, not as living, developing nations. Moreover, as represented in his static bas-reliefs, Pettrich drastically simplified the complex processes of the treaty talks, the multiple discussions, ceremonies, and engagements between the Sioux, Sac and Fox, and Creek and the US government.[70] Tellingly, the Vatican curators write of Pettrich's oeuvre using heroic terms and do not fully contextualize his work within the history of North America.[71]

Pettrich donated his collection to the Vatican in 1858, promoting it as unique and emphasizing his depiction of individuals. Writing to pope Pius IX on May 21, 1858, he asserted:

> Having had occasion during my long sojourn abroad—especially in South America and Rio de Janeiro—to undertake careful studies in sculpture of Indigenous Indian races, I succeeded with the help of my three sons, who are also sculptors, to create an Indian Museum composed of various statues, busts, and bas-reliefs of the most prominent of these tribes. In the judgment of the most celebrated sculptors of America and England, there may be no other museum like it in all of Europe. I desire no greater honor than that of being able to offer it to Your Holiness, humbly imploring that I be granted a provisional site to display it in the Vatican so that it might be considered by Your Holiness. I have no doubt that this museum will be pleasing to Your Beatitude as well as to the many tourists who will visit Rome.[72]

Pettrich's statement makes it clear that he is using the subject matter to gain Pius IX's interest and favor rather than from any commitment to support for or empathize with Indigenous peoples. Pettrich's term Indian Museum implies that the Indigenous nations represented belong in the past, thus aligning itself with the neoclassical imagery by Greenough, Crawford, and Persico found at the US Capitol, and throughout major American cities, which helped justify settler-colonial eradication of Indigenous peoples and their memorialization in marble as no more than statues and reminders of the past.

In a letter to Pius IX dated November 8, 1858, Nazarene painters Johann Friedrich Overbeck and Peter von Cornelius evaluated the statuary and emphasized the veracity of the artworks as a record of the destruction by the American settlers of Indigenous Americans and their homelands: "Mr. Pettrich places before our eyes, with startling verisimilitude, those unfortunate wild tribes of North America whom the cold-hearted selfishness of a nation that calls itself Christian is now succeeding in eradicating from the face of the earth, and whose few remnants, it seems, will not long survive the massacre unleashed by their brothers. In these faces, full of spirit and vigor, one can easily recognize a people of uncommon dispositions of mind and heart."[73] These Romantic German painters emphasized the complicity of American governments and citizens in the destruction of Indigenous American lifeways. They understood the artworks as records of a way of life that was under siege.[74] They also express the inevitability of the destruction of Native American life and a patronizing sympathy for the state of Indigenous Americans at the time. Indigenous Americans faced extreme conditions on all fronts, losing their homelands, removed to reservations, consigned to hunger, poverty, and dispossession. Westward expansion continued, as settlers and gold miners moved across the Great Plains. US treaty policy led to the annexation of over 1.5 billion acres of Indigenous lands across the US from 1766 to 1866 and to a series of Indian wars in which Indigenous nations battled for their traditional lands.[75] Overbeck and von Cornelius's letter, like Pettrich's Indian Museum, express a patronizing sympathy and sense of inevitability in line with settler-colonial attitudes of Indigenous eradication.

Pettrich's works are important for their record of Native American presence, yet at the same time they introduce broader questions about agency and the value of using colonial artworks to understand Indigeneity. Pius IX accepted the collection of thirty-three sculptures and busts in 1858, and they were displayed in the Gran Sala del Concilio of the Lateran Palace, the great hall through which visitors and dignitaries entered. Eight years later, Edmonia Lewis arrived in Rome. Perhaps she visited Pettrich's Indian Museum at the Vatican during the almost thirty years she lived in the city. Artists at the time were known to tour the Vatican galleries by candlelight, viewing the statuary in the flickering light. Perhaps Lewis critiqued Pettrich's representation of Indigenous people as solely belonging in the past when she thrived in Rome, creating sculptures that promoted and even celebrated Indigenous and Black life. I turn now to placing Lewis and Pettrich in "conversation" in order to consider the problem of representing Indigeneity in art and to rethink the complicated meanings of neoclassicism for Indigenous artists.

Edmonia Lewis: Defying Colonial Expectations

Edmonia Wildfire Lewis provides an example of the survival and resilience of Indigenous Americans and thus challenges the narrative epitomized by Pettrich's Indian Museum and Crawford's *The Indian*—works that promoted the eradication values of settler colonialism. An Indigenous woman with maternal ties to the Mississauga of the New Credit First Nation in present-day Ontario, Lewis lived and worked in Rome from 1866 to about 1895.[76] She was born on July 4, 1844, in Greenbush, New York, and died in London in 1907.[77] Her mother, Catherine Lewis, was raised on the Credit River Reserve, now known as the Mississauga of the New Credit First Nation, but when she married

Lewis's father, who was African Haitian, New Credit First Nation denied them Indian status and annual government support. After her parents died when she was four, Edmonia maintained a nomadic life. Raised along with her brother by her Ojibwe aunts, she sold souvenirs in Buffalo and Toronto.[78] The voices of Indigenous peoples, and especially Indigenous women, are rare in the archival record of the nineteenth century, and I begin this section by highlighting a statement by Lewis from an 1866 interview in the literary magazine *Athenaeum*: "My mother was a wild Indian and born in Albany, of copper color and with straight black hair. There she made and sold moccasins. My father, who was a Negro, and a gentleman's servant, saw her and married her . . . Mother often left her home and wandered with her people, whose habits she could not forget, and thus we, her children, were brought up in the same wild manner. Until I was twelve years old, I led this wandering life, fishing and swimming . . . and making moccasins."[79] By describing her mother as a "wild Indian" and saying she was brought up in a "wild manner," Lewis's statement plays into the standard tropes of American settler colonialism, which depicted Indigenous Americans as "primitive savages" and amounted at best to what Robert Penner describes as "the commodification of Indian—Christian or otherwise—as exotic entertainer."[80]

Lewis also marketed herself as Indian to capitalize on popular interest in Indigenous history and peoples. Perhaps it was easier for her to identify with her Indigenous ancestry than her Haitian American ancestry given the prevalence of anti-Black sentiment and her artistic development during the Civil War.[81] Lewis took risks in identifying with her Native heritage, but they paid off in the form of commissions for her work and her enjoyment of an international lifestyle and fame in American expatriate circles in Rome as well as in North America. By 1867, when Lewis had moved to Rome, missionary and settler-colonial attitudes toward Native people had firmly established them as belonging to the past and not the future, as "relics of an outmoded, prehistoric savagery."[82] Pettrich too, as a German artist in the xenophobic atmosphere of Washington, faced discrimination and hostility, and moved to Brazil after being attacked. However, Pettrich's peers never questioned his choice of subject matter or his ability to create art.

The "wild manner" Lewis articulated drew on popular ideas of Indians in touch with nature, another facet of neoclassicism. As a Native woman of her time, she articulated the romantic ideals surrounding the Indigenous American figure. She also played with these concepts and "performed her Indianness verbally and visually" for a primarily white audience in her press statements and her statuary.[83] Indeed, many contemporary Indigenous writers referred to themselves as wild children of the forest. Native American writers William Apess and Charles Eastman used the concepts of the "native of the soil" and the "free and natural life of an Indian" in their writings and autobiographies. Thus, through her articulation of the "wild Indian," Lewis expressed her awareness and identification with other Indigenous writers and thinkers of the time. In this way, she connected with an Indigenous community of scholars and artists creating from their marginal positions within society.[84]

Lewis emphasized the training and knowledge she had learned from her Ojibwe family and her exposure to Indigenous American art production. She made moccasins and helped her aunts create souvenir arts for the tourist trade, using the skills of beadwork, quillwork, and basketry, a form of employment and labor that many Indigenous artists engaged in to support themselves.[85] Tourists and travelers respected and admired the Mississauga Ojibwe in the northeast for their fine quillwork and beadwork on moccasins and other souvenir arts. "Because Native people successfully commoditized their arts," art historian Ruth Phillips explains, "these reinvented constructions of Indianness achieved wide distribution. Popular with members of nearly all classes of North American and European society, these objects traversed cultural boundaries and took their places in fashionable cosmopolitan displays in curio cabinets and cozy corners."[86] Like the souvenir arts that she sold, Lewis too navigated international boundaries in her artistic career. She lived most of her life abroad, studying at Oberlin College, Boston, then lived in Rome, never returning to the Anishinaabeg and her traditional territories near the Credit River in Ontario.[87] Because her mother married out and due to the colonial measures of the Indian Act, Lewis did not have Indian status. This significant factor in addition to the multiple forms of trauma Lewis faced on Turtle Island may be why she never returned to her traditional homelands but chose to make Rome her home instead.

The Studios of Edmonia Lewis as Indigenous Spaces

An 1867 guidebook, *A Handbook to Rome and Its Environs*, lists "Lewis, Miss (American), 27, Via della Frezza," the address of the former studio of Antonio Canova, a notable and celebrated Roman artist. The guidebook adds, "Among the characteristics of Modern Rome capable of affording high interest to the intellectual visitor, there are few that offer a greater charm than the artists' studios. Travellers in general are little aware of the interest which they are calculated to afford, and many leave Rome without making the acquaintance of a single artist."[88] Visiting this studio today, one can see ancient Roman fragments of putti, Latin inscriptions, and other pieces of the Roman past fixed to the exterior. The studio is a few minutes' walk from the busy Piazza di Spagna and the intellectual and artistic hub of Café Greco, then and now frequented by writers and artists.[89] Lewis took up this studio when she first moved to Rome, surely drawing inspiration from the larger-than-life papal figures, mythical goddesses, and Roman centurions created by Canova and left as models in the studio.[90] It is likely she walked up the Spanish Steps to sweeping views of Rome and perhaps even attended services at the church of Trinità dei Monti perched above the Piazza di Spagna. The street around the studio is narrow but dappled with morning rays of sunlight. The lighting, together with the fact that Canova worked here, surely inspired an ambitious sculptor like Lewis.

Harriet Hosmer and fellow women sculptors had homes in the Piazza di Spagna area, close to the studios of contemporaries such as Ferdinand Pettrich. A decade later, Lewis relocated from Canova's former studio near the Spanish Steps and across the way from the Fratelli D'Alessandri brothers' photographic studio to an atelier near Piazza Barberini. She moved to Via San Nicola da Tolentino, another area of Rome in Sallustiano, halfway between Piazza Barberini and Piazza di San Bernardo.[91] The Triton Fountain by Baroque artist Bernini in the main square of Piazza Barberini is a commanding presence; Lewis likely bought her fruit and vegetables at the market stands that used to surround the fountain. A later edition of *A Handbook of Rome* (1875) listed her again, evidence of her success as a sculptor in a competitive, international sphere and of the ongoing importance of her work and her many commissions from American, British, and European patrons.[92]

Lewis left an indelible trace on the artistic community in Rome. She purposefully chose to use a medium not associated with Native American souvenir arts and to create work that was part of the elite western art tradition. At the same time, she drew on the aesthetic traditions of Native American art, an element that would become important in her well-known work *Minnehaha*.[93] Lewis enjoyed a degree of social freedom not available to her in the United States, but, as one of a group of female artists, she was subjected to patronizing critiques from her male contemporaries.[94] As a person of color, she also faced discrimination from her female colleagues and had to negotiate a challenging politics of representation to avoid her colleagues pigeonholing her as a "colored artist." As art historian Charmaine Nelson argues, "Lewis was recognized as one of the flock, but in comparison with her white female contemporaries, the invisibility, visibility, or hypervisibility of her black-Native body within the Roman colony further complexified her experience as a female sculptor, since her racial identity challenged the 'regime of race' as it transgressed the entrenched western ideal of the white artist."[95] Thus, working in Rome among a group of other American sculptors, Lewis confronted ideas of who could create neoclassical sculpture and why. Her colleague, the white female sculptor Anne Whitney, wrote of Lewis as being "very much of an aboriginal, grateful, vengeful, a little cunning . . . I like her in spite of her faults and will help her all I can. I wish she were a little less of an aborigine."[96] Thus, although Lewis arguably had more freedom within the artistic and social circles of expatriate Rome than she would have had in the United States, she still suffered discrimination from fellow artists. While her works exemplify the technical standards of neoclassical art, her identity as an Indigenous woman unsettled her colleagues and challenged the neoclassical idea that Indigenous people lived only in the past. In this way, her presence in the Roman artistic community and her statuary left an indelible trace of Anishinaabe space-making within the city of Rome.

Negotiating Settler and Indigenous Ideals: *Minnehaha*

Lewis's sculpture *Minnehaha* draws inspiration both from Henry Wadsworth Longfellow's *The Song of Hiawatha* (1855) and her own Ojibwe heritage and experience growing up creating and selling quill and birch-bark baskets for the souvenir trade. The artistic community in Rome at the time included Longfellow, and Lewis made a bust of him, reputedly an excellent likeness. *The Song of Hiawatha* is an epic poem that gives a fictional account of the Ojibwe peoples of the Great Lakes region. Longfellow drew on the ethnographic studies of Henry Rowe Schoolcraft, an Indian agent married to an Ojibwe woman, Jane Schoolcraft, who was a direct source of inspiration and knowledge for him.[97]

With her marble bust of *Minnehaha*, created in 1868 (see figure 1.2), Lewis capitalized on the popular image of Minnehaha within American culture.[98] The bust, carved from Carrara marble, depicts a young girl with stylized eagle feathers that mesh into her hair. She wears a necklace of medium and small round and oval beads that recall Venetian glass beads used by Indigenous women to create beaded moccasins, vests, and other items of material culture. In this way the materiality of her sculpture, making glass beads into marble, pays tribute to the ancient trade routes between Italy and Turtle Island that Indigenous artists relied on for their artistic production. Minnehaha purses her lips in a serious expression, and Lewis depicts the young woman as she is coming of age. Her long hair flows over her shoulders, and her headband is a piece of hide.

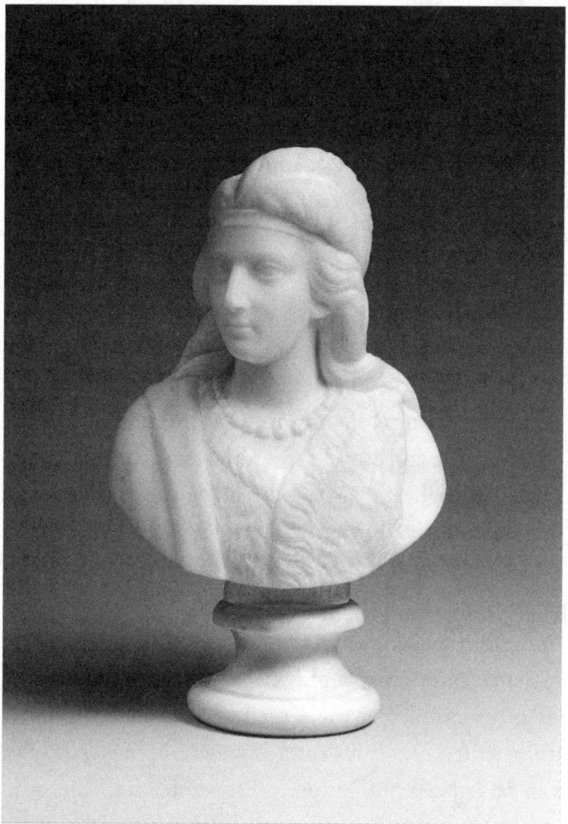

FIGURE 1.2. Edmonia Lewis, *Minnehaha*, 1868. Marble, 29.5 × 18.4 × 12.4 cm. Courtesy of the Metropolitan Museum of Art, New York.

Lewis, a beader and maker of Anishinaabeg material culture including moccasins and baskets, chose to work in the medium of marble, rendering Indigenous material culture markers such as trade beads and hide in a more permanent medium, stone.[99] Her choice to sculpt Indigenous subjects and Indigenous material culture in stone works against the destruction caused by anthropologists and government agents who, operating within a salvage mindset, seized cultural belongings of Indigenous communities without care.[100] The deliberate medium of marble suggests the immortality of the subjects represented, and thus works against the ideology of the Indian as vanishing and out of time that is prominent in collecting practices, world's fairs, and sculptures found throughout the United States. Another exciting and interesting possibility to consider is whether Lewis had a collection of Indigenous artifacts and belongings that she drew inspiration from for her works. She sculpted moccasins, hides, and different forms of trade beads in marble several times throughout her career, and likely garnered insight from collections she had seen, perhaps even the Cardinal Borgia collection at the Vatican. Thinking of Lewis as an artist-collector like West and Pettrich who accumulated Indigenous artifacts and used these as reference points in their art makes sense given her longstanding interest in and appreciation of Indigenous material culture, especially when she lived so far away from her traditional homelands.[101] Having a collection of Indigenous artifacts would also help authenticate the many stories she told about her Indigenous ancestry and grounded her position in the mercurial community of artistic expats.

Lewis did not want the artistic community to accuse her of having a male atelier complete the work, as her colleague Harriet Hosmer had done and been reprimanded and discredited for doing.[102] Working with the marble herself required a great deal of strength, tactility, and grit, and Lewis seems to have thought of herself as a modern Michelangelo, as she made several copies of his works, challenging herself against a prominent male artist of the Italian Renaissance and proving via sculpture that she was equal to the challenge.[103]

Viewers could interpret Minnehaha's aquiline nose and high cheekbones as reminders of Native American facial features, but they can also signify as European.[104] Thus, her facial features seem ambiguous, yet the eagle feather in her straight hair serves as a reminder of the sacred reverence that Ojibwe hold for the soaring creature; its feathers carry intercessions and prayers to the creator, and participants in sacred ceremonies use the eagle feather. The bust therefore evokes the idea that Minnehaha is protected by the spiritual powers of the eagle that watches over Ojibwe peoples. Lewis's bust, all in white marble, has no hint of color, unlike the tinted Venus done by her predecessor John Gibson, which had created a scandal in Rome.[105] Lewis chose to work in white marble for all her sculptural pieces, like the rest of the artistic community. Her use of white marble also allowed her to reference Eurocentric notions of racialized whiteness and to appeal to collectors, much like her contemporaries, including American sculptor Anne Whitney.[106] One exception was French artist Charles Cordier (1827–1905), who used polychrome marble for his busts of Algerian and Egyptian figures.[107] In other words, the medium of white marble allows artist and viewer to understand *Minnehaha* according to the racial prejudices of the time. Although not visible in this version, in her larger sculpture *Hiawatha's Marriage* (1871), Lewis used a Greek key motif (meander) on the hemline of Minnehaha's dress, visually aligning Indigenous Americans and the antique Greek past. She also included the Greek key motif in her *carte de visite* in Chicago, placing herself within the artistic legacy of Greek antiquity but also affirming her contemporary cultural capital.[108]

Lewis wanted to capitalize on the tourist market for images inspired by Longfellow's romanticized vision of Ojibwe peoples, and she did so far from her traditional territories, yet she also drew on her life experience as an Anishinaabe person of mixed heritage to create her works. This may be why Lewis sculpted Minnehaha's face to reference both European and Native American ideals. Lewis most likely made Minnehaha with ambiguous rather than individualized features in order to appeal more readily to a white audience hungry for images of the romantic, beautiful maiden who came to a tragic end in the famous poem. Perhaps she was also playing around with white audiences' expectations of "authentic" looking Indians, and thus the sculpture reflects those expectations in the facial features and the material culture the figure wears. At the same time, Lewis also drew on her childhood memories of selling baskets and souvenirs with the Ojibwe Mississauga band, even while working in Rome. She thus was layering elements of her own temporal experience as a beader and a maker of Anishinaabe visual culture onto the sculpture. Moreover, Lewis's unforgettable presence in Rome disrupted ideas about Indigenous people as belonging to the past, as suggested by the pathetic, defeatist poses found throughout sculptures by her contemporaries. Thus, her works and artistic experience create a different sense of time for Indigenous peoples through the medium of marble and suggest a longevity and even immortality that flies in the face of genocidal policies of elimination by the US and Canadian governments and made into physical form in the sculptural works of Pettrich.

The expatriate artistic community thrived in Rome during this period, and both Lewis and Pettrich worked in the same genre. The distance between Pettrich's and Lewis's studios was about a fifteen-minute walk, with major attractions such as the Café Greco along the way.[109] They both had studios beside Piazza Barberini from 1866 to 1872, and Pius IX supported both artists during his papacy (1846–78).[110] Both used the artistic language of neoclassicism for unique purposes. They were pragmatic sculptors who recorded Indigenous American life as they saw fit, and they did so for a popular audience and for commissions. Although romanticized, their depictions challenged the biases of neoclassical art in their different ways. Pettrich's sketches and statuary call for a substantial degree of skepticism when considering them as documentary evidence and require an engagement with the stakes that Indigenous peoples faced at the time, what anthropologist Laura Peers calls the "deeper challenges" of artworks like Pettrich's.[111] In his sketches, Pettrich used individual details to work against the neoclassical preference for a lack of ornamentation, but his *Dying Tecumseh* glorified death and heroic sacrifice, key tenets of neoclassicism, rather than the living presence of Indigenous nations that he witnessed in Washington, DC. For her part, Lewis complicated the expectations and meanings of Indigenous identities associated with neoclassical art through her presence as a modern artist, her cultural capital, and her marble renderings of Anishinaabe visual culture. Although her oeuvre remained fairly standard, drawing on literary inspiration from Longfellow, she also met the demands of a public hungry for an idealized Minnehaha, a mythical figure.

In a patronizing, pigeonholing judgment of Lewis's work as "appropriate," art historian William Gerdts had this to say: "The 19th-century American sculptor perhaps most involved with Indian subject matter was Edmonia Lewis—appropriately enough, since she was half-Indian as well as half-black (her mother was a member of the Chippewa tribe)."[112] This research works against this judgment of Lewis's oeuvre as merely autobiographical. Lewis created Native American statuary at a time when Indigenous Americans were experiencing massive upheaval and displacement; at the same moment, a burgeoning market had emerged in North America and Europe for representations of Indigenous peoples.[113] Popular culture, sculptures, and the collection of Indigenous visual culture, as well as world's fairs such as the 1876 Philadelphia Centennial International Exposition, participated in the capitalist market for the elimination of Indigenous lifeways and the search for American identity. As scholar Shari Huhndorf notes on world's fairs from this period, "while the exhibits frequently raised the specter of Native savagery, they also quelled viewers' fears by promising them that 'progress' would soon render the Indian threat meaningless."[114] In contrast to monolithic settler representations of Indigenous peoples in world's fairs and popular culture, Lewis occupied a complex position of creating Indigenous sculptures by drawing on her own life experience while simultaneously negotiating and achieving success in the art world that was not a safe or welcoming place for Indigenous and many other artists of color.

Her own story of expulsion from Oberlin College, the accusation of murder, and then success on an international level, is part of the tenacity of Indigenous Americans during an intense period of destruction and assimilationist policy. Lewis operated outside the expected boundaries imposed on Native American lives by US governmental rule and outside the confines of artistic expectation as well. The art market desired Native American artists to produce things that seemed ethnographically authentic and exotic, referencing some aspect of their heritage in a recognizably Indian mode, but Lewis complicates this assumption in a provocative way. She provides an exceptional way of thinking about how her life and work existed, and about the legacy of Native American representation within America and Italy. She challenged assumptions prevalent in neoclassical artworks throughout the nineteenth century that presented Indigenous Americans as out of time, such as Pettrich's *Dying Tecumseh*, which played into the dying warrior theme dominant in American art on Indigenous subject matter and solidified the idea of Native Americans as stranded in the past.

At the same time, Lewis's work adds to the historical narrative of Native artists abroad.[115] As a sculptor, Lewis was a contemporary of Pettrich in artistic output, medium, and subject matter, but, as an Indigenous and Black female artist working in Rome, she was a unique figure at the time. Considering her within the canon of art history helps to expand and broaden our definition of what Indigenous artists and artists of color created in the nineteenth century, as well as questions our assumptions about Native American art.[116] Lewis worked in the medium of marble, not beads and quills, the more "traditional" media for Ojibwe artists. She also worked and lived in Rome for most of her life. Her existence provides evidence against the settler-colonial assumption, often expressed in neoclassical sculptures, that all Indigenous Americans had died, or, in Tecumseh's case, were dying out. In the words of historian Lorenzo Veracini, "settler projects are inevitably premised on the traumatic, that is, violent, replacement and/or displacement of indigenous Others."[117] Whereas neoclassical artworks such as Pettrich's evidence complicity in the settler-colonial process of the denial of the modernity of Indigenous Americans, Lewis counteracts this denial through her presence and her sculpting of Indigenous material culture in marble, creating a permanence that outlasted the genocidal policies intended to eliminate Indigenous peoples in the nineteenth century. Lewis provides evidence of alterity in the artistic canon and thus requires our attention if we are to write more expansive and critical art histories.

Although Lewis drew on fictional characters such as Longfellow's Minnehaha, she also created work from her life experience as an artist of African American and Native American heritage. She was an artist of color working at a time when the US government fought a bloody genocide against Indigenous peoples across Turtle Island and began to confine Native American people to reservations, and while slavery continued. Battles for Indigenous territories lasted through this period, including the Wounded Knee Massacre of 1890.[118] The chapter has analyzed her as an artist of color who produced work contrary to nineteenth-century colonial assumptions about what artists of color could do and, moreover, who worked within the milieu of the American art community in Rome. Lewis played to an audience of largely white American collectors in an artistic atmosphere that represented Indigenous Americans as either nubile young pagans ready for conversion or doomed savages fleeing from civilization. Importantly, Lewis presented Indigenous peoples in her statuary as alive and well, countering the depictions of Indigenous subjects as dying or doomed that were prevalent in Pettrich's *Dying Tecumseh*, Crawford's *The Indian*, and many other works.

Thinking of Lewis as part of a history of Indigenous people abroad helps place her life and works within the larger movement of Native peoples transcending colonial expectations and genocidal policy in the nineteenth and early twentieth centuries. Lewis provides a much needed intervention into the canon and fractures expectations about neoclassicism as a movement. From the Indian Removal Act of 1830 through the end of the nineteenth century and beyond, the US government continued to legislate and enforce the removal and relocation of Native peoples. Lewis moved to Rome in 1867, the year the Treaty of Medicine Lodge began one of the most destructive periods for Indigenous peoples across Turtle Island. By the 1880s, throughout the Great Plains, they were forced onto reservations and genocidal boarding school policy commenced.[119] With buffalo by then nearly exterminated by the federal governments of the US and Canada, Plains Indigenous peoples experienced widespread starvation.[120]

Lewis made brief trips back to Turtle Island for the Philadelphia Centennial International Exposition and to attend the opening of her award-winning sculpture *The Death of Cleopatra* (1876), which reviewers praised for its ingenuity.[121] Yet for all her renown in the art world in the United States, Lewis chose to stay and likely felt more comfortable in Rome; she spoke fluent Italian and entertained patrons at her studios.

Rather than looking back, she carved out new territories for Indigenous peoples and artists of color, claiming with gravitas her place as an Indigenous woman in modernity, making her mark in marble, and complicating the colonial assumptions and simplistic binaries prominent in neoclassical art. Her life is also a testament to the tenacity of Indigenous artists in the nineteenth and early twentieth centuries, and thus forms an important precursor to thinking about Indigeneity in Rome and in the 1925 VME.[122]

In Closing: Edmonia Lewis Disrupting Ferdinand Pettrich's Indian Museum

Although Lewis's statuary was not displayed at the Vatican Missionary Exposition, one can imagine that if her work was showcased alongside Pettrich's, it would interrupt the logic of Pettrich's and pope Pius IX's Indian Museum that

Indigenous nations had disappeared by the early twentieth century. If Pettrich and Lewis had met, what types of conversations might they have had? Maybe they both would have debated their passion and interest in sculpting Indigenous nations for an international audience of collectors, tourists, and the Catholic Church. Maybe Lewis would have discussed her Indigenous ancestry as a point of importance in sculpting Indigenous works and examined white patrons' demands around authenticity and her reservations against reading *Minnehaha* as a self-portrait and an "unmediated autobiography."[123] They likely would have had some disagreements about method and the stakes for Indigenous artists and communities. Circling back to Lewis's *carte de visite* discussed at the opening of this chapter, it has been less than a decade since a curator discovered this evidence, and perhaps, as time passes, more details about Lewis's life will be revealed in the archival record that will complement the world-building in this chapter—and by that I mean more layered interpretations and imaginings of Lewis's life and works.

My intention with this chapter has been to create a space of possible imagining and imaging beyond the evidence in the limited archival record that for Lewis, unlike Pettrich, remains under documented. As for many artists of color, Lewis's archive is fragmented and to some extent unknown due to the colonial biases of nineteenth-century recordkeeping. For Lewis, a career in Rome meant a happier and more productive life. She was able to work in spite of the racist assumptions and violence of the United States and to carry on her art production and self-promotion to her advantage by discussing and celebrating her Ojibwe heritage. She created sculptures and busts depicting idealized and heroic Indigenous Americans based on *The Song of Hiawatha* and the legends of her people.

Lewis's life as an Indigenous artist contradicted the presumption found in works such as Pettrich's *Dying Tecumseh* that Native people had died out and were relics of the past. However, her works also conformed to the popular appetite for Native mythic heroes, as evident with sculptural works such as *Minnehaha*. Lewis used neoclassical art to present Indigenous peoples not as specters for processes of settler colonialism but to give presence to Indigenous women; in this light, it is important to note that she presented her figures not as nude but wearing hide, carved with an eye for textural details. Pettrich did give some visibility to Indigenous nations with his Indian Museum, but in general—and in line with other American sculptors—he presented Indigenous figures, including Tecumseh, as waiting certain death due to colonial takeover. For example, the sculptors Thomas Crawford and Erastus Dow Palmer presented Indigenous women as nude in a thinly veiled gratuitous way to be ogled by the white American viewer—the not-so-subtle subtext of these works being that the Indigenous woman is a resource to be exploited, much like the land in the wake of American westward expansion and Indigenous removal.[124] Lewis's presence as an Indigenous person worked against the homogenization appearing in the neoclassical form and in allegorical representations in which Indigenous people were passive bystanders.[125] The inclusion of Lewis's statuary and her life story in imperial spaces complicates the meanings associated with the neoclassical style and provides compelling evidence of the transatlantic circulation of Indigenous statuary and artists. Both Lewis and Pettrich benefited from the global interest in Indigenous American visual culture, and their works were important foundations for later American artists such as Augustus Saint-Gaudens and Hermon Atkins MacNeil, who worked in Rome creating Indigenous subjects.[126]

Global art history today seems a recent phenomenon. However, Indigenous imagery as created by Pettrich, together with Lewis's artworks and her personal experience, are evidence that First Nations art and people circulated in a global network.[127] This story builds a foundation for the following chapters, indicating the international boundaries that First Nations arts traveled and the reframing of images and conceptions of Indigenous archives across the booming metropolis of Rome.

Significantly, Lewis unsettled presumptions about Indigenous artists, and her legacy continues to this day. For example, the inclusion of Lewis's *Old Arrow Maker* (1872) in the ground-breaking 2019 exhibition *Hearts of Our People: Native Women Artists*, which circulated throughout the United States, is testimony to her wide-ranging inspiration for ongoing Native American arts.[128] *Old Arrow Maker* celebrates the close bond between father and daughter, as Minnehaha weaves rushes together into mats and her father carves jasper arrow heads. The sculpture also exemplifies Lewis's skill at creating textures with the hide that Minnehaha wears wrapped around her torso. Minnehaha has a feather in her hair and her neck is adorned with a beaded necklace, both signifiers of her Indigenous presence. Minnehaha's rush-weaving parallels the work of Lewis, who strove to weave together her experiences in both white and Indigenous worlds in order to create new sculptures that pleased a global audience of collectors. The weaver also signifies the agility of female makers and hints at the traditional knowledge involved in both harvesting and making work from rushes, which continue to be important for Anishinaabe cultures today. Lewis worked in the medium of marble, sculpting far away from her traditional lands, but her oeuvre, unlike if she had chosen to work only with rushes or sinew and hide and beads, creates a permanence and hints at the immortality of Indigenous life through this medium.

More broadly, tracing Lewis as an artist in relation to Pettrich allows insights into the ways that Indigenous artists succeeded on a global stage despite the epistemic violence of settler colonialism, overcoming hardships during her early career and raising awareness through works that promoted Indigenous and Black life. Lewis was not a passive or mute bystander, as typical in colonial renditions and allegories of Indigenous America, and her life and oeuvre provide an ancestral art history lesson of perseverance, creativity, and negotiation of both settler and Indigenous ideals and worlds. Considering Pettrich and Lewis together furthermore points to the problematic ideals of neoclassical art, which actively endorsed the destruction and eradication of Indigenous life via statuary. Through her presence and oeuvre, Lewis disrupted this attitude of elimination found in the sculptural sphere in the Capitol in Washington and in Rome. Lewis may now be considered as an Indigenous and Black celebrity, and her documented life and artworks push against the lack of awareness and absence of naming that occurred for Indigenous American artists at the 1925 VME. Considering that Lewis spent some time working and sketching at the Vatican in its many sculpture-filled hallways, perhaps she visited the exposition and haunts the place today, visiting with Anishinaabe material culture—ancestors who remain captives in the sealed vaults.

2

"THE MOST EXHAUSTIVE RECORD OF THE WORLD'S PROGRESS EVER DISPLAYED"

Pope Pius XI's Culture of Conquest and Visitors' Experiences at the Vatican Missionary Exposition

Journal: Fototeca, Vatican City

APRIL 2016. *I walked to the Vatican Museums yesterday and did some archival digging in a gray cubicle located outside the main museum overlooking a courtyard filled with pine trees. A museum worker snuck me into the Fototeca, a photo repository. I saw archival photographs from the closing of the Vatican Missionary Exposition in 1925 and from the 1926 opening of the Missionary Ethnological Museum in the Lateran palace. It was interesting because I could see evidence of the transitions of the museum after the closing of the exposition in the photos; some of the vitrines were open, and there were also newspaper scraps lying around on the floor; materials, including cultural belongings, were also scattered there. It reminded me of anthropologist Ann Laura Stoler's admonition to write about the unbalanced archival moments, the unpolished spaces.*[1] *This was evidence of the disorientation of the expo, an unofficial record that would never make its way into the official catalogs. I saw a plethora of cultural belongings from Turtle Island, including Yup'ik masks, amauti, woven baskets, pottery, miniature models of dogsled teams, and Očhéthi Šakówiŋ (Sioux) regalia. I also saw weapons, including arrows, an ax, a club, beaded octopus bags from the Great Lakes, a collection of parfleche, two masks from the Northwest Coast, Haida argillite miniature totem poles, ancient hide drums, birchbark baskets, and Diné (Navajo) textiles. The photographs provided clear material evidence of the contents of the collections. Front and center in these photographs were Pettrich's statuary and, on the walls, his bas-reliefs. I made a drawing of the Indigenous cultural belongings and asked if I could take photographs, but the curator said this was not allowed. Toward the end of the day, after the other curators in the small office had left, the curator whispered that my visit would be a one-time occurrence.*

At the Fototeca, the person who let me in had shaking hands as she showed me around; she seemed nervous about me being there. It made me feel uneasy and wonder why were they being so secretive? It was helpful, though, to see the photographs of the museum from the closing of the expo onward. I also wonder if some of the material no longer exists due to infestation or neglect. After my visit to the Fototeca, I met a former Vatican curator and ethnologist outside the Vatican walls. As the person said in the privacy of their own home, the Plains buffalo hides that were exhibited in 1925 were destroyed by insect infestation.[2] *At the former curator's home, I viewed some more photos from the conservation lab of the Americas collection, but it seemed an exercise largely in frustration, as the Vatican Missionary Ethnological Museum staff did not respond to my multiple requests for access and viewing the collection.*

On December 21, 1924, the winter solstice, with the sun at its lowest in the sky, pope Pius XI solemnly ascended the Vatican staircase and opened the door to the Vatican Missionary Exhibition (VME).[3] Standing in one of the central rooms, the Hall of North America, surrounded by cultural belongings stolen from Indigenous peoples of North America, he welcomed tourists and pilgrims into this unprecedented exposition, which would close just over a year later, on January 10, 1926. Assembled in the heart of the Vatican, the VME included specially designed pavilions showcasing art and artifacts seized by missions across the Americas, Asia, Oceania, and Africa.[4] Sponsored by Pius XI, and with the cooperation of the city of Rome and Italy's fascist dictator Benito Mussolini, the exhibition featured over one hundred thousand objects and attracted over one million visitors during its thirteen-month run.

Royalty, missionary scholars, the press, pilgrims for the Holy Year, and tourists all flocked to Rome.[5] Amid a flurry of world's fairs and colonial exhibitions during the first decades of the twentieth century, this exhibition was unique; it was the largest Catholic missionary exhibition in Europe during the early twentieth century. Organized by Father Wilhelm Schmidt, an Austrian anthropologist and the pope's curator, the exhibition operated as a show of propaganda to compete with Protestant exhibitions and world's fairs.

A grainy black and white photograph from 1924 in the *Rivista Illustrata della Esposizione Missionaria Vaticana*, the official print organ of the VME, shows a room chaotically stacked with overflowing boxes and crates, revealing a moment of slippage in colonial order (see figure 2.1).[6] Nuns and priests mill about among some of the numerous belongings that missionaries collected for the VME. In the middle foreground, a priest in a black robe with sheaves of papers at his feet looks up from unpacking. Behind him, missionary organizers in long dark robes and workers in civilian clothes take a pause from sorting materials. A missionary crouches on the ground, too busy unpacking to look up for the camera. Half-open boxes filled with flora and fauna, with sacred things and secular objects, wait to be sorted. Folded textiles rest on top of shipping crates stacked high. Rows of model colonial schoolhouses remain unsorted in the left background.

In the chaos of unpacking, missionaries have scattered shipping papers and textiles across the ground. These and the half-opened crates reveal an inevitable moment of disorganization but also suggest a larger context of colonial disorder, a slippage behind the totalizing mission of the VME, a glimpse of what Ann Laura Stoler describes as the "the febrile movements of persons off balance—of thoughts and feelings in and out of place" that underlies the entire colonial project.[7] This awkward, unpolished space, a back room of the Vatican Museums, expresses a palpable anxiety similar to the one I had sensed at the Fototeca Archive. The blurriness of nuns' hands unwinding some materials in the left foreground, the disordered space, the frantic attempt at organization, are also reminders of the failure of some materials to arrive in time.[8] Other items landed in a damaged condition, and some never arrived at all.[9] Port authorities, such as those at Hankou, China, retained objects, and organizers worried that not enough material would arrive for the opening of the exhibition. Missionaries sent boxes as heavy as 350 pounds that porters had to carry on their backs excruciatingly long distances to shipping points, a "veritable odyssey."[10]

Mill Hill Catholic Father Dreves described his experience of viewing the VME under construction: "I was greatly impressed by the many and extensive

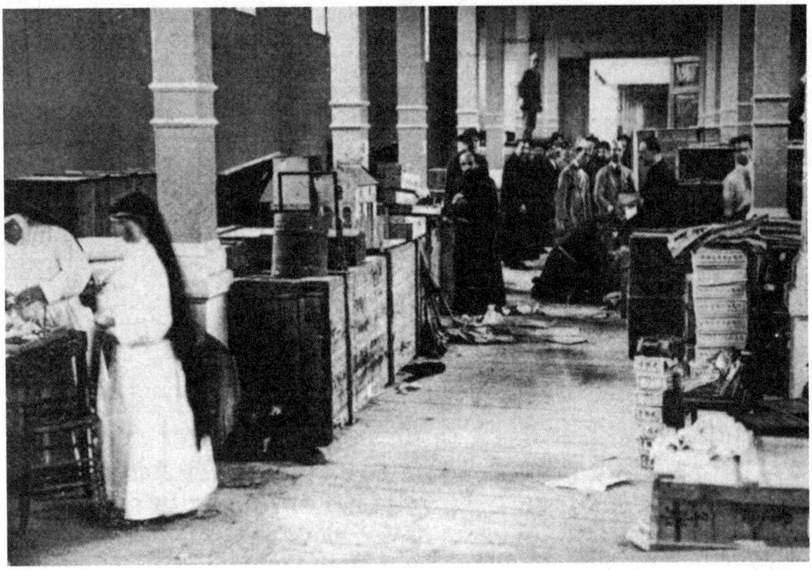

FIGURE 2.1. "Il lavoro di sistemazione della mostra" (The work of setting up the show). Source: *Rivista Illustrata della Esposizione Missionaria Vaticana*, December 15, 1924, 30. Courtesy of Propaganda Fide Library Collections, Pontificio Collegio Urbano "De Propaganda Fide," Rome.

pavilions that were already built or that were under construction. There was a feverish activity all round. Missionaries were engaged emptying boxes containing an immense variety of exhibits. Hundreds of boxes had already arrived, but hundreds more were still to come. I spent some anxious weeks awaiting the arrival of the Mill Hill Missions' exhibits. At last, most of these made their appearance early in December."[11] The VME required a complex and often untidy global system of effort and organization that remained invisible to those touring the carefully laid-out exhibits. When considering the significance of the VME, it is useful to remember this photograph documenting the moments of feverish activity beforehand. It is a marker of the anxieties and frustrations of missionary behavior. Analyzing the photographs and other missionary documents critically, attending to the gaps and inconsistencies, is part of the decolonizing work necessary to destabilize the apparent self-assurance of the Catholic Church's colonial missionary project. Applying a decolonizing lens and mode of inquiry to the archive of papal culture of the VME raises many questions and ways in of working and thinking with the material that move beyond a surface appreciation and unsettle the truth claims of the images.

At the time, journalist Gaultiero Campino observed in the *New York Times* that "this exhibition, both as an historical record and as an indication of future achievement, is expected to be the most exhaustive record of the world's progress ever displayed."[12] The arrangement and display of material culture, described using binary terms such as "beautiful" or "grotesque," and featuring "pagan idols" and other evidence of "witchcraft," shamanism, and other fantastical terms, made tangible its allochronic state.[13] This "denial of the coevalness," a lack of acknowledgment of Indigenous peoples' modernity and their cultural production and existence in time, relied on the paradox of inclusion.[14] This chapter contends that the arrangement and interpretation of Indigenous arts and material culture within the exhibition space and the *Rivista Illustrata* served the VME's goal by rendering Indigenous nations within a static and homogenizing vision that flattened makers and communities. The regime of the VME used Indigenous American visual culture to form what Pius XI called "silent eloquence," a description that positioned Indigenous visual culture as trophies and fetishes, mute objects of the pope's domain and his wish to glorify missionaries as heroes.[15]

The VME was a self-serving mechanism, an attempt to show the absolute control of papal activity and authority over Indigenous communities and their material culture "Urbi et Orbi" (in Rome and across the world). In fact, missionaries often had limited influence among the Indigenous nations they worked with and expressed their frustration at the display requirements of the VME. The chapter further contextualizes the exhibition by imagining a visitor walking through the grandeur and cacophony of 1920s Rome and Saint Peter's and into the VME. As a last point of comparison, I will argue the VME operated as a competitive spectacle and a form of papal culture of conquest in the age of world's fairs by considering it in relation to contemporaneous fairs and expositions. All the publications and the visual culture produced by the Vatican for the VME formed part of this papal culture, an ethos of conquest that continues the exploitation of Indigenous peoples.

Stealing, Collecting, and Displaying Indigenous Art

The VME, like other world's fairs and expositions, formed part of the collecting craze across Europe and the Americas for all things Indigenous. Middle-class Americans amassed Native American baskets, weavings, curios, handiwork, embroidered and beaded moccasins, dolls, clothing, ceramics, and other articles for their homes. Buying from mail order catalogs and department stores, artists, writers, and homemakers collected Native American materials and displayed them, usually in their parlors or studies, or wherever they entertained guests.[16] The passion for Native American handicrafts paralleled the "aesthetic reform" of the time, that is, the arts and crafts movement. Many Americans turned to Native American art as an antidote to the alienating effects of modern society.[17] Women's home-decor magazines esteemed the beauty and usefulness of Native art. Americans thought of Native Americans as in touch with nature, as "authentic," in order to construct their own identity.

While Americans sought out Indigenous material culture and fetishized sacred and secular Indigenous arts for their homes, Indigenous scholars and activists argued for the importance of Indigenous art for the survival of future generations. Native American critics saw art as having positive, redemptory qualities for American Indian civilization and reforms.[18] Santee Dakota scholar Charles Eastman wrote of the positive value of Native arts and their significance as having a "vital role" for modern living and compared them favorably with Japanese art.[19] Winnebago artist Angel De Cora taught Indigenous art forms to Native children at the Carlisle Indian School in Pennsylvania; she believed Native arts could make a unique and modern contribution to American society. The boarding schools like Carlisle—one of the most well-known of the assimilative schools in the United States and the first government-run institution, whose motto was "kill the Indian"—also capitalized on the craze for Native American-made souvenirs and material culture by selling the work, exploiting the labor of Indigenous children.[20]

The VME formed part of a demand for all things Indigenous American at the Vatican, too. Visitors could purchase guidebooks to support missionary orders, as well as souvenirs, postcards, and stamps. Father Dreves of the Saint Joseph's Missionary Society, part of the Mill Hill Missionaries, recalled that "having bought your ticket, costing three lire (seven pence) . . . you pass on your left a stand where you can purchase Anno Santo stamps, souvenirs, etc., and a little further up, a Refreshment room" (see plate 4).[21] The densely packed bibelot nature of the displays of Indigenous American material culture within the Halls of the Americas replicated the Indian curio-corner fashion found in department stores, museums, and magazine ads for Indian objects; the Vatican's display technique also emphasized that Indigenous material culture, although not for sale at the VME, was part of the larger world of cultural capital, a burgeoning aspect of modernity.[22] "Walls and roof and floor are covered with exhibits," Father Felix, OSFC (of the Franciscan religious order), observed, "one section more interesting than another."[23] Felix's observation suggested that the

VME mobilized pilgrims and visitors from around the world through a massive display strategy that utilized every available space.

Materials overflowed and appeared too crammed for many viewers, but this also replicated the conventions of the curio corners of domestic spaces. The overflow of materials imported a moralizing lesson that visitors took away from their experience. The exhibits contained and decontextualized stolen artifacts within the space of the Vatican display halls to illustrate the moral order of Catholic missionary vision. For example, in the Hall of North America, the VME organizers placed paintings by missionaries and the sculptural reliefs of German artist Ferdinand Pettrich high above the Indigenous belongings, thus reinforcing a hierarchy of the arts that also reinforced a hierarchy of value and race.[24] At the same time, the Vatican's display strategy aligned with the fashion for the presentation of Indigenous materials in one's studio or sitting room and paralleled surrealist artists' interest and appropriation of Indigenous American art. The surrealist André Breton, for example, had a collection of Haida and Yup'ik masks in his studio in Paris.[25] The VME forms part of a sustained interest in collecting and displaying Native American cultural belongings at the Vatican in a demonstration of papal control.[26] Pius XI sought to display material and visual culture as evidence of Catholic conversion and missionary progress, as well as to contend and compete with contemporary world's fairs and expositions (see plate 5).

Like Janus, Pius XI looked both ways to create an image of the Catholic Church as progressive and in step with colonial collecting and scientific advances in museums across the Americas, like the Smithsonian, as well as harkening back to the decadence of ancient Rome. Yet, in line with ethnographic museums of the time, including the American Museum of Natural History, the VME provided little education to visitors about the aesthetic, historical, or social aspects of Indigenous art or communities.[27] Moreover, the quality of the information provided to visitors needs to be questioned for its validity and biases, as the *Rivista Illustrata* contained racist and problematic assumptions about Indigenous communities.[28] The VME's homogenizing vision paralleled the ancient Roman past with displays of missionary strength and power, emphasizing mass quantity with no distinctions made for makers or communities. These power displays extend back to ancient Roman traditions of capturing and presenting materials and peoples in a show of imperial might, as well as to Catholic performance found throughout Rome in painted allegories such as Jesuit artist Andrea Pozzo's illusionistic allegories of the four continents (ca. 1691 at the Church of Sant'Ignazio in Rome). The visual culture of Rome as a Catholic empire extended into the creation of the VME, heightening visitors' experiences of the exhibition as an overwhelmingly colonial affair.

Approaching the Vatican Missionary Exposition

Rome is a kaleidoscope of ancient and baroque silhouettes and impressions. One can imagine visitors strolling the Ponte Sant'Angelo, which is guarded by larger-than-life angels outside the Castel Sant'Angelo, and taking in the Roman palette of burnt sienna, ocher, and sky blue. In 1924, looking from the bridge before Castel Sant'Angelo, visitors would have seen silhouettes of the churches of Rome standing like ancient sentinels leading up to the central heart of Christendom. Crossing the bridge, visitors would then have turned left and walked over the *sanpietrini* (cobblestones) toward the grand promenade with Saint Peter's at the apex. A promotional poster designed by Maurizio Rava, Mussolini's colonial administrator, envisions the scene, yet includes no representation of Indigenous arts, and emphasizes instead the Catholic iconography of Gian Lorenzo Bernini's avenging angels, a reminder of Catholic colonization (see plate 6). For visitors to the VME, the baroque architecture of Bernini's colonnades in Saint Peter's Square, the grandeur of Saint Peter's Basilica, and the hierarchical placement of fascinating objects throughout the many halls would have evoked a sense of Catholic ritual. In the rush of the crowds, the excited yet hushed and reverent voices of visitors and pilgrims, and echoes of Italian, French, English, Spanish, Hindi, Farsi, Arabic, and multiple other languages could be heard at any given moment.

Imagine an exposition occupying the space of several neighborhood blocks, filled with blooming gardens, ornately designed pavilions, and wax models of Indigenous peoples, all within the walls of the Vatican. All of these aspects worked on the visitors' senses to create an atmosphere of reverence.[29] The burial place of many saints and martyrs, Saint Peter's Basilica housed countless relics and reliquaries. The Vatican also functioned as both a sacred pilgrimage site and a reminder of overlapping pagan rites—Catholics built Saint Peter's on the pagan ruins of Roman antiquity. Proceeding through the grounds of the Vatican, visitors would have experienced the grandeur of Saint Peter's Square at the exhibition's starting point in the Pavilion of the Holy Land and the History of the Missions. Onward through the Halls of the Americas, Oceania, and India, they would have encountered what must have been an impressive and overwhelming collection of missionary paintings, statues of martyrs, and cultural belongings from diverse Indigenous communities from around the globe.

Scholars have discussed world's fairs and museums as contested spaces of competing influences, especially for the presentation and curation of Indigenous art.[30] Much important work has been done to articulate not only how Indigenous representation serves colonial narratives and disciplines of western progress but also how rereading colonial expositions and their archival holdings, such as the VME, can offer different lessons on the complexities of Indigenous experience within a context of international case studies. As Turtle Mountain Chippewa historian Danika Medak-Saltzman notes: "Examining the historical record to shed light on transnational Indigenous encounters is not about seeking a continuous resistance movement where there is none. It is about recognizing Indigenous resistance as a continual part of Native negotiations with colonial regimes and about considering how moments of colonial celebrations of empire may have inadvertently served anticolonial purposes by presenting the Indigenous participants with opportunities to interact across larger distances than had been practical or possible in the past."[31] This chapter's methodology builds on Medak-Saltzman's insights, especially her creative interpretation of archival documents and Indigenous resistance via close readings of photographs of Indigenous participants at the 1904 Saint Louis exposition. In addition to Medak-Saltzman, I draw inspiration from the work of Tanana Athabaskan scholar Dian Million, who argues for emotive histories—what she calls "felt theory"—that consider how Indigenous peoples work through trauma and the structures of colonial rule on Indigenous lives.[32] Million notes that Indigenous studies scholars, and particularly Native women, "feel our histories as well as think them."[33] When I think about the VME and papal culture, I feel a mixture of rage, horror, and ambivalence. I feel anger at the colonial dogma of the exhibition and its continued display today at the Ethnological Museum *Anima Mundi*, and I also wonder about the fatalistic aspect of the work, as the Vatican is such a Catholic colonial stronghold. Some of the missionary descriptions I have read through about the VME and Indigenous people almost make me sick. The Vatican remains a space for the denial of Indigenous people as human beings.

Missionaries stole materials for the exhibition from around the globe and described them as "gifts" and "offerings" to pope Pius XI, expressing an attitude of colonial amassing that aligns with the triumphal culture of ancient Rome.[34] Parsing the archival record, Indigenous communities did not give consent or permission to display their belongings.[35] Not inadvertently, missionaries framed the materials as trophies of the church and part of a long history of Roman ceremony. Indeed, the VME cannot be separated from its Roman environs.[36] It belongs to a tradition originating in the "glories" of ancient Rome.

Roman armies exhibited the spoils (books, antiquities, paintings, sculptures) and peoples (captives and slaves) seized in war and paraded them through the streets of Rome for the glorification of the empire.[37] Anthropologist Guido Abbattista notes that ruling powers in the Renaissance era paraded captives from the New World through the streets of Rome, which he calls the "trophying of human otherness."[38] Pius XI described the materials sent in for the exhibition—ranging from books, antiquities, paintings, sculptures, material culture, miniatures, and mannequins to flora and fauna—as a form of *lux in tenebris* (light in the darkness) that conveyed a message of "silent eloquence" about the heroism of missionary work, part of the papal culture of amassing goods for displays of imperial power.[39]

Visitors appreciated Indigenous cultural belongings sent in from missions as silent markers of conversion from supposed compliant subjects. Although anxieties surrounding Indigenous beliefs and the cultural belongings that represented them remained just under the surface, materials functioned as reminders of the triumph of missionary work and the suppression of alternative religious beliefs. Thus, Pius XI even situated the objects as part of the "spiritual wealth" and cultural heritage of Catholicism.[40] Paradoxically, the inclusion of Indigenous cultural belongings from the Americas bolstered the visual consumption and viewing experience of Catholic citizens through visual hierarchies that also reinforced a hierarchy of race and the arts. A 1924 account in the *New York Times* promised that the VME would "present to visitors the life, customs, and habits of the most obscure tribes in the remotest regions of the earth."[41] Visitors to the VME wanted to see things the newspapers had promised, and attending the exposition reinforced their beliefs through the observation of tangible things.

The organizers framed cultural belongings as material evidence of Catholic conversion and faith in the Americas, Oceania, Africa, and Asia, all the while denying the modernity of the makers and their artistic, cultural, and spiritual ancestries and iconographic traditions. For example, the organizers did not name the makers of belongings, nor acknowledge their communities, except if they were a white male European artist, like Pettrich, which perpetuated the idea and ideal of compliant powerless subjects. This could be because the missionaries in their colonial and racist mindsets did not believe it mattered and were not interested in considering Indigenous peoples' contributions as art or worthy of contextualization, but instead wanted to impress Pius XI with their displays to gain his blessing. This is likely, as during the 1920s the artwork and material culture created by anyone other than a white male artist was not considered art but rather as ethnographic and sometimes scientific material.[42] This colonial attitude morphed through various forms yet persisted in exhibition spaces and continues today in the *Anima Mundi* gallery at the Vatican Museums.

The Design of the Vatican Missionary Exposition

The VME occupied twenty-four specially designed pavilions in the Pine Court of the Vatican Museums.[43] From the moment visitors entered the VME, the Catholic ordering of vision pulled them into the space. Cultural belongings and other artifacts were crammed into glass cases and piled high on top of the exhibit cases, overflowing into the exposition. After the exhibition closed, the materials became part of the permanent Vatican Missionary Ethnological Museum, which Pius XI opened shortly thereafter.[44] Organizers of the VME noted that missionaries sent in one hundred thousand items, and from this they selected some forty thousand for inclusion.[45] From analysis of photographs of the Halls of the Americas and visits to the collection, the organizers also drew on items they already had in their collections; for example, two Inuit amulets, one depicting a medicine man and the other a seal, were from the Cardinal Borgia collection.[46]

Melding historical and contemporary missionary history, statistical data, dioramas, cultural belongings, "and a great variety of memorabilia," Father Wilhelm Schmidt, Pius XI's advisor for the VME, and his team created the exhibition like an adventure experience (see figure 2.2).[47] Visitors moved through a sequence of thirty-two rooms, with information posted in Italian and other languages that framed Catholic missionary efforts through a Judeo-Christian structure. They started with the early martyrs (the Pavilion of the Holy Land, the History of the Missions, and the Hall of Martyrs) and moved to the contemporary missions, beginning with the Ethnology Hall, Schmidt's special project. Analyzing the arrangement of the exhibition sheds insight into visitors' experiences of the spaces and the imposition of missionary order. Slow looking and study, taking time to visually unpack some of the spaces, are some of my art historical tools. In this chapter I aim to re-story the exhibition and provide a narrative for the materials both sacred and secular that remain largely undiscussed and unexplained.

Although he oversaw the entire exhibition, Schmidt took a special interest in the construction and display of the Ethnology Hall, which was created to reflect his theory of "primitive monotheism," an innovative idea at the time but one that is now discredited.[48] Schmidt was a Catholic missionary, linguist, and ethnologist and the founder of *Anthropos*, an important journal of ethnology,

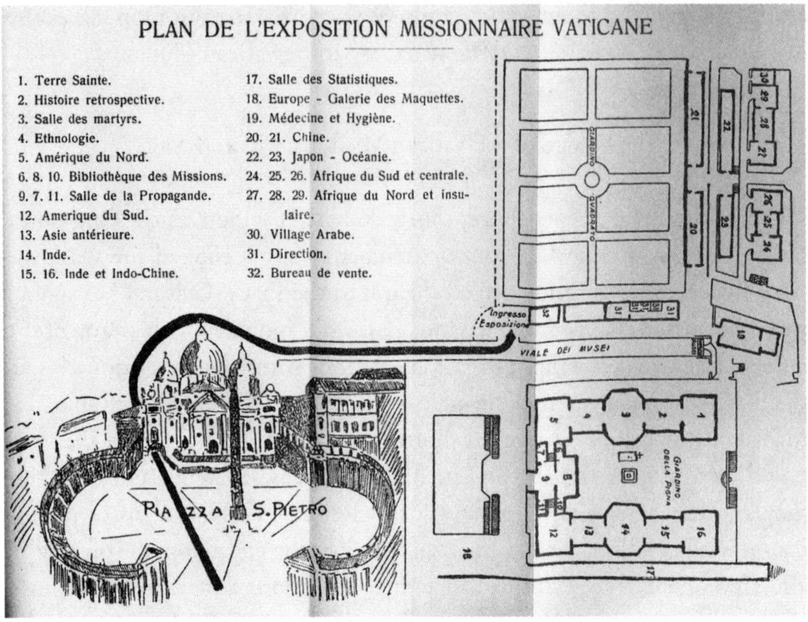

FIGURE 2.2. Map of the Vatican Missionary Exposition of 1925. Source: Noël Gubbels, *L'exposition missionnaire du Vatican et le Musée Missionnaire Ethnographique du Latran, 1925–1927* (1928), n.p. Courtesy of Propaganda Fide Library Collections, Pontificio Collegio Urbano "De Propaganda Fide," Rome.

anthropology, and missionary studies. He published many essays on his theory of "primitive monotheism" in *Anthropos*, which was essentially a sounding board for his Catholic version of anthropology.[49] Interested in understanding how "primitive" peoples maintained what he saw as their "monotheistic" beliefs, he argued that there was an inherent link between race and belief.[50] He suggested that, among tribal peoples, a belief in one god paralleled Christian principles.

The Ethnology Hall was arranged by Schmidt to show the "progress of civilization outside the influence of Christianity," complete with many fetishes and other occult objects.[51] A founder of the tradition of *Kulturkreis* (cultural complex), Schmidt took a missionary-based approach to anthropology that emphasized understanding the particular histories of individual societies rather than placing cultures within a universalizing discourse of human nature.[52] He believed anthropology should be "a scientific discipline, proving the ability of Catholics to work in this field, and an apologetic discipline, proving the natural foundations of Catholic doctrine."[53] Schmidt's thesis, based on his studies in

Africa, did not address the complexities of religious belief for the Indigenous peoples of the Americas nor appreciate the religious structures of communities in Africa. In line with the normative perspective showcased by missionary expositions and world exhibitions at the time, his curatorial method contributed to an understanding of Indigenous Americans as "primitive" and outside the "rational" time and space of western exposition visitors.[54] As anthropologist Alison Kahn notes, "the 'pre-contact heathen objects' were presented 'en masse' with the implicit message to the visitor that indigenous cultures were lost and in need of guidance. Conversion to Christianity was portrayed as simultaneous with an enriched material culture."[55] By this, Kahn means that these displays suggested that by converting to Christianity, Indigenous peoples would achieve both greater material wealth and the ability to assimilate the values of western societies.

It is important to add to Kahn's observations that many anthropologists, scholars, and others employed a salvage ethnography mindset during this period. Indian agents, collectors, hucksters, and anthropologists acquired Indigenous cultural belongings both sacred and secular from Indigenous communities using coercive means in the belief that Indigenous people would soon die out.[56] This attitude of salvage collecting as a colonial and societal mindset of ownership and entitlement infiltrated missionary behaviors at the VME as well. A *New York Times* journalist noted that the Ethnological Hall of the exhibition included "a wealth of material relating to the pagan cults and rites, witchcraft, and conditions of life," emphasizing the spectacle rather than the science.[57] After these first rooms, deemed the "scientific" section, visitors to the Halls of the Americas moved on to the larger work and accomplishments of Catholic missionaries abroad.[58]

For this vast and ambitious exhibition, Schmidt and his team worked with a plethora of cultural belongings and ephemera, including pottery, textiles, paintings, pamphlets, books, and photographs.[59] Because Pius XI had sent out a call for submissions to the broader community of Catholic missionaries and converts, Schmidt had to work with whatever the missionaries offered. The unpredictability of the submissions and their variety formed part of the importance of the exhibition as pop and papal culture. As Father Penkowski, former curator of the Vatican Missionary Ethnological Collection, noted regarding the array of material stolen: "They included objects from every part of the world where Catholic missions carry out their activities. The systematic display of this heritage, arranged according to geographical criteria, provided in itself a wonderful panorama of the life and wide-ranging activities of many non-European peoples in the economic, social and artistic fields, as well as that of their magical practices and their multifarious beliefs."[60] Penkowski hints at the collision between Indigenous belief systems and Catholic dogma throughout this period of intense missionization, which was founded on a salvage paradigm of collecting "magical practices." Visitors admired cultural belongings for their status as objects created by Indigenous peoples who were either described as converts or pagans.[61] Materials functioned as uneasy reminders of alternative religious beliefs, but also of the triumphs and trophies of missionary work. Under the gaze of Pius XI, these objects were all situated as part of the spiritual wealth and cultural heritage of Catholicism, yet they did not always fit this framework neatly, as reflected in the archival record by Father Dreves and others.

These discrepancies created some anxieties on the part of organizers.[62] Writing from Holy Cross, Alaska, to the Provincial Reverend Father Joseph M. Piet, Jesuit missionary Phillip Delon noted his distress at his inability to send in a comprehensive account to the VME:

> Personally, I knew nothing about the upcoming exposition till I received a letter from Father Ruppert, a short while before his death, telling me about it, and all the work he intended to do to make it a success . . . having but little time to do anything towards the exposition, the more so as I had not yet received the instructions or directions from Father Cicera on how to prepare the exhibit. These instructions reached me in the early part of spring, or some time before Easter. In the meantime, I had of course, requested our fathers in the various missions to do all they could to come up to the expectations of the Father General. But all of them were all taken up with their missionary work, and they had neither the inclination, nor the money to gather any objects of interest. However, some of them took pains to meet the requirements. But the time was too short, the difficulties of communication among ourselves were too great, and the penury of interesting or valuable objects was too deeply felt for one to become much "inspirited" about the matter.[63]

Father Delon's behind-the-scenes reflection expresses the anxiety he shared with other missionaries about their ability to meet the Father General's expectations, as well as ambivalence about participating in an exposition in Rome.

This personal correspondence contrasts sharply with newspaper reports and other visits to the exhibition that praised it as an organized albeit overwhelming space. Delon's use of the word "penury of interesting or valuable objects" suggests his bias against Indigenous cultural belongings and his view that they were not of adequate aesthetic or scholarly interest for a metropolitan exposition.[64] The term "penury" also suggests Delon's view of Indigenous nations as poverty-stricken. In fact, Indigenous nations had and still have multiple forms of wealth that do not conform to Delon's materialist standards: songs, stories, and cultural teachings, for example, form part of the vast richness of Indigenous arts. In contrast to Delon's ambivalence about the VME, the arrangement of visitors' movement through the space imposed a sense of order on the otherwise unruly collection of largely unexplained materials and cultural belongings.

Visitors then moved from the Ethnology Hall to the Hall of North Americas through the Library of the Missions.[65] After this, they entered the Hall of Propaganda of the Faith, then on to South America and sections on Asia and India. During this sequence, visitors also had access to the Pine Court, where they could move outside into the gardens and encounter the reconstructed dwellings and wax models of Indigenous peoples from South America and Africa.[66] Back inside, they continued through the Statistical Hall, replete with scientific data on Indigenous converts and "infidels," then on to Europe and the Gallery of Statues. From there, they might re-enter the Pavilion of the Holy Land, which depicted the missionary origins of the church, complete with a miniature reconstruction of Palestine that visitors could walk around.[67] From the Holy Land, visitors would move on to the History of the Missions, which traced the church's missionary aims from the time of the Roman Empire through to the early twentieth century. Visitors then came to the Hall of Martyrs, where relics, paintings, sculptures, tapestries, and instruments of torture depicted the sufferings endured by missionaries around the world, including China and Japan.[68] One reporter for the *Catholic Historical Review* declared that seeing the tunic and cowl of humble Saint Francis of Assisi perched above the entrance to the Hall of Martyrs was the highlight of his trip.[69] Visitors then moved on to the Hall of Medicine, and from there to China, Japan, Oceania, North and South Africa, an Arab village, and finally the gift shop (see figures 2.3 and 2.4).[70]

The setting of the Vatican, the principal pilgrimage site for millions of Catholics annually, along with the architecture of the halls and the placement of the objects, contributed to visitors' experience of the VME as a ritual space. Pilgrims entered the exhibition through the *porta sancta* (holy door) of Saint Peter's Basilica, which is open only during the holy jubilee year. Treading in the footsteps of millions of pious devotees through the ages of Christendom, they waited on bended knee for the blessing of the Holy Father in the Apostolic Palace.[71] They could stop and admire the beauty and grandeur of the

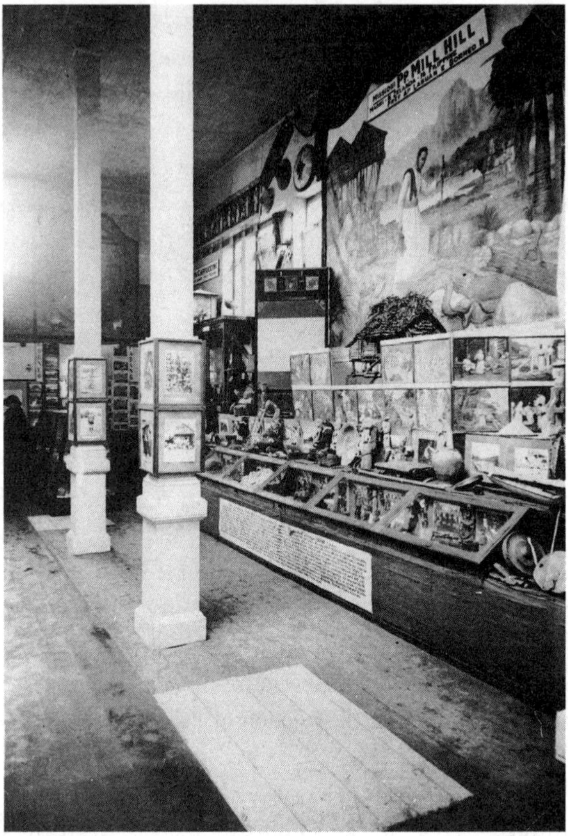

FIGURE 2.3. Borneo Mission stand, Vatican Missionary Exposition, 1925. Archival note on image: "The collection generated tremendous interest and gave a fair idea of the way of life of both of the indigenous peoples and of the missionaries working among them." Courtesy of Mill Hill Missionaries Archive, Liverpool.

architecture of Saint Peter's, the opulence of the Vatican's Italian Renaissance paintings, and the ornate interior featuring a wealth of sculpture, antiquities, and decorative arts. A Dominican priest, Father J. Bowen, recalled his peaceful experience: "There is a happy absence of stallholders anxious to exhibit their wares, self-advertisement or noise; instead, a welcome sense of peace and calm pervades the atmosphere, with the blue sky of Italy overall."[72] Implying a contrast to the more raucous and lively experience of other world expositions of the time, Bowen's account makes clear the reverence he (and other Catholics) had for the space. The processional walk from the holy door of Saint Peter's through to the gardens, where visitors contemplated the wonders of the Catholic faith in its illuminated artworks and vast collections, functioned as a practical, intellectual, and spiritual gateway that prepared them for the experience of the exhibition.

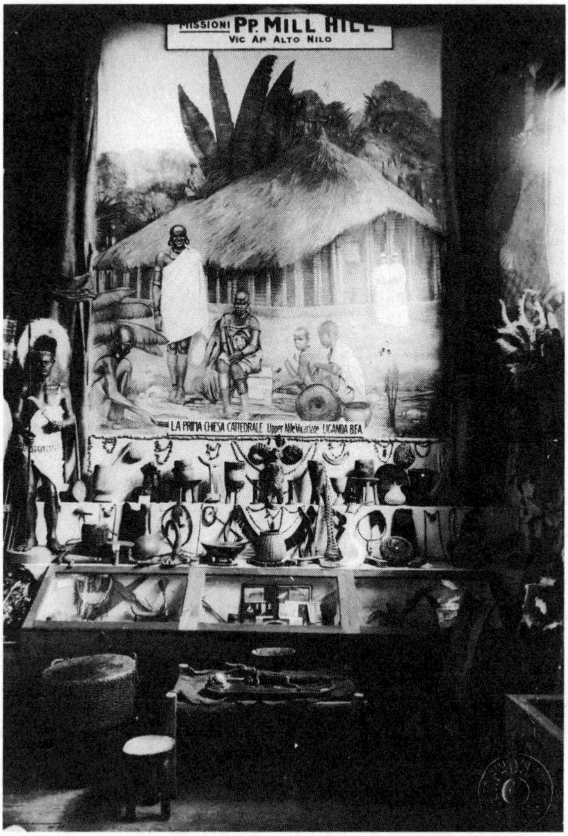

FIGURE 2.4. Uganda mission stand illustrating the Vicariate of the Upper Nile, including carvings, basketwork, and wax models, Vatican Missionary Exposition, 1925. Courtesy of Mill Hill Missionaries Archive, Liverpool.

Halls of the Americas: Pius XI's Culture of Conquest

Catholic orders represented in the Hall of North America at the VME included Franciscans with missions in Wisconsin, Michigan, New Mexico, California, Arizona, and Tobique, New Brunswick. Jesuit missions from Alaska, Montreal, Montana, and California also contributed displays. The Oblates of Mary Immaculate provided displays of Indigenous artworks from Ottawa, Saint Boniface of Edmonton, and missions in Vancouver, Prince Rupert, Yukon, Mackenzie River, Athabaska, and Keewatin. So too did the Catechist Missionaries of Santa Fe; the Franciscan Sisters, the Missionaries of Mary, and the Missionary Works of the Propagation of the Faith in New York; and the Society for the Extension of the Faith in Chicago and Toronto.[73] Indigenous children's embroidery and beadwork, created in residential schools operating across Turtle

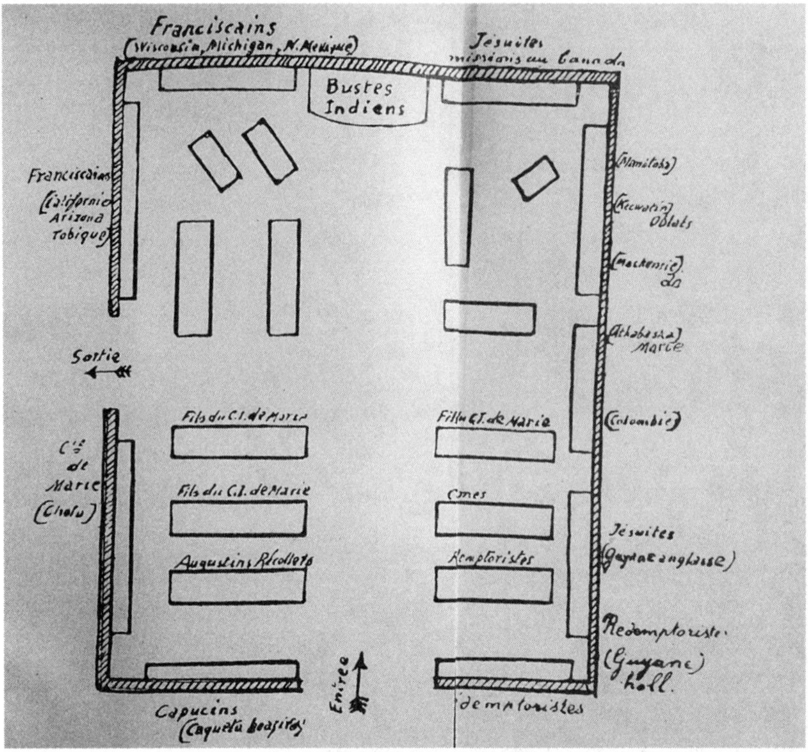

FIGURE 2.5. Map of the Hall of North America, Vatican Missionary Exposition, 1925. Source: Noël Gubbels, *L'exposition missionnaire du Vatican et le Musée Missionnaire Ethnographique du Latran, 1925–1927* (1928), n.p. Courtesy of Propaganda Fide Library Collections, Pontificio Collegio Urbano "De Propaganda Fide," Rome.

Island, was exploited at the VME, described by missionaries as "offerings" and "gifts" to Pius XI.[74] Missionaries also sent in objects from the Day Schools of Pine Ridge and Rosebud in South Dakota, and the Saint Francis of Assisi Mission on the Fort Apache Reservation, Whiteriver, Arizona, part of the Bureau of Catholic Indian Missions.[75] Yet although missionaries sent in Indigenous cultural belongings from a vast and diverse array of Indigenous territories and cultural traditions, this diversity and complexity was not highlighted in the exhibition strategy.

Standing in the Hall of North America, visitors entered a syncretic space overflowing with materials, from paintings by missionaries on the walls to thousands of stolen cultural belongings from diverse Indigenous nations in glass cases.[76] A hand-drawn map by a French missionary provides clues for

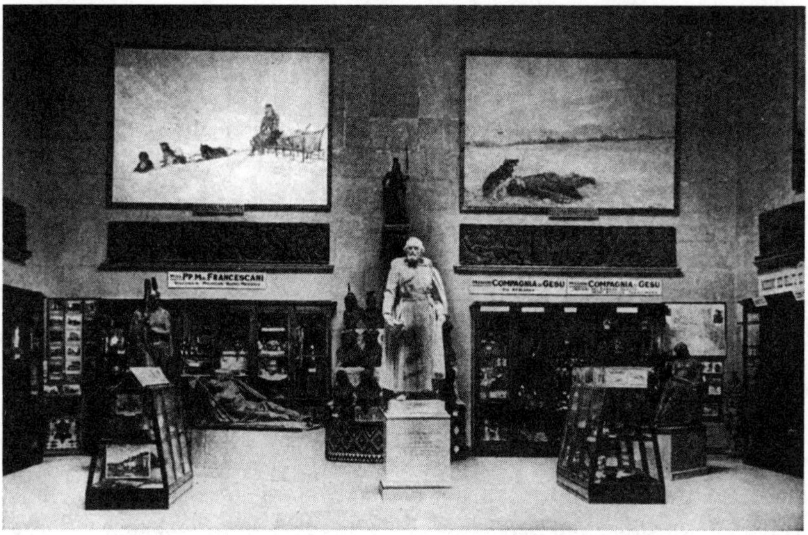

FIGURE 2.6. Hall of North America, Vatican Missionary Exposition, 1925. A statue of Father J. Marquette is at center; Ferdinand Pettrich's *Wah-pe-kec-suk* and *Dying Tecumseh* are at left, and his *Sauk-Fox Girl* at right. Source: John Joseph Considine, *The Vatican Mission Exposition: A Window on the World* (1925), 59.

deciphering the space (see figure 2.5). Facing north, visitors saw three life-size sculptures of Native Americans by Ferdinand Pettrich: *Dying Tecumseh* (discussed in chapter 1), *Wah-pe-kec-suk*, and *Sauk-Fox Girl* in neoclassical style (see figure 2.6).[77] The Lateran Palace had displayed them in the Indian Museum as a reminder of the devastation experienced by Native Americans, and they were subsequently centered in the Hall of North America. The curators placed Pettrich's sculpture of Tecumseh, the great Shawnee chief who had led a resistance movement against British settlement, surrounded by display cases of cultural belongings. As if watching over him, the influential spiritual leader and prophet of the Sauk-Fox, Wah-pe-kec-suk ("White Cloud Medicine Man"), leans against an obelisk-shaped pillar that Pettrich inscribed with Egyptian-inspired hieroglyphs. Wah-pe-kec-suk wears a buffalo hide over his upper torso, as well as fringed buckskin breeches, a loincloth, and bear-claw necklace. Like *Dying Tecumseh* and *Wah-pe-kec-suk*, the other life-size sculpture, *Sauk-Fox Girl*, fulfills an ornamental role in the static space.

On the plinth near Tecumseh, the organizers placed sixteen busts, also by Pettrich, and, beneath the busts, finely woven rugs by Diné (Navajo) weavers of the Southwest created in an eye-dazzling design known as the Germantown style pattern (see figure 2.7).[78] These busts depicted Native American leaders from the Winnebago, Creek, Sauk-Fox, and Očhéthi Šakówiŋ nations in their prime, including Black Hawk, Keokuk, Wah-pe-kec-suk, Ha-sa-Za, Wath-hat-tu-kah, Rowley McIntosh, Nah-se-us-Kuk, Wee-sheet, Tah-tape-saa an unnamed Očhéthi Šakówiŋ warrior, and three more unidentified men. Along the top row of busts were Sauk-Fox leaders Black Hawk and Keokuk, and below them, Wah-pe-kec-suk, priest and prophet of the Sauk-Fox, with Ha-sa-Za ("The Elk's Horn"), chief of the Yankton Sioux, beside him. Pettrich observed Ha-sa-Za, a member of the Yankton delegation, in treaty talks in Washington, DC, on October 21, 1837, on the ceding of territory.[79] A drawing in Pettrich's sketchbook of Ha-sa-Za (ca. 1837) depicts the chief deep in meditation.[80] He smokes a pipe, holding a staff wrapped in buffalo skin with eagle feathers, a marker of the integrity of the Yankton Sioux people and of his prestige as a leader. On the brutal practice of treaty-making, historian Kevin O'Donnell observes that "the treaty work itself was grim—during this period, most of the tribes were in the process of ceding their remaining best lands. Travel to the city was hard, and diseases in the city typically took their toll on the Indians."[81] The US government promised portraits to Native participants in treaty meetings as a form of flattery and persuasion in the brutalizing process of land cession.[82] Pettrich created his artworks within this tradition. The archival record is not clear on whether Pettrich's Indigenous sitters took home a lithograph made by him, but this would not be unheard of during this period. Given Pettrich's intimate access to the treaty processes represented in his art, he likely strived to become a bona fide portrait artist for the US Department of War, like Charles Bird King, the official portrait painter of Indigenous nations and treaty processes for the department's Gallery of the American Indian in Washington. King, George Catlin, and Paul Kane created a collection of portraits of Indigenous leaders for the War Department Gallery that memorialized Native leaders during the 1837 treaty process.[83] Visitors described Pettrich's works both as "beautiful" and as "pagan idols," terms that do not account for the presence of the Indigenous individuals depicted. The placement of the busts over the Diné textiles reinforced an ideological order of the arts—the dominance of western art over the communal weaving arts of Diné women—as well as an aesthetic choice.

Importantly, the busts of the Indigenous men and women, unlike the life-size sculptural works, look upward and out into the Hall of North America, as if challenging viewers to recognize their individuality. The organizers included three busts of women on the plinth as well as a Sauk-Fox woman with a child. The bust that Pettrich created is almost a direct replica of a drawing he did in his studio in Washington (see figure 2.8). Pettrich used his sketches to cre-

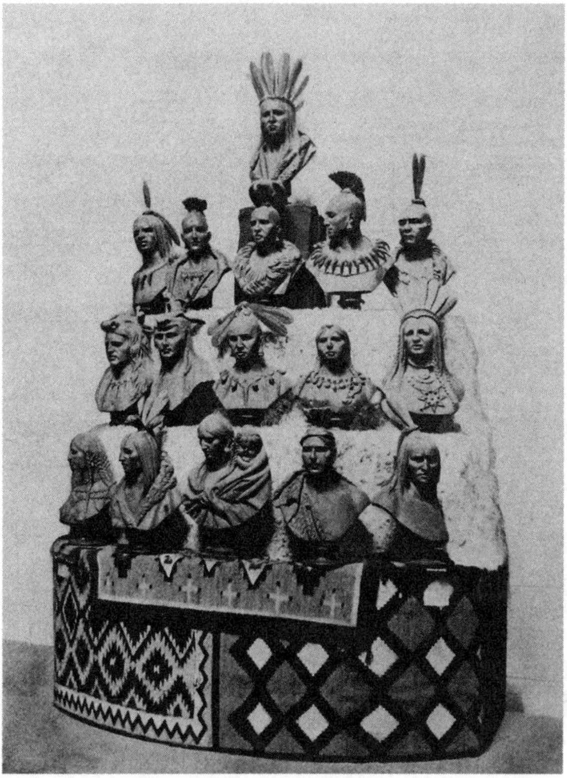

FIGURE 2.7. Sixteen busts of Native Americans by Ferdinand Pettrich displayed above Diné textiles, Hall of North America, Vatican Missionary Exposition, 1925. Source: *Rivista Illustrata della Esposizione Missioniaria Vaticana*, November 15, 1925, 736. Courtesy of Propaganda Fide Library Collections, Pontificio Collegio Urbano "De Propaganda Fide," Rome.

ate a sense of the sitter's individuality for his busts and bas-reliefs. However, in none of his drawings and sculptures did he identify the women by name, suggesting that he never knew the subjects on a personal level; and that he, like government officials, ignored the names of the women as part of a Eurocentric male vision of Indigenous Americans.[84] Comparing the sketchbook of 1837 with the sculptures, we can see that Pettrich reused certain details, such as a tin-thimble earring that features in many of his profile drawings of male sitters, such as Keokuk, and in his busts. The US government gave the tin earrings as part of the exchange of gifts during the treaty process. Pettrich also added certain details, such as the bear-claw necklace for Wee-sheet, a member of the Sauk-Fox, creating a sense of the Native men's personalities. It is notable that Pettrich did not depict elderly men or women, but only men and women in their prime, in keeping with an idealism that aligned with the neoclassical standard of warrior youths and innocent maidens. Alternatively, perhaps only younger men and women could make the arduous trip to Washington. Another sketch, *A Band of Sioux Musicians,* shows men with very short chopped-off

FIGURE 2.8. Ferdinand Pettrich, *Sauk-Fox Woman*, ca. 1837. Ink and wash on paper, 22.9 × 33 cm. Source: Ferdinand Pettrich, Sketchbook 33. Courtesy of Edward E. Ayer Special Collections, Newberry Library, Chicago.

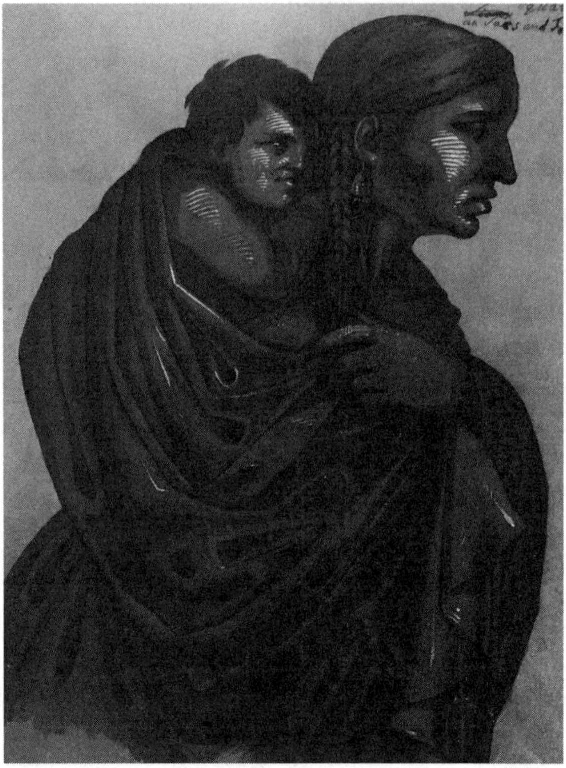

hair. It is likely they had cut their hair in a sign of mourning for the deaths of fellow delegation members (see figure 2.9).[85]

Placed in front of these busts and towering above them on a plinth, the curators centered a life-size sculpture in white marble of Father Marquette, missionary to the Iroquois and martyr. His likeness blocked the view of the busts of the Indigenous men and women.[86] Throughout the exhibition, in the Hall of Martyrs and the Halls of the Americas and other geographical sections, the organizers and visitors celebrated missionaries as heroes. On the walls, underneath a painting depicting the missionary Father Ruppert in northern Canada, who froze to death, one could see bas-reliefs by Pettrich, one of which depicted Sauk-Fox leader Keokuk, along with members of his tribe, negotiating a treaty with the secretary of state, John Forsythe, who smokes a pipe.[87] Pettrich's sketches, completed between 1837 and 1842, provided direct inspiration for his bas-reliefs; he only changed the compositions slightly (see figure 2.10). The other reliefs depicted musical scenes of Winnebago, Creek, and Očhéthi Šakówiŋ musicians, aligning once again with the neoclassical

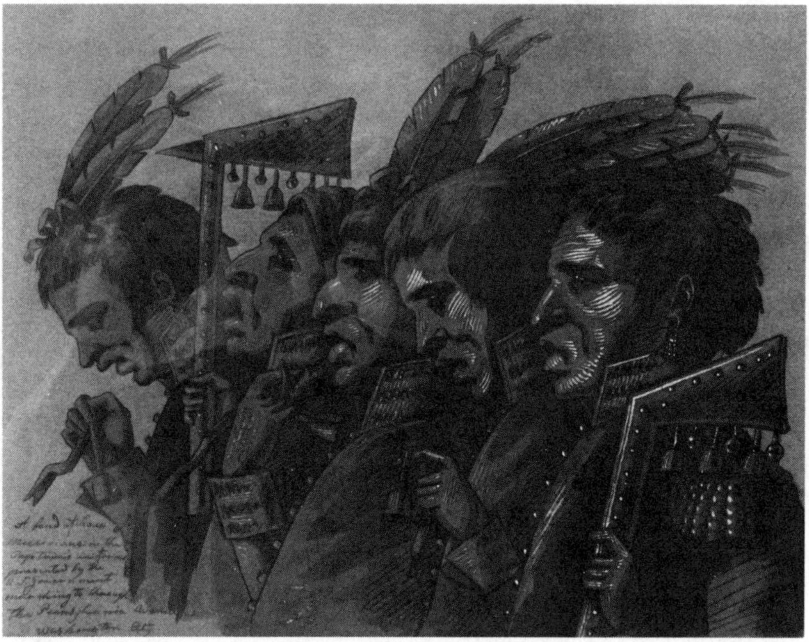

FIGURE 2.9. Ferdinand Pettrich, *A Band of Sioux Musicians*, ca. 1837. Ink and wash on paper, 25.4 × 38 cm. Source: Ferdinand Pettrich, Sketchbook 25. Courtesy of Edward E. Ayer Special Collections, Newberry Library, Chicago.

ideal of emulating classical models. To the left of the busts, the viewer could see the stolen contributions of the Franciscan order (adherents to Saint Francis of Assisi's teachings of humility and poverty), with artifacts from their missions in Wisconsin, Michigan, New Mexico, California, and Arizona.[88]

Belongings taken without consent by the Canadian missionaries, mostly Jesuits, with additional material from Franciscans and Oblates of Mary Immaculate from the Athabasca and Mackenzie River areas, surrounded Pettrich's statuary.[89] The materials displayed in the Halls of the Americas included baskets, ceramics, beaded and embroidered gloves, amulets, and textiles from diverse Indigenous nations across the Americas. The organizers included photographs from the *Rivista Illustrata* and statistical data on "heathens and saved" laminated on small cards and placed on top of the glass cases. In other geographic areas of the exhibition, such as the South-Central Africa section, they left some material out in the open or used rope to control how visitors could interact with objects. In the two rooms on Asia, the organizers placed fans on the walls rather than behind glass cases.[90] This display strategy conformed with

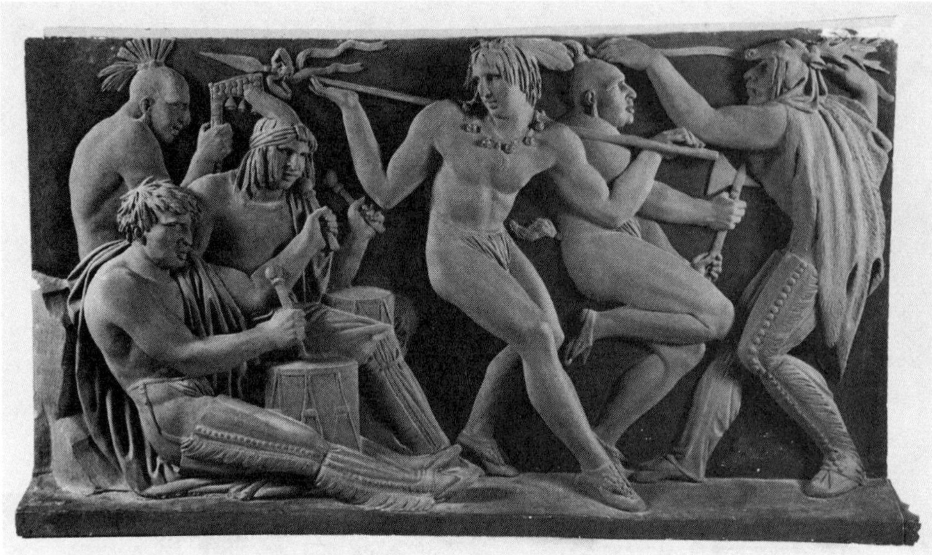

FIGURE 2.10. Ferdinand Pettrich, *The Sauk-Fox and Sioux Nations of the Mississippi Engaged in a War Dance*, ca. 1856. Gesso and pigment, 87 × 143 × 22.5 cm. Vatican Museums, Vatican City, MV.101586.3.1. https://catalogo.museivaticani.va/index.php/Detail/objects/MV.101586.3.1.

the curio-corner fashion in homes and department stores of the period. The organizers included charts in the Halls of the Americas and in the exposition's guidebooks that provided statistical breakdowns of souls saved and pagans, lending a surface impression of authority. The VME promoted itself as at the leading edge of science with its exhibition Hall of Medicine, yet it relied on overpacked display cases like a messy department store to showcase materials, which created an effect more of spectacle and confusion than science.

The overloaded vitrines clashed with the aim of presenting an objective, rational approach to viewing the Indigenous materials, and many visitors expressed feelings of being overwhelmed by the vast scale of the exposition and the overpowering presence of objects. As Father Felix noted of his visit, "thirty-one pavilions there are in all—it is nothing short of immense. To view it properly without stopping to study it in detail takes four hours."[91] The organizers wanted visitors to understand missionary goals and the life of Indigenous Americans primarily through what they saw with their own eyes. They provided little contextual information, perhaps because missionaries did not send in the information or lost the supplementary materials, as discussions with a former curator confirm.[92] Yet this lack of interpretive texts also aided their goal of creating a portrait of missionary life itself as overcoming the challenge of being confronted with a cacophony of foreignness.[93]

Reviewers emphasized the visibility of the objects and understood them as tangible objects of faith. Guidebooks and photographs, sometimes with handwritten captions, along with charts and graphs in the statistical section, highlighted the visual. The Catholic Church wanted to show through the statistical data that it, too, like Protestant missionary exhibitions, harnessed the latest technology to evidence conversion. Visualizations of statistical data created for the exhibition emphasized geography and souls. The charts showed the souls of the heathens and souls of the saved along with those yet to be converted, creating a pseudoscientific veneer of data collection that was supported by country and region distinctions. The charts reported data for the United States and Canada along with missionary orders and tribal specifications.[94] For example, the introduction to a small handbook that accompanied the exhibition reads:

> The Mission Exposition has for its purpose to set before the eyes of the faithful who come from every part of the world how much has been done and is being done by the Missions and in the Missions. This sight will arouse and intensify the interest of all in the important problem of the conversion of the infidels, and the visitor will be able to form an exact idea of the Missionaries' work, of the physical and moral surroundings in which it is carried on, of the many difficulties of it, and also what successes have been obtained, and how much still remains to be done.[95]

Viewers may have been transfixed by the tremendous and intense array of instructions and images they encountered in the library section of the exhibition and throughout the various halls. Yet if they saw a plethora of fascinating things, including a huge diversity of cultural belongings, they did not understand them.

Sometimes the missionaries had very few materials available, so they sent in whatever items they could; for example, a missionary from northern Canada sent in a picture made of parasites, claiming it as the "only one in the world."[96] This curious artwork made by a missionary occupied a position out of place both because of the odd medium and the fact that it was not made by an Indigenous artist. Mounted fleas portray the image of a man and his dogsled team, with the necessities of his labor surrounding him, including snowshoes, a paddle, a gun, and a canoe. The juxtaposition of Pettrich's sculptures, busts, and reliefs from a century earlier, done in a neoclassical style that romanticized Native Americans, together with the more recent contributions of Indigenous cultural belongings (parfleche bags, photographs, pottery, textiles), and strange missionary artworks such as the flea painting, collapsed the temporal and geographical boundaries of diverse Indigenous groups into a homogeneous presentation.

In the Halls of the Americas, viewers visually encountered a variety of interesting objects, from sculpture and textiles to ethnographic "specimens," including minerals, flora, and fauna. Although they displayed cultural belongings, the organizers did not present the historical realities of the Indigenous communities featured. They were not interested in individual makers. This tension between the anonymous and therefore "vanishing" Indigenous maker and named European artists such as Pettrich remained consistent throughout the displays. The organizers included photographs throughout the various exhibition areas but did not incorporate any didactic panels, a fact that led Father J. Bowen to criticize the display strategy.[97] This lack of didactic materials emphasized the importance of visual consumption; visitors read the exhibition as part of a visual world that denied the modernity of Indigenous peoples.[98]

The visual regime of the VME, reiterated in numerous accounts by travelers, settlers, pilgrims, priests, and government officials, created a narrative of Indigenous Americans as tragically doomed, in line with colonial-era accounts of settler takeover and expansion in America and Italy. The constructive logic of the Halls of the Americas, together with its model dioramas, worked to place the Indigenous person outside of the time of "rational" western viewers. As Ho-Chunk scholar Amy Lonetree notes, museum displays emphasized stasis by "depicting Indians as frozen in time and by displaying them near dinosaurs and other extinct animals . . . Objects were presented and defined by Western scientific categories—anthropological categories of manufacture and use—and not by Indigenous categories of culture, worldview and meaning."[99] Much as Lonetree observes of turn-of-the-century museum displays, the VME did not discuss Indigenous worldviews and combined eerie wax models with flora, fauna, and material culture in a vast array that emphasized the quantity of goods amassed by missionaries. No distinctions were made between communities or care shown for the material cultures displayed. In this way, the overflowing space justified the supposed need for the redemption—physically, mentally, and spiritually—of Indigenous peoples and thereby provided motivation for Catholics who visited the exhibition to pursue or support missionary work abroad.[100]

Pius XI's description of the materials as having a "silent eloquence" framed this culture largely as an ethnological collection to be compared with other areas displayed at the VME rather than as having any artistic value. However, reviews of the Hall of North America lauded the sculptures by Pettrich and the paintings by missionaries as the epitome of artistic achievement. As Father Dreves noted, "beautiful and very artistic mural paintings and groups of natives in terra cotta, further adorn the walls of these places."[101] Dreves's observation reinforced the hierarchy of values established in western art historical traditions, placing emphasis on painting and sculpture that conformed to the standards of the time while ignoring Indigenous artistic ability. This kind of looking at Pettrich's work and the lack of acknowledgment of Indigenous material culture, both sacred and secular artworks, reinforced the papal culture of conquest. The approach also bolstered a mindset of mass quantity to show imperial might, an idea of the wealth of the church via physical things, taken without consent, to make tangible the colonizing mission of the church.

No reviewers discussed the Indigenous American basketry, pottery, handiwork and textiles. Instead, "silent eloquence" eclipsed the labor of Indigenous artists, some of whom were children based on the evidence of correspondence about the VME in the *Indian Sentinel*, a publication of the Bureau of Catholic Indian Missions in the United States.[102] Missionary organizers and viewers did not see the Indigenous American materials as having any artistic merit and described them in dichotomous terms as either "beautiful" or "grotesque."[103] Within the Hall of North America, Pettrich's sculptures, which acted as a stand-in for western European artistic traditions, presented a tension with the Indigenous American materials, and were placed in front of and even blocking them. Reviews of the VME lauded Pettrich's sculptures and busts as artworks but ignored the textiles displayed beneath them. The lack of discussion surrounding the Indigenous belongings speaks to Pius XI's desire that the materials remain silent, creating a romantic perspective and colonial framework that denied the modernity of the Indigenous makers.[104] The objects taken under coercive circumstances from Indigenous communities functioned like trophies of war.

Evolutionary dogma perpetuated the denial of the modernity of Indigenous cultures and artists in VME reviews. Evaluating the VME, Father Felix noted: "The simple, care-free, happy lives of those tribes is purely romance. Their minds clouded in error—every horrid belief finds a resting place there; their bodies are tortured by disease—it must be so, they have no sense of cleanliness, no organizing powers to fight disease, no knowledge of medicine, and added to all is their practice of crude superstitions which often prevent them applying the most obvious remedies to the disease."[105] Felix's racist and ignorant observations reflect his own biases more than any Indigenous reality. His words also show the intensity of his animosity for Indigenous bodies and beliefs, and reflect his anxiety that Indigenous methods might present a challenge to western medicine. More broadly, the scholarship of the late nineteenth and early twentieth century discussed Native American pictorial traditions as evidence of the "primitive" state of Native Americans within discussions of North American art and history. When American artists and ethnologists considered such Native American pictorial traditions as tattooing, hide painting, and hieroglyphs, they positioned Indigenous subjects in the past, outside the time, history, and artistic traditions of western American artists. As art historian Michael Gaudio notes, "in this pictorial civilization of the 1880s, a civilization in which a picture could be a kind of writing and writing a kind of picture, evolution provided a logic of interpretation."[106] Scholars, artists, and writers framed pictorial traditions of Indigenous cultures as "evidence" of their unevolved state.[107] Writers and theorists saw syllabics, for example, and hieroglyphic markings on pottery, textiles, and hide as evidence of a "primitive" state of mind.[108] This evolutionary perspective continued unchallenged and unchanged with the VME's display techniques, which resembled a packed storehouse with no distinctions made between communities or sacred and secular cultural belongings.

Complementary to the visual regime, a narrative of western progress emphasized the allochronic space and time of Indigenous cultures at the VME. In a parallel example, scholar Maureen Perkins notes that conceptions of time played an important role in the colonial discourse of Australia. Perkins observes that "time was a means of imposing order on 'disorder,' and the colonial experience involved temporal domination as much as territorial control."[109] Perkins's point resonates with the premise of the VME in that intellectuals, government officials, and artists constructed and understood Indigenous peoples as outside the picture of Christian linear time and progress created at the VME.[110] For example, the History of the Missions and the Hall of Martyrs were completely separate from the Halls of the Americas, placing Indigenous peoples and their cultural belongings outside visitors' frame of reference rather than considering the multiple ways that Indigenous peoples, settlers, and missionaries impacted each other.

Contemporary Fairs and Expositions

1911: The World in Boston

The scope and diversity of materials collected and displayed by Schmidt and his team of missionaries at the VME created a unique exhibition space unprecedented at the Vatican and within Europe, although it paralleled many missionary

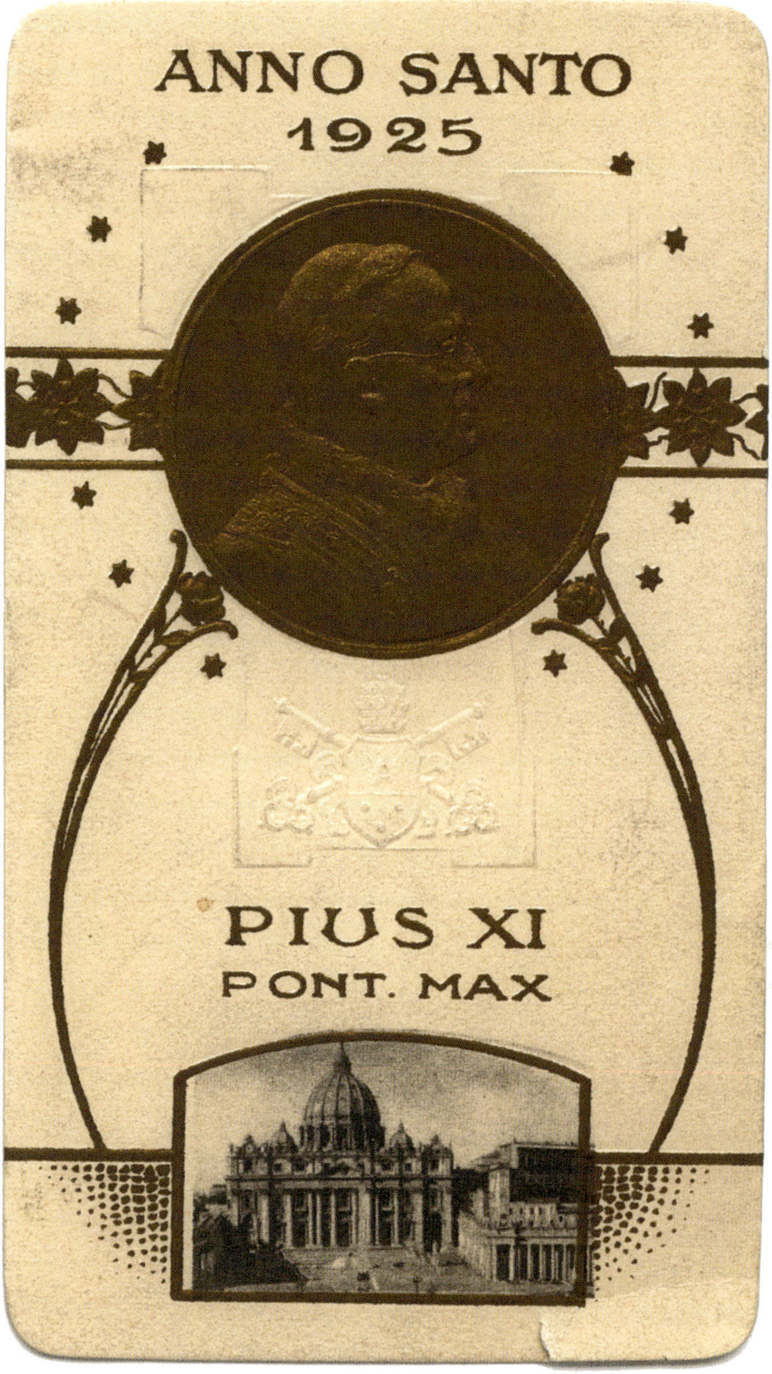

PLATE 1. Anno Santo 1925, Pius XI, Pont. Max. (Holy Year 1925, Pius XI, Pope). Commemorative card for the jubilee year 1925, with photograph of Saint Peter's Basilica. Collection of the author.

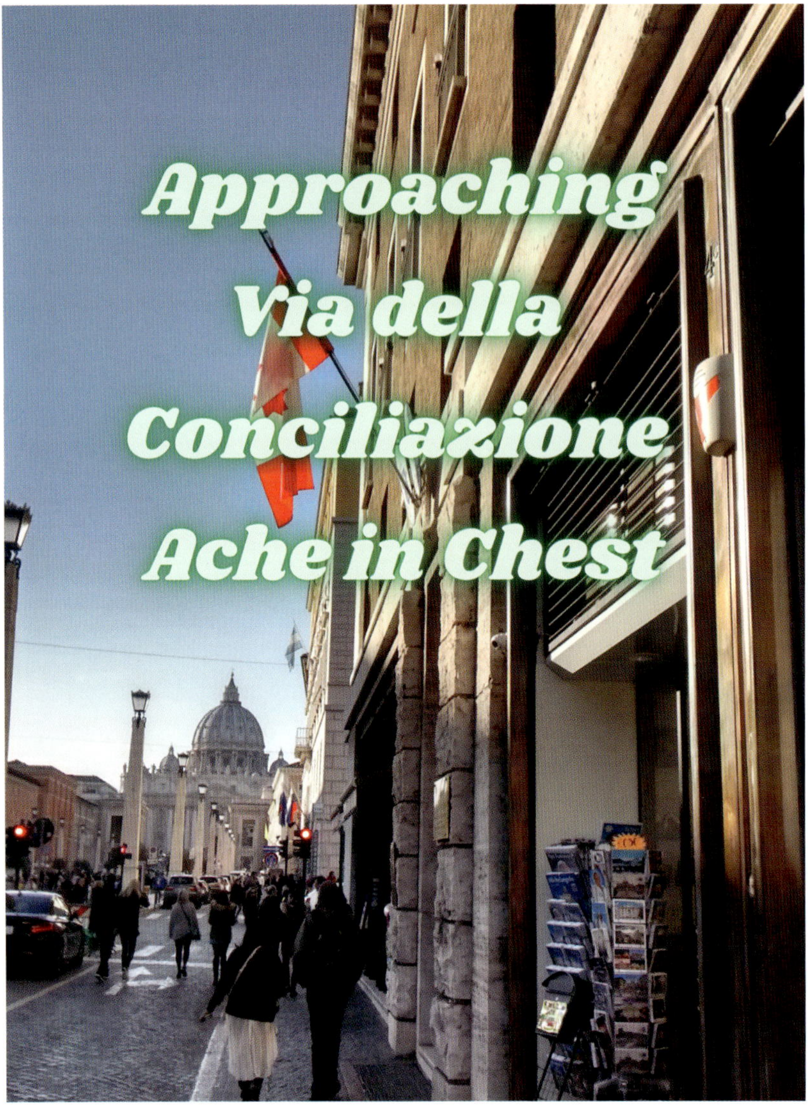

PLATE 2. *Approaching via della Conciliazione, ache in chest*, 2023. Photograph with lettering by the author.

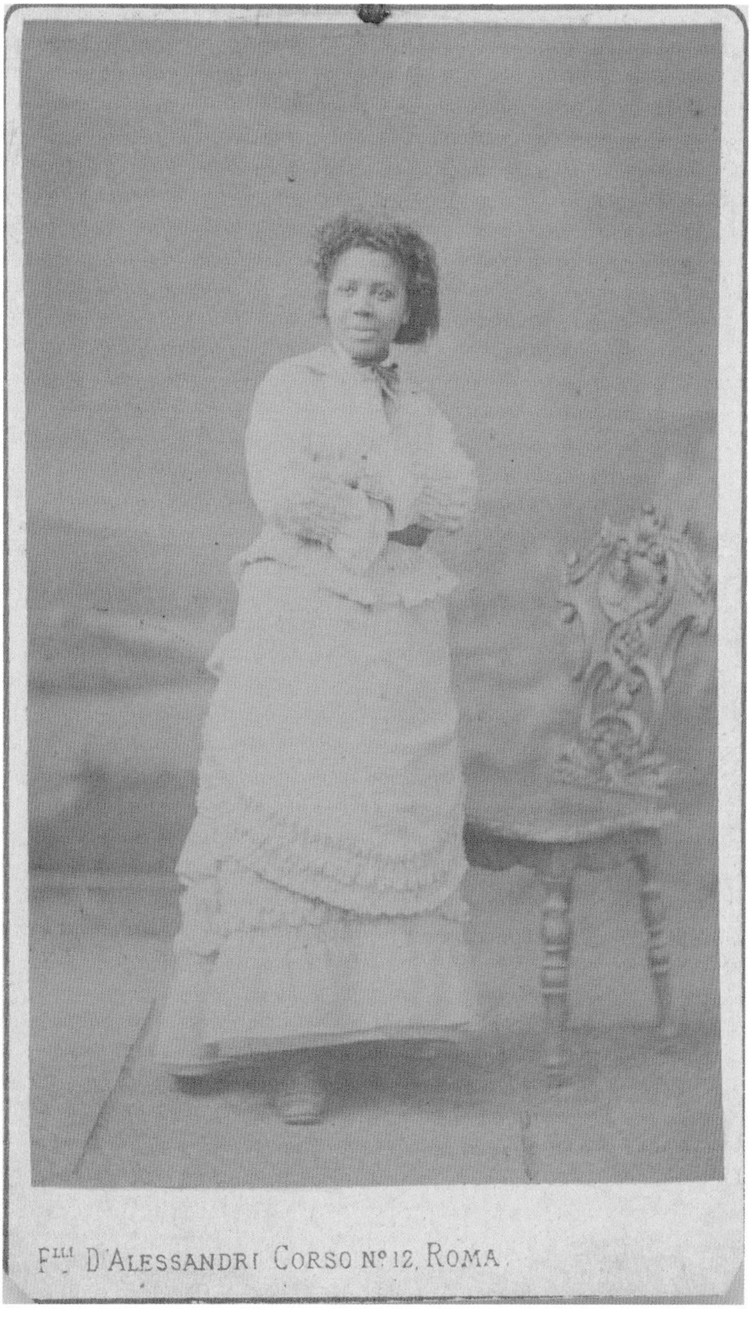

PLATE 3. Edmonia Lewis's *carte de visite* featuring a photograph of her by Fratelli D'Alessandri, Rome, ca. 1874–76. Albumen silver print mounted on card, 10.16 × 6.35 cm. Courtesy of Walters Art Museum, Baltimore.

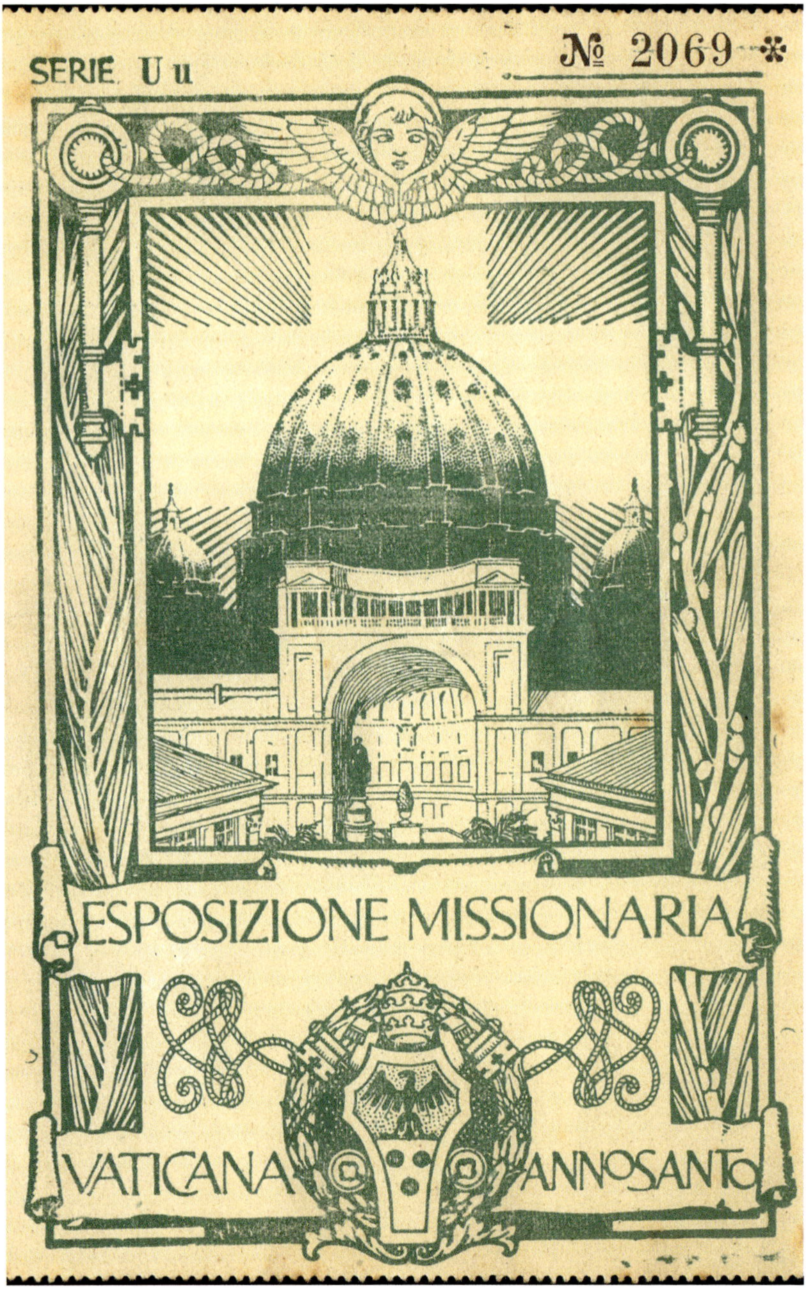

PLATE 4. Ticket for the 1925 Vatican Missionary Exposition. Collection of the author.

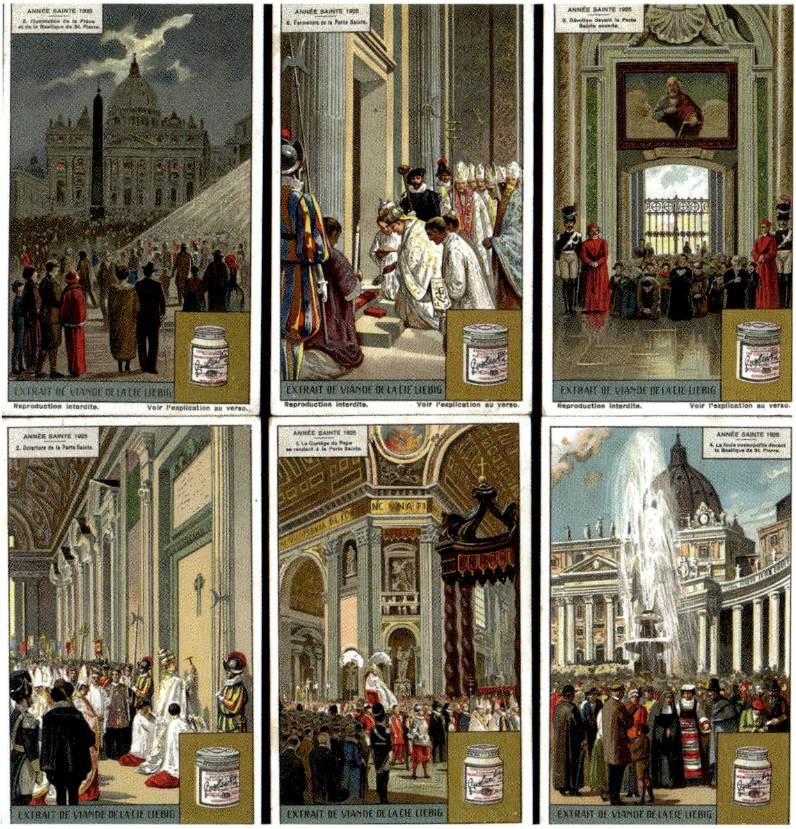

PLATE 5. Six scenes from the opening of the Vatican Missionary Exposition, 1925. Series of commemorative cards. Collection of the author.

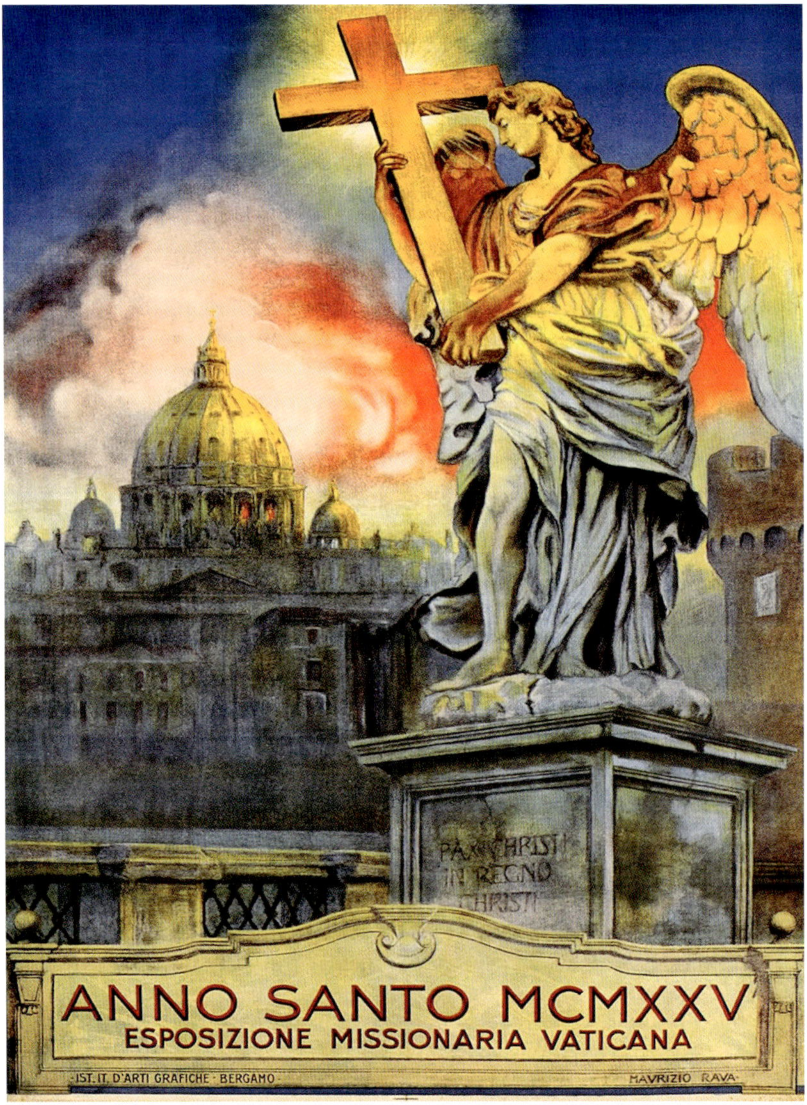

PLATE 6. Maurizio Rava, *Anno Santo MCMXXV, Esposizione Missionaria Vaticana* (Holy Year 1925, Vatican Missionary Exposition). Poster. Courtesy of Mill Hill Missionaries Archive, Liverpool.

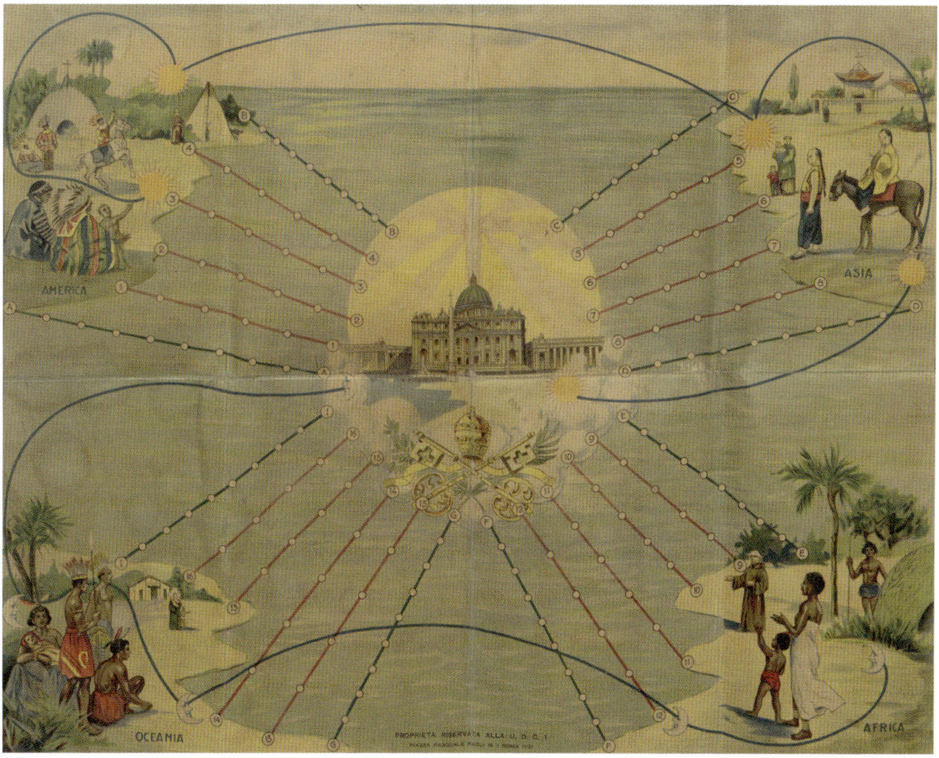

PLATE 7. *Viaggi missionari* (Missionary voyages), board game, ca. 1930. Chromolithograph. Courtesy of Missionary Ephemera Collection, RG 221, Special Collections, Yale Divinity Library, New Haven, CT.

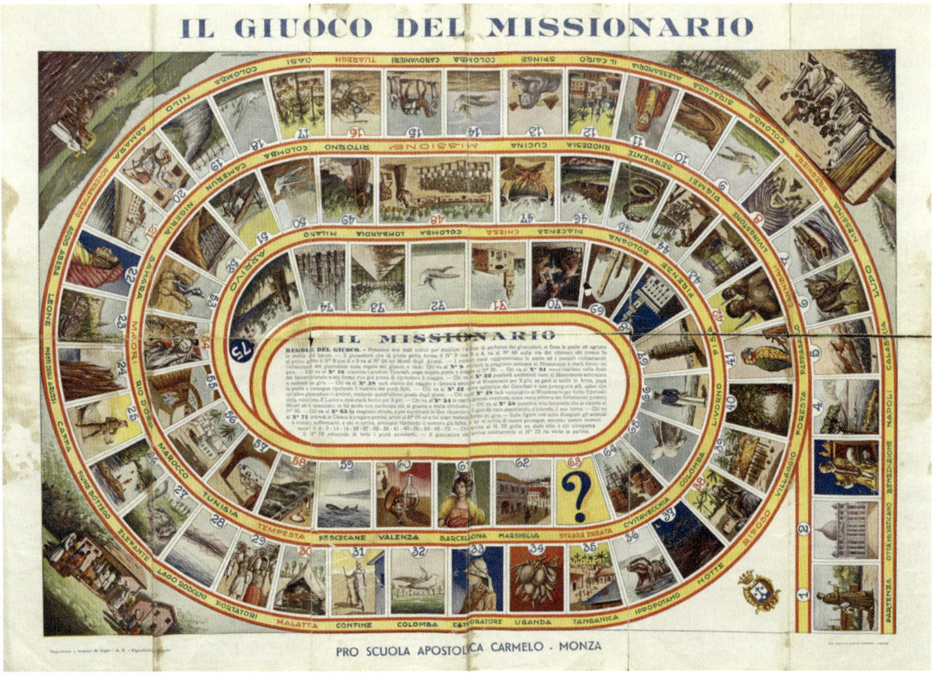

PLATE 8. *Il giuoco del missionario* (The missionary game), board game, ca. 1930. Chromolithograph. Courtesy of Missionary Ephemera Collection, RG 221, Special Collections, Yale Divinity Library, New Haven, CT.

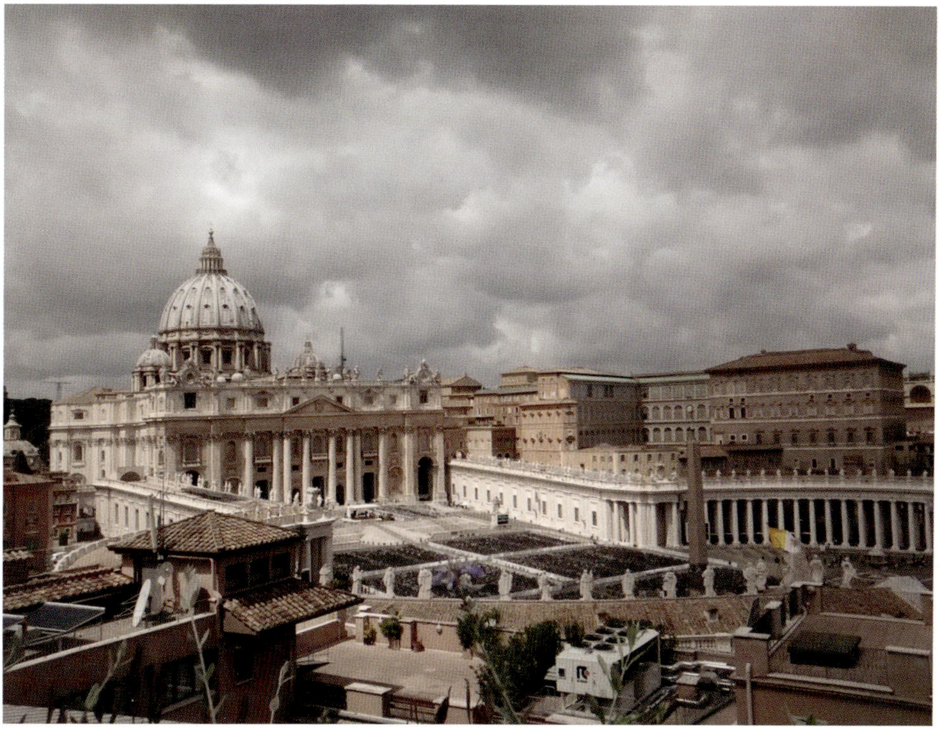

PLATE 9. View of Saint Peter's from Propaganda Fide College, Janiculum Hill, Rome, 2017. Photograph by the author.

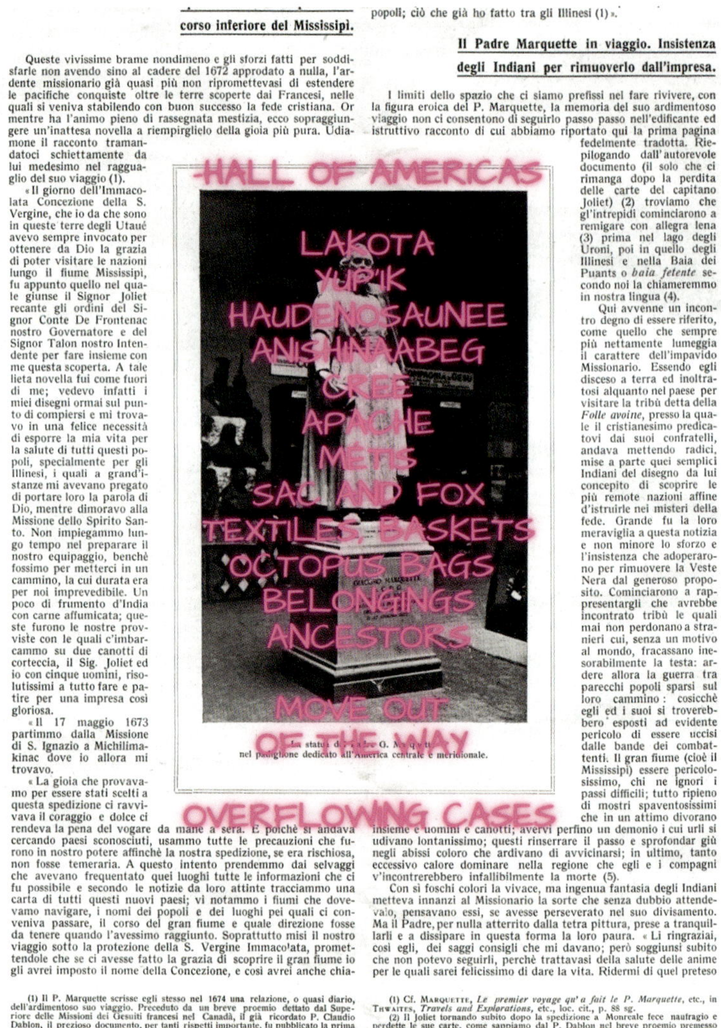

corso inferiore del Mississipì.

Queste vivissime brame nondimeno e gli sforzi fatti per soddisfarle non avendo sino al cadere del 1672 approdato a nulla, l'ardente missionario già quasi più non riprometttevasi di estendere le pacifiche conquiste oltre le terre scoperte dai Francesi, nelle quali si veniva stabilendo con buon successo la fede cristiana. Or mentre ha l'animo pieno di rassegnata mestizia, ecco sopraggiungere un'inattesa novella a riempirglielo della gioia più pura. Udiamone il racconto tramandatoci schiettamente da lui medesimo nel ragguaglio del suo viaggio (1).

« Il giorno dell'Immacolata Concezione della S. Vergine, che io da che sono in queste terre degli Utaué avevo sempre invocato per ottenere da Dio la grazia di poter visitare le nazioni lungo il fiume Mississipi, fu appunto quello nel quale giunse il Signor Joliet recante gli ordini del Signor Conte De Frontenac nostro Governatore e del Signor Talon nostro Intendente per fare insieme con me questa scoperta. A tale lieta novella fui come fuori di me; vedevo infatti i miei disegni ormai sul punto di compiersi e mi trovavo in una felice necessità di esporre la mia vita per la salute di tutti questi popoli, specialmente per gli Illinesi, i quali a grand'istanze mi avevano pregato di portare loro la parola di Dio, mentre dimoravo alla Missione dello Spirito Santo. Non impiegammo lungo tempo nel preparare il nostro equipaggio, benchè fossimo per metterci in un cammino, la cui durata era per noi imprevedibile. Un poco di frumento d'India con carne affumicata; queste furono le nostre provviste con le quali c'imbarcammo su due canotti di corteccia, il Sig. Joliet ed io con cinque uomini, risolutissimi a tutto fare e patire per una impresa così gloriosa.

« Il 17 maggio 1673 partimmo dalla Missione di S. Ignazio a Michilimakinac dove io allora mi trovavo.

« La gioia che provavamo per essere stati scelti a questa spedizione ci ravvivava il coraggio e dolce ci rendeva la pena del vogare da mane a sera. E poichè si andava cercando paesi sconosciuti, usammo tutte le precauzioni che furono in nostro potere affinchè la nostra spedizione, se era rischiosa, non fosse temeraria. A questo intento prendemmo dai selvaggi che avevano frequentato quei luoghi tutte le informazioni che ci fu possibile e secondo le notizie da loro attinte tracciammo una carta di tutti questi nuovi paesi; vi notammo i fiumi che dovevamo navigare, i nomi dei popoli e dei luoghi pei quali ci conveniva passare, il corso del gran fiume e quale direzione fosse da tenere quando l'avessimo raggiunto. Soprattutto misi il nostro viaggio sotto la protezione della S. Vergine Immacolata, promettendole che se ci avesse fatto la grazia di scoprire il gran fiume io gli avrei imposto il nome della Concezione, e così avrei anche chiapopoli; ciò che già ho fatto tra gli Illinesi (1) ».

Il Padre Marquette in viaggio. Insistenza degli Indiani per rimuoverlo dall'impresa.

I limiti dello spazio che ci siamo prefissi nel fare rivivere, con la figura eroica del P. Marquette, la memoria del suo ardimentoso viaggio non ci consentono di seguirlo passo passo nell'edificante ed istruttivo racconto di cui abbiamo riportato qui la prima pagina fedelmente tradotta. Riepilogando dall'autorevole documento (il solo che ci rimanga dopo la perdita delle carte del capitano Joliet) (2) troviamo che gl'intrepidi cominciarono a remigare con allegra lena (3) prima nel lago degli Uroni, poi in quello degli Illinesi e nella Baia dei Puants o *baia fetente* secondo noi la chiameremmo in nostra lingua (4).

Qui avvenne un incontro degno di essere riferito, come quello che sempre più nettamente lumeggia il carattere dell'impavido Missionario. Essendo egli disceso a terra ed inoltratosi alquanto nel paese per visitare la tribù detta della *Folle avoine*, presso la quale il cristianesimo predicatovi dai suoi confratelli, andava mettendo radici, mise a parte quei semplici Indiani del disegno da lui concepito di scoprire le più remote nazioni affine d'istruirle nei misteri della fede. Grande fu la loro meraviglia a questa notizia e non minore lo sforzo e l'insistenza che adoperarono per rimuovere la Veste Nera dal generoso proposito. Cominciarono a rappresentargli che avrebbe incontrato tribù le quali mai non perdonano a stranieri cui, senza un motivo al mondo, fracassano inesorabilmente la testa: ardere allora la guerra tra parecchi popoli sparsi sul loro cammino: cosicchè egli ed i suoi si troverebbero esposti ad evidente pericolo di essere uccisi dalle bande dei combattenti. Il gran fiume (cioè il Mississipì) essere pericolosissimo, chi ne ignori i passi difficili; tutto ripieno di mostri spaventosissimi che in un attimo divorano insieme e uomini e canotti; avervi perfino un demonio i cui urli si udivano lontanissimo; questi rinserrare il passo e sprofondar giù negli abissi coloro che ardivano di avvicinarsi; in ultimo, tanto eccessivo calore dominare nella regione che egli e i compagni v'incontrerebbero infallibilmente la morte (5).

Con sì foschi colori la vivace, ma ingenua fantasia degli Indiani metteva innanzi al Missionario la sorte che senza dubbio attendevalo, pensavano essi, se avesse perseverato nel suo divisamento. Ma il Padre, per nulla atterrito dalla tetra pittura, prese a tranquillarli e a dissipare in questa forma la loro paura. « Li ringraziai, così egli, dei saggi consigli che mi davano; però soggiunsi subito che non potevo seguirli, perchè trattavasi della salute delle anime per le quali sarei felicissimo di dare la vita. Ridermi di quel preteso

La statua d[illegible] G. M[illegible]
nel p[illegible]glione dedicato all'America centrale e meridionale.

(1) Il P. Marquette scrisse egli stesso nel 1674 una relazione, o quasi diario, dell'ardimentoso suo viaggio. Preceduto da un breve proemio dettato dal Superiore delle Missioni dei Gesuiti francesi nel Canadà, il già ricordato P. Claudio Dablon, il prezioso documento, per tanti rispetti importante, fu pubblicato la prima volta in Parigi il 1682 a cura del Thévenot che l'inserì nella sua opera, oggi sì rara, *Recueil des voyages*. Rivide poi la luce nel 1885 in Albany negli Stati Uniti. Noi qui facciamo uso della edizione più recente, condotta, come la testè ricordata, (pur troppo con deplorevoli criterii) sullo stesso autografo che conservasi in Monreal nel Collegio di S. Maria presso i Padri della Compagnia di Gesù, ed inserita nella grande collezione americana del *Thwaites, Travels und Explorations*, già ripetutamente qui sopra citata.

(1) Cf. Marquette, *Le premier voyage qu'a fait le P. Marquette*, etc., in Thwaites, *Travels and Explorations*, etc., loc. cit., p. 88 sg.

(2) Il Joliet tornando subito dopo la spedizione a Monreale fece naufragio e perdette le sue carte, come sappiamo dal P. Dablon nel breve proemio premesso all'autografo del P. Marquette. Loc. cit., p. 88.

(3) « Nous faisons jouer joyeusement les avirons ». Così il P. Marquette, loc. cit., p. 92.

(4) Per sentimento del P. Marquette così nomasi questa baia a cagione della molta melma o belletta donde esalavano sgradevoli vapori. Cf. Marquette, loc. cit., p. 96.

(5) Marquette, loc. cit., p. 94 sg.

PLATE 10. *Marquette move out of the way*, 2023. Photograph with lettering by the author.

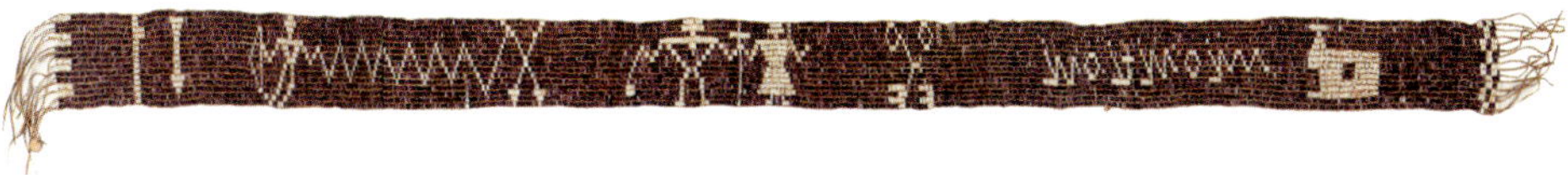

PLATE 11. Anishinaabe, Nipissing, and Kanien'kehá:ka, wampum belt, ca. 1830. Deer hide, shell, and cotton, 231 × 11.5 cm. Vatican Museums, Vatican City, inv. 107525. https://catalogo.museivaticani.va/index.php/Detail/objects/MV.107525.0.0.

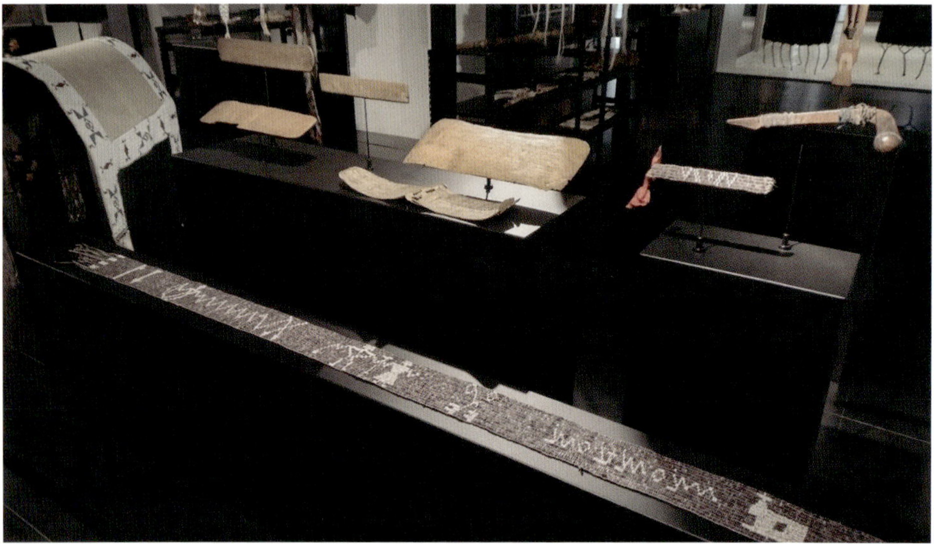

PLATE 12. Installation view, Anishinaabe, Nipissing, and Kanien'kehá:ka, wampum belt, Ethnological Museum *Anima Mundi*, Vatican Museums, Vatican City, March 2023. Photograph by the author.

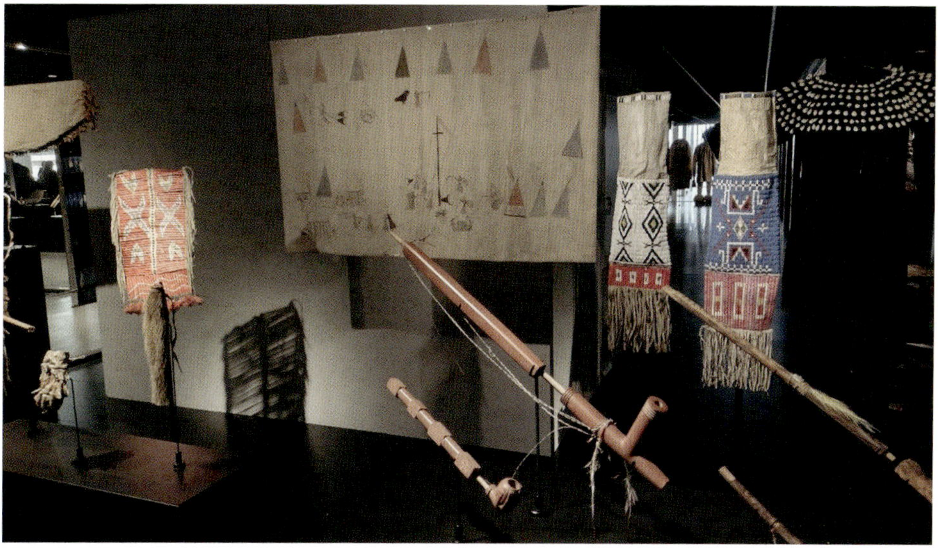

PLATE 13. Installation view, Lakota Sioux, Sun Dance drawing (figure 4.4), Ethnological Museum *Anima Mundi*, Vatican Museums, Vatican City, March 2023. Photograph by the author.

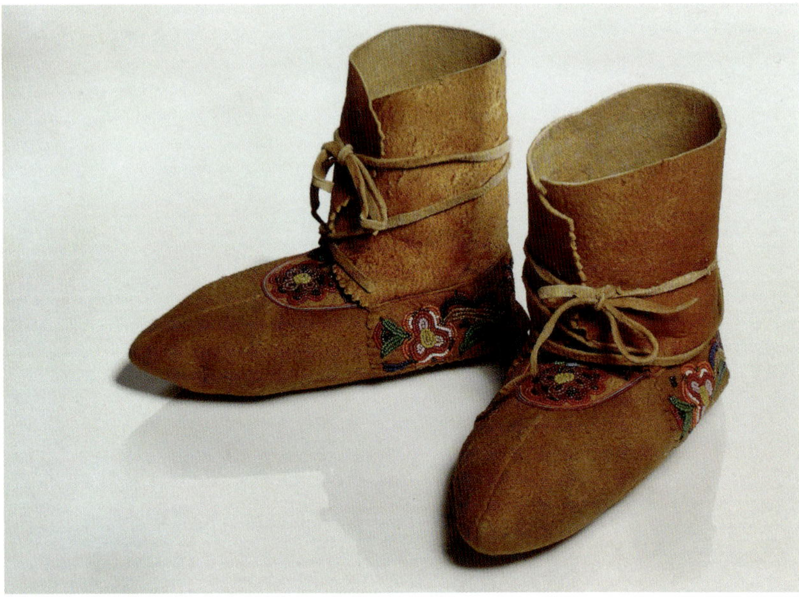

PLATE 14. Cree, moccasins, ca. 1900. Moose hide, beads, 21 × 27.5 × 12 cm. Vatican Museums, Vatican City, inv. 106048. Source: Katherine Aigner et al., *The Americas: Collections from the Vatican Ethnological Museum* (2015), 66.

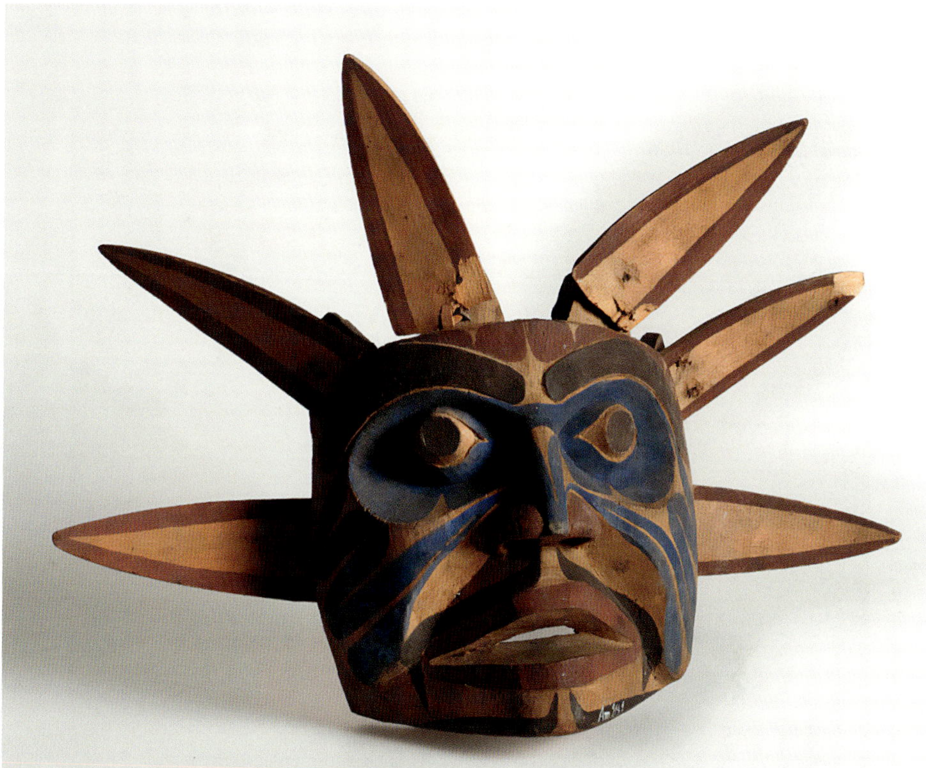

PLATE 15. Kwakwaka'wakw, Sun Dance mask, ca. 1920. Cedar, pigments, 53 × 37 × 19 cm. Vatican Museums, Vatican City, inv. 101600. Source: Patrons of the Arts in the Vatican Museums, https://www.patronsvaticanmuseums.org/en/restoration/projects/six-ritual-masks.

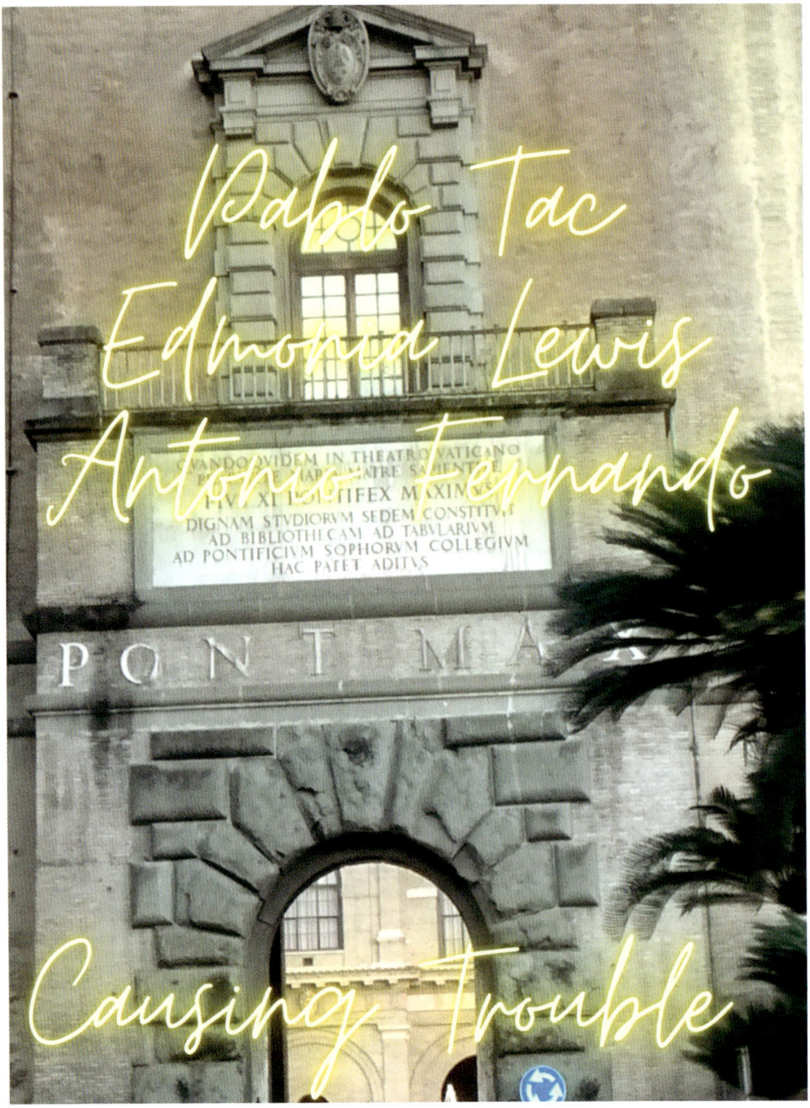

PLATE 16. *Causing trouble*, 2023. Photograph with lettering by the author.

exhibitions at the time in terms of the missionary-cum-hero narrative. The World in Boston Missionary Exposition in 1911, organized by Boston Protestants, featured exhibition display halls, costumed reenactors, missionaries and some of their "converts," pageants, and illustrated lectures.[111] The exhibition organizers aimed to show objects from around the world and, through them, the worthiness of Protestant missionary efforts. Over three hundred denominations participated. Anthropologist Erin L. Hasinoff notes that the material culture collected by the missionaries helped create a tangible connection for viewers to comprehend "faith in objects." Material things provided "object lessons" and examples of American heritage through which viewers could understand missionary work and Protestant Christian ideologies, and at the same time cultivate a sense of American identity.[112] At the exhibition, which over four hundred thousand people attended, twenty thousand stewards encouraged support for and pursuit of Protestant missionary work.

A portion of the exhibition featured Native American textiles and other arts. The inclusion of textiles, basketry, and pottery aimed to show how Native Americans could "become" industrious under the influence of Christianity. Hasinoff argues that, "displayed in a missionary exposition, such objects demonstrated Native American ingenuity and industriousness, qualities that during the Progressive Era were thought to position Natives for upliftment."[113] Visitors saw Native artisans and their work as evidence of their ability to make progress and assimilate into American society. As she observes, "the Indian's weaving was an object lesson of the latent possibility of the Indians of the Southwest, and the American Indian in general, to be civilized and educated in Western habits and demeanor."[114] At the same time, I would argue, Native Americans were positioned as "primitive" outsiders in relation to the development of American modernity, and the use of costumed reenactors at the fair further solidified the imagined position of Native Americans as separate from the time and space of the American citizens who visited. Stewards from the Young Peoples Missionary Movement spent months in training, studying Native American art and life, before the exhibition. Organizers divided the American Indians section into four categories: Indians of the Southwest, Indians of the Great Plains, Indians in the woods, and Alaskan Indians. The interpreters of the World in Boston wore Native American attire of the "Plains" and the "woods," essentially performing a dress-up version of their ideas of Native American life. "Playing Indian" was a popular practice also found at colonial celebrations of empire, as in the next example discussed.

1924: Pageant of Empire at Wembley

The Pageant of Empire ran at Wembley Park, London, from April to October 1924 and was repeated in 1925. Featuring a Wild West show, a midway with games, a pageant, lectures, sporting events, and many pavilions, it showcased the industrial and natural resources of the British Empire. The organizers aimed to celebrate the empire through a massive performance display, and the pageants were extensive, with music, animals, and costumed performers. One reviewer described "Westward Ho!," one of an extensive series of pageants, as "a good object lesson in the history of the Empire."[115] The pavilions and pageants celebrated British imperialism while presenting a spectacle of material culture to the thousands of visitors.[116]

The Pageant of Empire also featured living people from around the world, with craftsmen demonstrating arts and crafts, and a "races in residence" experience, which was a display of living people.[117] This encounter affirmed colonial attitudes of racial superiority and the brutalizing equation of Indigenous bodies as colonial resources to be exploited and displaced. Indigenous Americans faced immense pressure for integration and assimilation into mainstream society in the 1920s and 1930s, a period when residential schools became obligatory for Indigenous children. According to curator Jonathan King, throughout this period playwrights, filmmakers, and other artists in popular culture stereotyped Native peoples as either bloodthirsty raiders or doomed heroes.[118] In the European imagination, the image of the Indian often oscillated between an idealized noble savage and a predator who threatened the British Empire and its settler-colonial ideals. The Wembley pageant, with its gross historical inaccuracies—including a tableau sculpted of butter with Native women, children, a tipi, and Edward, Prince of Wales, playing Chief Morning Star, a Stony Chief—was no exception.[119]

1927: Native and Modern Exhibition of Canadian West Coast Art

The 1927 Native and Modern Exhibition of Canadian West Coast Art at the National Gallery of Ottawa, organized by Eric Brown, the gallery director, featured a mixture of settler artists, including the Group of Seven and Emily Carr, alongside Indigenous artists' works from the Northwest Coast, among them landscape paintings by Frederick Alexcee, a Tsimshian artist. The exhibition featured sculpture, paintings, and Indigenous cultural belongings in several rooms of the National Gallery. All the artworks were given ample space, a radical curatorial move that presented Indigenous works as artworks rather than as ethnographic specimens. However, equality was present only at first glance. Brown promoted the Group of Seven's work as Canadian art for a Canadian nation and silenced alternative traditions, including those of Indigenous peoples and French Canadians, in order to convey a single story of an Anglo settler nation.[120]

In relation to Indigenous peoples, Brown promoted a discourse of disappearance by strategically excluding contemporary Indigenous art from discussions of Canadian art and identity.[121] For example, he included the work of Alexcee in the exhibition but did not list him as a "Canadian artist" in the exhibition booklet.[122] Anthropologist Marius Barbeau organized the show to prominently feature a Nuxalk ancestor figure opening his arms as if in blessing. Barbeau did not seek permission, nor did any First Nations give it, to display the masks and other sacred items of the Indigenous Northwest Coast. He simply believed he could do so as part of the broader assumption by settler colonials and settler artists that Indigenous cultures were theirs to appropriate.[123] Brown included Emily Carr's weaving, pottery, and paintings, which drew inspiration and appropriated knowledge from Northwest Coast First Nations, alongside the paintings of Lawren Harris and other members of the Group of Seven. Canadian painters used Native Art at the exposition as a jumping-off point to establish their own modernity and to create a Canadian art distinct from British and European art. The exhibition traveled to London and then Paris. In London, Brown separated Indigenous art from the Group of Seven's work in order to underline the idea of Canadian identity as a single narrative.

However, French critics of the exhibition's Paris version at the Musée de Jeu de Paume received Native Northwest Coast art enthusiastically and criticized the Group of Seven's works. Brown hid the evidence of this criticism, but art historian Leslie Allan Dawn has recovered it in the archives. Given elevated status at the Paris exhibition, Haida-made argillite sculptures caused problems for Brown's monocultural vision of Canadian art as a "primitive wilderness" and Barbeau's aim to position Indigenous art in a mythic past.[124] Meanwhile, many artists, writers, and cultural workers used a discourse of "primitive art" in the 1920s to justify their appropriations. The surrealists recognized Native Northwest Coast art, but only in order to situate themselves as modernists and use Native art as foils for their creative inspiration.[125] Ultimately, Native artworks challenged the idea of a "primitive" wilderness and the imaginary Indian constructed by Emily Carr, the Group of Seven, and Eric Brown, and their vision of Canadian identity as lacking Indigenous presence.

1931: Exposition of Indian Tribal Arts, New York

Like the Native and Modern Exhibition, the Exposition of Indian Tribal Arts in New York City promoted Indigenous cultural belongings as art, not ethnography, a significant shift in curatorial method in the United States.[126] Grand Central Art Galleries held the exposition, which primarily featured paintings juxtaposed with Indigenous cultural belongings from museums in New York. The curators divided the Indigenous artworks into cultural areas and emphasized the aesthetic qualities of the artworks; they were interested in displaying the "Native esthetic."[127] Organized by John Sloan and Elizabeth White, the exposition aimed to elevate Native American art as fine art, but it also emphasized the tribal, racial status of the artists, "patterned by tribal identities," and thus encouraged perception of them as embodying the opposite of modern individualism.[128] Janet Berlo notes: "Its curators sought to convince the American public that Indian art was 'at once classic and modern,' representing 'thousands of years of development' on American, rather than European, soil."[129] Like the exposition at the National Gallery in Ottawa, with its desire to project a Canadian national identity, American exhibitions relied on Indigenous American art to create a unique character for Americans. Curators emphasized that Indigenous art promoted national pride and distinguished Americans from Europeans. The interest in Native art in the United States positively impacted Canadian policies on the support and development of Native arts.[130] For example, later in the twentieth century the Canada Council for the Arts founded several programs to support and exhibit contemporary Indigenous art and hire Indigenous curators.

1932: Venice Biennale

Six years after the VME, the American pavilion in Venice showcased the work of Indigenous American artists, the first occurrence of Indigenous art at a contemporary art exhibition outside North America. Then as now, the Venice Biennale featured contemporary art from around the world, with national pavilions showcasing artworks chosen by artists of that nation. Visitors could attend over a period of several months. The American pavilion included the work of Hopi artist Fred Kabotie and other Indigenous artists from the Southwest alongside the efforts of American settler artists.[131] In addition to the display of paintings by Kabotie, another room in the American pavilion included weaving, pottery, and jewelry, but the Indigenous artists in this room remained anonymous, reaffirming the hierarchy of manual ("primitive," collective mentality, unnamed) versus fine arts (modern, individual, named). Nevertheless,

John Sloan, who organized the American section at the Venice Biennale, marketed the Native artworks as truly American and modernist, although "steeped in an ancient tradition," as part of the American pavilion's quest for a truly "national aesthetic."[132] Art historian Jessica Horton notes that the 1932 display of Indigenous art at the Venice Biennale has been forgotten and explains that "the organizers' initial plans to circulate the works to other European cities dwindled in the wake of the disappointing press and Depression-era financial constraints."[133] It was not until 1995 that the Canadian pavilion at the Venice Biennale featured the work of Métis artist Edward Poitras, the first Indigenous artist shown at the Venice Biennale since 1932.

The VME has also fallen out of the official annals of art history, yet it had many similarities with other world's fairs and art expositions of the early twentieth century and still operates as a reminder and marker of pope Pius XI's sense of entitlement and brutal missionary violence. Just as the organizers of the World in Boston presented Indigenous American cultural belongings as trophies to be admired, so too did the VME.[134] And just as Boston, like Wembley, celebrated American and British imperialism through material things, so too did the VME praise Catholic missionary work. The expositions in Boston and Wembley emphasized western "progress" and "civilization" through the "heroic" colonial efforts of missionaries and other agents of British imperialism. Whereas the VME resorted to wax models and dioramas, the Pageant of Empire included live people, and Boston used costumed reenactors and "recent converts" to entertain visitors.[135] The fairs in Boston and Wembley, along with the VME, featured packed display cases of Native American art and artifacts, resorting to nineteenth-century museum techniques to emphasize the Indigenous materials as ethnographic specimens rather than as art. In contrast, Brown, in his curation of the Native and Modern Exhibition, did not pack the Northwest Coast Native art into cases like a curiosity corner or the collecting parlor of a surrealist artist, and instead placed the artworks sparingly throughout the gallery.[136] The organizers of the Exposition of Indian Tribal Art and the Venice Biennale also used a spatial technique that emphasized Indigenous art as fine art. This marked a decisive shift in the treatment of Indigenous art—a recognition of Indigenous artists as artists rather than anonymous makers—that continued to build throughout the twentieth century.

In marked contrast to the other exhibitions, the VME did not focus on individual makers and instead promoted a homogenizing discourse that rendered Indigenous communities as static and their artforms as artifacts. Pius XI and his curatorial team were not interested in the individuality of Indigenous

FIGURE 2.11. "Norme circa gli oggetti destinati all'esposizione" (Norms for objects destined for the exposition), 1923. Papal document listing Pius XI's demands for the VME. Courtesy of Archivum Generale O.M.I. Romae, Rome.

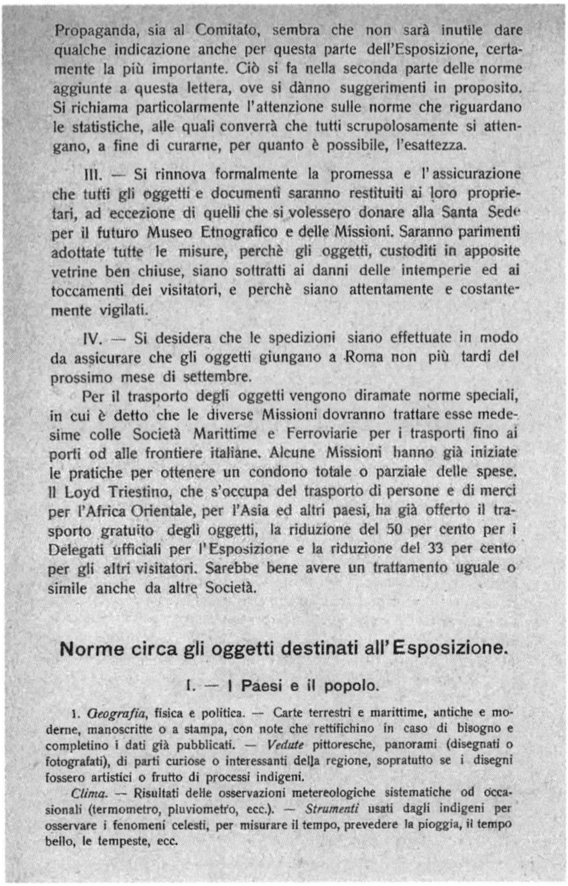

Propaganda, sia al Comitato, sembra che non sarà inutile dare qualche indicazione anche per questa parte dell'Esposizione, certamente la più importante. Ciò si fa nella seconda parte delle norme aggiunte a questa lettera, ove si dànno suggerimenti in proposito. Si richiama particolarmente l'attenzione sulle norme che riguardano le statistiche, alle quali converrà che tutti scrupolosamente si attengano, a fine di curarne, per quanto è possibile, l'esattezza.

III. — Si rinnova formalmente la promessa e l'assicurazione che tutti gli oggetti e documenti saranno restituiti ai loro proprietari, ad eccezione di quelli che si volessero donare alla Santa Sede per il futuro Museo Etnografico e delle Missioni. Saranno parimenti adottate tutte le misure, perchè gli oggetti, custoditi in apposite vetrine ben chiuse, siano sottratti ai danni delle intemperie ed ai toccamenti dei visitatori, e perchè siano attentamente e costantemente vigilati.

IV. — Si desidera che le spedizioni siano effettuate in modo da assicurare che gli oggetti giungano a Roma non più tardi del prossimo mese di settembre.

Per il trasporto degli oggetti vengono diramate norme speciali, in cui è detto che le diverse Missioni dovranno trattare esse medesime colle Società Marittime e Ferroviarie per i trasporti fino ai porti od alle frontiere italiane. Alcune Missioni hanno già iniziate le pratiche per ottenere un condono totale o parziale delle spese. Il Loyd Triestino, che s'occupa del trasporto di persone e di merci per l'Africa Orientale, per l'Asia ed altri paesi, ha già offerto il trasporto gratuito degli oggetti, la riduzione del 50 per cento per i Delegati ufficiali per l'Esposizione e la riduzione del 33 per cento per gli altri visitatori. Sarebbe bene avere un trattamento uguale o simile anche da altre Società.

Norme circa gli oggetti destinati all'Esposizione.

I. — I Paesi e il popolo.

1. *Geografia*, fisica e politica. — Carte terrestri e marittime, antiche e moderne, manoscritte o a stampa, con note che rettifichino in caso di bisogno e completino i dati già pubblicati. — *Vedute* pittoresche, panorami (disegnati o fotografati), di parti curiose o interessanti della regione, sopratutto se i disegni fossero artistici o frutto di processi indigeni.

Clima. — Risultati delle osservazioni metereologiche sistematiche od occasionali (termometro, pluviometro, ecc.). — *Strumenti* usati dagli indigeni per osservare i fenomeni celesti, per misurare il tempo, prevedere la pioggia, il tempo bello, le tempeste, ecc.

people as makers, as is evident in the stockpiling of materials, including cultural belongings, in glass display cases and the absence of discussion of Indigenous makers throughout archival records. This could also be because missionaries did not value nor study Indigenous artworks or belongings. Operating with a salvage mindset, missionaries with their limited and often brutal racist attitudes then stole belongings both sacred and secular from Indigenous communities of Turtle Island to please the pope and try to fulfill his extensive list of demands for the exhibition (see figure 2.11).

The belongings, stolen treasures, today remain secured like prisoners in inaccessible vaults and in *Anima Mundi*, in the basement of the Vatican Museums. Indigenous communities never gave their permission or consent to display their belongings. The artifacts today function as trophies of war during this colonial and genocidal period of Indigenous assimilation and missionary violence. The Vatican Museums have not repatriated anything to date, despite multiple requests from Indigenous communities across Turtle Island. The belongings are not unlike much Nazi-looted art, taken under duress from vulnerable communities during the early decades of the twentieth century.

In Conclusion: Weird Images and Overflowing Spaces

Let us turn to another fantasy image in the *Rivista Illustrata* that parallels the odd syncretism and the pope's propaganda found in the Halls of the Americas. The front cover of an issue of the December 31, 1924, issue offers another allochronic image: two stylized "Indians," a Plains Indian on the left and, on the right, a man from "India" (see figure 2.12). The Plains Indian man wears a war bonnet and a ribbon bow around his neck as well as a necklace with a medallion. His torso is a stylized column; he is presented as a glyph, a sculpted figure. The artist could have drawn inspiration from Little Falcon, the Očhéthi Šakówiŋ man featured in the issue. Above his head is a scallop shell, a prominent symbol used in Renaissance and baroque art and architecture. The shell emphasizes his status as a pagan, in line with pagan iconography that was plentiful throughout Rome that used the same scallop motif, such as Bernini's Triton Fountain (1643). On the right, the Indian man wears a turban with hoop earrings, and around his neck he sports elaborate jewelry. Like the companion who flanks him on the left, his torso is also a stylized column, his head sheltered by a scallop shell, again emphasizing his spiritual difference. At the bottom of both glyphs are laurel-leaf bundles, another symbol of ancient pagan Rome. Across the bottom a Latin inscription reads "All nations will adore him." The two figures frame a reproduction of a painting of the Nativity by Gherardo delle Notti, dated circa 1622. This strange image is the cover illustration for the issue of the journal that featured an in-depth examination of the VME, with accounts from missionaries and of their genocidal work in the Americas as well as around the world. The figures that frame the Nativity scene seem to act like gods, surrounding the site like protectors, but they are not Christian, as their status as glyphs and the shell motifs suggests. The sculptural decor of the Plains Indian man, likely based on Little Falcon, and an "Indian man" suggest the broader pan-Indianism that was present within artistic fantasies and conceptions of "Indianness" at the VME and within Rome. The gods frame the baroque painting as glyphs, creating a kind of temporal distancing in the image

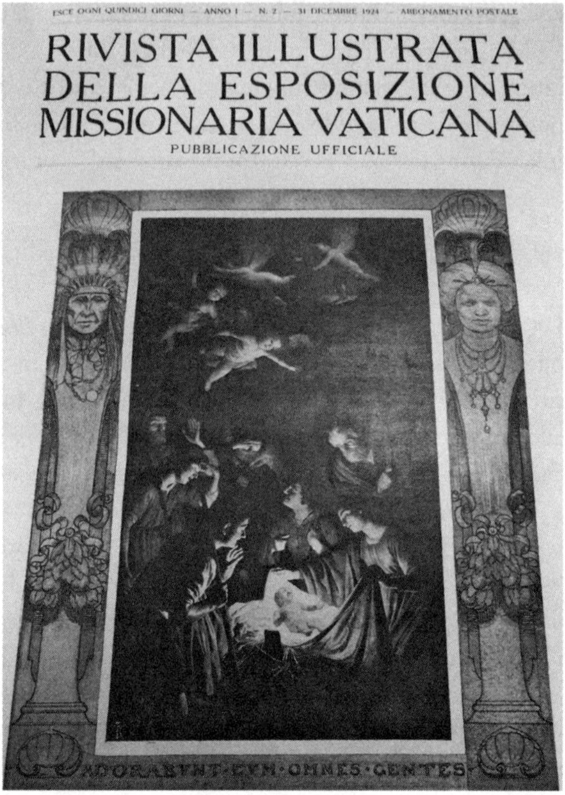

FIGURE 2.12. Cover of *Rivista Illustrata della Esposizione Missionaria Vaticana*, December 31, 1924. Courtesy of Propaganda Fide Library Collections, Pontificio Collegio Urbano "De Propaganda Fide," Rome.

that duplicated the temporal distancing for visitors to the VME. The gods are mute allegories of "India" and "America," part of the silent eloquence of Pius XI's culture of conquest.

This odd syncretic image resonates with the allochronic space of the Halls of the Americas as a form of propaganda. The image depicts an idealized, imaginary Indigenous figure from the Great Plains rather than a specific individual and collapses distinctions between the imaginary and the real.[137] Pictures like this one reverberate with the denial of Indigenous modernity present throughout the Halls of the Americas and underscore the need to closely reread VME imagery to unpack papal logic. Analyzing the extensive archival record of the Halls of the Americas and the VME also parallels the many impasses I encountered in my research experience at the Fototeca and in archives throughout Rome and Turtle Island, as the archives are muddled, inarticulate spaces wherein history is submerged, documents go missing, and researchers are not always welcome. The VME ultimately functioned as a propaganda machine both in the construction of the exhibition and in the production of fantasy knowledge in the *Rivista Illustrata*. Pius XI, cognizant of the power of world's exhibitions, sought to compete with other world's fairs, particularly Protestant ones, in the race to convert souls, killing in the name of Catholicism with images and celebrations of missionary work that equated children's games with the missionary labors of genocide.

3

"A WINDOW ON THE WORLD" OF COLONIAL UNKNOWING

Dioramas, Children's Games, and Missionary Perspectives at the Vatican Missionary Exposition

Journal: Societas Verbi Divini, Pyramid of Cestius

MAY 2016. *The giant, creamy-white pyramid of ancient Roman Caius Cestius greeted me as I got off the bus and walked over to the Societas Verbi Divini. The Verbites of the Divine Word Missionaries is the order that Father Wilhelm Schmidt, the curator of the Vatican Missionary Exposition, had trained in and that still holds some of his papers. I had been calling the archivist for a few days, and finally he had agreed that I could come. The archivist buzzed me into the gated structure. I wandered around the outside of a massive building and through a dark green garden. Finally, after I had walked about ten minutes not sure where to go, a large door opened and a tall man in a black robe stood in the entryway. I walked up the stairs feeling a bit nervous. The archive of the Verbite order is situated in the College of the Divine Word, an imposing place with lush vegetation. I was brought down two flights of steep stairs by Herbert Scholz, an elderly priest. Located in the basement, the archive was essentially a desk with files behind it. It was dark and quiet, and I worked in silence. The correspondence was on wrinkled, translucent paper sheets, some handwritten in black or blue ink and some typewritten. There were three separations in the file I examined, including one for the Museo Laterano and another for the business of the museum up until the 1960s. The third section, labeled* Ausstellung *(exhibition), was for the Vatican Missionary Exposition.*

I had come to the archive to see their folder on the exposition, and I found some interesting correspondence, including lists of materials and cultural belongings sent in from China and from Paraguay. I felt disappointed that there were not any lists of Indigenous cultural belongings from North America, but I guess that would have been a researcher's dream. Moreover, things are rarely what you hope or think they will be in an archive. The correspondence regarding the exhibition was in German, French, Italian, and English. The faint scratches of curator Father Schmidt's pencil and his messy lists had faded in time.

Seeing the vast amount of correspondence, I began to understand the sense Schmidt must have had of being overwhelmed when he started to organize the exposition for the pope. I photographed relevant materials. I also found a letter in French regarding the loss of some missionary objects bound for the exposition in a shipwreck. After almost four hours in the archive, I had looked through the entire folder and found a few interesting letters and documents. Nothing related directly to the Americas, however, although the lists of materials from China and Paraguay were intriguing. As I walked out to get a glass of water, Scholz noted that behind one of the locked doors in the basement was a massive photographic archive. I was not sure if I would be able to use any of the material I had seen in my search, but only time would tell. It piqued my interest to know that lists were made, but many materials were lost, objects being a bit unruly in their way.

Scholz was up to speed on the history of the order, and as we wandered through the archives in the basement he told me that the director of the Vatican Museums Missionary Ethnological Museum had been an member of the Verbites up until the 1990s. After sifting through documents in the archive, I went to the adjacent library. A couple of times, Scholz came into the library where I was searching through books, speaking in fast German. He went on for a few minutes before he looked up and realized I did not know what he was saying. It was disorienting. I planned to return to the Verbite archive and check out their library and look further at the Annali Lateranensi *and some of the other periodicals from the 1920s, as they had a small but impressively full collection. I said a prayer or two to the divine for help with the project.*

American Catholic Father John Considine's *The Vatican Mission Exposition: A Window on the World* (1925) is perhaps the best contemporary account of the importance of the Vatican Missionary Exposition (VME). His emphasis on the exposition as a lens through which to understand the global efforts of the Catholic Church builds on the popular metaphor of an exhibition as a "window." After climbing the cupola of Saint Peter's to survey the infrastructure of the VME, Considine makes this observation:

> What a wonderful thing is a window! A tiny opening barely the width of my eye, in this otherwise pitch dark globe, gives the prospect of a whole countryside. Yes, what a wonderful thing is a window that can lay before the vision in an instant more ground than can be traversed in a day. What a wonderful thing is any instrument that gives us in panorama great vistas of loveliness and inspiration. And if the expanses that are laid before us are visions of whole continents, of whole peoples, of the thoughts and aspirations of those peoples and the struggles of the Church of God to bless those peoples with their birthright of the Faith, what a marvelous handmaid for mind and soul is such an agency! And is not the Vatican Mission Exposition such? It is, indeed, a window on the world.[1]

Considine's experience of viewing the exhibition from multiple perspectives—first from the cupola of Saint Peter's and then at ground level, moving through the VME and encountering and experiencing the material cultures on display—gave him, along with the million other viewers who attended the exposition, an overwhelming panorama. Visitors frequently emphasized the difference between themselves and the subjects, such as the Indigenous Americans who were represented in photographs, wax mannequins, children's games, and Pettrich's artworks. The seeming veracity and authenticity of what visitors saw with their eyes reinforced this sense of difference and separation. At the same time, the predominantly visual nature of the VME, with its stereotypical and idealized dioramas and children's games, allowed visitors to ignore how Catholic missionaries, supported by the federal government, subjected Indigenous children and adults to a process of genocide and cultural eradication.

The Jesuit C. Howard Morrison, reviewing the VME six months after it opened, described the experience of a visitor: "On the streets and in the basilicas, he sees bishops, priests, and people from every civilized country on the globe, while at the Vatican Missionary Exhibition the whole pagan world is presented to his gaze. Mission booths from India, China, Japan, Africa, the islands of the Pacific, frozen Alaska, and the tropics of the Amazon attest the truth that the Church is Catholic not only in name but Catholic also in fact."[2] However, the dioramas and children's games provide an alternative way to analyze the exhibition. Visitors, government officials, and pilgrims viewed the exhibition through a dichotomy of "civilized" and "pagan" that focused on Catholic "facts" rather than the realities of Indigenous American life. Building on the account of visitors' experiences at the VME in chapter 2, which argues that the VME created an exhaustive vision of pope Pius XI's culture of conquest, this chapter examines the material culture—namely, the dioramas and children's games—that the missionaries used to teach, educate, and inform visitors to the VME. Considine and Morrison viewed the entire VME as a sweeping panorama, but visitors also encountered dioramas and games, and even handled objects, in a direct engagement with tangible things to reinforce their colonial learning.[3]

Missionaries placed the materials in the Halls of the Americas behind glass so that they would not be within reach of visitors. However, one photograph, dated 1925, shows an interesting exception and provides evidence that sometimes visitors could and indeed did touch materials (see figure 3.1). Mill Hill Missionaries Archive, in Liverpool, captioned this image "The lady visitors admire the texture of some eastern cloth," and the photograph shows visitors physically handling materials.[4] Dioramas, by contrast, were cordoned off: in some of the dioramas depicting missionaries and Indigenous peoples, such as one showing a Capuchin missionary and Arachin people, a barrier separated the diorama from the viewing public; other dioramas used ropes.[5] Thus, in collecting and producing colonial knowledge about Indigenous peoples, the VME—with some exceptions, as indicated by the photo of the "lady visitors"—relied on *viewing*; visitors had to *see* the exposition and were expected to depend almost exclusively on their eyes. Morrison's and Considine's accounts read almost as if they had taken a snapshot with a camera, producing a form of knowledge to be sure, but one that was not considerate of the realities that Indigenous Americans faced.[6] Their vision went hand in hand with a greedy form of looking and refracted what Ann Laura Stoler calls the "panoptic glare" of the official archival record.[7]

This chapter contends that the many dioramas and children's games at the VME, while seeming to be supplements to engage younger visitors, were in fact essential pieces of the exhibition that celebrated missionaries as heroes. Together they form a "window on the world" that was replete with what American studies scholars Manu Vimalassery, Juliana Hu Pegues, and Alyosha

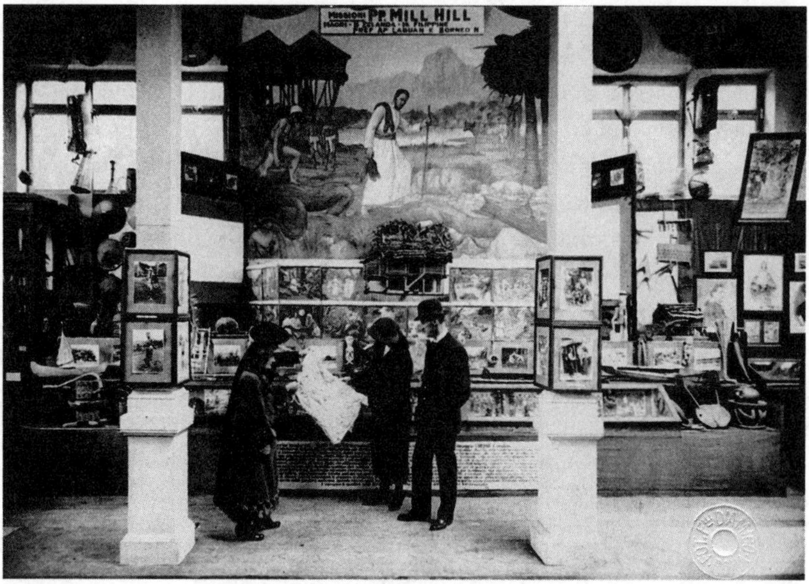

FIGURE 3.1. "The lady visitors admire the texture of some eastern cloth," 1925. Courtesy of Mill Hill Missionaries Archive, Liverpool.

Goldstein call "colonial unknowing," a term that denotes the process of containing and controlling Indigenous presence in the Americas.[8] Colonial unknowing is an ongoing disavowal of the colonial foundations of conquest and genocide that settler nations such as Canada, the United States, and Australia are based on. This deep obfuscation erases settler-colonial histories of violence and dispossession.[9] Complementing visitors' accounts, the material culture, dioramas, children's games, and certificates, in presenting stereotypical and idealized imagery, displayed a tangible form of Pius XI's disavowal.

To counter this elision of colonial realities at the VME, the second half of this chapter will incorporate a discussion of the realities that Indigenous children of the Americas faced in residential schools run by Catholic missionaries in the early twentieth century. The VME functioned, like the residential schools, as part of the settler-colonial project for the eradication of Indigenous lifeways. The VME included models of colonial schoolhouses, making visible and celebrating missionary work as heroic and noble. The schools and the VME both funded missionary work and relied extensively on visual, artistic pedagogy. While the VME was representing Indigenous peoples as "primitives" doomed to exist in the past to largely white European audiences in Rome, residential schools were forcibly teaching Indigenous children assimilative values and exploiting their labor to make souvenir arts and crafts to fund missionary work.[10] Thus, to understand the VME more fully, it is necessary to consider the overarching impact of residential schools on Indigenous life in North America and the ways in which vision and art making played a significant role in that process. The VME's games and dioramas offered a "window on the world" of the ideologies of missionaries with regard to Indigenous peoples; these missionary perspectives and attitudes—this colonial way of seeing, looking, and understanding—flowed one way. The colonial gaze did not acknowledge Indigenous realities and settler-colonial violence against Indigenous peoples in the Americas; in so doing, it actively reinforced these realities. Missionary organizers and artists constructed Indigenous peoples in the dioramas and the games as mute, compliant subjects; only the Catholic stewards animated the discussions.[11] Since the viewer would encounter the dioramas before the games and other ephemera such as postcards, this chapter commences with them.

Cringey Dioramas and Colonial Records

Throughout the VME, the organizers used finely made wax models to represent both missionaries and Indigenous peoples in lifelike reproductions. These models recall the histories of captive and forced Indigenous peoples in world's fairs and colonial and missionary exhibitions, a practice that has been widely discussed in critical scholarship, starting with Raymond Corbey's work on ethnographic showcases and the exploitative relationship they suggest between empire and the display of colonized peoples.[12] In the lead-up to the opening of the VME, a journalist observed the preparations and reported in the *New York Times* that "one of the most attractive features for the general public will be placed in the Vatican garden, where the various nations of the earth will be represented in native environment by natives brought specially to Rome."[13] The journalist noted that the VME would be "showing the customs and modes of living from the Arctic to the Antarctic, from Red Indians to Papuans, including cannibal tribes."[14] In Pius XI's official call for participation in the exposition, he urged missionaries to send in Indigenous people from all corners of the earth if the missionary orders could cope with the costs and difficulties of doing so.[15] In preparation for the opening, missionaries often discussed including Indigenous peoples at the exposition. A 1923 missive to the Oblate Missions from Vatican City, noting Pius XI's recommendation, commented: "One does not exclude the idea of bringing natives to make them participate in the Exhibition; But in this case, the idea must be studied in time and prepared in agreement with the Organizers of the Exhibition."[16] I have surveyed missionary pamphlets, photographs and films of the exposition, maps, and accounts in English, French, and Italian, as well as examined the exhibition's official journal, the *Rivista Illustrata della Esposizione Missionaria Vaticana*, and have only found references to wax dioramas. Considering this newspaper account, it is possible, but not likely, that individuals from Indigenous nations attended. On the evidence, it seems that living Indigenous people did not participate in the VME—except in protest, as in the case of Anthony Martin Fernando, whom I discuss in the epilogue of this book.

However, there remains some ambiguity as to whether Schmidt and his team of organizers brought any Indigenous peoples to Rome for the VME. Reviewers discussed the idea, but it remained an open question. If the VME did put Native peoples on display, this would not have been an anomaly at the time, as discussed in chapter 2. For example, the 1905 Lewis and Clark Centennial Exposition in Portland, Oregon, featured a "live" Igorot village as part of the Philippines section. The display attracted thousands of visitors eager to view "barbaric tribes," and newspaper reviews praised the village for its scientific and anthropological value.[17] Other sections of the Lewis and Clark Centennial that displayed living peoples included Fair Japan, the Streets of Cairo, an "Eskimo" village, and a colonial plantation with African Americans.[18] World's fairs like these also included living ethnology sections. Seattle's Alaska-Yukon-Pacific Exposition of 1909 had, in addition to a Filipino display, an "Eskimo" village and a display of African Americans.[19] Living displays of non-whites that presented them as "vanishing" peoples and "last survivors," fictional or not, conveyed the imperialist mindset of the organizers.[20] Many Indigenous Americans died due to poor living conditions in these missionary and colonial exhibits.[21] Fair organizers gradually shifted to wax mannequins as stand-ins for living Indigenous bodies, but the displays continued to attract high numbers of visitors who wanted to see "primitive" peoples in their inferior stages of evolutionary development.[22] These displays helped shape the evolutionary mindset of visitors throughout the late nineteenth and early twentieth century in America and elsewhere.

Fair organizers frequently included Native Americans from "Indian" villages across Turtle Island, as well as their cultural belongings, in displays that trumpeted American imperialism. For example, incarcerated Apache leader Geronimo posed for tourists at the 1904 Saint Louis World's Fair while the US War Department supervised his ongoing status as a prisoner.[23] The fair espoused the colonial ideology of Native Americans as vanishing and "primitive" peoples, yet Geronimo sold buttons, hats, and photographs of himself in a successful business enterprise.[24] At the same exposition, organizers stationed people from Pueblo nations of the Southwest at displays of their dwellings and had them wear Plains-style feather bonnets, a stereotype of the Indigenous American.[25] Reviewers praised these living displays for their educational aspects while also underscoring the need for white Americans to bring civilization, industry, and economic development to the Indigenous nations of the Americas and other nations globally. On seeing Geronimo, one reviewer noted that he "had been tamed and looked alright," emphasizing the assimilative values promoted at St Louis.[26] Fair promoters and the government explicitly used living displays to justify white imperialism in America and globally.[27]

What distinguished the VME from other world's fairs of the era was its espousal of a specifically Catholic vision of progress. The organizers portrayed unbelievers, represented in the dioramas and other sections of the exposition, as "primitive," devilish heathens who occupied a space antithetical to civilized Christians. Throughout this period, European and American artists, writers, and anthropologists drew inspiration from "exotic" living displays and the Indigenous cultural belongings presented at world's fairs, and "primitive" art and cultures became a major inspiration for the modernist art movement.[28] In other words, Rome followed in the footsteps of global world's fairs, not to mention its Roman ancestors, in the "success of display no less than the display of success."[29] As historian Mary Beard writes, the Roman Empire "brought the margins of the Empire to its centre."[30] At the VME, the Catholic Church did the same for its global empire of faith. The VME's wax mannequins have an eerie quality, perhaps because the history of the exploitation of Indigenous peoples remains under the surface, and one cannot forget their ties with the classical Roman tradition of triumphal display.

Missionary scholars discussed Indigenous Catholic priests in the *Rivista Illustrata*, drawing on examples from Oceania and China.[31] Missionary reports emphasized the importance of training Native priests and nuns so that they, already fluent in the local Indigenous language, would be able to evangelize their fellow people more effectively. The legacy of Indigenous peoples at worlds' fairs and colonial and missionary exhibitions has a long, sad history but needs a brief mention here. Ever since Columbus captured Taino peoples and forced them to walk through the streets of Seville, monarchs, explorers, scientists, and hucksters had displayed Indigenous peoples from the Americas for the amusement and gratification of European audiences. Among missionary exhibitions, the Catholic Church was the first to display Indigenous peoples in the name of science and religion.[32]

As in the missionary games made for children examined later in this chapter, the viewer at the VME traveled through diverse lands like a hunter and explorer, gathering clues through visual evidence about the missionary's efforts abroad. In the process, the viewer encountered carefully constructed dioramas populated by wax models of Indigenous people, complete with glass eyes and human hair. In the Pine Court, for example, visitors would have encountered the reconstructed huts of Indigenous peoples from Ecuador and Africa, and could enter and walk through a diorama of Indigenous models lying or squatting in the dark in states of apparent stupor, the dirt floors of the huts covered with debris.[33] Missionaries constructed the dwellings to look unkempt and in a state of slovenly disrepair in order to emphasize the need for the missions to bring Indigenous peoples to a more "progressive" and "civilized" condition.

The displays were also designed to inspire fear and horror. For example, in the Oceania section, the organizers included a diorama depicting cannibalism, complete with the tools used in necrophagy. The diorama contained a staged photograph of Indigenous Samoans displaying two clubs, a conch shell, and a human skull. Considine's caption reads: "Cannibals preparing victims for the feast: This scene was posed for the missioner's camera by natives of the Solomon Islands. In the days of man-eating, dead enemies were disjointed, stacked in piles, surrounded with hot stones, covered with grass, and baked. The fork attached to frame at the left of the picture was actually used to eat human flesh."[34] The inclusion of the fork created a veneer of authenticity and seeming veracity while also sensationalizing cannibalism for VME visitors. Missionaries staged the scene for a public eager for tales of cannibalistic pleasures.[35] In reality, the VME itself acted as a kind of cannibal. As Michael M. Ames, the former director of the Museum of Anthropology at the University of British Columbia noted, "Museums are cannibalistic in appropriating other peoples' material for their own study and interpretation."[36] This diorama staged necrophagy for the gratification of a populace primed for stereotypes.

Dioramas are part of popular culture and expected aspects of natural history and anthropology museums. However, the use of dioramas, both lifesize and miniature, also harkens back to their religious use for reflection and meditation by Catholic orders such as the Franciscans in northern Italy during the Counter-Reformation. Art historian Noémie Étienne describes how "the startling lifelikeness of these dioramas was understood at the time to encourage viewers to become absorbed in the story and to place themselves imaginatively in the represented scene."[37] Thus, the use of dioramas in the VME maintained a Catholic devotional tradition as well as aligned with the organizers' interests in showing the church as scientific and adept at using the latest display technology.[38] Dioramas invited the viewer to "see through" the construction and imagine themselves within the display, while missionaries and other church personnel would have recognized the dioramas as part of a longer trajectory of meditative images.

Writing about the wax models used at the VME, Considine, the missionary who described the VME as a window on the world, comments that "the people are graphically portrayed by models, and the missioner's work of course, is made clear. In this respect, the scenic group of the Capuchin missioner teaching catechism among the Araucanian wigwam dwellers of Chile is most impressive."[39] Considine first describes the spectacular, awe-inducing taxidermied animals before briefly discussing the human models, and without mentioning anything of the inhumane history of living Indigenous peoples being exhibited or the ongoing work of missionaries in residential schools. Stoler calls ignorance like his "the well-tended conditions of disregard" in the colonial agent's perspective, which resonates with the colonial unknowing found throughout the VME.[40]

Consider, for example, the photograph of a diorama of a "Mapuche family" (also described as Araucanian, the generic colonial name for Indigenous peoples of South America) being preached to by a Capuchin missionary, which Considine also notes (see figure 3.2). The diorama artist has used white mannequins with blond hair to depict the Mapuche family, which appears to be a slip or an exhibition error, since all the other dioramas of Indigenous peoples were painted nonwhite; the Mapuche family stands out. This slippage is a gap in the totalizing mission of the VME, or evidence of what Stoler describes as "the febrile movements of persons off balance—of thoughts and feelings in and out of place."[41] These glitches in the system allow for a reconsideration and alternative reading of the colonial representations of the VME.

Like the strange composite image of the "Indian" men who acted as glyphs on the cover of the *Rivista Illustrata* (see figure 2.12), this mannequin display also unsettles the overarching colonial narrative of the VME. The Mapuche family consists of a mother and father, a girl, a boy, and a baby propped up on a back carrier. They all wear woven jackets of fine wool, the traditional dress of the Mapuche. The Capuchin missionary gestures with his hand, and one can see the rosary hanging from his waist. The family, outside their hut, faces the missionary, seemingly grateful with their heads turned toward him, accepting what he offers. They conform more to missionary idealizations of a heteronormative family unit than to actual Indigenous conceptions of kin and sexuality, which are more expansive than those on display here.[42] Through their not dissimilar use of models, the VME organizers connected themselves more

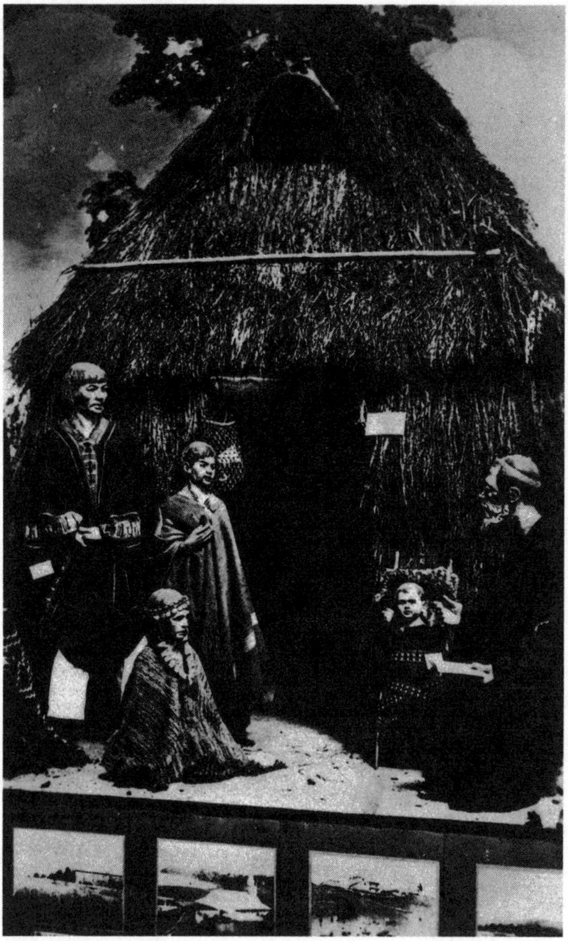

FIGURE 3.2. "A missioner teaching Araucanian Indians." Source: John Joseph Considine, *The Vatican Mission Exposition: A Window on the World* (1925), 83.

broadly, beyond a papal culture of conquest and greed, to a pop culture history of world's fairs, edutainment, and department-store consumption.

Their goal, however, was to use the dioramas to illustrate the strengths and achievements of the church's missionary work. The dioramas served as moralizing lessons on the efficacy of the missionaries' reach and the need for continued intervention. An example can be seen in a photo of Pine Court models representing "Aborigines of Ecuador" living in squalor (see figure 3.3). The diorama consists of two women: one stirs something in a pot as if preparing a meal, while the other reclines on a woven mat facing her. An Ecuadorian man sits in the background, looking out. Sticks and debris are strewn on the ground, and the women wear makeshift robes tied with string. The organizers staged

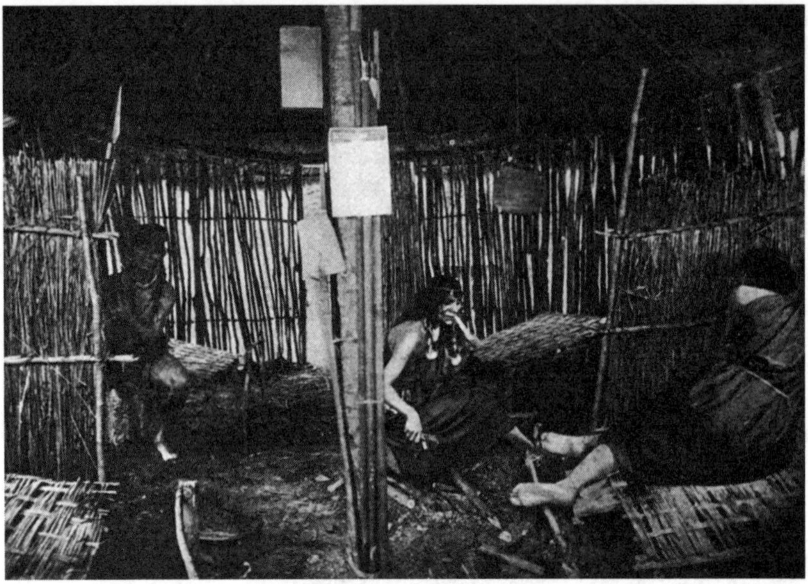

FIGURE 3.3. "Models of a native hut and Aborigines of Ecuador." Source: John Joseph Considine, *The Vatican Mission Exposition: A Window on the World* (1925), 81.

the living quarters in a state of squalor to reflect and justify their assumptions about the degraded lives of Indigenous peoples. As Father Felix observed in his review of the Indigenous cultures represented at the VME, "They have no sense of cleanliness, no organizing powers to fight disease, no knowledge of medicine."[43] Indigenous Americans were out of time, "primitive," and unclean, but the visual displays also constructed Indigenous peoples as humble converts, urgently in need of both physical and spiritual healing. As if to underscore this message, organizers situated the wax models in the Pine Court on the borders of the exposition—literally outside and exposed to the elements. This worked to emphasize visually the idea that Indigenous peoples were outside the civilized order of western space but still enclosed within the Catholic worldview and the pastoral care of the church (see my reflection on this dynamic in figure 3.4). Anthropologist Erin Hasinoff observes of the World in Boston Missionary Exposition of 1911, a comparable Protestant exhibition discussed in chapter 2, that missionaries used housing models as part of a strategy to emphasize the need for missionary intervention: "Like other ranked forms of material culture, the dwellings were not only a visible illustration of the prehistoric state of progress reached, or inscribed in a particular hierarchy, but also of the necessity for missionaries to uplift their inhabitants from their sullied contemporary state."[44]

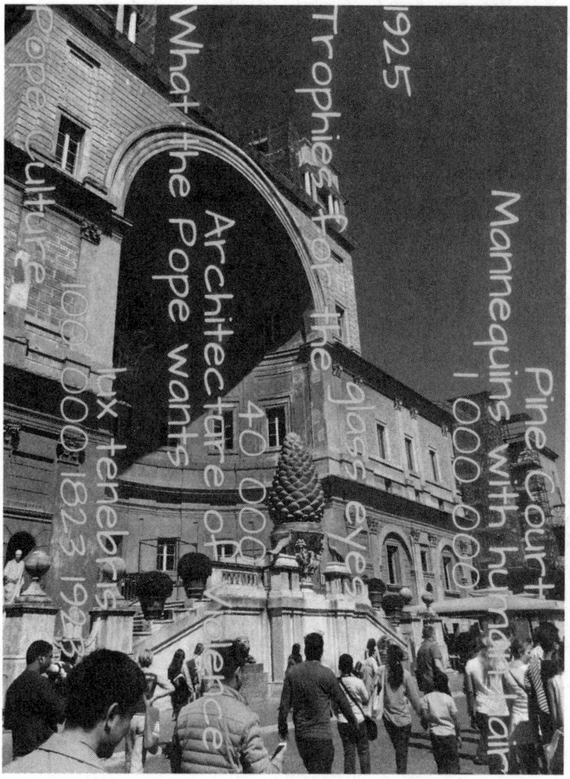

FIGURE 3.4.
Architecture of violence, 2023. Photograph with lettering by the author.

A grainy photograph of a section of the Hall of North America reveals a wax model of an Indigenous woman wearing a Gwich'in pointed summer tunic, beautifully beaded, as well as a baby belt, seized by Jesuit and Oblate missions in northern Alberta and the Yukon River area.[45] When I think about the broader significance of this regalia, the confiscation of this Gwich'in woman's beaded tunic and the baby belt is a reminder of loss and especially the violence of residential schools as genocidal spaces, with their separation of mother and child. Beaded octopus bags from the Great Lakes, Yup'ik ceremonial masks, stone tools, handwoven baskets from British Columbia, and Cree beaded moccasins and gloves surround the mannequin in the display window (see figure 3.5). Missionaries piled the materials high in the display cases like trophies with no regard for their sacred or secular importance and, in this way, decontextualized the cultural belongings. They displayed snowshoes and miniature models of canoes above the top of the case. On the right side of the mannequin, belongings stolen by missionaries from Indigenous communities on the Northwest Coast were shut behind the glass, including a Haida ceremonial rattle.[46] As

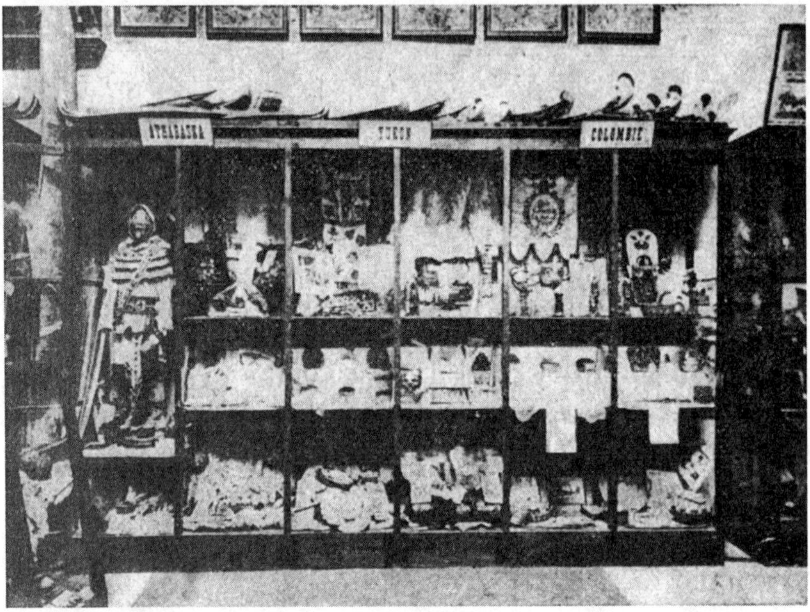

FIGURE 3.5. Hall of North America, Vatican Missionary Exposition, 1925. Source: P. Giovanni, *L'Esposizione Missionaria Vaticana e l'Ordine dei Frati Minori Cappucini* (1925), 44. Courtesy of Paul Bechtold Library Special Collections, Catholic Theological Union, Chicago.

discussed in chapter 2, this overcrowded crammed case resembles the earlier cabinet of curiosities tradition, and thus frames the Indigenous artifacts as part of an ethnographic spectacle rather than offer any understanding of their importance as cultural markers and sacred beings.

At the entrance to the Hall of South America, the curators placed wax figures of an Indigenous man and a woman (see figures 3.6 and 3.7). The man wears a woven blanket and seems more realistic, at least in skin color and facial features, than the Mapuche family discussed previously. Behind him are examples of some of the fauna of South America, including a stuffed ibis in a small diorama. Stuck between the glass cases packed with his cultural belongings, the man appears quaint, part of a narrative of social evolutionary "progress."[47] As in other dioramas, the seemingly realistic status of the mannequins played with visitors' powers of perception and contributed to the larger visual spectacle of the exhibition. The diorama experience of the Americas, Oceania, and Africa forwarded a narrative of Indigenous people as romantic and doomed to tragedy, out of time and history. Ferdinand Pettrich's individual yet idealized statuary

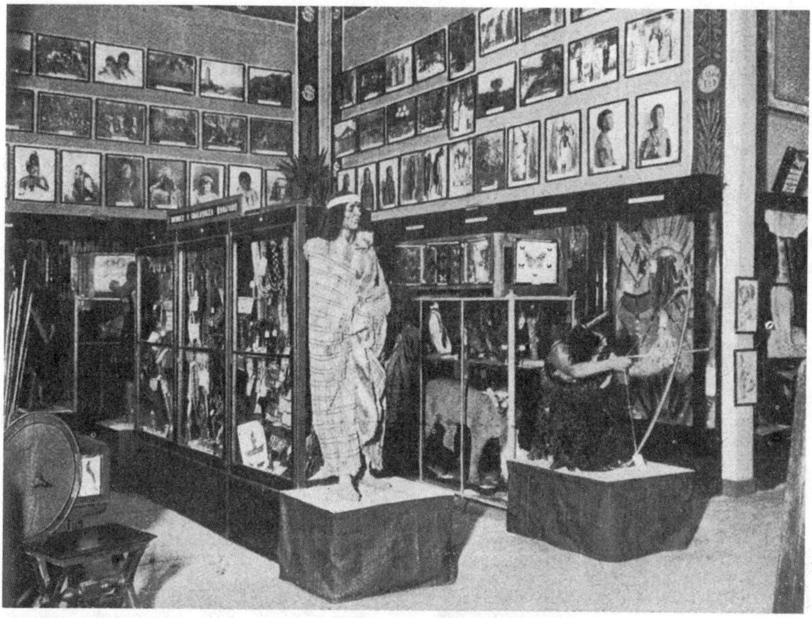

FIGURE 3.6. A corner of the Hall of South America, Vatican Missionary Exposition, 1925. Collection of the author.

in the Hall of North America echoed this perspective. Missionary organizers constructed the Indigenous people as humble converts, often in positions of prayer, on their knees, accepting missionary blessings.[48] The diorama artists at the VME probably did not base their models on real people, more likely using "types" amalgamated from photographs. The stiff poses of the mannequins reinforce this unchanging impression.

To this day, museums display dioramas of Indigenous cultures. Natural history museums, such as the American Museum of Natural History in New York, still employ wax dioramas like those at the VME. By using the dioramas, the VME aligned itself with curatorial strategies used by natural history and science museums in the early twentieth century and thereby promoted itself as scientific and on the cutting edge of technology and public education.[49] Dioramas functioned like windows onto unknown worlds, through which viewers could glimpse finely crafted scenes complete with flora, fauna, and people.[50] They gave visitors a chance to view a world they might never otherwise experience, given that not everyone could travel to distant lands. A prime example is the Great Hall of Dioramas at the American Museum of Natural History, opened in 1903, where visitors flocked to immerse themselves in "nature." In

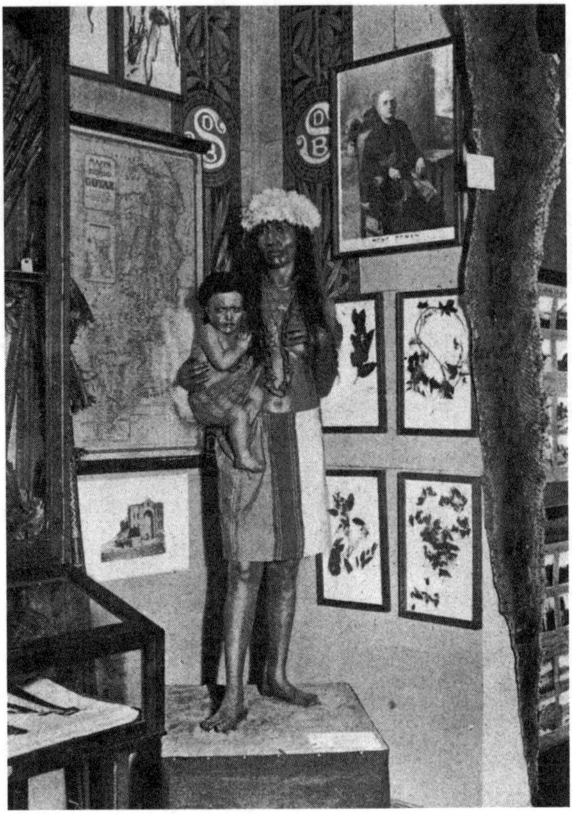

FIGURE 3.7. Hall of South America, Vatican Missionary Exposition, 1925. Collection of the author.

addition to exhibitions during the early twentieth century, museums also used dioramas to promote the value of conservation. Exhibitions were seen as an important way to "produce permanence, to arrest decay."[51] Complete with flora, fauna, and models with a waxy pallor, the dioramas seemed natural, and their almost lifelike scenes must have stopped many visitors in their tracks.

For Indigenous people, however, dioramas tell a very different story, and they usually receive mixed reviews from Indigenous communities. On visiting the Pequot Museum in Mashantucket, Connecticut, in 1998, for example, some Pequot visitors expressed shock to see themselves represented in dioramas.[52] To the Māori, dioramas are a reminder of forced removal, violence, and genocide. As Conal McCarthy, Director of the Museum and Heritage Studies program at Victoria University in Wellington, notes, "When real Maori proved to be too much of a handful or refused to live up to their ethnic stereotype, wax models were found to be a much more malleable substitute, their mortuary pallor signifying their fate in a much more acquiescent way."[53] Indeed, the representation of individuals by mannequins is particularly problematic for Māori, who view them as in-between figures, neither alive nor dead.[54] Anthropologist Franz Boas, a prominent scholar during the twentieth century, protested the use of dioramas, describing them as ghastly. The waxy pallor, static poses, and eerie silence of the models seemed to him to represent the dead rather than the living.[55] Yet Boas also used mannequins representing Indigenous life on the Northwest Coast in his own work as pedagogical models and edutainment at the American Museum of Natural History throughout the twentieth century.[56] At the Buffalo Nations Luxton Museum in Banff, Alberta, the Blackfoot agreed to the use of dioramas based on models of individuals to represent the Sun Dance and other sacred events. Although some did not approve, many Blackfoot in the community praised the dioramas.[57] Thus, the relationship between Indigenous peoples, missionaries, anthropologists, and dioramas is ongoing and fraught, and continues to be the subject of much scholarship and critique.[58] The dioramas used by Pius XI at the VME are no exception in this fraught relationship. They are, like the games discussed in what follows, a reminder of forced assimilation, missionary brutality, and markers of modern tourism.

Pop Culture to Papal Culture: Genocide as Children's Games

Visitors to the VME departed through the gift shop, where they could buy souvenirs and memorabilia such as children's games that would remind them of pope Pius XI's greedy vision.[59] Missionary expositions sold children's games as a form of income to support proselytizing. Sifting through the missionary archives at the Yale Divinity Library, I came upon two Italian children's games that missionary orders created during the papacy of Pius XI (1922–39). As is often the case with ephemera in archives, the games were accompanied with little explanation as to their provenance. Missionaries sent games to the VME, but they are listed only as "games" from Tobique First Nation, with no further details.[60] However, considered in their historical context, they provide a unique window onto the stereotypes and assumptions of the missionary modeling of the Catholic empire. The VME relied on these stereotypes and assumptions, but they also informed the colonizing goals of the fascist Italian state during the period of Pius XI's papacy. Although there is a paucity of information about the games in the archives, the materials themselves remain telling fragments of the missionary project.

The VME placed Rome, and the Vatican, at the center of the hearts and minds of believers and tourists around the world. As Corbey notes, "Rome was represented as the centre of the world—a role that on medieval world maps was still reserved for Jerusalem and in imperialist discourse was given to the metropoles of the leading imperialist nation-states."[61] Indeed, a game that Pius XI issued during that period (ca. 1930) contains a visual motif of the Catholic missionary ideals that the VME emulated (see plate 7).[62] The Catholic Women's Union of Italy sponsored the game, which was about how to "save, baptize, educate and Christianize the unbelieving children."[63] On the game board, one can see the so-called "primitive" unbelievers of four regions—Asia, Africa, Oceania, and America—represented stereotypically. In the upper left corner, America is symbolized by a Native American couple sitting on the ground in a passive pose. The man wears a Plains feather war bonnet and a richly colored, striped blanket which could be a Diné chief blanket. In the background, another man sits astride a white horse, and behind him there is an adobe dome with a cross, typical of the US Southwest. In the far-right corner, a missionary waits beside a tipi, a popular image of the Plains nations. There is no indication of the complexity or diversity of Indigenous peoples. The idle and idyllic Indigenous characters on the game board all turn toward Rome: the motif of Saint Peter's Basilica in the center pulls like a powerful magnetic force.

The stereotypical depictions of Indigenous peoples reveal the artist's shallow understanding of the diversity of Indigenous groups and would have provided an easy way for children to identify and distinguish the role of the "primitives" from the role of the missionary. The game encourages a surface understanding of and instruction in the role of the missionary, whose life is represented as an exotic adventure of traveling around the world to save "heathen" children. The missionary is represented as active and in control, moving across continents, standing, and often holding children. The Indigenous peoples are presented in passive poses, crouching, creating an impression of easy acceptance of missionary work and conveying an idyllic image of peace and harmony. This shallow understanding of missionary and Indigenous lives, as imagined through the game, is in tension with the dedication and time required by some missionaries to learn Indigenous languages and customs, not to mention the active resistance of Indigenous peoples in the struggle to retain their beliefs, cultures, and languages.[64] The game, with its veneer of authenticity, parallels the aim of the VME to convey a surface understanding of the languages, customs, social practices of, and scientific data about nonbelievers around the world through missionary collections.[65]

The aesthetics of the game, with its bright colors and kaleidoscopic quality, parallels the ritual of the exhibition in its overwhelming emphasis on the visual as well as in its stereotypical representations of Indigenous peoples. The viewer's gaze is drawn to the central motif, the Vatican and the heraldry of the Catholic Church, uniting the eye with the church's central aims and power of saving souls. It is a visionary, dogmatic image; viewers are invited to use their imagination to take them from the four corners of the world to the heart of Rome.[66] Indigenous children, it suggests, are in touch with the heavens only through missionary interaction. In the Americas, the child in the far-left corner reaches out to touch the path of the sun, the celestial orbit of Catholic influence. It seems that in this case the sun never sets on the Catholic "empire" any more than it does on the British Empire. The Catholic Church never sleeps in its mission to convert.

The process of Catholic faith and conversion is, in fact, not a mystery, and the image, with its instructions to bring "heathen infidels" for baptism to the heart of Catholicism at Saint Peter's Basilica in Rome, is not subtle. The game, like the VME dioramas, forms part of a process of unseeing and colonial disregard of the realities for Indigenous children of residential and boarding schools, for example, and ultimately becomes a visual justification and celebration not just of missionary work but also of the dehistoricizing of Indigenous peoples.

The game denies the living diversity of Indigenous children in North America while celebrating the work of missionaries. The complexity of Indigenous nations has been narrowed down to a few stereotypes, while the missionaries bide their time in the background, either holding children or waiting beside the dwelling places. Cringey! In a parallel example, art historians Bret L. Rothstein and Karen M. Inouye note how in American games from the late nineteenth century "an object that gives visual form to bigotry does not simply appeal to or depict stereotypes but in fact instantiates them, activating those stereotypes perceptually, intellectually, and even physically."[67] Thus, far from being mere images, stereotypes in these children's games reinforced a limited concept of Indigenous peoples in an embodied experience when children and adults played them. Games and dioramas were thus part of the racist microcosm of colonial visual culture, encouraging the misunderstanding and misrecognition of Indigenous cultures and peoples and promoting and furthering the settler-colonial project.[68] If one reads this game literally, one might think of the conversion of souls as child's play in pastel colors. However, the lurking, shadowy figures of the missionaries remind the child of the seriousness and dangers of duty. The church's aim was to inculcate its values in children at a young age, effectively converting them to the Catholic worldview for life.[69]

The game therefore acts as a microcosm of the church's efforts at the VME to seize not only thousands of cultural belongings from the missions abroad but, by implication, the souls of unbelievers as well.[70] In the game, players chose their mode of transport: steamboat, sailboat, or airplane. If they chose the airplane, they traveled in the opposite direction of the ships, paid fifty cents to land in Indigenous territories, and returned to Rome with an unbelieving child, thereby bringing the child to the light and reason of the Catholic faith. The game's monetary aspect, in which players received twenty-five to fifty cents after every round, depending on mode of transport, might be thought of as symbolizing the heavy expenditures the Catholic Church made to host the VME, as it spared no expense for the conversion of souls.[71] The temporal aspect of the game—the players traveled counterclockwise from Rome outward—parallels the route visitors followed in the VME and hints at the broader aims of both Italy and the Catholic Church to expand their empires, something I will return to in my analysis of the second missionary game. At every completed round, according to the instructions written on the bottom of the game board, players were required to utter an "Ave Maria" (Hail Mary) with the invocation "Virgin Mary, pray for me and the poor swaddled infidel children" and then commit an act of virtue.[72] The ritual-like aspects of the game, with its recitals of "Ave Maria" after every turn, together with the incitement of a monetary reward, make it part of a long tradition of games for children and adults alike. Along all the various routes in red, green, and deep blue, players would eventually land in Rome, the epicenter of Catholic belief and their spiritual home.

This game was only one part of the indoctrination and education of Catholic children, but such games inspired a lifelong interest in the geographic aspect of missions, something visitors would also have familiarized themselves with in attending the various sections of the VME.[73] The game and the VME are also evidence of Catholic outreach to diverse corners of the planet, and of a transnational faith in the uncertain social and economic climate following World War I.[74] The cultural belongings in the exhibitions, together with other didactic material such as these games, played a central role, inspiring hope, faith, and security in material things. Games were sold to VME visitors in order to promote missionary work and raise money while also serving as an interactive souvenir of the visit.[75]

Whereas the missionary game I discuss above portrays America, Oceania, Africa, and Asia, a second missionary game (ca. 1930) depicts only Africa and offers a unique opportunity to further understand missionary efforts through visual culture during Pius XI's papacy. It was created by the Province of the Discalced Carmelite Friars at the Scuola Apostolica Carmelo and dedicated to the education of young novices.[76] The Carmelites produced the game explicitly to promote their work in Africa.[77] The game's artist clearly designed it to capture Italian children's imaginations and excite their interest in missionary work (see plate 8). The game resembles a popular family pastime called Game of the Goose. Players roll dice and compete to reach the last square first without succumbing to various perils along the way. The circular layout of the game parallels the cyclical layout of the VME. After receiving a benediction from the pope, the players, in the role of missionaries, set out by ship on a pilgrimage from Italy to Egypt, and then tour Egypt and other African countries. They encounter wild animals (wolves, elephants, hippopotamuses, snakes, parrots) and the natural elements (storms), as well as face physical hardship and sickness, again emphasizing the perilous but exciting nature of missionary endeavors. Players are enmeshed in the colorful route of the missionaries, and if they make it through the adventure, they can return to the *vita contemplativa* (contemplative life) in Italy. The game reads like an encyclopedia entry on Africa, complete with various ethnographic illustrations of the peoples and wildlife, and emphasizes a simplistic understanding of "primitive" peoples. As in popular adventure fiction from the time, children were encouraged to voyage in their imaginations through dangerous foreign lands and colonies, creating an illusion of experience and subjectivity.

Whereas the first game presents an idyllic image of missionaries working among Indigenous peoples throughout the world, the second focuses on the perils and heroics of traveling through Africa. Moving along the squares of the game and entering the African forest, players first encounter cannibals with sharpened spears. In the small image, two figures can be seen threatening the player-cum-missionary's life. Players then take on the role of benevolent missionaries as they greet pygmies. On the next square, players slide into the mouth of a poisonous snake, which devours its prey. Players' heart rates are presumably meant to pulse rapidly as they imagine getting eaten alive. In the next square, players encounter an image of a large pot over a fire. The relationship between the players, the fire, and the cooking pot is ambiguous; the square may convey the risk that, as a missionary, one might be boiled alive over a fire or simply symbolize the scarcity of food rations on a perilous journey in the wilderness. The missionary fantasy of encountering wild "primitives" culminates in the next image on the game, where players again assume the role of missionaries preaching and proselytizing to Indigenous peoples. Tellingly, the Indigenous characters are half the size of the missionary, who reaches out his hand in benediction, evoking a sense of his God-given right to convert. As art historian Annie E. Coombes observes of the work of British missionaries in Africa and their frantic collecting and stealing of material belongings: "This presence derived its sanction from the supposedly God-given right of the missionaries to impose their religious beliefs on the colonised races; a mission executed in the name of salvation and civilisation, arbitrarily designated as the prerogative of European culture."[78]

Scholar Gareth Griffiths notes that the goals of missionaries as they relate to imperial discourses remain underexamined. These two games, issued at the height of missionization as part of the visual culture of missionary work and Christian empire, highlight these tensions.[79] Readers of imperial adventure fiction also bought missionary tales. The missionary presses adopted the narrative themes, styles of cover art, and formats of popular secular works to capitalize on this large market. Griffiths notes the strong parallel aims in missionary and secular fiction as well as their rivalry: "the very popular secular adventure tales of exploration, soldiering, and hunting in various far-flung parts of the Empire were also increasingly influential on the mission publications competing for the new readership."[80] Building his argument in an analysis of missionary and popular journals, Griffiths contends that missionary texts often deployed oversimplified representations of missionary lifestyles. Within the texts, missionaries downplayed the subjects of conversion and economic processes, as compared with the more exciting and romantic adventurous aspects. Secular values of adventure and excitement "disrupted" the texts' Christian purpose, however.[81] As Griffiths notes, "such fractures between an overall discourse of Christian charity and forbearance and the rhetoric of the hunter/adventurer seeking to conquer and subdue the worlds he encounters is a common ideological and discursive rupture in these texts."[82] This rupture, I would argue, can be found not only within popular mission texts for children but also in missionary games and the VME.

Griffiths's analysis of missionary texts reveals the attitudes of missionaries working at the time and also hints at how a broader readership understood missionary lives. Missionaries expressed their paternalistic attitudes toward the Indigenous peoples they worked with through the stereotypical descriptions in their accounts. They often explain how they hunted wild game, portraying a dangerous and exciting lifestyle so that readers could conflate the largely sedentary lifestyle of a missionary with that of an active hunter-explorer.[83] As the general population in Europe and America became increasingly literate, sales skyrocketed for these exciting tales. Griffiths notes, and I agree, that we should not underestimate the relevance of missionary fiction in the promotion of imperial ideologies. He argues that "the powerful audience created by the mission presses in the late nineteenth century remained in place much later than we might imagine and continued to influence domestic imperial attitudes much later than we might imagine."[84] Thus, it is important to consider how these tales conveyed a romantic and adventurous image of missionary work and how their oversimplifications and idealized dramas fed into the popular image, and attraction, of missionary activity. The physicality of them as games was part of their attraction; children and adults playing them could insert themselves into the colonial fantasy, somewhere between reality and illusion. Thus, the games also reinforce the role of the imagination in the illusory project of encounter and conquest in Catholic missionary work.

The children's games emphasized the missionary as a daring explorer and adventurer, yet the impact of missionaries on Indigenous children of the Americas was not a game; it resulted in abuse and death, unmarked graves, and produced trauma that survivors and their families are still working through.[85] At the VME, missionary organizers created a separation between the history of the missions, the triumphs of missionary work, and the Halls of the Americas. On the other side of vision are lack of care and disavowal. The piling of materials into glass cases with no regard for secular or sacred values created an overwhelming effect in which visitors and missionary organizers denied the contemporary realities of Indigenous adults and children. More specifically, through a visual process in which Indigenous Americans existed outside the frame, missionary organizers and visitors bypassed the ongoing processes of Indigenous dispossession in the Americas. Historian Lorenzo Veracini calls this "strategic disavowal of the colonizing act" an allied form of denial with colonial unknowing.[86] Processes of settler colonialism refute the violence of settler colonialism as a historical and ongoing act and, at the same time, dispossess Indigenous peoples of their lands.[87] In a parallel example of the strategy of seeing and not seeing in Australia, Alison Ravenscroft describes the underlying power relation and the resulting privilege of seeing as the "logic of colonization which disavows Indigenous sovereignty, dispossession, and ongoing presence."[88] Building on Veracini's and Ravenscroft's argument about the logic of settler-colonial vision and eradication, and grounding this chapter in the historical reality for Indigenous children in North America during this time, the next section examines the overarching impact of residential schools on Indigenous children. As in Australia, the reality for Indigenous children in residential and boarding schools during the period of the VME, and more broadly within historical memory, largely remains a history of denial, unrecognition, and disavowal.

FIGURE 3.8. Letter from Florentin Digmann SJ to Father Hughes, with photograph of Očhéthi Šakówiŋ children. "Many thanks for informing us that the Indian articles have been sent to the Vatican Missionary Exposition. I hope that the articles will be as welcome as dessert at the feast." Source: *Indian Sentinel*, May 23, 1925, 115.

THE INDIAN SENTINEL 115

vine Faith shine upon these simple souls. They, above all others, are of the category, "of such is the Kingdom of Heaven."

Please, Father, pray for us. We do not forget you.

Very respectfully in Xto,
(VERY REV.) P. I. DELON, S.J.

ALWAYS BETTER
St. Francis Mission, S. D.,
May 23, 1925.

DEAR FATHER:

Many thanks for informing us that the Indian articles have been sent to the Vatican Missionary Exposition. I hope that the articles will be as welcome as dessert at the feast. The prairie fire came pretty near St. Francis, but not near enough to do any harm. Our recent entertainment "The Blind Princess," was rendered very creditably by our girls. Mr. McGregor, Government superintendent, said: "Always better. This is the best given on our stage." Father Zimmerman has bought farm implements for extensive farming. The investment will pay in the end, but at present it runs us into debt. If you can do anything to help along, you will greatly oblige us.

Very sincerely yours,
(REV.) FLORENTIN DIGMANN, S.J.

CATHOLIC OUTING SYSTEM
San Luis Rey Mission, California,
May 23, 1925.

DEAR FATHER HUGHES:

Let me first of all thank you for the check of $100 and for the promise to transport twenty-five Catholic Indian children from Arizona to Los Angeles, where they will be put on the Catholic Outing System. Margaret Shosh has done exceptionally well under the Outing System. Under all circumstances she knows how to deport herself as a lady. The people of St. Joseph's, her home mission of Mescalero, esteem her highly because of her ladylike behavior and her holy life. She goes to Holy Communion almost daily at St. Joseph's. In a few weeks Margaret intends to write you about her four years under the Catholic Outing System. She hopes to go home this summer.

In Los Angeles there are many Catholic Indian boys and girls. They are beginning to hear of our little crowd and want to become acquainted. All of them say we must form a society for the Catholic Indians in Los Angeles. As time goes on Los Angeles is becoming a center to which the Indians of the Southwest are flocking. Already there are Comanche, Pueblo, Apache, Hopi, Yuma, Navajo,

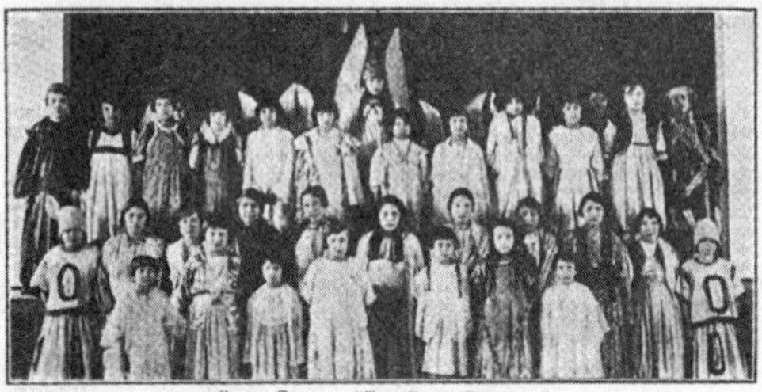

SIOUX GIRLS IN "THE BLIND PRINCESS"

Residential Schools and Missionary Exhibitions

Photographs in the *Indian Sentinel* of Očhéthi Šakówiŋ children at residential schools, alongside missionary discussions of material sent in for the VME, are evidence that missionaries sent materials made by Indigenous children at residential schools to the VME. For example, Reverend Florentin Digmann of Saint Francis Mission, Rosebud Reservation of South Dakota, wrote on May 23, 1925, in a letter accompanied by a photograph of young Očhéthi Šakówiŋ girls: "Dear Father, many thanks for informing us that the Indian articles have been sent to the Vatican Missionary Exposition. I hope that the articles will be as welcome as dessert at the feast" (see figure 3.8).[89] Digmann's wording is reminiscent of the cannibalistic tendencies of museums, and the VME was no exception.[90] The VME through its reliance on the material and the visual implicitly endorsed and trumpeted missionary labors as acts of faith allowing visitors to not account for the exploitation and abuse of Indigenous children in acts of colonial unknowing.

Expositions across Turtle Island as well as in the Eternal City featured homogeneous Indian arts and crafts made by students from residential schools.[91] The Catholic Church sold souvenir arts and crafts by Native children to make money as well to ensure a future source of cheap labor for the Church and settler society. Of a parallel example in Australia, historian Fiona Paisley observes that "unless they were expected to become priests, for most Aboriginal children education and religious training were designed to prepare them for a life of servitude."[92] Missionaries subjected Indigenous children in North America and Australia to religious and educational teachings and provided training in trades such as carpentry, laundry, and agriculture.[93] The federal government expected Indigenous people to contribute and assimilate to American society, leaving behind all aspects of Indigenous cultures and lifeways.

Pius XI organized the VME at a time when the Canadian and US governments were forcing Native children to attend residential and day schools (Canada) and boarding schools (United States).[94] The Roman Catholic Church operated the majority of residential schools from the nineteenth century onward, although some were run by Methodist and Presbyterian organizations.[95] Parallel programs for the assimilation of Indigenous children occurred in Canada, the United States, and Australia; children endured physical, emotional, and sexual abuse in all these settler systems. The US and Canadian governments set up institutions, including day schools and boarding schools, for the training and education of Native children and their assimilation into Euro-American and Euro-Canadian settler society.[96] The government separated Indigenous children from their parents. As one aspect of the broader assimilationist policy adopted in the United States and Canada, missionaries at the boarding schools operated under a mandate to "kill the Indian and spare the child."[97] Missionaries required children to complete manual labor tasks, such as cleaning, and provided some education in basic English, trades, farming, and cooking. Schools did not offer education at high-school level. The government underfunded and poorly regulated the schools. Understood as "primitive," uncivilized, and heathen by missionaries and governments, Indigenous nations were regarded only as objects of assimilation.[98] Only recently has a Truth and Reconciliation Commission been established in Canada to address the abusive history of residential schools, and the process is ongoing.[99]

The work of Duncan Campbell Scott, deputy superintendent of the Department of Indian Affairs from 1913 to 1932 and one of Canada's most celebrated poets of the time, perhaps best epitomizes the values and goals of residential schools as well as the attitudes of missionaries and governments.[100] He described "the Indian" as a problem to be eradicated, and by 1920, an amendment to Canada's Indian Act made attendance at residential and day schools compulsory for Indian children aged seven to fifteen.[101] By 1927, a year after the VME had closed, the Canadian government made further amendments to the Indian Act to make it impossible for Indigenous nations to hire lawyers or raise money to pursue their land claims. Under Scott's administration, attendance at residential schools was increased and stricter policy measures implemented to ensure the suppression of Indigenous cultural practices.

Organizers at the VME displayed stolen sacred materials never intended for public viewing, such as an ancestral sun mask of the Kwakwaka'wakw and a human face mask from Haida Gwaii, making no distinction between cultural groups.[102] Missionaries seized not only cultural belongings but also children, the most precious heritage, during this period of attempted assimilation and genocidal violence.[103] Residential school attendees experienced severe physical and emotional abuse and terrible living conditions, resulting in the suicide or death from illness or neglect of many attendees, and causing mental and emotional trauma that survivors and their families continue to work through.[104] Residential schools had destructive effects on Indigenous cultural traditions, languages, and lifeways that artists, academics, and thinkers are still grappling with today in an effort to address traumatic colonial histories and their reverberations in contemporary society.

Missionaries forbade Indigenous children from wearing their customary clothing, speaking their own languages, and other forms of creativity that would remind them of their identities. Instead, they instructed Indigenous children in a program of "Native" styles of arts and crafts that contributed to funding the schools. Some schools had an art program; others did not. Curator Scott Watson notes: "In the 1920s, children in some residential schools were encouraged to make objects based on 'Native' design provided them by the staff of the Provincial Museum. Thus, in its very inception, the attempt to make a space for the reception of native art in white high culture rested on the notion that the indigenous and historical forms of native arts and crafts production were dead or dying out and could only be revived through the reintroduction of native design into native communities—in this case, those held captive in residential schools."[105] Missionaries forced children to make "Indian"-style arts and crafts to sell to support missionary work, and the VME was no exception in describing them as "dessert at the feast."[106] In these horrific spaces, missionaries kept children against their will during the most aggressive assimilationist period; so too were their cultural belongings kept as prisoners and displayed under glass at the VME. Like the residential and day schools, the VME also capitalized on the promotion and dissemination of Indigenous art to fuel the "Indian craze" and relied extensively on the visual to mobilize viewers in a narrative that equated missionaries as noble and Indigenous communities as willing converts.

In Canada, the Department of Indian Affairs encouraged acculturation and assimilation of Native culture into mainstream Canadian society specifically through Native arts.[107] The historian Marinella Lentis traces art education as part of the assimilation process in boarding schools for Native American children in the United States and describes how teachers used art training to assimilate students' Native identities. As Lentis notes, "the education of American Indian Children started with a physical transformation and expanded to a linguistic, moral, religious, social, and ultimately cultural 'renovation' at an individual as well as a group level."[108] Missionaries forbade the production and practice of any ceremonial arts and suppressed the links between art and spirituality. Instead, children were taught to make generic "Indian" art that bore no connection to distinct tribal aesthetics or designs. Missionaries did not foster children's creativity.[109] "Native children had to learn how to draw and see things from a Western perspective," Lentis notes, "that did not take into account their Indigenous knowledge or social and natural environments."[110] Rather, art instruction was an extension of the industrial, educational, and moralizing training the children received in order to become productive workers and rule-abiding citizens in Anglo-Saxon America. In the early twentieth century, government policy enforced by missionaries meant Indigenous students were expected to spend their lives in low-paying jobs and contribute to settler society via menial labor, forgetting any aspect of their Native identity and assimilating into mainstream American and Canadian society. As sociologist Andrew Woolford notes, "benevolence was not the primary, motivation behind assimilative schooling, for discourses of benevolence were underwritten by a settler colonial desire for land, resources, and national consolidation."[111]

Despite the schools' unremitting efforts of assimilation, several Indigenous artist-educators were able to integrate Indigenous artistic practices into the curriculum. Winnebago artist, designer, and activist Angel De Cora taught at Carlisle Indian School in Pennsylvania from 1906 to 1915, and Cherokee educator Arizona Swayney had an active art practice and worked at Hampton School in Virginia from 1902 to 1906. Both encouraged Indigenous creativity rather than assimilation. Swayney urged Native children to embrace their Native heritage and create art that referenced their multiple traditions and ancestries visibly.[112] Meanwhile, De Cora's approach explicitly rejected assimilationist policies: "on taking up the work at Carlisle I found one of the necessary things to do was to impress upon the minds of my pupils that they were Indians, possessing native abilities that had never been recognized in the curriculum of the Government schools."[113] De Cora advocated the inclusion and training of Native arts and designs in Carlisle's school program, and encouraged students to express themselves freely without heavy-handed guidance from teachers, explaining that "the simple dignity of Indian design lends itself well to ways of conventional art and the American people must . . . give recognition to another phase of the Indian's nature, which is his art."[114]

One of the innovators in forwarding a tribally specific decorative arts and design program, De Cora encouraged students to research particular aesthetic traditions and apply them to modern design and everyday items. Students incorporated Native design elements into wall friezes and embroidery, home furnishings such as textiles, even opera bags, and eventually pottery. Where previously students had copied European masters in exercises such as easel painting as well as in music, De Cora inspired students to see Native art as part of the broader spectrum of American art.[115] However, De Cora and Swayney are some of the only teachers that emphasized the importance of incorporating Indigenous perspectives. Sadly, De Cora's curriculum only lasted the nine years that she taught at Carlisle, although in the 1930s Indigenous teachers in the United States reintroduced the program after Indian education reforms.[116] Elsewhere, most other educators policed Native children in an attempt to stamp out their Native identities, languages, and lifeways—anything that might connect them to their Indigenous heritage. In the name of pedagogy and civilization, missionaries in particular promoted cultural and spiritual disconnect.

Like the VME, Indian boarding school displays at expositions in the United States relied on mobilizing Indigenous art created by children to promote missionaries as heroic workers. Displays of Native American materials to showcase the progress of Indian children first occurred at the 1876 Philadelphia Centennial International Exposition. The Smithsonian organized the display in Philadelphia, which included a plethora of materials such as maps of the schools, photographs, paintings by Native Americans, models of canoes, wigwams, and papier-mâché replicas of Native people, tools, and weapons. The organizers also included essays, drawings, and other material by children in boarding schools as "stable indicators of academic progress."[117] Throughout the display, organizers constructed Native American cultures as static, "primitive," and barbaric, in an irredeemable position compared with the American visitors who attended. Lentis notes that "the endless and apparently chaotic displays, the predominance of primitive objects and tools, and marked emphasis on the warlike nature of Indians did not help visitors in gaining a better understanding of these Indigenous cultures."[118] Although writing about an exhibition nearly fifty years before the VME, Lentis could have been commenting on the VME's use of eerie dioramas and stereotypical imagery, also found in the two examples of games previously discussed. Like the Philadelphia exposition of 1876, the VME encouraged only a shallow engagement with materials, which were arranged in such a way as to overwhelm visitors. The disconnect between the reality of Indigenous children's experiences in residential schools and in the arrangement of the Halls of the Americas reinforced the sense of Indigenous Americans as "primitive" and stuck in the past. The VME promoted the idea that Indigenous people would only enter the present or participate in the future through Catholic conversion.

To force their assimilation into American society and to develop American pride rather than a tribal-based identity, teachers at the residential and boarding schools required Indigenous children to perform music, pageants, games, sports, art, and plays with American themes. Like the dioramas and mannequins at the VME, the teachers used constructions of settler-colonial "model homes" with settler-colonial "model families" to instruct Indigenous parents and children. At the same time, instructors separated children from their siblings, and students rarely saw their families after entering school. Teachers became the children's only emotional support, but this support was also a tool of coercive assimilation.[119] Instructors used games as part of the general arts curriculum, along with marching and breathing exercises, in an enforced style of learning instead of the voluntary learning and expression promoted by De Cora. Ultimately, in most residential and boarding schools, missionaries did not encourage intellectual development, but rather how to become "subservient, docile, and physically regimented Indians who would follow federal directions."[120]

Nevertheless, some children who attended boarding schools went on to become successful and famous artists, belying federal policymakers' assumptions that Indigenous children could only succeed by assimilating. For example, young Kiutus Tecumseh, a Yacama survivor of a boarding school, performed songs on the radio in the 1920s and promoted awareness of Indigenous history and policy.[121] Another musician, Tsianina Redfeather, a Creek-Cherokee, started her musical education at Eufaula Indian Boarding school in Oklahoma. Traveling through the United States as a soloist, she performed for American troops and general audiences throughout the early twentieth century.[122] Another advocate for the arts, Zitkala-sá (Gertrude Simmons Bonnin), a Dakota, attended several residential schools as well as Earlham College, Indiana. A visionary and staunch advocate of Indigenous rights and sovereignty, she wrote essays critiquing federal policy and published Lakota legends in *Harper's Weekly*. With her partner, she created the National Congress of American Indians to support and promote Indigenous rights, politics, and cultural traditions in the early twentieth century.[123]

The experiences of residential school attendees like Zitkala-sá and Kiutus Tecumseh had no place at the VME. Instead, missionaries used an immersive display technique in the Halls of the Americas to construct an eerie, cringeworthy vision of Indigeneity. This technique erased details and created a homogeneous mass. The dioramas and games, for example, did not present Indigenous peoples as individuals with agency but instead emphasized only the heroism of the missionaries.[124] Both the games and the dioramas required a physical and intellectual engagement, commanding viewers to move through space figuratively, imaginatively, and literally. They also required an element of colonial unknowing in that the games and dioramas involved no response from or consideration of the Indigenous subjects represented. The dioramas and games, created for Italian children, ignored the realities that Indigenous children experienced in residential schools, discussed earlier as a process of disavowal. The artists certainly did not consult Indigenous Americans regarding how they were presented. Visitors often bought postcards of the dioramas as they exited through the gift shop, and these as well as collectible cards, stamps, and papal paraphernalia in multiple languages created an afterlife for the exhibition and its values. Indeed, some of these items are still available for purchase on eBay as collectible, nostalgic reminders of decrepit twentieth-century museum display techniques. The VME dioramas and games reinforced Pius XI's culture of conquest and became a blueprint for genocidal labors and missionary exhibitions across the globe. The experience of the dioramas and games were essential in the making of modern tourists and pilgrims who, after being visually persuaded and educated by the exhibition, could buy souvenirs to further rationalize the colonial project.

In Conclusion: *Lux in tenebris* and Pius XI's Colonial Unknowing

In the uncertainty and devastation following World War I, the VME used the apparent permanence of material things to celebrate missionary work as represented in the material culture of children's games, dioramas, and certificates of participation. The certificate shown in figure 3.9, which records Pius XI's blessing of the Oblates' contribution to the VME, epitomizes the self-congratulatory nature of missionary orders. Like the children's games and dioramas, the certificate shows vignettes of subservient Indigenous converts. Pius XI, crowned by the keys of Saint Peters and surrounded by winged Roman putti, occupies the center. The vignettes on the left and right showcase Saint Peter's Basilica and Vatican City. The remaining five vignettes show missionaries, male and female, instructing Indigenous peoples from Africa, Asia, and the Americas in agriculture and in prayer. They also depict missionaries teaching in classrooms and proselytizing. The missionaries are active, but the Indigenous people remain static, again conforming to the dioramas and the motifs in the children's games.

The VME showcased missionaries as heroes in their endeavors to save souls and bring *lux in tenebris* (light in the darkness), thus aligning them with the "benevolent experiment" of the residential and boarding schools for Indigenous American children in North America.[125] Pius XI's tagline for the exhibition built on this ubiquitous metaphor in missionary ideology.[126] In claiming that the VME would bring light in the darkness, Pius XI assumed that "primitive"

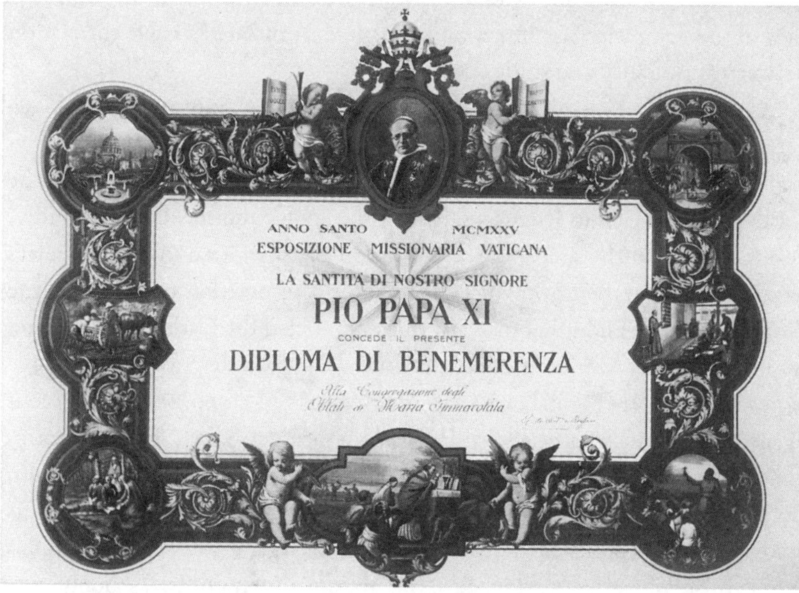

FIGURE 3.9. Certificate of participation in the 1925 Vatican Missionary Exposition. Courtesy of Archivum Generale O.M.I. Romae, Rome.

Indigenous peoples existed in a state of spiritual darkness. This binary perspective ignored the complex realities of Indigenous experience, in particular, the sophisticated spiritual structures of Indigenous belief systems. Missionary pageants at the time promoted the literal "light in the darkness" idea. For example, in the Pageant of Darkness and Light (1909), a British missionary "rescued" an Inuit child from an Inuit shaman.[127] Considine also makes use of the darkness metaphor in his vision of the VME when he describes the earth as a "pitch dark globe" except for the light of the "window" of the VME.[128]

The VME organizers constructed a narrow vision that aligned with the goals of Catholic residential schools to force Indigenous peoples to assimilate and adopt the role of compliant American and Canadian citizens. Physiognomy studies went hand in hand with experiments in phrenology, which would later lead to craniometry, and promoted the idea that studying a person's facial features would reveal their moral character. This type of thinking led to the Carlisle Indian School's obsession with before-and-after portraits of Native American youths.[129] Government policymakers and missionaries used these before-and-after photographs of Indian children attending school as evidence of progress and civilization. Art Historian Peter Hayes Mauro points out the importance of the visual in the "civilizing" process: "the school's founders and subsequent administrators deployed visual imagery in the forms of life masks, photographs, and pseudoscientific illustrations to show the efficacy of the institution's assimilationist mission . . . through a naive correlation between appearance and reality."[130]

As part of their eradication of Indigenous lifeways, missionaries also targeted how Indigenous children saw themselves, that is, their self-visioning. They cut their hair, forced them to wear school uniforms, and forbade the speaking of Indigenous languages.[131] As in the games and the dioramas, Indigenous children at the residential schools were not permitted to see themselves as having agency; their own voices were never considered or represented. The dioramas, games, and other material things modeled the Catholic empire and its imposition of Christian order. Andrew Woolford describes this imposition as the "settler colonial mesh," an "uneven process comprised of numerous agents—government officials, military and police personnel, settlers, reformers, politicians, teachers, Indigenous leaders, parents, and children, but also nonhuman actors such as disease, land, time, and food."[132] Woolford's insights resonate with accounts of the VME. The dioramas, games, and other materials sent in by missionaries as evidence of the "progress" of residential schools justified missionary work for visitors. In other words, the material things mattered in their shaping of visitor's perceptions, biases, and assumptions.

It is imperative to think critically about the role that the VME and its plethora of stolen Indigenous belongings and Catholic material culture, now securely deposited at the Ethnological Museum *Anima Mundi*, had in inspiring the devotion, awe, and amazement of millions of Catholics worldwide and tourists to this day. One visitor to the exhibition on the History of the Missions section recalled that "the testimonials of heroism in spreading the Gospel of Christ through the centuries, gathered in these four sections, fill the heart with emotion and pride. They are so profuse and touching they cause constant wonder."[133] As discussed throughout this chapter, visitors based their sense of wonder and belonging on the celebration of brutal missionary practices in the Americas and the denial of Indigenous realities.

Visitors to the VME and players of the missionary games found clues to match their illusions about the Indigenous "primitives" who existed only in their imaginations. Players of the game boards took tentative steps in an adventurous trek that paralleled the perilous and exploitative adventures of the missionaries working across Africa and Turtle Island. Within the VME, visitors could imagine themselves as missionaries, with the cultural belongings, dioramas, and massive collections of sculptures and paintings serving as the tangible inheritance of missionaries and Catholic believers, and helping to solidify their illusions while simultaneously denying any Indigenous presence. Often inspired by missionary fiction, missionary games, and accounts such as Considine's, exhibitions like the VME served as mediations between knowledge and imagination, and helped to perpetuate Italian goals of expansion in the Catholic missionary vision and within the Italian settler colonies of Libya, Eritrea, Somalia and Ethiopia.[134] The VME also visualized and made material a justification for residential and boarding schools in its celebration of missionaries and their schools as heroic and noble.

The next chapter explores Indigenous American understandings of some of the cultural belongings displayed at the VME. Perhaps one can imagine the glass boxes being shattered and a different type of transcendent vision being ushered in—one in which Indigenous perspectives are acknowledged and respected.[135] One must remember that pope Alexander VI created the papal bull *Inter caetera* (1493), used to justify and endorse slavery and violence against Indigenous peoples through centuries of Indigenous dispossession in the Americas. The VME functioned as a physical, moral, and spiritual extension and manifestation of the papal bulls issued in the Renaissance, and it contains an important lesson to unpack. The apology to Indigenous survivors of residential schools issued by pope Francis in Rome in the spring of 2022 was a step in this broader reckoning with the colonial period of missionary and settler brutality, but much more needs to be done to understand some of the darker "truths" through a process of truth and reconciliation. Re-storying Indigenous cultural belongings helps unsettle the VME in an anticolonial gesture and raises awareness in the ongoing fight for human rights and the rematriation and repatriation of Indigenous art and ancestors globally.

4

ETERNAL SOVEREIGNS AND ANCESTRAL ART

Ancient Archives, Relatives, and Travelers at the Vatican Missionary Exposition

Journal: Propaganda Fide College and the Janiculum Hill

FEBRUARY 2017. *After a few visits to the Vatican Museums and discussions with the archivist at the Jesuit Archive in Rome, I decided to head to Propaganda Fide College, which holds the Propaganda Fide Library and a collection of missionary documents from the Vatican Missionary Exposition. Propaganda Fide College is, to this day, a place of missionary study and training. Situated on Janiculum Hill, it is a rusty-red, brick-walled fortress housing an archive, library, and school. After walking past Saint Peter's, I faced a steep uphill climb. Occasionally, nuns in gray habits and priests with white collars brushed past me on the skinny footpath up to the college. On one side, the narrow path abuts a steep brick wall that climbs for 100 feet and frames the edge of the complex of Propaganda Fide. On the other side are two lanes of speeding traffic full of tourist buses and Vespas. The wall is interspersed with pink and green plants hanging on to bits of soil in the crevices. Sometimes walking up the medieval path I imagined myself like one of the little pink plants, clinging on to the side and not daring to look down at the thick trails of traffic. Passing through the gates of Propaganda Fide, I walked under two large bronze globes, symbols of the doctrine of Propaganda Fide and its mission of global conversion. After checking in with security, I followed a long path lined with palm trees and climbed another set of stone stairs that was worn down in the middle by legions of priests and nuns in training. I headed to the library but stopped first at the archive. After verification of my academic status, I inquired about the 1925 exposition, but the archivist told me that scant documents were available. He directed me to the Propaganda Fide Museum, so I went there, only to find it had closed for renovation six years ago and showed no signs of reopening anytime soon.*

No conversations or whispers disturbed me when I returned later to the library. There were two librarians at work who told patrons where to find books and to keep quiet. Nuns in gray habits with gold rings on their left hands—the only flashy display in their comportment—and priests in training, mostly in black, with their bibles and religious tracts open, hunched over their studies. After a brief conversation, the mustachioed librarian, wearing a dark-gray jacket, brought me the tomes of the Rivista Illustrata, *the official publication of the exposition. Many thoughts and what-if scenarios rushed through my mind as I first flipped through the publication's more than eight hundred pages, full of miscellaneous missionary accounts and anecdotes from around the world. Propaganda Fide holds many documents and accounts from the expo, including some Indigenous language dictionaries, missionary flyers, and a variety of guides to the exhibition. Some duplicates are also held at the Vatican Apostolic Library.*[1] *The sun streamed through the windows, and inside the library no one whispered or chatted. In the quiet and faced with the immense piles of archival ephemera, I felt hopeful and optimistic in one moment and plagued with uncertainty the next.*

A pleasant breeze washed over me the next morning as I had my foamy cappuccino at the café near the library. It was a surreal feeling—like I was floating—to be in Italy with the privilege of being engaged in scholarship. On my lunch break, as I walked past Propaganda Fide College and looked over the panorama of Saint Peter's, the apostles were in full view. I could see and feel the power and glory of the Roman Catholic world. Propaganda Fide College, situated above Vatican City, offers breathtaking panoramic views of Rome, the Tiber river, and Saint Peter's itself (plate 9). *This is the heart, the epicenter, of Catholic dogma and the Catholic world. I almost felt like Professor Langdon in Dan Brown's* The Da Vinci Code, *but I pinched myself to prove that the experience was not fictional. The encounters I had had in Rome thus far—whispered conversations with curators just outside the fortress walls of Vatican City, documents that had gone "missing" in my archival searches, and other barriers I had faced—created a cloud of secrecy around me. The centuries-old pine trees that line the walk along the Saint Peter's vista towered above me, standing like soldiers and smelling of spice in the sun. Rose-ringed parakeets, olive-green monk parakeets, sparrows, and gray-and-black jackdaws flew overhead, unrestricted by the boundaries of access that I confronted.*

I reflected on the fact that Pablo Tac had also studied here at the college, and that encouraged me to keep going, despite the many opportunities I had had to give up. A Luiseño scholar and priest-in-training, Tac lived and studied in Rome during the 1830s. He compiled the first Luiseño dictionary and was fluent in Latin. His life and writings are an example of an Indigenous person from the Americas living in Rome during the early nineteenth century and thus are outside the parameters of this project, but his work remains an inspiration. I first came across Tac's work when I was thinking and researching about Indigenous scholars abroad. Historian Lisbeth Haas notes that "Tac's death follows an all-too-common pattern among native scholars, diplomats, and translators who traveled to Europe: many died there, and their bodies never returned home. Although Tac is buried in Rome, his unique contribution remains."[2] Like Tac, I came to the Propaganda Fide College to study at the library and spent a good deal of time there. The college remains a walled fortress, and it is fascinating to consider that Tac and I have looked out over the same vistas onto Saint Peter's. Often during my lunch break, I would glance over the wall onto Saint Peter's and feel the glory and power of being in Rome. As I peered over the Catholic stronghold my heart fluttered. Sadness and feelings of annoyance plagued me, largely due to the immensity of my task and the bureaucracy and power plays at the Vatican Museums, as well as the snaking paper trail surrounding the Vatican Missionary Exposition. I wondered what Tac contemplated when he was here, studying Latin, writing his Luiseño dictionary, and sketching memories of home. I guessed he may have experienced similar feelings of sadness and homesickness, pondering the future of Indigenous peoples. Could he foresee that other Indigenous scholars from the Americas would follow in his footsteps? Tac attended Propaganda Fide College with several other Indigenous scholars from the Americas, including Cherokee scholars.[3] Tac's legacy as the first to write a Luiseño dictionary for his people and sketch cultural memories in Rome, during a period of intense missionization for Luiseño peoples, provides creative inspiration for thinking about the impact of scholarly Indigenous Americans abroad and the importance of centering Indigenous stories right in the heart of the Vatican.

Displacing Father Marquette in the Hall of North America

Jesuit Father Marquette (1637–75) founded missions at Sault Ste. Marie in Michigan and mapped the northern portion of the Mississippi relying on the intelligence of the Illinois people. In a gesture of goodwill, the Illinois fed him *sagamité*, a food of ceremonial importance, when they welcomed him back into their territories in what is now known as Chicago after his journey along the Mississippi in 1673.[4] Marquette labored to convert the Indigenous nations he encountered to Christianity, but his plans were cut short. He contracted dysentery on his Mississippi expedition and died in 1675 at the age of thirty-seven.[5]

In the Hall of North America at the Vatican Missionary Exposition (VME) in 1925, a statue of Marquette by Italian artist Gaetano Trentanove (1858–1937) occupied the center of the room, blocking the visitor's view of Indigenous cultural belongings around him. The statue celebrated and idealized the Jesuit's missionary work among the Illinois 250 years earlier (see figure 4.1). Visitors to the Hall of North America, as well as contributors to the *Rivista Illustrata della Esposizione Missionaria Vaticana*, praised the statue of Father Marquette and his spiritual labors but ignored the Indigenous cultural belongings behind him. "With exquisite majesty, master Gaetano Trentanove, creator of the marble statue that in the Capitol of Washington exalts all the heroism of the promoter of the faith and the excellence of Italian art," wrote a contributor to the *Rivista*, "portrayed admirably Father Marquette in accordance with the venerable tradition and such dear imagination that he exceeded tradition."[6] The same article features a map of Marquette's route and a photograph of a page of the *Jesuit Relations*, the chronicles of the Jesuit mission, as evidence of the Jesuit's labors.[7] By celebrating Marquette as a "grand explorer" of the Mississippi, the same reviewer ignored the fact that Marquette relied extensively on Indigenous knowledge. Trentanove's statue is a celebration of missionary labors that worked to eradicate Indigenous belief systems and the cultural imaginary across Turtle Island.

The position of the statue of Marquette in front of Indigenous cultural belongings represents a collision of sovereignties.[8] Indigenous cultural belongings draw us to a form of sovereignty and cultural imagining that obscures the lens on Marquette, privileges Indigenous artworks, and rewrites the canon of papal

RIVISTA ILLUSTRATA DELLA ESPOSIZIONE MISSIONARIA VATICANA 699

Spedizione alla scoperta del corso inferiore del Mississipi.

Queste vivissime brame nondimeno e gli sforzi fatti per soddisfarle non avendo sino al cadere del 1672 approdato a nulla, l'ardente missionario già quasi più non ripromettevasi di estendere le pacifiche conquiste oltre le terre scoperte dai Francesi, nelle quali si veniva stabilendo con buon successo la fede cristiana. Or mentre ha l'animo pieno di rassegnata mestizia, ecco sopraggiungere un'inattesa novella a riempirglielo della gioia più pura. Udiamone il racconto tramandatoci schiettamente da lui medesimo nel ragguaglio del suo viaggio (1).

« Il giorno dell'Immacolata Concezione della S. Vergine, che io da che sono in queste terre degli Utauè avevo sempre invocato per ottenere da Dio la grazia di poter visitare le nazioni lungo il fiume Mississipi, fu appunto quello nel quale giunse il Signor Joliet recante gli ordini del Signor Conte De Frontenac nostro Governatore e del Signor Talon nostro Intendente per fare insieme con me questa scoperta. A tale lieta novella fui come fuori di me; vedevo infatti i miei disegni ormai sul punto di compiersi e mi trovavo in una felice necessità di esporre la mia vita per la salute di tutti questi popoli, specialmente per gli Illinesi, i quali a grand'istanze mi avevano pregato di portare loro la parola di Dio, mentre dimoravo alla Missione dello Spirito Santo. Non impiegammo lungo tempo nel preparare il nostro equipaggio, benché fossimo per metterci in un cammino, la cui durata era per noi imprevedibile. Un poco di frumento d'India con carne affumicata; queste furono le nostre provviste con le quali c'imbarcammo su due canotti di corteccia, il Sig. Joliet ed io con cinque uomini, risolutissimi a tutto fare e patire per una impresa così gloriosa.

« Il 17 maggio 1673 partimmo dalla Missione di S. Ignazio a Michilimakinac dove io allora mi trovavo.

« La gioia che provavamo per essere stati scelti a questa spedizione ci ravvivava il coraggio e dolce ci rendeva la pena del vogare da mane a sera. E poichè si andava cercando paesi sconosciuti, usammo tutte le precauzioni che furono in nostro potere affinchè la nostra spedizione, se era rischiosa, non fosse temeraria. A questo intento prendemmo dai selvaggi che avevano frequentato quei luoghi tutte le informazioni che ci fu possibile e secondo le notizie da loro attinte tracciammo una carta di tutti questi nuovi paesi; vi notammo i fiumi che dovevamo navigare, i nomi dei popoli e dei luoghi pei quali ci conveniva passare, il corso del gran fiume e quale direzione fosse da tenere quando l'avessimo raggiunto. Soprattutto misi il nostro viaggio sotto la protezione della S. Vergine Immacolata, promettendole che se ci avesse fatto la grazia di scoprire il gran fiume io gli avrei imposto il nome della Concezione, e così avrei anche chiamato la prima Missione che riuscissi a stabilire presso questi nuovi popoli; ciò che già ho fatto tra gli Illinesi (1) ».

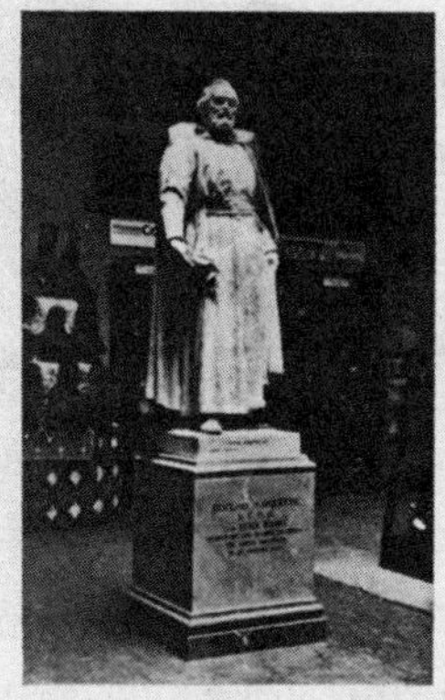

La statua del Padre G. Marquette nel padiglione dedicato all'America centrale e meridionale.

Il Padre Marquette in viaggio. Insistenza degli Indiani per rimuoverlo dall'impresa.

I limiti dello spazio che ci siamo prefissi nel fare rivivere, con la figura eroica del P. Marquette, la memoria del suo ardimentoso viaggio non ci consentono di seguirlo passo passo nell'edificante ed istruttivo racconto di cui abbiamo riportato qui la prima pagina fedelmente tradotta. Riepilogando dall'autorevole documento (il solo che ci rimanga dopo la perdita delle carte del capitano Joliet) (2) troviamo che gl'intrepidi cominciarono a remigare con allegra lena (3) prima nel lago degli Uroni, poi in quello degli Illinesi e nella Baia dei Puants o *baia fetente* secondo noi la chiameremmo in nostra lingua (4).

Qui avvenne un incontro degno di essere riferito, come quello che sempre più nettamente lumeggia il carattere dell'impavido Missionario. Essendo egli disceso a terra ed inoltratosi alquanto nel paese per visitare la tribù detta della *Folle avoine*, presso la quale il cristianesimo predicatovi dai suoi confratelli, andava mettendo radici, mise a parte quei semplici Indiani del disegno da lui concepito di scoprire le più remote nazioni affine d'istruirle nei misteri della fede. Grande fu la loro meraviglia a questa notizia e non minore lo sforzo e l'insistenza che adoperarono per rimuovere la Veste Nera dal generoso proposito. Cominciarono a rappresentargli che avrebbe incontrato tribù le quali mai non perdonano a stranieri cui, senza un motivo al mondo, fracassano inesorabilmente la testa: ardere allora la guerra tra parecchi popoli sparsi sul loro cammino: cosicchè egli ed i suoi si troverebbero esposti ad evidente pericolo di essere uccisi dalle bande dei combattenti. Il gran fiume (cioè il Mississipi) essere pericolosissimo, chi ne ignori i passi difficili; tutto ripieno di mostri spaventosissimi che in un attimo divorano insieme e uomini e canotti; avervi perfino un demonio i cui urli si udivano lontanissimo; questi rinserrare il passo e sprofondar giù negli abissi coloro che ardivano di avvicinarsi; in ultimo, tanto eccessivo calore dominare nella regione che egli e i compagni v'incontrerebbero infallibilmente la morte (5).

Con sì foschi colori la vivace, ma ingenua fantasia degli Indiani metteva innanzi al Missionario la sorte che senza dubbio attendevalo, pensavano essi, se avesse perseverato nel suo divisamento. Ma il Padre, per nulla atterrito dalla tetra pittura, prese a tranquillarli e a dissipare in questa forma la loro paura. « Li ringraziai, così egli, dei saggi consigli che mi davano; però soggiunsi subito che non potevo seguirli, perché trattavasi della salute delle anime per le quali sarei felicissimo di dare la vita. Ridermi di quel preteso

(1) Il P. Marquette scrisse egli stesso nel 1674 una relazione, o quasi diario, dell'ardimentoso suo viaggio. Preceduto da un breve proemio dettato dal Superiore delle Missioni dei Gesuiti francesi nel Canadà, il già ricordato P. Claudio Dablon, il prezioso documento, per tanti rispetti importante, fu pubblicato la prima volta in Parigi il 1682 a cura del Thévenot che l'inserì nella sua opera, oggi sì rara, *Recueil des voyages*. Rivide poi la luce nel 1885 in Albany negli Stati Uniti. Noi qui facciamo uso della edizione più recente, condotta, come la testè ricordata, (pur troppo con deplorevoli criterii) sullo stesso autografo che conservasi in Montreal nel Collegio di S. Maria presso i Padri della Compagnia di Gesù, ed inserita nella grande collezione americana del Thwaites, *Travels and Explorations*, già ripetutamente qui sopra citata.

(1) Cf. Marquette, *Le premier voyage qu'a fait le P. Marquette*, etc., in Thwaites, *Travels and Explorations*, etc., loc. cit., p. 88 sg.

(2) Il Joliet tornando subito dopo la spedizione a Montreale fece naufragio e perdette le sue carte, come sappiamo dal P. Dablon nel breve proemio premesso all'autografo del P. Marquette. Loc. cit., p. 88.

(3) « Nous faisons jouer joyeusement les avirons ». Così il P. Marquette, loc. cit., p. 92.

(4) Per sentimento del P. Marquette così nomasi questa baia a cagione della molta melma o belletta donde esalavano sgradevoli vapori. Cf. Marquette, loc. cit., p. 96.

(5) Marquette, loc. cit., p. 94 sg.

FIGURE 4.1. Statue of Father J. Marquette, Hall of North America, Vatican Missionary Exposition, 1925. Source: *Rivista Illustrata della Esposizione Missionaria Vaticana*, October 31, 1925, 699. Courtesy of Propaganda Fide Library Collections, Pontificio Collegio Urbano "De Propaganda Fide," Rome.

history (see my reflection on rewriting in plate 10). Pope Pius XI declared that the materials sent in to the VME shone like a light in the darkness (*lux in tenebris*) to highlight missionary work.[9] In closing the exposition, he further professed that all the things sent in for the VME conveyed a "silent eloquence."[10] Instead, I propose the concept of "eternal sovereigns" to counter Pius XI's silence. Considering the suppression of Indigenous voices at the VME and the celebration of missionary genocidal labors as heroic, such as those at residential and day schools, there is no eloquence in silence. Countering the reviewers who ignored the materials surrounding them in the Halls of the Americas, I write against a paucity of information on the Indigenous cultural belongings displayed at the VME and, in this chapter, make them central participants in a counternarrative that displaces the statue of Marquette and, more importantly, the legacy of silent eloquence and Pius XI's greed.

Unsettling the Vatican Missionary Exposition: Indigenous Cultural Belongings as Eternal Sovereigns

Focusing on the Indigenous cultural belongings at the VME foregrounds the eternal sovereignties of Indigenous artisans within the space of the Vatican and moves beyond the ethnographic gaze of the VME curators, which claims a form of colonial sovereignty over all that was exhibited. Instead, I read the cultural belongings as "eternal sovereigns," a term I use to present an alternative dominion to that represented by the statue of Marquette. These cultural belongings serve as ancestral art history lessons that form an alternative text to the one presented and celebrated by the VME curators. *Eternal Sovereigns* as a scholarly project offers up an analytic framework and counternarrative to Pius XI's culture of greed and conquest. There is a conceptual and moral imperative to look again at Indigenous cultural belongings in the Vatican. The belongings discussed in what follows give a sense of the diversity of Indigenous American cultural production held at the Vatican. This chapter offers a reading of their importance as ancient and living archives, markers of diplomacy, ancestors, and travelers, and their ongoing significance in the fight for cultural autonomy.

Indigenous artworks displayed in the exhibition, including an Anishinaabe, Nipissing, and Kanien'kehá:ka wampum belt, a Passamaquoddy cross, a Lakota Sun Dance drawing, Cree beaded moccasins, and a Kwakwaka'wakw ancestral sun mask, are central participants in this story.[11] The order in which I analyze this material is inspired by the chronology of their making, while recognizing also that linear models of time do not always account for the multiplicities of Indigenous time and space. Despite missionary positioning of sacred and secular materials as gifts to the pope and, by implication, as additions to a triumphal Roman heritage, the presence of the Indigenous materials speaks to the unacknowledged Indigenous labor and the artistic and spiritual wealth of many Indigenous nations across Turtle Island and the globe. Rather than see them solely as silent objects of Vatican contemplation and confiscation, they are travelers, subjects, and actors with lives that continue beyond the hands of their creators. This book therefore takes up the challenge posed by scholars and activists to unbind historical silences and reread colonial archives, which are inherent "repositories of colonial privilege," in order to recenter Indigenous perspectives and open up rather than obscure colonial histories.[12]

Terms such as "object" and "gift" do not account for the sacred and embodied understandings of materials that Indigenous perspectives bring to this discussion. Indigenous artworks, many of which are sacred and important historical markers, should be thought of as having a presence, both physical and spiritual, within the walls of the Vatican. Indeed, some VME visitors expressed their anxiety about this sacred aspect, describing it as the "domain of the head-hunter, the witch-doctor, the cannibal," indicating that the cultural belongings signified far more than just silent markers of missionary progress.[13] The materials are also powerful, enchanting belongings, ancestors and relatives, that carry Indigenous spiritual ideas and thought processes.[14] The power of Indigenous cultural belongings are ancestral art history lessons that unsettle Pius XI's logic and the pervasive but not all-encompassing views of missionaries and visitors. Cultural belongings made using Indigenous methods and hands resonate beyond missionary anxiety and past the allochronic space of the Halls of the Americas. Although Pius XI and his missionaries considered them as silent markers of missionary progress, visual analysis reveals them to be ancestral art history lessons full of persuasive power and aesthetic brilliance.

An "Ancient Archive" and an Eternal Assertion of Sovereignty: The Anishinaabe, Nipissing, and Kanien'kehá:ka Wampum Belt

In 1916, Seneca historian Arthur Parker described wampum as an "ancient archive" in the Iroquois Constitution: "For many generations its knowledge has been preserved by a collection of wampum belts and strings, each of which served to recall each law or regulation. Many of the belts and strings became lost or destroyed, and fearing a total destruction of their *ancient archives*, the Six Nations of New York Indians in 1898 elected The University of the State of New York the official custodian of their wampums."[15] This makes clear the importance of wampum as a mnemonic device. In the United States, the New York State Museum became custodian of the wampum belts Parker discusses, but in Canada, the government seized wampum belts and other important documents from the Six Nations in 1924 in an overt display of colonial seizure of cultural belongings.[16] This confiscation confirms the settlers' awareness of the inherent power of wampum as a device of cultural teaching and historical documentation.[17]

In November 1924, at a theater in Geneva one month before the VME opened, Cayuga Chief Levi General Deskaheh, dressed in Iroquois regalia and holding his booklet *The Redman's Appeal for Justice*, discussed some of the wampum treaties made with the British Crown.[18] His reading of wampum and publication of the booklet were part of his larger campaign to raise awareness of the ongoing struggle for recognition of the sovereignty of the Haudenosaunee (People of the Long House) Confederacy at the League of Nations, based in Geneva.[19] In particular, he presented a case for recognition of the sovereignty of the governing structure of the Iroquois Confederacy and appealed to the League of Nations to respect the treaties and mediate the ongoing dispute with the Canadian government, which was encroaching on Haudenosaunee lands and refusing to recognize the Haudenosaunee governing structure.[20] Deskaheh used the wampum as part of a "complex diplomatic strategy" to articulate Haudenosaunee political autonomy and sovereignty, and to resist the Department of Indian Affairs' colonial aim to assimilate First Nations.[21] He also made wampum visible as a central participant in international diplomacy for Indigenous peoples in the early twentieth century.[22] The First Nations' tradition of wearing wampum for delegation purposes is perhaps most perfectly epitomized by the famous series of paintings by Jan Verelst made in 1710 and known as "Four Indian Kings," located today in the Library and Archives Canada, Ottawa.[23] These paintings, like the belt, are evidence of the visual circulation of wampum and cultural diplomacy in the global imaginary.

Deskaheh's wampum, like the wampum at the Vatican, holds an important position in articulating sovereign relationships and making Indigenous arts and acts visible on an international scale. Wampum belts circulated within the international imaginary and formed part of a long tradition of wampum diplomacy on behalf of Haudenosaunee rights in the Northeast.[24] Parker, Deskaheh, and other Native historians contemplated the value and purpose of Indigenous cultural belongings at the time of the VME, articulating complex Indigenous histories through cultural belongings. Wampum, like the other ancestral belongings discussed herein, form an integral, ancient, and living archive for Indigenous peoples and art historians that continues to resonate today.[25]

A powerful marker of Indigenous women's labor presents itself in the wampum belt that was displayed in the "Algonquin" section of the VME (see plate 11).[26] In 1831, this belt had been sent as a diplomatic gift to pope Gregory XVI from the Anishinaabe, Nipissing, and Kanien'kehá:ka of Kanehsatà:ke, the Lake of Two Mountains, near Montreal in the Saint Lawrence Valley.[27] Female artisans carefully crafted purple and white shells into delicate beads and then wove them into wampum. In another image of the belt, the photographer has placed it like a sash with a fold in the center, giving an impression of the belt's use as a stole, an item usually worn like a scarf over the shoulders and also used as a liturgical garment in Catholic ceremonies.[28] Both missionaries and Indigenous people wore wampum sometimes as belts and as scarves or sashes.[29] The wampum belt records the signing of a peace treaty between the Haudenosaunee, Algonquin, and the Catholic Church. Catholics established missions at Kanehsatà:ke, in the eighteenth century, and many had converted to Catholicism by the early nineteenth century, although many retained their Indigenous beliefs, often in tandem with their Christianity.[30] The belt functions as a memory tool that speaks to the relations between the Mohawk, Algonquin, and the Catholic Church as well as to the dynamics of Indigenous oratorical practices. The artisan made it with delicate care and handling. The wampum belt is not a silent marker of missionary practice, but a belonging with mnemonic presence and power carefully crafted with almost ten thousand beads.

The belt has been the object of some scholarship over the years—it is perhaps one of the most famous examples of Indigenous American art in the Vatican collection—and its power continues to resonate. The artisans wove the wampum belt fifteen rows wide with a deer hide fringe. Looking at the belt from right to left, it is a woven image featuring, in this order, a chapel, Haudenosaunee writing, two keys crossed (symbolizing Saint Peter's "keys to the kingdom"), a missionary holding a cross, and a Native man beside him holding the same cross but also holding wampum, and then two crisscrossed arrows and a bow held by another Native man. At the far left are an arrow and a calumet, a pipe used in diplomatic events and other important ceremonies. There is a checkered border at the right end, while the left ends in alternating white and purple shells. The white and purple abalone shell, with the symbols in white against a purple background, are majestic colors and suitable materials for this sacred mnemonic document and device. White was often used by the Haudenosaunee weavers to symbolize peace and purple to depict political matters. The belt has fringes at both ends. Historian David Bushnell's enthusiastic account of the wampum belt from 1895, in which he describes it as an extraordinary "specimen," is typical of the language of the time, but it provides a basis for the visual analysis.[31]

More recently, anthropologist Marshall Becker has worked on the significance of the belt.[32] He suggests that the belt depicts Catholic and Indigenous iconography. Although Becker's research is useful, he does not acknowledge the ongoing importance of wampum belts for the Indigenous peoples of Turtle Island, a glaring oversight that the Vatican catalog *The Americas: Collections from the Vatican Ethnological Museum* (2015) repeats.[33] Although the wampum is not a two-row belt evidencing the mutually respectful relationship between colonial governments and Haudenosaunee, it does represent the "diplomatic convention" of using wampum in negotiations between the Haudenosaunee and other governments—in this case, the Vatican.[34] As Abenaki scholar and wampum specialist Margaret Bruchac notes: "Wampum belts have long been used by Native American peoples to encode and facilitate intertribal and international relations. Federal legislation and national museums have identified wampum belts as iconic and inalienable items of cultural patrimony, and

Haudenosaunee (Iroquois) tribal leaders have been actively seeking to repatriate wampum for more than a century."[35] Wampum belts represent part of the richness of ongoing Haudenosaunee and Algonquin iconographic traditions.

The Vatican curators emphasized that the practice of making wampum has died out and credited the missionaries with preserving "specimens" of it. This colonial attitude has not changed since the time of the VME. The Vatican's catalog *The Americas* lists this as the most famous piece of wampum in the collection, although it holds another wampum by the Penobscot, who along with the Passamaquoddy, Mi'kmaq, Maliseet, and Abenaki, form the Wabanaki Confederacy.[36] Present-day Vatican curators still insist that the practice has died out. They state that "since the belt-making tradition was lost by 1831, the production of the Vatican Wampum Belt was an attempt by the missionaries to help revitalize a disappearing tradition."[37] However, their assumption of an inevitable decline of Indigenous artistic traditions is limiting and misinformed. The making and use of wampum belts as historically binding documents continues to this day in various ceremonies, including the inauguration of chiefs in the Haudenosaunee Confederacy.[38] As a mnemonic device, the wampum belt complements the oral tradition of the Haudenosaunee and Algonquin and is another way of articulating Indigenous presence and Indigenous literacies other than through paper and ink.[39] Anishinaabe legal scholar John Borrows is clear about the continuing significance of the wampum belt: "The two-row wampum belt illustrates a First Nation/Crown relationship that is founded on peace, friendship and respect, where each Nation will not interfere with the internal affairs of the other."[40] This sovereign relation between the Vatican and the Haudenosaunee and the Algonquin represented by the wampum belt was not recognized by the VME curators in their display techniques, nor is it recognized to this day.

Through the discussion here, I hope to further awareness of this wampum belt and contribute to the restorative methodologies that Bruchac and her network of scholars are building. Bruchac's methods include cataloging wampum belts across the globe, creating digital records, and working with a variety of scholars and community members to resituate and narrate wampum and its ongoing cultural importance. I hope also to bring the wampum belt at the Vatican into the discussion out of respect for the "ancient archive" and the woven-in stories it holds.[41] The wampum belt's trajectory in the archives was a bit of a mystery. Giovanni Pizzorusso noted in 1990 that the belt "was presumably moved to the Museo Missionario Ethnologico at the Lateran in 1926, but it does not survive today."[42] However, the photograph of the belt in *The Americas* catalog indicates it is still in existence.[43] In fact, as of March 2023, the powerful wampum belt is on display in the Ethnological Museum *Anima Mundi*, with limited curatorial information provided (see plate 12). *Anima Mundi* was closed for almost a decade, and at the time of this writing, some Indigenous American artworks are on partial display, evidence that the gallery is a work in progress, and the curatorial team is beginning to bring out some of the cultural belongings for tourist consumption at the Vatican. In any case, the belt remains evidence of the cultural practice of beadwork and its central importance in Haudenosaunee and Algonquin cultural identity, and it is a reminder of the vital role of wampum in complex acts of Indigenous diplomacy and of the varied ways in which cultural belongings matter in asserting sovereignty for Indigenous nations across the world.[44] The belt at the Vatican is a reminder of the onetime reciprocal relations of respect and tolerance and a recognition of sovereign states—the Haudenosaunee, Algonquin, and the Vatican—yet, held now at the Vatican, it does not get the full respect it deserves.

In the fall of 2023, after nearly two hundred years of being in the stronghold of the Vatican, the belt did travel back to its homelands and was briefly put on display for a few weeks as part of the *Wampum: Beads of Diplomacy* exhibition at the McCord Stewart Museum in Tiohtiá:ke Mooniyang (Montreal). The Vatican Museums loaned the belt but with a lot of restrictions and disregard for Indigenous patrimony; the belt will not be repatriated. The restrictions regarding the belt's display and lack of restitution are evidence of the curatorial disregard of the Vatican Museums and the inability to engage in an important step toward decolonization.[45] The belt is essentially a prisoner of the Vatican Museums. The wampum belt's voyage to Montreal and brief appearance in the exhibition may be the only time the belt will ever be seen by its Indigenous relatives. Indigenous women and their ancestors who made the belt and other pieces of wampum in the Ethnological Museum *Anima Mundi* collection are not getting the full respect they need. Seeing the belt at the McCord Stewart Museum was an important moment for me to think about the artistry of the Algonquin and Mohawk women who made it, their skill and care, and its complex iconography, and to reckon with the competing sovereignties at play. The belt should be rematriated, but it remains in a prison of glass in the Vatican Museums.

A Birch Cross of the Passamaquoddy: Carving Indigenous Spiritualities

The VME's Hall of North America included materials sent in by the Franciscan mission of Tobique and the Saint Ann Parish in New Brunswick from the Maliseet Wolastoqiyik community on the Tobique reserve.[46] Father Noël Gubbels, the Belgian Franciscan who cataloged the material, described the belongings as "savage curiosities," not concealing his contempt for the Maliseet people, whom he thought of as "primitive," stuck in the past, and incapable of producing art. Among the items he cataloged were: a map of New Brunswick detailing the missions and the location of the Maliseet; a group of "Indian types" (perhaps wax models or photographs); a map of Tobique; photographs of the mission, the school, and clothing he called "parade costumes." He also listed model birchbark canoes, twelve "fantastical" baskets, model rackets, moccasins, texts of prayers and legends in Maliseet, and a painting of the mission.[47] This record is unique in providing a thorough account of materials sent in. Most other accounts I have encountered do not give such specific details.

Miniature canoes, such as those from Tobique, are still on view today in the entrance to the Vatican Museums along with other miniature models from Africa, Asia, Oceania, and South America (see figure I.1). The present-day display conveys a sense of Maliseet culture as part of an antiquated past. No individual details, such as artists' names or communities, are provided; instead, the Wolastoqiyik cultural belongings are jumbled together with miniature canoes from Alaska and Chile. The missionary biases evident in Gubbels's language—"savage curiosities," "fantastical"—also reflect the broader racist attitudes of the time toward Native people, particularly the belief that they could not adapt to modern society. Despite these biases, Gubbels's account also provides important clues for tracing some of the material back to a specific community and location. I have contacted the Franciscan mission that is still there, but no records of the VME have been preserved; the parish church burned down in 1923, and it was not rebuilt until 1925.[48] The Maliseet and Passamaquoddy are part of the Wabanaki Confederacy of Algonquin-speaking peoples, whose traditional lands extend south from Newfoundland in Canada to the Merrimack River Valley in New Hampshire and Massachusetts, and west on both sides of the US-Canadian border.[49] They are known for their beautiful and intricate chip carving, splint baskets, and beadwork, and have made many souvenir artworks for the tourist trade from the eighteenth century onward. By the 1920s, the Passamaquoddy actively encouraged tourism to their territories in Maine through a series of travel booklets, pageants, and tourist arts.[50]

An example of Passamaquoddy culture displayed in the VME, and still in the Vatican collections, is a statue of Christ on the cross that provides a powerful example of Passamaquoddy carving ingenuity (see figure 4.2).[51] Father Pancrazio Maarschalkerweerd, a former museum assistant of the Vatican Missionary Ethnological Collection, described the statue in 1937 as "an art object that is of importance, being from the historical period and also representing the question of Indigenous art."[52] Maarschalkerweerd's phrase "the question of Indigenous art" suggests he at least considered the shifting hierarchies of

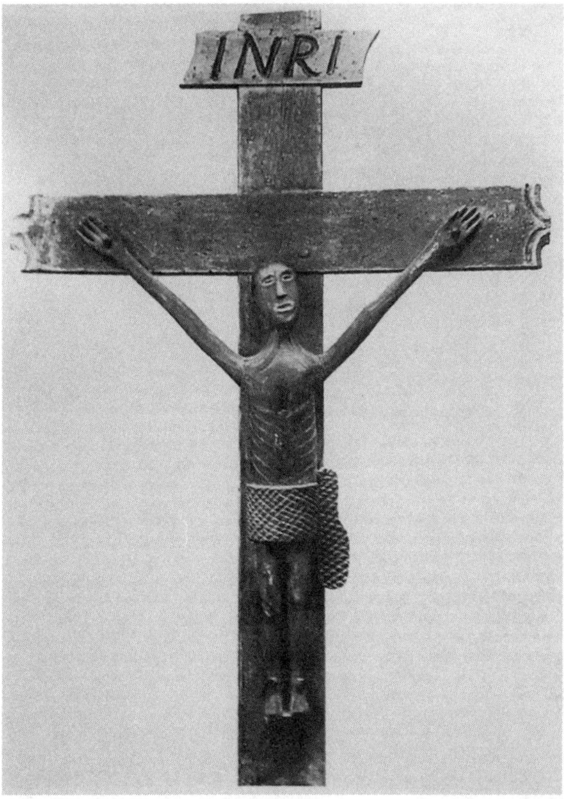

FIGURE 4.2. Passamaquoddy, Christ on cross, ca. 1830. Wood with pigment, 72 × 36.5 × 5 cm (cross); w. 29.5 cm (Christ). Vatican Museums, Vatican City, inv. 101612.0.0. Source: Maarschalkerweerd, "Plastiche cristiane," 19. Courtesy of Propaganda Fide Library Collections, Pontificio Collegio Urbano "De Propaganda Fide," Rome. https://catalogo.museivaticani.va/index.php/Detail/objects/MV.101612.0.0.

value surrounding Indigenous art in this period, ranging from the anonymity of "primitive" artists presented at the VME as part of the "Indian craze" to arts of diverse peoples worthy of recognition as art rather than as ethnography. Catholic missionaries working in the Passamaquoddy community sent in the carving as part of the Museo Borgia della Propaganda al Museo Lateranense collection.[53] It is the work of a Passamaquoddy artist from the first half of the nineteenth century.[54]

Some seventy-two centimeters in height, the statue is carved out of wood from yellow birch, an old-growth forest tree with multiple layers of importance for Indigenous groups across the Northeast of Turtle Island, including the Anishinaabe and Algonquin. Potawatomi writer Robin Wall Kimmerer observes that "the birch forests maintained by indigenous burning were a cornucopia of gifts: bark for canoes, sheathing for wigwams and tools and baskets, scrolls for writing."[55] The tinder of the birch is also used to light fires. Kimmerer notes that fires are central to Anishinaabe creation stories. A particular fungus that grows on birch is also highly valued in traditional medicine.[56]

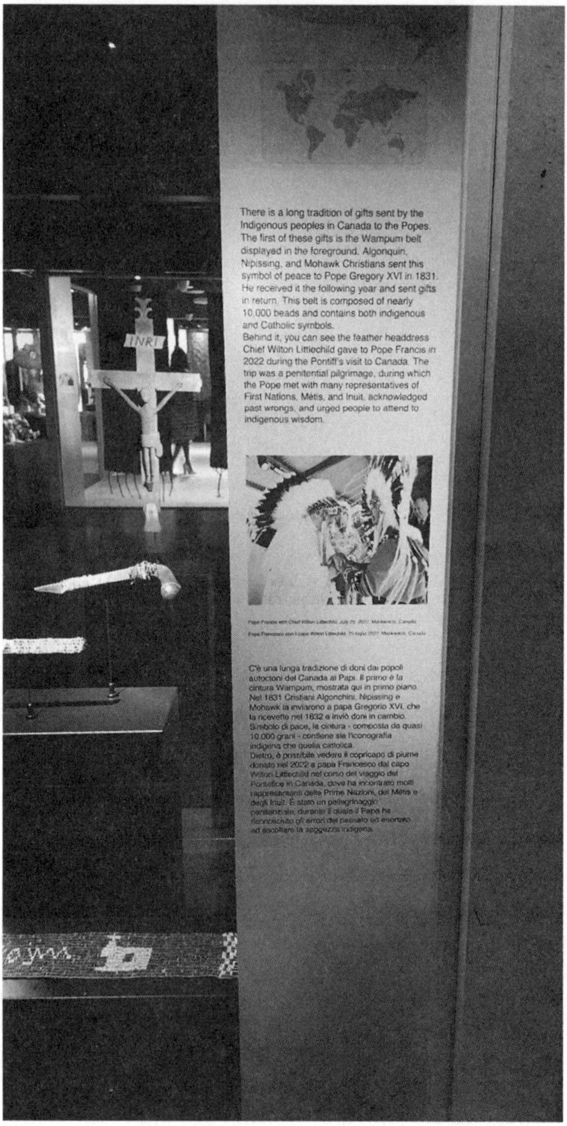

FIGURE 4.3. Installation view, Passamaquoddy, Christ on cross, Ethnological Museum *Anima Mundi*, Vatican Museums, Vatican City, March 2023. Photograph by the author.

Passamaquoddy use birch to make baskets and carrying bags as well as for ropes and other utility items for hunting.[57] Passamaquoddy and Wendaki continue to use birch for birchbark writing.[58] In Indigenous ontologies, birch is part of a holistic system of relationships between people and the earth, and a vital part of the ecosystem for animals, plants, and humans.[59] The materiality of the carving matters on multiple levels of the collective memory of Indigenous peoples of the Northeast. Yellow birch continues to remind Indigenous peoples of the respect they hold for the tree within creation stories, and of the ability of this sense of connection to strengthen and nurture Indigenous communities across Turtle Island. On an intellectual level, birch plays a central role in sustaining their mythologies. At a material level, it forms the literal basis for many arts practices, including basketry and carving traditions.[60]

The arms of the cross taper into points formed by curves marked with an incised line that draws the eyes to the figure's pierced hands and parallels the carved lines of his ribcage. He is an Indigenous savior. Throughout the eighteenth and nineteenth centuries, Northeast carvers used design motifs such as incised lines on effigies for Indigenous spiritual practices, on ritual belongings for burial, and on arts that functioned for many community purposes and the everyday. Indigenous artists of the Northeast were influenced by the impact of trade with Europeans, creating gifts of exchange for diplomacy.[61] Above the figure of Christ is the Latin acronym INRI (Iesus Nazarenus, Rex Iudaeorum/Jesus of Nazareth, King of the Jews). The body of Christ and the cross he rests on is a deep rose-bronze color, and black nails pierce his hands and feet. The lettering above the figure also has black pigment. The artist carved the figure out of a single piece of yellow birch and then attached it onto the larger cross behind it. The minimal rose-and-black color palette creates a stark mood for the piece, suitable for the agony of the figure; the viewer is meant to empathize with the suffering of the Indigenous man on the cross.

The artist presents the viewer with the tangible suffering of the emaciated body; the pain manifests in the open grimace carved into his face and the marks incised thickly across the figure's chest to indicate straining of breath. Notably, he is an Indigenous redeemer, wearing a garment wrapped around his waist, the crosshatching meant to evoke hide or beaver fur. The crosshatch technique of the loincloth presents an Algonquin approach to the iconography of sacred beings. The oval shape of the face and the incised eyes and lips are reminiscent of faces of sacred beings on catlinite pipes and feast bowls, part of the carving traditions of figurines and effigies used in medicine bundles and other sacred practices of Algonquin peoples of the Northeast.[62] Considering also that Passamaquoddy may have used this statue in processions, it showcases how Passamaquoddy adopted rather than assimilated Catholic practices into their carving traditions and spirituality, presenting a First Nations man as the human face of the divine.[63]

The adoption of Christian mythology using an Indigenous lens and an Indigenous approach to image-making is evident in this sculpture through the carving method that presents the suffering of a Passamaquoddy man as Christ.

Theologian R. Murray Thomas admits that "many Indians' faith may well be a synthesis of traditional Indian and Christian beliefs, because over the centuries Christian missionaries continually noted—usually with distress—how easily Native Americans adopted portions of Christian doctrine without abandoning tribal practices."[64] The statue is evidence of the ongoing Passamaquoddy worldview and its characteristic approach to sculpture, using a distinct visual language as part of the long continuum of visual culture practices in the medium of birch, which also includes birchbark writing and basketry.[65] This understudied carving is also a telling reminder of the series of transitions and hardships that the Passamaquoddy peoples went through, such as removal from their lands and attempts by missionaries and the federal governments of Canada and the United States to force their assimilation into settler society. It is also evidence of the persistence of the chip-carving method and of the ingenuity of Passamaquoddy carving traditions, yet in the earliest discussion of Native American material in Vatican collections, by David Bushnell in 1906, there is no mention of it.[66] The statue is also not in *The Americas* catalog, the most recent Vatican publication on its holdings from the Americas. This could be evidence of curatorial disregard as well as sporadic record keeping and the colonial conditions of the archive.

The finely carved statue is a marker of Indigenous Passamaquoddy presence in the Vatican and in the VME, and a reminder of the ongoing use of the arts by Native people to assert their identity and adapt Christian mythologies to Indigenous worldviews. The Indigenous figure on the cross reminds one of the seventeenth-century conversion of the Passamaquoddy and their adoption of Catholicism but also shows how Passamaquoddy peoples retained their Indigenous spiritual beliefs and cultural practices.[67] Like many of the cultural belongings featured in the VME, the location of the statue remained a mystery for quite some time. Pizzorusso noted that "no further collection history [of the statue] is available as old inventories were not copied at the time of the transfer."[68] My interviews with a former Vatican curator corroborate Pizzorusso's claim.[69]

The afterlives of many of the Indigenous cultural belongings sent in for the VME remain a mystery. Many cultural belongings of the Americas have been lost or destroyed, or have disappeared. Others, such as buffalo hides from the Great Plains, disintegrated due to insect infestations.[70] The disappearance of such sacred items as the Passamaquoddy statue evokes the utter curatorial disregard for Indigenous cultural belongings in addition to the erosion of history through time and neglect. The fact that the Ethnological Museum *Anima Mundi* does not allow Indigenous researchers access to its historical collections is also a major factor in the lack of scholarship on these belongings.[71] Yet an interesting turn of events has happened. As of spring 2023, the statue has reappeared in the *Anima Mundi* museum and is located behind glass not far from the Haudenosaunee and Algonquin wampum belt and sacred Menominee carvings from the Cardinal Borgia collection (see figure 4.3).[72] The statue provides an ancestral lesson in our larger research project to remember and articulate the contributions of Indigenous artisans within the VME and within the Vatican collections that missionaries neglected.

When I first encountered an image of the Passamaquoddy statue at the Propaganda Fide in Rome, its immediacy struck me. I paused for reflection during my research as I felt moved on a mental and spiritual level. I thought perhaps the artist and their carving were there guiding me, being a symbol for my research. When I encountered the sculpture itself at the Ethnological Museum *Anima Mundi*, it was almost hiding in plain sight, behind many other important belongings all taken from Indigenous communities, at the back of a display case. The sculpture was lit from above, making the features of the Indigenous Christ more dramatic, drawn out, and visible. I thought about all the Indigenous artists who were never named at the VME but were once known. I paused for a moment, and I could hear the low hum of chatter. I saw many stolen treasures in the display cases, and I could hear their screams. The suffering painstakingly carved into the Christ's face and within his body became more tangible and real.

The mental, physical, and spiritual struggles that scholars face in pursuing reparative archival work are part of affective labor practices that inform and motivate my research. The suffering and emaciated man on the Passamaquoddy cross reminds me of the eternal sovereignties of Indigenous artworks in the strongholds of the Vatican; it also serves more broadly as a reminder to trace and honor Indigeneity in the archives. In the following section, I recount my research and archival findings and a conversation I had with multimedia Lakota artist Dana Claxton regarding a Lakota Sun Dance drawing that reflects that aim.

A Lakota Sun Dance Drawing: Imaging the Great Mystery Wakan'tanka

> Grandfather,
> a voice I am going to send,
> hear me.
> All over the universe
> a voice I am going to send.

Hear me,
grandfather,
I will live,
I have said it.[73]

Red Bird recorded this prayer song in 1911 at Fort Yates, North Dakota, when he was twenty-four years old. It is an opening prayer of the Sun Dance. Perhaps the artist who created the muslin drawing seized for the VME heard a similar song as he first witnessed this sacred event (see figure 4.4). Pine Ridge and Rosebud Reservation German Jesuit missionaries seized and sent in the drawing as part of the ledger art tradition that extends from Plains hide painting and, along with other sacred and secular materials, formed a large collection of Lakota Očhéthi Šakówiŋ (Sioux) cultural belongings in the VME.[74] German Jesuit John Jutz worked among the Lakota and established the Saint Francis Mission on the Rosebud reservation in 1885. He also worked among the Lakota at Pine Ridge, and thus it is likely he sent in the drawing by an unidentified artist.[75]

The Sun Dance is a sacred and important spiritual event of prayer and body modification, with intercessions sent to Wakan'tanka (the Great Mystery). Devotions, offerings, and self-sacrifice in the form of the piercing of flesh are essential to this revered religious occasion. The Sun Dance has existed for hundreds, perhaps thousands, of years.[76] Across the Great Plains, dancers send supplications for healing to the Creator after time spent fasting and preparing for the rite. It is a sacred event to honor the Creator in which dancers envision and enact prayers for Indigenous futures. Dancers make kin ties with relatives in the human and other-than-human realm in honor of the cosmos. Under the Indian Act of 1885, the Canadian government banned the Sun Dance; the ban was not lifted until 1951.[77] The US government also banned the dance in 1904, condemning it as "pagan," and did not lift the ban until 1978. The bans were part and parcel of the outlawing of Native religious ceremonies and practices undertaken in order to suppress Indigenous knowledge, languages, and lives. The practice went underground, but due to its suppression, the Lakota people experienced cultural strain around the events that typically happen at the ceremony, including marriage and other social and economic practices. Thus, the bans disrupted and negatively affected the kinship ties made during the Sun Dance.

Missionaries seized this drawing and other Sun Dance material at the same time that Buffalo Bill and a large group of Native American men (including Lakota artist Mató Nájin Standing Bear) were traveling through Europe, with two stops in Italy at Bologna and Rome.[78] Missionaries then positioned the Sun

Dance materials at the VME as markers of missionary progress.[79] However, they are also important archives of Lakota cosmologies. As curator Louise Lincoln observes of Lakota arts, they "can reveal much about their makers and their time: the intellectual and emotional struggles of coping with assaultive change, the often-effective strategies Plains peoples put to use, and the ways in which they preserved, sometimes covertly, the traditional grounding of their lives."[80]

From the Lakota Rosebud Reservation, German missionaries sent in the Sun Dance ceremonial drawing, created with colored pigments on muslin. The Vatican's catalog *The Americas* does not explain the item's exact provenance, evidencing the lack of care that the VME curators had when amassing Indigenous American cultural belongings and perhaps the lack of thorough record taking in collecting.[81] The curators describe it as a "donation" from the Jesuits, but there is no evidence that consent was ever given for this belonging to be added to a museum collection or for it to be displayed, like the majority of the Indigenous belongings exhibited at the VME, almost a century ago, and today at *Anima Mundi* (see plate 13).[82] Pigments of blue, red, green, and black connect the drawing with the upper world, the lower world, and the four directions of the Lakota Očhéthi Šakówiŋ cosmos. Artists made the colors using local pigments they harvested and then mixed with buffalo fat or water. Anthropologist Frances Densmore notes that "on the Standing Rock Reservation is found a yellow ocherous substance which after being reduced to a fine powder, is used by the Indians in making yellow paint. This substance, when treated by means of heat, yields the vermilion used on all ceremonial articles as well as in painting the bodies of the Indians."[83] Očhéthi Šakówiŋ artists harvested, ground, and mixed their pigments, evidence of the symbiotic connection between art, creation, and ceremony.[84] I sat down with Lakota artist Dana Claxton and *The Americas* catalog to decode this drawing. We also talked about some of the ethics around discussing Lakota drawings but in the end decided it is better to have a conversation and bring this drawing into broader public awareness than have no dialogue at all.

The drawing shows several scenes in a continuous narrative depicting ceremonial dancers in body paint holding shields, burning medicine, and performing other actions of the ceremony.[85] The artist has used the bold graphic of the thin black pole as a focal device that attracts the eye, drawing attention to the Lakota warriors that encircle it at the bottom. The figures are following the path of the sun, a graphic visual motif of the event. Red, blue, green, and black tipis surround the scene, indicating the large number of attendees and the artist's rendering of a bird's eye view of the event, making an ephemeral occasion vividly present in the viewer's mind. The artist took an all-encompassing

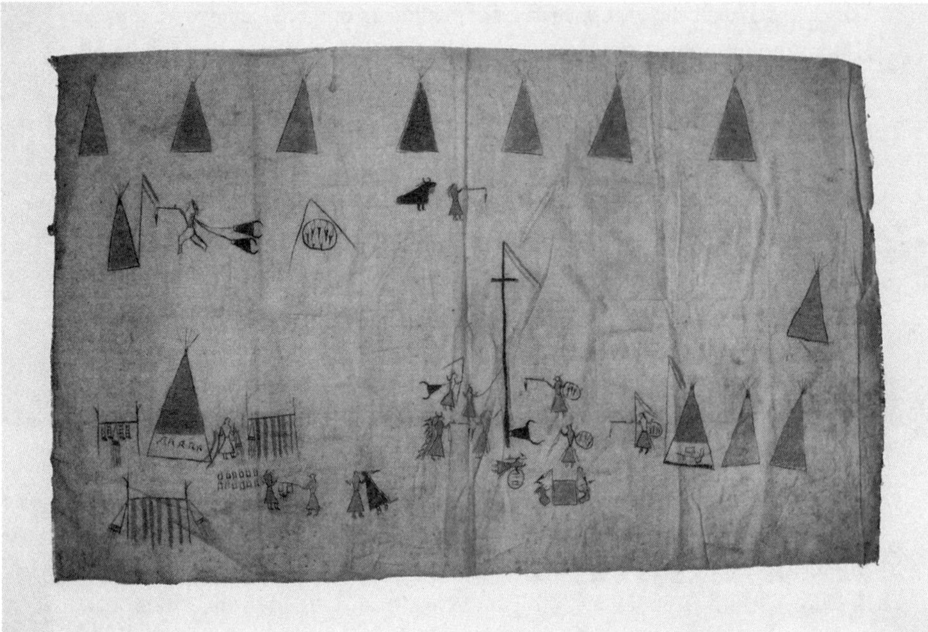

FIGURE 4.4. Lakota Sioux, Sun Dance drawing, ca. 1875. Pigments on muslin, 83 × 138 cm. Vatican Museums, Vatican City, inv. 107323. Source: Katherine Aigner et al., *The Americas: Collections from the Vatican Ethnological Museum* (2015), 95. https://catalogo.museivaticani.va/index.php/Detail/objects/MV.107323.0.0.

view of the ceremony, their deep knowledge of the event indicating that the artist was also likely a dancer.

A counterclockwise description of the Sun Dance provides an understanding of the sacred nature of the experience and reveals the complexity of interactions. Next to the red tipi in the upper left corner, a dancer has pierced his back. Blood flows out as he drags two buffalo skulls behind him. He holds his pipe with the bowl facing him and the stem facing out, pointing toward the sky. His prayers float upward, connecting him to the Great Mystery, as Dana observed in our discussion. As Oglala Lakota artist Arthur Amiotte notes, "through sacrifice, through being made sacred, through being transformed, his very spirit selves are attached to That Which Is Sacred."[86] Beside him, a shield embellished with seven eagle feathers rests. In the lower left, a blue tipi has geometric designs on the bottom reminiscent of people's faces. The artist has not colored in the entire tipi but has left the lower section with the geometric-like lines, creating an X-ray-like technique that allows the viewer to see the activities happening inside the tipi.[87] "X-ray" is used by art historian Janet Berlo and others to describe the way the artist's drawing technique enables viewers to peer through multiple layers of the image.[88] This method was also used by Swift Dog, a Hunkpapa Lakota.[89] Across the drawing in the lower right corner, the artist has used the same method with a red tipi to depict a singer pounding his drum and singing for the dancers outside.

Dana and I talked about the importance of medicine and the burning of sage in this sacred event. Outside the blue tipi in the lower left corner, a woman carries a pipe bag filled with medicine and prayer cloths that sweep across the corners of the tipi, suggesting the animated movements of her walk.[90] Prayer cloths surround the woman, and porcupine-quill work bags hang on the edges. Below her, a woman in red and a woman in green hold two tins over a flame. Dana shared with me that throughout the ceremony they would have burned the sage with its sweet and spicy odor. In the center of the image, a woman in red holds a pipe with the bowl facing toward her, the stem facing out. Beside her stands a two-legged bull. The two legs hint that it may be an other-worldly attendant, a peek into the relations between the seen and unseen narrative of the Sun Dance.[91]

Two women sit around a green square, creating a sacred space in the center of the image. Dana observed that in this space, a woman in blue lies on the ground; a vision has overcome her.[92] She holds a pipe and a shield. To the left of the pole, there are men tied with ropes to the cottonwood tree. They have pierced themselves, in an act of sacrifice. One of the dancers still has the skull that was attached to his back in the process of piercing. Blood flows from his back. A woman in blue with an eagle-feather headdress holds a pipe with the bowl toward her. Prayer cloths in red, blue, and green extend from the top of the tree, drawn at a diagonal to create a sense of movement. The breeze that carries the prayer cloths, together with the steps of the dancers as the buffalo skulls pierce them, indicate that the ceremony is in progress. Like the Lakota culture, which continues to grow and adapt, the drawing, too, is not static, as it takes on meanings through time and interpretations. For this I am thankful to Dana for illuminating more deeply the spiritual significance of this sacred image. Through the movement of the viewer's eye around the drawing, the viewer is invited to witness a sacred ceremony that continues to this day.

The composition and vivid choice of colors bear some similarity to ledger drawings of the time, including some that imprisoned Cheyenne warriors made at Fort Marion, circa 1875. In particular, the work invites comparison with artwork by Minneconjou Lakota/Teton Sioux, Mató Nájin Standing Bear (1859–1933).[93] Like the unidentified artist, Standing Bear created epic narrative drawings, often on muslin, using sparing but finely placed details. After witnessing Sitting Bull's

Sun Dance at Rosebud River in the summer of 1876, Standing Bear went on to paint images of the Sun Dance, of animal dreamers. He traveled with Buffalo Bill's Wild West to London in 1887 and Paris in 1889, defying expectations as an Indigenous traveler in the age of federal restrictions on any Native American travel outside the reservation system.[94] In 1900, he made images of the iconic Battle of the Greasy Grass (Battle of the Little Big Horn) of 1876.[95]

In 1902, another Indigenous traveler from the Plains, Sicangu and Oglala Luther Standing Bear (1868–1913), journeyed with Buffalo Bill throughout Britain and Europe, escaping the police state of the Rosebud Reservation.[96] Regarding the Sun Dance, Luther Standing Bear explained: "The Sun Dance started many years before Christopher Columbus drifted to these shores. We then knew that there was a God above us all. We called God 'Wakan Tanka' or the 'Big Holy' or sometimes 'Grandfather' . . . It was a sacrificial dance."[97] Luther Standing Bear emphasizes the longevity of the Sun Dance tradition, and his conceptual framework has a parallel with the artwork by the artist Mató Nájin Standing Bear. With the inclusion of multiple sacred figures, as well as the all-encompassing perspective, the epic drawing by the once-known artist displayed at the VME creates a visionary moment.[98]

More than half of the people featured in the drawing are women, a noteworthy detail given that usually only men danced in the Sun Dance. However, Lakota traditions are flexible. Although in the historical record men created ledger drawings, this is changing in contemporary Lakota art, and the unidentified artist's work here indicates at least an affinity with women artists.[99] Lakota artist Colleen Cutschall notes the ongoing importance of historical documents like this drawing: "while ledger art itself is not sacred art, images like these speak directly to our sacred traditions. That these traditions survive at all speaks to the tenacity of the Lakota people. Historical arts of this kind are important to generations of Native people who have lost their sacred traditions and are in the process of recovering them today."[100] This drawing, like the other Indigenous arts discussed in this chapter, forms part of an epic historical tradition that is both persistent and flexible.

To make an important point about the limits of understanding sacred events and the need to respect their processes, I turn to a story about the experience of Father Jutz, a German Jesuit missionary among the Lakota. Although Jutz worked among Lakota people from 1885 to 1897, he never learned the Lakota language and, throughout his writings, used colonial terminology that denigrated Indigenous people.[101] He observed at least one Ghost Dance, but his understanding remained cursory at best. In the 1890s, the Ghost Dance was part of a resistance movement across the Great Plains inspired by the vision of Paiute spiritual leader Wokova, a prophet who foresaw Indigenous futures and protested against settler colonialism.[102] Like the Sun Dance, the Ghost Dance forms an important example of the visionary movements of Indigenous peoples across the Plains and continues to impact the religious ceremonies and activism of Indigenous communities today.[103] Jutz stood in the center of a Ghost Dance at the White Clay Reservation in 1890. He witnessed dancers caught in a trance and asked them to tell him what they had seen, even offering payment. He described the (to him) frustrating experience in a journal entry:

> During the dance I took up my position in the middle of the circle, dressed in my religious habit, and from my place of observation I could see everything that went on. I went over to those who were "resurrected from the dead" and asked them if they had spoken with their deceased friends. I offered them a dollar if they would tell me their experiences, but they would not answer me. I offered them two, three, four, five dollars, but they only looked at me and said not a word.[104]

Shortly after this, the US Army massacred hundreds of Indigenous men, women, and children at Wounded Knee Creek in an attempt to wipe out Indigenous peoples across the Plains and facilitate white settlement, part of the broader practice of genocide in the wave of settler colonialism throughout the nineteenth and early twentieth centuries on Turtle Island.[105]

This anecdote about Jutz represents his cultural insensitivity and an example of Lakota cultural sensitivity that reverberates with my counternarrative of the VME, in that although missionaries like Jutz sent in a plethora of things, their colonial gaze did not include understanding them. The Sun Dance drawing presents an artistic response and a recording of traditional Lakota practices, an eternal sovereignty, that continues to exist in the face of intense missionary intervention, settler colonialism, and misunderstanding. Despite many hardships, Indigenous peoples continued to follow their cultural practices, although the practice of religious ceremonies, including the Ghost Dance and the Sun Dance, went underground. Still situated in the Vatican and now on display in *Anima Mundi* with sparse information posted, the Sun Dance drawing and other Lakota materials continue to offer up visionary lessons of mobility and of the Great Mystery, Wakan'tanka, for historians of Indigenous art today.

We can understand some of the dynamics of Indigenous presence in a material but also spiritual way by considering the movement of cultural belongings like the Lakota drawing from Turtle Island to the Eternal City. Contemplating the Lakota drawing as an eternal sovereign allows researchers to think in more expansive and critical ways about the VME, especially when pondering archival research as a form of ceremony that complements the sacred and secular materials discussed.[106] If we contemplate eternal sovereigns as ancestral art history lessons, then following the movement of the belongings and their eternal mobility defies the Vatican's missionary imposition of Indigenous art as the pope's domain and "gifts" on earth.

Thinking of the arc of the Lakota drawing, both the motifs present in the drawing and the biography of the belonging, opens a dialogue on the ongoing importance of the Indigenous material collections at the Vatican Museums and the need for such institutions to acknowledge the brutish legacies of violence and dispossession toward Indigenous American communities.[107] Many of the belongings sent in by missionaries remained in the permanent collections of the Vatican and formed the Vatican Missionary Ethnological Museum now called *Anima Mundi*. As discussed in the introduction, *Anima Mundi* lies beneath the Pinacoteca within the walled fortress of the Vatican Museums. This telling placement of Indigenous artworks in a basement at the exit with minimal information provided, underneath the masterpieces of Italian art, reinforces the hierarchy whereby Indigenous art is seen and experienced as beneath western art, a framework that the VME organizers also promoted.[108] This book challenges the existing papal narrative of Indigenous erasure by centering Indigenous cultural belongings and iconographic traditions in ancestral art history lessons that continue to resonate.

Cree Moccasins: Beaded Beauty for Self-Sustaining Practices

Like the Sun Dance drawing, moccasins have an important place in asserting Indigeneity across the earth and in the spiritual realm. A fine pair of moosehide, high-top moccasins included in the VME exhibition is evidence of Cree and possibly Métis artistry by an unidentified female artisan (see plate 14).[109] The Vatican Americas catalog gives only "Cree" as the description, noting that the artist made them sometime between 1880 and 1900.[110] There is no sign of wear or tear on the hide, and the beadwork is also in pristine condition. The tanned and smoked moose hide is a russet-brown color, and the artist has edged it with a serrated pattern. The process of hunting the moose, and then cleaning and tanning the hide so it will be soft and pliable, is a practice still carried on today, and for many it is an important aspect of Cree ways of being in the world.[111] It is a labor-intensive practice that connects Cree ontologies extending back centuries. The English word *moccasin* comes from the Cree word *maskisina*, meaning footwear.[112]

Moccasins resonate with me on a personal level. They remind me of the beadwork practices of my sisters and me, and of my Métis ancestry. I find beadwork a meditative and reflective practice that requires patience and persistence. Bead artists are only limited in their imagination in terms of the imagery produced and the colors used. Examining the evidence of Métis and Cree beadwork, I am very proud of the ingenuity and perseverance of Métis and all Indigenous women.[113] The floral beadwork designs of the moccasins held at the Vatican resonate with both Cree and Métis design and history. The Métis had a sweeping and dramatic impact on the designs used by First Nations quill and bead artisans in the eighteenth and nineteenth centuries, bringing fresh floral designs and imagery into dialogue with First Nations designs, which were largely geometric.[114] Certainly, bead workers now reference historical imagery, but we also draw inspiration from the dynamics of today. The artistry of Métis and Cree people flourished across Turtle Island, and these floral moccasins are a reminder of that deep knowledge and productivity.

The artist used red, green, yellow, pink, orange, blue, and bronze beads to create the floral beadwork on the vamp (the moccasin top) and around the base of the ankle in a floral rosette pattern. The artist used bronze beads at accent points on the leaves and the tips of the tendrils, which would have caught the light and shone when the wearer put them on. A thin strip of red and blue silk outlines the vamp design and complements the beadwork. Notably, the floral beadwork design has not been filled in; instead, the moose hide provides the background. This is characteristic of Cree and Métis beadwork, unlike Crow beadwork, for example. The floral beadwork style is reminiscent of Athabaskan floral designs as well, conveying the multiple influences that Cree and Métis women worked with, including beadwork examples from their neighbors to the west.[115] Also of note are the moose hide ties that the artist made for the wearer to wrap around the ankles. This feature speaks vividly of the elegance of late nineteenth-century moccasin style. Artisans made the moccasins functional to keep the foot protected and warm, but the footwear was also beautifully beaded, filled with floral patterns found in northern Canada and imaginatively rendered depictions of plants that could also have had medicinal significance.[116]

The finely beaded moccasins are evidence of Cree artwork that is functional and demonstrates that Cree women made many articles to sell to tourists, missionaries, and collectors to support themselves. Considering the style of the moccasins and the archival note, they were made for a woman.[117] Cree and Métis women were also making finely beaded belongings for an audience of hunters, travelers, missionaries, and their own husbands and lovers. As art historian Sherry Farrell Racette notes, “Métis women responded to the needs of the people they dressed and consciously created consumer desire for the goods they produced, often using the bodies of their own men for advertisement.”[118] Whereas the organizers of the VME did not recognize Cree and Métis beadwork as art nor historical document in the Hall of North America, and Indigenous people were seen as dependent on missionaries for instruction and guidance, these moccasins offer up a different reading. The Cree moccasins are an example of artistry and a testament to this other way of thinking of beadwork as an ongoing archive of Indigenous experience and care for the community.

By referencing a variety of imagery and media, Indigenous bead workers break down old stereotypes about Indigenous creativity and hierarchies within collecting histories that distinguish between “traditional” (that is, precontact) and “contemporary” arts practices. Moccasins also signify as reminders of the importance over the past three centuries of the beadwork economy for many communities of Native women across Turtle Island in supporting their families by selling tourist art.[119] For Cree and other Indigenous nations of Turtle Island, beadwork exists within a framework of artistic expression as an Indigenous methodology that connects current Indigenous makers with their ancestors through creativity.[120] Beadwork is a tactile and visual form of storytelling with subversive potential. Cree moccasins, along with other Indigenous cultural belongings discussed here, are evidence of the Cree artisan’s worldview. They present us with a story that has up to this point been ignored in the context of the VME. This story I detect in the artist’s engagement with the moose hide—the curving tendrils of the beadwork, the uniformity of design, and the experimental color choice—and shows the hand of an accomplished bead worker. The floral beadwork is evidence of the Cree artist’s knowledge of flora and the “regenerative potential” of medicinal plants, connecting her with a landscape of Cree ontologies.[121] The curving tendrils and finely made petals of the flowers evoke the artist’s relationship with the animate Cree universe, wherein humans and other-than-humans are deeply connected. In short, Cree artisans, like other Indigenous makers, are cognizant of the spiritual, sacred nature of the natural world and honor their place in it as artists, teachers, makers, and scholars. Considered as cultural belongings and primary documents, the moccasins and materials discussed here present an alternative narrative to that of western “progress” and “civilization” and Native obsolescence espoused at the VME.

The moccasins visualize a narrative of the sacred artistic relationship that artists such as this once known Cree maker had with her creation and the infinite world around her. Moccasins unite the wearer with the infinite world, and visual analysis of these moccasins connects us with all our relations. For

Indigenous peoples, the wearing of moccasins symbolizes and solidifies the multitude of relationships we hold with the Creator and our respect for all realms of the universe in the now and hereafter. The footwear of this unknown Cree artisan presents an Indigenous way of knowing and being in the world. As Siksika (Blackfoot) curator Gerald McMaster notes: "As we begin to rearticulate our cultural identities, lifeways, values, and beliefs, Native Americans must realize that objects such as these moccasins are more than a reflection or representation of the past—they are products of the past that point to the future; they signify the potential that exists within our communities. The objects speak to individuals, families, tribal groups, students, and scholars, and help to define our humanity on earth."[122] Thus, moccasins signify on a multitude of levels, and the Cree pair at the Vatican are no exception. The culturally distinctive patterns participate in an iconography created by Indigenous women that connects the observer with dynamic tribal histories of trade and exchange among Indigenous communities, fur traders, missionaries, hunters, travelers and settlers, and are a prominent symbol of Indigenous pride.[123] Moccasins have a long history of asserting Indigeneity, with more recent initiatives on social media such as #rockyourmoccs and Métis artist Christi Belcourt's *Walking with Our Sisters* moccasin vamp exhibition honoring missing and murdered Indigenous women.[124]

Stolen Heritage: Kwakwaka'wakw Ancestral Sun Mask

In all published accounts of the Vatican Museums, at the Vatican website, and within curatorial wall texts at the Ethnological Museum *Anima Mundi*, cultural belongings are always described as "gifts."[125] Indigenous communities did not give consent to have their belongings taken or displayed at the VME, and this terminology of "gift" denies the violent acquisition period of the 1920s and pope Pius XI's greed, a time of missionary brutality.[126] Operating under the aegis of Pius XI's culture of conquest, missionaries never asked Indigenous communities for their cultural belongings; they just seized them. The theft and looting of Indigenous art and ancestors from communities across Turtle Island and the globe were couched in a Catholic colonial language and propaganda of "gifts" and "offerings" for the VME and is still reiterated today throughout the Vatican Museums. In 2019 the Vatican Museums dropped the term "missionary" from the Vatican Missionary Ethnological Museum and changed the name to Ethnological Museum *Anima Mundi*. This rebranding effort largely is a whitewash of the missionary origins and violent acquisition history of the collection in a practice to forget and draw attention away from the history of plunder and missionaries' genocidal labors.[127] This confiscation of heritage created a legacy of annihilation and severed familial and community ties that Indigenous communities and museum professionals are still wrestling with today. The VME and the collection that stems from it, which is now the Ethnological Museum *Anima Mundi*, remains an uneasy and unresolved reminder of this violent history.

The term "gift" elides and denies the fact that missionaries also *stole* sacred materials from Native communities under the Indian Act and the potlatch ban and to meet Pius XI's list of demands for the VME.[128] Both the Canadian federal government and the missionaries viewed the potlatch, an important celebration of First Nations life and history, as a threat to progress and as an impediment to the conversion of Indigenous nations to Christianity. Missionaries opposed the potlatch, arguing it hindered the spiritual health of Native people.[129] For these reasons, in 1885 the federal government passed a potlatch ban, which remained in force until 1951 and devastated First Nations potlatch practices.

To give just one example of the enforcement of this ban, a raid took place on the Northwest Coast in 1921 on Chief Dan Cramer, during a potlatch in the Kwakwaka'wakw village of 'Mimkwamlis (Village Island), about one hundred and ninety miles northwest of Vancouver. Indian Agent William Halliday (1913–51) and Royal Canadian Mounted Police officers seized more than six hundred cultural belongings, including sacred masks and other regalia, rattles, and family heirlooms.[130] The government also imprisoned twenty dancers at the potlatch, both men and women, for refusing to hand over their cultural belongings.

Halliday exhibited the seized items in Alert Bay, a village on Vancouver Island, and charged visitors to view them. He later sold them to the Canadian Museum of History in addition to museums and exhibitions in the United States, Britain, and across Europe, including the VME.[131] Museum curators have returned some of these cultural belongings.[132] Although the ancient potlatch practice continued in secret, the policy of erasure and intolerance has left a destructive legacy.[133] The federal government seized Kwakwaka'wakw cultural belongings in an overt attempt to eradicate Kwakwaka'wakw spiritual and cultural traditions and, furthermore, to assimilate First Nations to a Christian and "civilized" worldview. In other words, the Indigenous cultural belongings, considered living beings for Kwakwaka'wakw, threatened the foundations of settler-colonial society.[134]

Belongings stolen and sent in to the VME by the Jesuits and Oblates operating on the Northwest Coast and Alaska included Yu'pik masks, Haida rattles, baskets, masks and argillite miniature totems made during the height of the potlatch ban.[135] The Oblates seized and then displayed an ancestral sun mask of the Kwakwaka'wakw at the VME. (see plate 15). The sun mask is considered an animate mask, the sun being an ancestor of the Kwakwaka'wakw. The sun mask was and is danced during the potlatch by the families that have exclusive hereditary privileges to the mask.[136] Out of respect for this mask, which was used in dance ceremonies and may be considered as an active being, I will not go into a visual analysis of it here, but mention it to make an important point about unwilling travelers that were displayed at the VME.[137]

Missionaries did not ask permission to present sacred cultural belongings, nor did the Kwakwaka'wakw authorize their display. The treatment of this mask is evidence of how missionaries worked with the government and Pius XI to degrade the cultures and values of Indigenous peoples across Turtle Island. As Kwakwaka'wakw curator Gloria Cranmer Webster notes, "We do not have a word for repatriation in the Kwak'wala language. The closest we come to it is the word *u'mista*, which describes the return of people taken captive in raids. It also means the return of something important. We are working toward the *u'mista* of much that was almost lost to us."[138] Processes of repatriation have begun on the Northwest Coast, with museums such as the Canadian Museum of History now involved in repatriating sacred materials, but discussions surrounding the Vatican returning belongings to Indigenous communities on the Pacific Northwest Coast have not even begun. The seizure of the Kwakwaka'wakw cultural belongings and their subsequent display at the VME as "gifts," along with other Indigenous cultural belongings from across Turtle Island, is evidence of the iconoclastic and genocidal measures that missionaries used and the brutal and brutalizing force that the Vatican Museums continue to exert today.

The VME's description of the materials as "gifts" continues to this day in exhibition panels at the Vatican Museums in a gross negligence, which erase the history and importance that cultural belongings have for the prosperity and survival of Indigenous communities. Scholar Alison Brown describes the ongoing consultations between museums in the UK and First Nations in Canada: "Given that many founding collections were assembled at a time when indigenous peoples were thought to be assimilating or dying out, the use of these collections by their descendants testifies to the resilience of indigenous peoples, to their present moral and legal rights of ownership, and to the responsibility of museums to make collections accessible."[139] Museums have a responsibility to work with Indigenous communities given the nature of collections created under duress and involving lack of consent. Indigenous artists and knowledge keepers and scholars will keep advocating for access to cultural belongings. Although some museums, such as the Pitt Rivers in Oxford, have worked with First Nations and other Indigenous communities, there are currently few legal precedents in the UK for repatriation.[140] Many countries and institutions prefer to work on a case-by-case basis and collaborate with advisors from Indigenous communities.[141] The same legal limbo pertains in Italy, as the laws against repatriation are very strict and museums do not have the same proactive attitude toward repatriation as in other countries.[142] It is encouraging that visits by Indigenous scholars to museum collections are on the rise, but there is still a long way to go to address the colonizing mindset of the Ethnological Museum *Anima Mundi* displays and to make the collections accessible to researchers.

Promising developments in the field of digital repatriation, digital archiving, and the decolonizing of archival methods are shifting the hegemony of museum spaces and our understanding of who has the right to control, interpret, and research Indigenous cultures. At the Vatican, however, the story is different.[143] Brown notes that many museums in the UK and Canada now "collaborate with originating community and diaspora colleagues to develop technologies that address cultural protocols and also challenge the legacies of colonial collecting practices and existing institutional structures so as to enable interpretation of heritage materials that takes account of alternative knowledge systems."[144] As of this writing, the Vatican has not implemented any processes of repatriation. An Indigenous delegation from Canada in spring 2022 had a very brief viewing of a few cultural belongings from the collections, but there was not a sustained research visit. The delegation had very mixed reactions to the viewing opportunity, as the Vatican curators insisted throughout the meeting that they were stewards of the collection, and delegates were not given any documentation or further explanation of the collection.[145] The Vatican curatorial team composed of Father Mapelli and conservationists policed the visit, as the delegates also were not allowed to handle their own belongings. The Vatican Museums' imprisonment of Indigenous cultural belongings and Indigenous life and dictations of care, claiming that they are the rightful stewards, are disturbing. My discussions of this matter with a former Vatican curator corroborated that there had been one Indigenous researcher about twenty years ago, but the consultation did not proceed well, as the perspectives of the researcher and the Vatican curators clashed.[146]

The Ethnological Museum *Anima Mundi* remains firm in its colonial stance that Indigenous cultural belongings are the pope's "gifts." The usage of the term "gift" does not begin to address the complex social relations and colonial dynamics that need to be unpacked, and it obscures the narrative of missionary violence and plunder. It is simplistic terminology and thinking that shuts down any type of conversation, when, now more than ever, conversations and action need to happen to move away from the rhetoric of truth and reconciliation. I am referencing here the panels I have seen most recently in curatorial exhibition spaces, Vatican publications, and the recent Indigenous delegation visit. The text panels and current publications do not acknowledge their importance to Indigenous communities of Turtle Island. We can suppose that the Vatican does not encourage or permit researchers for several reasons. They would need to have curatorial staff with proper training to ensure the protocols for sacred items. The current exhibition space is dedicated to the conservation lab in which sacred belongings are on very partial display and within visible access for museum visitors, showcasing their work as conservators rather than sensitivity to Indigenous communities' cultural belongings. The white sheets they place over the cultural belongings give an eerie impression of death. The prevalence of sacred items and human remains and their lack of awareness and sensitivity to statutes such as the 1990 US Native American Graves Protection and Repatriation Act are also factors in their gate-keeping. In Canada, the Task Force for First Nations and Museums has called for more cultural sensitivity toward Indigenous American cultural belongings, although it is up to each museum's discretion to repatriate materials, whereas in the United States repatriation is federally mandated.[147] In 2015, Canada's Truth and Reconciliation Commission made a recommendation and issued call to action #67 for the Canadian Museums Association to come up with a series of guidelines and best practices for museums in Canada to work proactively with Indigenous communities on museum collections and restitution. "Don't wait, repatriate!" is their motto.[148] In fact, in a conversation with a conservator in Rome, they did admit that this mask and several others in the collection were stolen but that restitution was not their priority.[149]

A major ongoing issue is that the Vatican Ethnological Museum *Anima Mundi* beholds itself to no ethical museum policy or recommendation, such as the Canadian Museum Association's guidelines or the United Nations Declaration on the Rights of Indigenous Peoples (2007). Indigenous conservators and curators are not employed or consulted. The handling of the stolen treasures by conservators at Ethnological Museum *Anima Mundi*, if we think again of the handling of the Inuvialuit kayak, pointing to its dimensions and emphasizing it as a papal trophy, is part of the ongoing violence of the Vatican Museums. The Indigenous belongings are bereft from their makers and have had the curious gaze and prolonged stare of popes Pius XI and Francis upon them. I think about Pius XI walking through *Anima Mundi* late at night wringing his cold hands in all his greed.

Elizabeth Povinelli's research reminds me, however, that archival power can also work against itself. She notes that "archival power is also, and perhaps most profoundly, about the orientation of truth to some lost trace of the real."[150] Furthermore, colonial archives, as Indigenous studies scholars Zoe Todd and Crystal Fraser note, always remain partial narrations, and my experience working in religious archives and the Vatican archives in Rome thus forms part of a movement of counternarratives that challenges the one-sided story espoused by the VME.[151]

Stolen Treasures: Eternal Sovereigns in the Eternal City

J. Garvin of the Venerable College of Rome, a missionary-in-training, gave this rather romantic account of the VME experience: "It is impossible even to enumerate all the different sections of this wonderful exhibition—one passes from the snows of Alaska and Canada to the tropical dwellings of Africa and India, a few yards from China and one is walking through Australasia; in Mesopotamia one can hear Oriental music on the gramophone, and Japan is delicious with orange blossom and the sound of silver bells."[152] The VME overwhelmed Garvin's senses. By the end of his experience, he confessed that the exhibition had thoroughly exhausted him: "This Exhibition has the disadvantage of being too big—its immensity leaves the mind crushed, but not one English Catholic can visit it without being a little more proud of the Church and the Empire, the two greatest institutions which the world has ever known."[153]

Rather than our minds being closed and exhausted, I hope our perspectives have been opened to considering the compelling evidence that Garvin did not sense. This chapter has explored the eloquence of Indigenous cultural belongings, their spiritual presence and persuasive power, and the beauty and diversity of Indigenous iconographic traditions. Indigenous artists across Turtle Island survived and adapted to the shifting cultures and social conditions of the nineteenth and early twentieth centuries, and made their eloquent cultural belongings in the face of severe challenges. Contrary to the western representations and evolutionist theories reiterated in inter/national expositions like the VME, Indigenous peoples were not silent or dying out; we were fighting for our inclusion as modern citizens. To this day, Indigenous arts in Vatican City are weighty reminders of that negotiation with and adaptation to the modern world.

Missionaries misinterpreted cultural belongings displayed at the VME using the simplistic terminology of "beautiful" or "grotesque."[154] Indigenous cultural belongings now lodged firmly behind the closed doors of the Ethnological Museum *Anima Mundi* are reminders of the ongoing colonial dynamic that Indigenous nations and scholars are still working against in a broader movement to decolonize museums, archives, and classrooms. In this way, I echo the observations of Royal Ontario Museum curator Trudy Nicks about the ongoing need for Indigenous responses to museum collections: "the restudying of old collections from new angles may help to explain to museum visitors how Aboriginal peoples have maintained vital and distinct cultures in spite of contact with dominant societies which have long expected them to vanish."[155] The need for more investigation into the Vatican collections and other collections of Indigenous American cultural belongings in Italy is an open challenge that will require grit and determination. As Gerald Conaty notes: "countless items currently languish in museum collections worldwide, bereft of their cultural contact and their human creators. Many of these objects are ordinary, of the sort in everyday use; many others, however, are charged with cosmological and spiritual meaning . . . Although the ways in which the museum community is currently addressing their responsibilities give us some cause for hope, the legacy of colonialism is proving to be remarkably stubborn."[156] Ominously, Conaty adds that it is often the directors and global museum leaders that are the "most insidious obstacle to repatriation," and the Vatican fits this pattern.[157] When pope Pius XI concluded the VME in 1926 as part of the closing ceremony of the Holy Year, he declared that he wanted the museum and its collections to remain as an open book for researchers, which is a far cry from the *Anima Mundi* collection and its conditions of access today. Pius XI kept forty thousand of the cultural belongings for the museum collection that would open one year later.[158] Indigenous cultural belongings have waited almost a century since the VME, long forgotten and ignored, but today more than ever they need care, research, attention, and rematriation.

Placing Indigenous cultural belongings at the center of this story as markers of Indigenous cultural and intellectual sovereignty flips the colonial script that prevails throughout the archival records of the VME.[159] Reclaiming Indigenous artifacts as cultural belongings opens an Indigenous spatial orientation that acknowledges the contemporary reality of diverse Indigenous nations and artistic practices. Eternal sovereigns defy the papal and missionary logic of dispossession. The stories here present the arc of materials and souls, and suggest the multiplicity of aesthetic, intellectual, and spiritual practices for Indigenous communities across Turtle Island. Although missionaries disregarded the sovereignty of Indigenous cultural belongings in a gross neglect that continues to this day in Vatican displays, they present us with ancestral art history lessons that continue to inspire. Eternal sovereigns confront silent eloquence and form part of resistance tactics. If we read Indigenous cultural belongings as articulations of subversive potential, we can unsettle colonial sovereignty claims and undermine the colonial unknowing prevalent throughout the VME. Watching some of the footage from the Indigenous delegation visit to the *Anima Mundi* collection, the words of Norman Yakeleya, a residential-school survivor and member of the Dene Nation of the Northwest Territories, ring in my mind, "For God's sakes, give them back to our people."[160] The analysis here of Indigenous cultural belongings as overlooked archives provides evidence of the need for a vast re-storying and restoring of Indigenous cultural belongings to decolonize the Vatican's art history and collecting practices of plunder.

Epilogue

DEUS EX MACHINA

An Indigenous Protester at the Vatican Missionary Exposition

Although barred at the entryway to the Vatican Missionary Exposition (VME), Anthony Martin Fernando (1864–1949), an Australian Aborigine of the Dharug people, activist, and toymaker from Woolloomooloo, leafleted visitors to the VME in 1925 while standing outside Saint Peter's Basilica in the Vatican.[1] Pilgrims came from around the world to complete their penance at the seven Holy Year churches, ending with Saint Peter's, and thousands of Australians uttering "Viva Australia!" attended.[2] Dressed in a dark coat embroidered with many tiny skeletons, Fernando handed out protest leaflets that called for an inquiry into the colonial genocide of thousands of Australian Aborigines. As Australian settlers, colonial officials, and pilgrims came to Rome to obtain blessings from the pope, Fernando demanded action for the injustices Indigenous peoples faced.[3]

While Fernando was protesting Aboriginal genocide, Benedictine missionaries at New Norcia in Western Australia and the Missionaries of the Sacred Hearts of Jesus and Mary had seized and sent in ancestral art, regalia, and many cultural belongings for display at the VME.[4] Boomerangs, healing tools such as a bundle of eucalyptus leaves, ceremonial belts, and bark paintings were included in the exhibition to illustrate Australia as one of the founding "primitive" civilizations of the world.[5] A photograph shows a Belgian missionary of the Sacred Hearts order at the VME, surrounded by Aboriginal cultural belongings, including boomerangs and sacred ancestral figures from Oceania seen at right above his head (see figure E.1). The glass display case beside him is filled with cultural belongings such as necklaces of shell and ancestor figures, including one of a divinity, Rogo, associated with fertility.[6] At far right, a case contains material culture from Hawai'i, including *kapa*, or mantels of pounded bark cloth (a method of dressing that dates back centuries before missionary contact); grass skirts; intricate feather fans; and *lei*, or necklaces, made of whale bone.[7] Along the top of the case, a miniature catamaran, possibly from Papua New Guinea, is also visible.[8] On the right side of the image, one can see that the display case is wide open; this too was a moment of colonial disorder, an unofficial image of the archive off balance.[9]

In his leaflet and in his journal, Fernando wrote about Aboriginal uses of the boomerang to illustrate the logical, scientific methods Australian Aborigines used in their daily practices. His writing implies that he visited the VME, perhaps even the display shown in the photograph mentioned above, and he wanted to illustrate Aboriginal uses of the boomerang in a nuanced and non-static way—in other words, counter to how Indigenous culture was framed at the exhibition.[10] In any case, he was arrested, questioned, and detained in Rome, but his leaflet and protest still stand as a reminder of an undoing of colonial unknowing (see figure E.2). The leaflet headline is "I pochi Aborigeni che rimangono ancora in Australia" (The few Aboriginals that still remain in Australia). In the text, Fernando calls on the pope during the Holy Jubilee Year of 1925 to address the injustices faced by Aboriginal Australians: "From the forests and the woods, they [Aboriginal Australians] appeal to the Lord and through the pope to the Christians to protect them from their vile and ruthless assassins." If Fernando did see the VME, surely he derided the simplistic binaries it promoted, and he most certainly would not have described the collection of cultural belongings taken from Oceania as gifts.[11] He certainly would have critiqued its lack of acknowledgment of the devastating impact of settler colonialism on Indigenous lands, an issue he strongly highlighted in his oratory and leaflet. The Italian police, operating under Mussolini's fascist system of surveillance, arrested

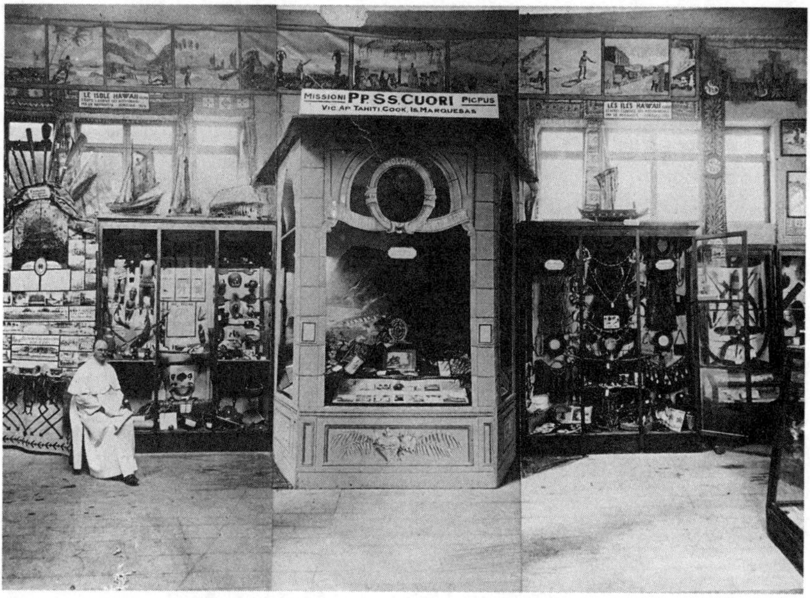

FIGURE E.1. Sacred Hearts of Jesus and Mary missionary with cultural belongings from Oceania, Vatican Missionary Exposition, 1925. Courtesy of Damiaanmuseum, Tremelo, Belgium.

Fernando, and he was held as a prisoner, like Antonio Gramsci and many others who critiqued the cultural hegemony of Italian society. When a British legal friend learned of Fernando's destitute situation, he petitioned the Italian government, an ally of Britain at this time, to release him. Italian police then forcefully escorted him to the Alps, where he had to make his way on foot over the mountains and then on to Britain.[12] Fernando's deportation was an overt attempt on the part of Italian authorities to quash his activism and silence his voice.[13]

As far as the historical record shows, Fernando operated largely as a lone activist and protester, although he must have had assistance to produce the more than ten thousand leaflets that he distributed. Historian Fiona Paisley notes that Fernando is an exceptional case, and her model of inquiry forms an important stepping stone and timely interlude in understanding the Jubilee Year at the Vatican and its impact not only on one Aboriginal man's life, but on Indigenous peoples globally. Fernando's activism also raises the question whether there might have been other Indigenous protesters at the VME. I have not found any evidence that other Indigenous activists attended the VME as visitors or protested like Fernando, but they were there, represented in artworks and via their cultural belongings.[14] Although Fernando may have thought of

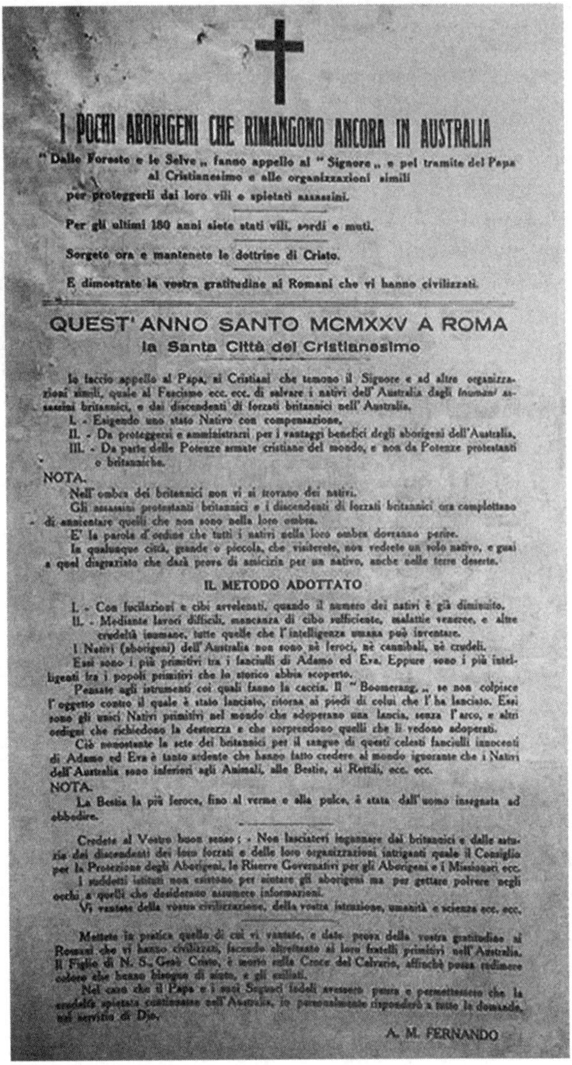

I POCHI ABORIGENI CHE RIMANGONO ANCORA IN AUSTRALIA

"Dalle Foreste e le Selve„ fanno appello al "Signore„ e pel tramite del Papa al Cristianesimo e alle organizzazioni simili per proteggerli dai loro vili e spietati assassini.

Per gli ultimi 180 anni siete stati vili, sordi e muti.

Sorgete ora e mantenete le dottrine di Cristo.

E dimostrate la vostra gratitudine ai Romani che vi hanno civilizzati.

QUEST' ANNO SANTO MCMXXV A ROMA

la Santa Città del Cristianesimo

Io faccio appello al Papa, ai Cristiani che temono il Signore e ad altre organizzazioni simili, quale al Fascismo ecc. ecc. di salvare i nativi dell' Australia dagli *inumani* assassini britannici, e dai discendenti di forzati britannici nell' Australia.

I. - Esigendo uno stato Nativo con compensazione.

II. - Da proteggersi e amministrarsi per i vantaggi benefici degli aborigeni dell'Australia.

III. - Da parte delle Potenze armate cristiane del mondo, e non da Potenze protestanti o britanniche.

NOTA.

Nell' ombra dei britannici non vi si trovano dei nativi.

Gli assassini protestanti britannici e i discendenti di forzati britannici ora complottano di annientare quelli che non sono nella loro ombra.

E' la parola d'ordine che tutti i nativi nella loro ombra dovranno perire.

In qualunque città, grande o piccola, che visiterete, non vedrete un solo nativo, e guai a quel disgraziato che darà prova di amicizia per un nativo, anche nelle terre deserte.

IL METODO ADOTTATO

I. - Con fucilazioni e cibi avvelenati, quando il numero dei nativi è già diminuito.

II. - Mediante lavori difficili, mancanza di cibo sufficiente, malattie veneree, e altre crudeltà inumane, tutte quelle che l' intelligenza umana può inventare.

I Nativi (aborigeni) dell' Australia non sono nè feroci, nè cannibali, nè crudeli.

Essi sono i più primitivi tra i fanciulli di Adamo ed Eva. Eppure sono i più intelligenti tra i popoli primitivi che lo storico abbia scoperto.

Pensate agli istrumenti coi quali fanno la caccia. Il "Boomerang„ se non colpisce l' oggetto contro il quale è stato lanciato, ritorna ai piedi di colui che l' ha lanciato. Essi sono gli unici Nativi primitivi nel mondo che adoperano una lancia, senza l' arco, e altri ordigni che richiedono la destrezza e che sorprendono quelli che li vedono adoperati.

Ciò nonostante la sete dei britannici per il sangue di questi celesti fanciulli innocenti di Adamo ed Eva è tanto ardente che hanno fatto credere al mondo ignorante che i Nativi dell' Australia sono inferiori agli Animali, alle Bestie, ai Rettili, ecc. ecc.

NOTA.

La Bestia la più feroce, fino al verme e alla pulce, è stata dall' uomo insegnata ad obbedire.

Credete al Vostro buon senso: - Non lasciatevi ingannare dai britannici e dalle astuzie dei discendenti dei loro forzati e delle loro organizzazioni intriganti quale il Consiglio per la Protezione degli Aborigeni, le Riserve Governativi per gli Aborigeni e i Missionari ecc.

I suddetti istituti non esistono per aiutare gli aborigeni ma per gettare polvere negli occhi a quelli che desiderano assumere informazioni.

Vi vantate della vostra civilizzazione, della vostra istruzione, umanità e scienza ecc. ecc.

Mettete in pratica quello di cui vi vantate, e date prova della vostra gratitudine ai Romani che vi hanno civilizzati, facendo altrettanto ai loro fratelli primitivi nell' Australia. Il Figlio di N. S., Gesù Cristo, è morto sulla Croce del Calvario, affinchè possa redimere coloro che hanno bisogno di aiuto, e gli esiliati.

Nel caso che il Papa e i suoi Seguaci fedeli avessero paura e permettessero che la crudeltà spietata continuasse nell' Australia, io personalmente risponderò a tutte le domande, nel servizio di Dio.

A. M. FERNANDO

FIGURE E.2. Anthony Martin Fernando's leaflet, which he distributed at the entrance to the Vatican Missionary Exposition, 1925. Source: Fiona Paisley, *The Lone Protester: A. M. Fernando in Australia and Europe* (2012), fig. 11.

himself as a lone activist—and certainly the title of his leaflet conveys that he considered himself as one of a few—his actions may be understood more broadly as one of countless Indigenous acts of survival and resistance during the VME and the 1920s in general. Could Fernando have imagined his protests as being in solidarity with other Indigenous artists and writers of the time, such as educators Angel De Cora and Charles Eastman? Fernando, De Cora, and Eastman imagined futures for Indigenous peoples that extend across time and space.

Afterlife of the Vatican Missionary Exposition: Inspiration for Fascism?

Although I have found no direct evidence that Mussolini attended the VME, he likely did, given that over one million visitors attended during its thirteen-month run. Mussolini worked with pope Pius XI during this time to solidify and bolster his relationship with the Catholic Church. In fact, 1925, the same year as the VME opened, was also the year of the national congress on fascist culture in Rome, at which attendees discussed the relationship between Italian identity and fascism in its early developing stages.[15] On February 11, 1929, Mussolini signed the Lateran Pacts with the Vatican, which established the Vatican state (of 144 hectares) and paid financial compensation for losses suffered in 1870 with the takeover of Rome by the newly unified Italian state. The treaty was welcomed with massive celebrations in the Eternal City.[16] As historian Peter Neville observes: "Mussolini received official endorsement from the Church for Fascist candidates in the elections of 1929 and 1934. Priests might now lead their flocks to the polling booths and might be seen giving a Fascist salute."[17] In terms of the relationship between visual culture, the VME, and fascism, the VME set the scene in some ways, with its emphasis on martyrdom and heroes, Christian ritual, and the hierarchy of race and culture legitimized by brutal colonial missionary expansion, all of which would be taken up by the fascists in Italy in the 1932 *Mostra della Rivoluzione Fascista* (Exhibition of the Fascist Revolution).

Housed in the neoclassical Palazzo delle Esposizioni on via Nazionale in Rome, the *Mostra della Rivoluzione Fascista* championed key ideas of the new fascist state: sacrifice, the importance of ritual, and aggressive colonial expansion. Like the Hall of Martyrs at the VME, it included a shrine of martyrs with a large metal cross in the gigantic circular room.[18] This space celebrated the heroism of the unknown soldier and recalled earlier ancient and imperial Roman spaces such as Saint Peter's Basilica, which was built over the spot where the blood of thousands of Christian martyrs had been shed. It also echoed the monument to the fallen soldier, Altare della Patria (1925), overlooking Piazza Venezia. As at the VME, visitors experienced the space through a series of carefully constructed rooms, complete with a chronology, and also moved procession-like through the space. The incorporation of the recorded voices of martyrs in the space made the experience almost like a mass for visitors, and they were overwhelmed with the visual and aural record.[19]

As with the VME, there was an emphasis on the documentary quality of the exhibition. It included relics, such as the bloody clothes of martyrs of the faith (similar to artifacts on display at the VME, such as the robe of Saint Francis of Assisi), and photographs, letters, and memorabilia, all in glass cases, that emphasized the exhibition as a type of museum space and propaganda machine.[20] Ideals associated with neoclassical art and architecture—white marble, classical references, artworks glorifying death and sacrifice like Pettrich's *Dying Tecumseh* in the Hall of North America—were taken up by artists and architects in the designing of the 1932 exhibition, in a display of what art historian Hugh Honour calls neoclassical's "bastard progeny."[21] Pius XI's description of the VME as providing "light in the darkness," thereby enlightening visitors, also foreshadowed the fascist ideals of purity and whiteness, and in 1938 would eventuate in the passage of Italian racial purity laws.[22] As the VME articulated the colonial agenda of the church, connecting itself with eons of expansion through the Roman tradition of triumphal display and plunder, so too did the fascist exhibition showcase and celebrate colonial expansion in East Africa, in areas encompassed by Eritrea, Ethiopia, Libya, and Somalia.[23] Through the display of stolen Indigenous cultural belongings, the VME provided a physical and intellectual panorama of colonial presence over the Americas and the other continents, and, at the same time, a collision of sovereignties.[24] If the VME was a "window on the world," as Father John Considine remarked on viewing the exhibition from the cupola of Saint Peter's, it was also a fantasy of colonial unknowing that perpetuated the denial of Indigenous artists and communities.[25]

Voyages beyond Turtle Island: Indigenous Artists, Activists, and Travelers in the Eternal City

Although the VME occurred more than ninety-nine years ago, the exhibition's history, the Indigenous cultural belongings, and the stories they tell are just as relevant today.[26] As Canada's federal policies, specifically the Truth and Reconciliation Commission, move toward addressing the legacy of genocide of Indigenous children in residential schools and the confiscation of secular and sacred Indigenous belongings, this project adds to the field of Indigenous knowledge and its ongoing confrontation with North America's colonial histories. This project also adds to the growing field of scholarship working to establish critical expansive histories of Indigenous arts and peoples across and beyond Turtle Island. This study creates new intellectual spaces for generative inquiry amid archives and histories that are replete with colonial unknowing. In traditional historical terms, this inquiry, documented by examples drawn from the archives on the material artifacts of the VME, can be considered a historiography of what could not be articulated, either at the time of the exhibition or even later in the Catholic Church.

Reading through some records of the Oblates of Mary Immaculate again, after months and years spent in the archives on both sides of the Atlantic, I came across a young girl's name: "Elisa." The Oblate missionary Goalven Trébaol wrote of her work, "It is an offering from the Indian children of the convent of Saint Angel of Fort Chipewayan, Athabaska." He further noted the materials and maker: "soft caribou skin, prepared and embroidered by Elisa, child of the school."[27] What was her life like? The display of Indigenous children's handiwork at the VME, described as "offerings" and "gifts" and then at *Anima Mundi* today is unsettling. Analysis of the archival record raises many more questions that have yet to be answered. How many of the Indigenous artworks in the collection were made by Indigenous children in residential and boarding schools? Thousands of stolen treasures made by Indigenous artisans wait in the collection and vaults. When will the Vatican Museums employ Indigenous curators and rewrite and re-right their narratives of looting and plundering? Why did pope Francis not rematriate the Inuvialuit kayak stolen by missionaries for the VME when he flew to Iqualiut for a brief visit on his penitential trip? I have found methods of opening a discourse of historical weight and significance through dialogue with the stolen treasures that remain at the Vatican Museums, using evidence of the exhibition practices that pertained at the VME and the ongoing colonial dynamics employed today at *Anima Mundi*. The research presents a new historiography that focuses on the legacies of Indigenous Americans in Vatican City through visual culture: statuary, children's games, Indigenous cultural belongings, and archival documents. While previous scholars have focused on the Catholic theological and anthropological aspects of the VME, this book presents a new perspective that centers the fraught, unsettled relationships between Indigenous American visual culture and the papal culture of conquest and greed. In doing so, this book has examined the multiple ways that Indigenous visual culture matters—as eternal sovereigns and as ancestral art history lessons that continue to resonate beyond the frame, the Vatican, and the Eternal City (see plate 16).

Journal: Roma, non basta una vita

JUNE 2022. *Not much to note today other than that I am feeling a bit anxious and excited about upcoming trips, my departure from Italy, and my travels to the archives at the Yale Divinity Library to see the Italian children's games with missionary themes. I can hardly believe I have been here in Rome nearly a year. I have this sense of being here but also not here, a floating sensation. Feeling the strong Roman sun on my face, walking through the old Roman churches and amid the ruins with Italian friends, I get this in-between feeling. It is not quite an out-of-body experience, but almost as if, recognizing my body being in this place but knowing I will leave soon, my spirit identifies a sense of magic that still exists in some very old parts of Rome. I remember a conversation on Janiculum Hill with an elderly Roman lady who reminded me of the words of Roman author and Vatican correspondent Silvio Negro, "Roma, non basta una vita" (Rome, a lifetime is not enough).*[28] *I hear Beyoncé's song on the radio once again, "Baby, I can feel your halo."*

Appendix. Letters on Accessing the Vatican Missionary Ethnological Museum

Below are two examples of the many letters I sent to officials in the Canadian government and at the Vatican in 2017, as I sought access to the collections of the Vatican Missionary Ethnological Museum. My addressees included Pope Francis and Prime Minister Justin Trudeau as well as curators at the Vatican Museums. The Vatican Missionary Ethnological Museum, now called the Ethnological Museum *Anima Mundi*, remained closed to researchers and the public for more than a decade. I was trying to access archival documents and museum records as well as Indigenous cultural belongings that were not on public display. To some of the letters, I received responses, and to some I did not. As of March 2023, *Anima Mundi* is now open in a new wing of the Vatican Museums, but the majority of the Indigenous cultural belongings remain sealed away, kept in storage areas, bereft of their makers. Many of the Indigenous cultural belongings and artifacts I discuss in this book were available to see and study in person at various museum spaces throughout Rome and Turtle Island; visiting them was a crucial part of my research process. As of 2024, records of some Indigenous cultural belongings at the Vatican Museums are viewable in the museums' online database; before this, very scant records were available. Thousands of Indigenous cultural belongings remain today like prisoners in the Vatican Museums.

LETTER 1. To Pope Francis

His Holiness, Pope Francis
Apostolic Palace
00120 Vatican City

January 16, 2017

Dear Pope Francis,

I am writing to you to tell you about my PhD research and to ask for your help. I am a PhD Candidate at the University of British Columbia, in Vancouver, Canada, and am here living in Rome for my PhD research. I have conducted research at several archives in Rome including Propaganda Fide, the central Jesuit archive, Vatican Secret Archive, and the Vatican Apostolic Library. I applied to consult the Vatican Missionary Ethnological Museum at the Vatican Museums and was refused access. I am part of a larger group of scholars who have been refused and I would like to bring this issue to your attention and also ask for your help.

My PhD is titled "Object Lessons: An Analysis of Indigenous Art at the 1925 Pontifical Missionary Exhibition." My particular focus seeks to understand the plethora of art and material culture (beaded bags, kayaks, carvings, masks) that were made by Native Americans and sent in for the exhibition as well as photographs and other ephemera that were sent in by missionaries. By using the term "Indigenous" as an Indigenous studies scholar, I also hope to connect my project with the broader political project of recognition and rights for Indigenous peoples and Indigenous studies worldwide. My perspective on this project has been shaped by my training in art history and Indigenous studies, and my personal experience as an Indigenous person with heritage ties to the Métis peoples of Canada. I have spoken with journalists, art historians, archivists, and other scholars regarding this issue of access to the Vatican Missionary Ethnological Museum but I have not made progress in accessing this archive.

The Vatican Missionary Ethnological Museum has material of importance for many Native American communities, and it would be an important step for the Vatican Museums to allow access for researchers. Indeed many Indigenous communities consider materials in the Vatican collections as sacred and special, and allowing access would be a profound step forward in repairing relationships between Indigenous communities and the Catholic Church. Considering also that Pope Pius XI intended the 1925 Vatican Missionary Exhibition and the objects therein to be as a resource for scholars and an "open book" for the understanding of missionary endeavors and Indigenous faith around the world, it would be also fitting of his intentions and for the future of the collection that it be open for researchers and Indigenous peoples to consult.

I really appreciate that you have taken the time to read this letter and I look forward to your response.

Sincerely,

Gloria Jane Bell
Vanier Canada Scholar
University of British Columbia

LETTER 2. To Justin Trudeau, Prime Minister, Canada

August 4, 2017

Dear Right Honorable Prime Minister Justin Trudeau, Ottawa, Canada,

I am writing to you to tell you about my PhD research as I thought it may be of interest to Indigenous and Northern Affairs Canada. I am a PhD candidate and Vanier Scholar at the University of British Columbia, in Vancouver, Canada. I have conducted archival research in Rome, Italy, for the past year. I have collected data at archives in Rome including Propaganda Fide, the central Jesuit archive, the Vatican Secret Archive, and the Vatican Apostolic Library, as well as archives in Canada and the United States.

My PhD is titled "The Eloquence of Things: An Analysis of Indigenous Art at the 1925 Pontifical Missionary Exhibition." My particular focus seeks to understand the plethora of cultural belongings (beaded bags, carvings, souvenirs, masks) that were made by diverse Indigenous communities in Canada and the United States and sent in for the exhibition, as well as photographs and other ephemera that were sent in by missionaries. By using the term "Indigenous" as an Indigenous studies scholar, I also hope to connect my project with the broader political project of recognition and rights for Indigenous peoples and Indigenous studies worldwide. My perspective on this project has been shaped by my training in art history and Indigenous studies, and my personal experience as an Indigenous person with heritage ties to the Métis peoples of Canada. The manuscript examines the importance of the history of the exposition, Indigenous collections at the Vatican, and the dynamics of relations between missionaries and Indigenous peoples from the late nineteenth century until the 1920s. Central to this story are material things including: Indigenous cultural belongings, Catholic children's games created by missionaries, wax dioramas, and photographs of Indigenous Americans in Rome.

While in Rome, I applied to consult the Vatican Missionary Ethnological Museum at the Vatican Museums and was refused access. I am part of a larger group of scholars who have been refused. The Vatican Missionary Ethnological Museum has material of importance for many Indigenous communities, and it would be an important step for the Vatican Museums to allow access for researchers. Indeed, many Indigenous communities consider materials in the Vatican collections as sacred and special, and allowing access would be a profound step forward in repairing relationships between Indigenous communities and the Catholic Church. Considering also that Pope Pius XI intended the 1925 Vatican Missionary Exhibition and the objects therein to be a resource for scholars and an "open book" for the understanding of missionary endeavors and Indigenous faith around the world, it would be also fitting of his intentions and for the future of the collection that it be open for researchers and Indigenous peoples to consult. Despite this archival obstacle, I remain confident that my research will promote thinking about the history of this forgotten global missionary exposition. I wrote this letter as I think more connections need to be made between

Indigenous and Northern Affairs, governmental policy, global studies, and academic research.

I appreciate that you have taken the time to read this letter. I welcome any questions or suggestions regarding my research.

Sincerely,

Gloria Jane Bell
Vanier Canada Scholar
University of British Columbia

Notes

INTRODUCTION. A NOMAD IN THE ROMAN ARCHIVES

1. Pius XI's demands and coercive methods of collecting for the 1925 Vatican Missionary Exposition (VME) then formed the basis of the Vatican Missionary Ethnological Museum, established in 1926. In 2019 the museum changed its name to Ethnological Museum *Anima Mundi*. The VME was one of the largest Catholic missionary expositions in Europe during the early twentieth century and showcased stolen Indigenous art as well as sacred and secular belongings taken from Indigenous communities across the globe. The museum and its collections were largely closed off for approximately twenty years from the early 2000s until 2023, with funding being dedicated to the establishment of a conservation lab in 2000, which remains the priority today. The majority of the collections remain in the sealed vaults. To this day, the artworks and belongings have not been returned or repatriated to communities despite requests in a brutish battle that continues.

2. The Musée du Quai Branly–Jacques Chirac has a vast array of photographs and cultural belongings from Indigenous America. See Musée du Quai Branly–Jacques Chirac, "History of the Collections," accessed August 28, 2023, https://www.quaibranly.fr/en/collections/all-collections/history-of-the-collections.

3. My use of the term *cultural belonging* is inspired by the 2015 series of exhibitions *Ćəsnaʔəm: The City before the City*, which traced the ancestral presence of the Musqueam, dating back five thousand years, to their current presence in Vancouver across three sites: the Museum of Vancouver, the Museum of Anthropology, and the Musqueam Cultural Centre. See Museum of Vancouver, "Ćəsnaʔəm: The City before the City," accessed August 18, 2023, https://museumofvancouver.ca/csnam-the-city-before-the-city/. The use of the term is also inspired by the artistic practice and oeuvre of Lakota multimedia artist Dana Claxton.

4. "Silent eloquence" is the term pope Pius XI used to describe the VME. Pius XI, *Rerum Ecclesiae*.

5. Important studies in the field include Lonetree, *Decolonizing Museums*; Nahwegahbow, "From Great-Grandmothers to Great-Granddaughters"; Racette, Corbiere, and Migwans, "Pieces Left along the Trail"; Igloliorte and Taunton, "Continuities between Eras."

6. Like other collections of Indigenous American material in Italy, the Vatican collections extend back several centuries. Of importance here, the first missionary museum in Rome was established by the German-born Jesuit polymath and collector Athanius Kircher (1602–80), who amassed various materials from the Americas, including ceremonial pipes and wampum belts that were sent in by Jesuits along with cultural belongings from the four corners of the globe. Kircher's museum, a "theatre of nature and art," was housed in the Jesuit Collegio Romano collection and was later amalgamated into the Vatican Museums. See Rowland, *Ecstatic Journey*. See also Lugli, "Inquiry as Collection." Recent scholarship in Renaissance studies of the early modern period, such as the work of art historian Lia Markey, explores Indigenous art collections of the Americas in Florence, namely material things in the "New World" collections that include feather paintings. Markey focuses primarily on South America. See Markey, *Imagining the Americas*. The Beltrami collection of Indigenous art in Bergamo is also an important and understudied collection. See Museo Civico Scienze Naturali Enrico Caffi, "Nord America," accessed January 24, 2024, https://www.museoscienzebergamo.it/senza-categoria/nord-america/. See also Marino, "Preview of the Beltrami Collection."

7. For an anthropologist's view of the exhibition, see Kahn, "Mind over Matter." See also Amaral, "Exhibiting Faith."

8. On sovereignty, see Raheja, "Visual Sovereignty," 29; Rickard, "Sovereignty," 51; D'Angeli, "Dancing Chiax, Dancing Sovereignty."

9. Foster, "Archival Impulse," 4.

10. For more information on this genocide, see Truth and Reconciliation Commission (Canada), *They Came for the Children*.

11. On transnational studies of Indigenous travelers, artists, and missionaries, see Harney and Phillips, *Mapping Modernisms*; Burns, *Transnational Frontiers*; Friesen and Chladiuk, *Lakota Performers*; Horton, *Art for an Undivided Earth*; Voelker, "Unfixing the Frame."

12. Tuck and Yang, "Decolonization Is Not a Metaphor."

13. Crosby, "Construction of the Imaginary Indian."

14. Todd and Fraser, "Decolonial Sensibilities."

15. Medak-Saltzman, "Transnational Indigenous Exchange"; Deloria, *Indians in Unexpected Places*; Vizenor, "Aesthetics of Survivance"; Mithlo, *Knowing Native Arts*; Lonetree, *Decolonizing Museums*.

16. Stoler, *Along the Archival Grain*. See also Schweitzer and Henry, *Afterlives of Indigenous Archives*.

17. Papafava, *Vatican*, 44.

18. "Ethnological Museum Anima Mundi," Vatican Museums, accessed February 6, 2024, https://www.museivaticani.va/content/museivaticani/en/collezioni/musei/museo-etnologico/museo-etnologico.html.

19. Fabian, *Time and the Other*, 91.

20. Meetings with conservator, American Academy in Rome, February, and March 2022.

21. Cole, *Performance*.

22. My usage of the term *stolen treasures* is inspired by Lou-ann Neel's practice as a Kwakwaka'wakw artist and museum specialist. See also the interdisciplinary symposium, "Restitution Dialogues: Exploring the Vatican Archives," University of Toronto, Faculty of Law, January 18, 2023; see https://www.law.utoronto.ca/events/restitution-dialogues-exploring-vatican-archives.

23. I am one of a number of scholars from across the Americas and Europe who have been refused access to the archives and collections of the Ethnological Museum *Anima Mundi*. Conversation with Alison Kahn, anthropologist, Rome, November 2016, and ongoing correspondence. I was also a recipient of a letter that further outlines the Ethnological Museum's colonial dynamics: "In contrast to what Dr. Bell reports, I have had welcome access as a nonindigenous researcher to these collections and their records." Letter copied to the author, March 2022.

24. Pohlandt-McCormick, "In Good Hands," 316. She expands on her fieldwork, "As I focused my topic and placed it in the time of the Soweto Uprising of June 16, 1976, I came up against what, at the time, seemed like the intransigent barriers of the South African archival system and the laws that—not unlike those in other countries—prevented insight into documents younger than thirty years. It was clear that the archives were also rooted in a historical context and reflected the conventions and habits of the apartheid past as much as the rapid pace of historical change in South Africa during the 1990s." Pohlandt-McCormick, "In Good Hands," 303.

25. Historian Jace Weaver notes that "by the grace of God and declaration of the Holy Pontiff, Indians were found to possess divine souls and were thus eligible for salvation." Weaver, *Native American Religious Identity*, 22.

26. "Pope Inspects Exhibition," 5.

27. Ghosh et al., *Archive Stories*, 10.

28. The Propaganda Fide Library now holds many Indigenous-language books taken by missionaries for the VME.

29. Todd and Fraser, "Decolonial Sensibilities."

30. McMaster and Martin, "Introduction," 11.

31. For more of the altered photographs, please see my research newsletter; see access information at https://www.mcgill.ca/ahcs/people-contacts/faculty/gloria-bell.

32. Sweet, "Reimagining the African-Atlantic Archive." See also Gell, "Vogel's Net."

33. Derrida, *Archive Fever.*

34. See "The Pope Has a Rare Antique Kayak and Many More Indigenous Artifacts Hidden away in the Vatican Museums," *Globe and Mail,* November 31, 2021, https://www.theglobeandmail.com/world/article-the-pope-has-a-rare-antique-kayak-and-many-more-indigenous-artifacts/; and Testore, "L'Evangelizzazione degli Esquimesi."

35. I recently participated in an interdisciplinary symposium about the Vatican's nonresponse to restitution: "Restitution Dialogues: Exploring the Vatican Archives," University of Toronto, Faculty of Law, January 18, 2023; https://www.law.utoronto.ca/events/restitution-dialogues-exploring-vatican-archives.

36. Throughout the text I will refer to Edmonia Lewis as Anishinaabe and/or Ojibwe. Both are acceptable terminology and also represent the complexity and importance of naming for Indigenous artists. See Buffalo, "Knowing All My Names"; Buick, "Ideal Works."

37. Vimalassery, Pegues, and Goldstein, "Colonial Unknowing," 1042.

38. See Aigner et al., *The Americas.*

39. The leaflet headline is "I pochi Aborigeni che rimangono ancora in Australia" (The few Aboriginals that still remain in Australia). For more on Fernando, see Paisley, *Lone Protester.*

CHAPTER 1. UNSETTLING THE INDIAN MUSEUM IN ROME

1. Richard Payne Knight wrote about West's experience in a footnote to a poem entitled "The Landscape: A Didactic Poem in Three Books" (1794). See fuller discussion in Pratt, *American Indians*, 22–23.

2. Historian Marilyn Richardson notes that Lewis garnered permission to sketch at the Vatican collections. Richardson, "Friends and Colleagues," 104. For more about Canova, see Honour, "Canova's Studio Practice I" and "Canova's Studio Practice II."

3. Salenius, "Introduction," 16; "Personal" (1870).

4. Curator Jacqueline Copeland discovered this *carte de visite* of Lewis, and it is now in the collection of the Walters Art Museum, Baltimore.

5. Lewis received a papal blessing for her work. See James, James, and Boyer, *Notable American Women*, 398.

6. "An interesting novelty has sprung up amongst us, in a city where all our surroundings are of the olden time. Miss Edmonia Lewis, a lady of color, has taken a studio in Rome, and works as a sculptress." Wreford, "Negro Sculptress." See also Tufts, "Edmonia Lewis."

7. Nelson, *Color of Stone*, 180.

8. Nelson, *Color of Stone*, 180.

9. Nelson, *Color of Stone*, 17.

10. Buick, *Child of the Fire*, 12.

11. Nelson, *Color of Stone*, 174.

12. Buick, *Child of the Fire*, 14.

13. Buick, *Child of the Fire*, 27.

14. "Seeking Equality Abroad."

15. Blackman notes that "in the frontier city of Victoria, *cartes de visite* of Indians were made over about a ten-year period beginning in 1862 and represent, by a few years, the earliest photographs of British Columbia's native population. Although it is doubtful that these *cartes* were purchased by the Indian subjects of the images, they were sought by local colonists and particularly by visitors to Victoria." Blackman, "Studio Indians," 68.

16. A contemporary of Lewis, the Haida carver Charles Edenshaw (1839–1920), would make an interesting comparison but is outside the parameters of this study.

17. My analysis focuses on the rare photograph of Edmonia Lewis in Rome. The other set of six *cartes de visite* of Lewis made in Chicago, and wearing a Phrygian cap and shawl, were made by prominent Chicago photographer Henry Rocher between 1868 and 1870 and have been widely discussed. See Shaw, *Portraits of a People.*

18. Nelson, *Color of Stone*, 27, quoting a letter by Anne Whitney to Adele Manning, August 9, 1864.

19. See, e.g., American sculptor Horatio Greenough's commission for the Capitol, *The Rescue* (1837), which celebrates Indigenous displacement in the wake of settlers. Ciregna, "Example in the Right Direction," 30.

20. Buffalo, "Knowing All My Names"; Buick, "Ideal Works." See also Gubernatis and Matini, *Dizionario degli artisti italiani viventi.*

21. On Pettrich, see Edenheiser and Nielsen, *Portrayals of Native Americans.*

22. Cavina, *Geometries of Silence*, 4.

23. Honour, *Neo-Classicism*, 146.

24. Art historian Hugh Honour uses the term "contradiction" in his discussion of neoclassical art. He does not discuss, however, the contradiction of the treatment of Indigenous Americans by American settlers and the US government and their parallel representation in neoclassical art. Honour, *Neo-Classicism*, 15.

25. Nelson, *Color of Stone*, xiii.

26. Nesselrath, "Points of View," 69.

27. Edenheiser, "Introduction," 16.

28. "An attempt at assassination—One of the most atrocious attempts to take away the life of a respectable citizen that it has ever befallen our lot to record occurred last Sunday night about ten o'clock, in the first ward of this city, at a building not far from the Executive Mansion. Two assassins entered the studio of Mr. Pettrich, the sculptor, and after a severe struggle, stabbed him in two places. This fiend-like and cowardly attack was made,

as it is thought, by two white men with their faces blacked." News report of May 31, 1842, reprinted in Stehle, "Ferdinand Pettrich in America," 403.

29. Stehle, "Ferdinand Pettrich in America," 402.

30. Stehle, "Ferdinand Pettrich in America," 403.

31. The Indian Removal Act (1830) passed by the US Congress and President Andrew Jackson implemented a policy of removal of all Native peoples from east of the Mississippi onto reservations in present-day Oklahoma to make way for American settler colonials. This policy continued to be implemented for two decades. Witgen, "American Indians," 605. See also Dunbar-Ortiz, *Indigenous Peoples' History*.

32. Witgen, "American Indians," 605.

33. Bowes, "US Expansion," 96–97. See also Fixico, "How We Remember Black Hawk."

34. Scheckel, *Insistence of the Indian*, 99. See also chapter 2 for more discussion of Pettrich's works.

35. Torre, "Le plastiche a soggetto indigeno nordamericano," 34.

36. Viola, *Diplomats in Buckskin*, 61.

37. Stehle, "Ferdinand Pettrich in America," 410. Only a few copies of the booklet survive, including one held by the New York Public Library; see https://www.nypl.org/research/research-catalog/bib/b14311954.

38. Pettrich sketchbook cover, Edward E. Ayer Special Collections, Newberry Library, Chicago.

39. Pettrich, *Portraits of Distinguished Indians*, title page.

40. Quoted in the February 2012 research notes of Karen Lemmey, curator of sculpture at the Smithsonian American Art Museum ([Lemmey], Research notes), which cite Gurney and Son, *On the Exhibition*, a catalog produced by the New York gallery of Jeremiah Gurney in about 1860, when it showed work by Pettrich.

41. [Lemmey], Research notes, citing Gurney and Son, *On the Exhibition*.

42. [Lemmey], Research notes, citing Gurney and Son, *On the Exhibition*.

43. [Lemmey], Research notes.

44. The plaster version of *Dying Tecumseh* (89 × 197 × 155 cm) is dated ca. 1856. For the Vatican's catalog record see "Statua a Grandezza Naturale di Te-cum-seh o Tecumseh," Vatican Museums, https://catalogo.museivaticani.va/index.php/Detail/objects/MV.101568.0.0. For the catalog record of the marble version, see "The Dying Tecumseh," Catalog of American Portraits, National Portrait Gallery, Smithsonian, https://npg.si.edu/object/npg_IT050005?destination=edan-search/catalog_of_america%3Fpage%3D430%26edan_fq%255B0%255D%3Ddate%253A%25221840s%2522.

45. Sugden, *Tecumseh*, 216.

46. Charles Bird King painted a beautiful portrait of Tecumseh's brother, the prophet Tenskwatawa. See McKenney and Hall, *History of the Indian Tribes of North America*, 47.

47. Sugden, *Tecumseh*, 179.

48. Tecumseh, "'Father! Listen to Your Children,'" 62.

49. The Dying Gaul (marble, 94 × 186.5 × 89 cm, Capitoline Museums, Rome) is a first-century BCE Roman copy of a Greek bronze of the late third century BCE. See "Statue of 'Capitoline Gaul,'" Musei Capitolini, https://www.museicapitolini.org/en/opera/statua-del-galata-capitolino; and Picón and Hemingway, *Pergamon*, 176.

50. Sugden, *Tecumseh's Last Stand*, 138.

51. Torre describes Tecumseh as inhaling and exhaling his last breath. Torre, "Le plastiche a soggetto indigeno nordamericano," 53. Pettrich's sculpture is unusual in that it is a sculpture and not a painting or drawing of the Shawnee leader. John Dorival's print *Battle of the Thames* (1833), based on a painting, was widely distributed and depicts Tecumseh as a large man engaged in combat with the Kentucky commander Richard Johnson and about to throw an axe at invading American forces.

52. Cikovsky, "Ravages of the Axe," 626.

53. On the equation between the tree stump and the end of Indigenous American life, see Cikovsky, "Ravages of the Axe," 626. See also Thomas Crawford's *The Progress of Civilization* (1863), a pediment on the Capitol in Washington, DC, which celebrates Indigenous removal. See Architect of the Capitol, "Progress of Civilization Pediment," accessed August 19, 2023, https://www.aoc.gov/explore-capitol-campus/art/progress-civilization-pediment.

54. Fryd, *Art and Empire*, 110.

55. Nekona Gokey, Shawnee artist, email communication with the author, October 25, 2017.

56. Haltman, "Towards Immobility," 52.

57. In Samuel Morse's painting *The House of Representatives* (1822), one can see the Pawnee Indian Chief Petalasharo in the visitor's gallery watching the debate on American Indian land rights and policy. Pettrich's *Dying Tecumseh* was placed in this room above the place where there was a designated crypt for George Washington. See the section by R. David Edmunds in "Carving Myths out of History: Ferdinand Pettrich's Sculpture 'The Dying Tecumseh,'" video, Smithsonian American Art Museum, 2014, https://americanart.si.edu/artwork/the-dying-tecumseh-19670.

58. Fryd, "Two Sculptures for the Capitol."

59. Sugden, *Tecumseh*, 180.

60. Sugden, *Tecumseh's Last Stand*, 17.

61. "Chevalier Pettrich's Sculptures."

62. Kort and Hollein, *I Like America*, 16. Pettrich's Indian Museum is less well known, and he never received as broad recognition as other European artists who traveled to Native America, such as Carl Bodmer, George Catlin, or Peter Rindisbacher, but his works are central to this discussion as they were an early iteration of the "Indian gallery" tradition and featured prominently in the Hall of North America at the VME.

63. Baedecker, *Italy*, 272.

64. Pettrich's Indian Museum remains in near obscurity, likely because the Ethnological Museum *Anima Mundi* and its collections remained closed for nearly two decades, on and off from the early 2000s until 2023. In 2000, the museum was turned into a conservation lab, which it remains today. Pettrich's marble *Dying Tecumseh* at the Smithsonian American Art Museum is well known. Sculptures from the Indian Museum are now placed around the perimeter of the Ethnological Museum *Anima Mundi*, which I hope to discuss in future work.

65. Bresciani, "Manuscript on the Indian Statues," 247.

66. On Benjamin West and the connection between American Indians and ancient Greece, see Prown, *Art as Evidence*, 99. See also Reinhardt, "British and Indian Identities in a Picture."

67. Visitors and travelers to the US equated the mound cultures of Indigenous Americans with the pyramids of the ancient Egyptians. This created an artistic and architectural link between Egypt and the Americas as well, although Indigenous Americans were not seen as the direct descendants of the mound builders but as less culturally developed relatives. Sayre, "Mound Builders." Art historians such as Aby Warburg would later go on to explore these associations further, although today such simplistic comparisons are often viewed as reductive and uninformed. See, e.g., Freedburg, "Warburg's Mask."

68. Germany has a long and complex history of reenactments of "authentic" Native American peoples at ongoing summer fairs every year. This started with the novel *Winnetou and Shatterhand* by Karl May, a popular novelist at the turn of the nineteenth century. See, e.g., Green, "Tribe Called Wannabee."

69. Edenheiser, "Introduction," 18.

70. Viola, *Diplomats in Buckskin*, 35.

71. Aigner, "Vatican Museums and Native Americans," 87.

72. Torre, "Le plastiche a soggetto indigeno nordamericano," 86. See also Aigner, "Vatican Museums and Native Americans," 91.

73. Torre, "Le plastiche a soggetto indigeno nordamericano," 87.

74. Kort and Hollein, *I Like America*, 6.

75. Tindall and Shi, *America*, 554.

76. Buick, *Child of the Fire*, 4. On the history of the Ojibwe and the Mississauga New Credit First Nation, see Bohaker, "Reading Anishinaabe Identities"; Nelson, "Hydromythology of the Anishinaabeg"; Smith, *Mississauga Portraits*; Penner, "Ojibwe Renaissance."

77. Edmonia Wildfire Lewis was buried in London. Buick, *Child of the Fire*, 4.

78. Buick, *Child of the Fire*, 4.

79. Wreford, "Negro Sculptress."

80. Penner, "Ojibwe Renaissance," 85. Scholarship by Edward Said and many others following Penner's lead describes how the European and American fine arts of the nineteenth century exoticized, misrepresented, and misunderstood many cultures, including Africa and Asia. See Said, *Orientalism*. Said does not write explicitly on neoclassicism, but the primitivizing discourse he discusses has a parallel in the exoticization of First Nations cultures of Turtle Island. Indeed, many Americans imagined the Southwest United States as an "American Orient," a romanticized and mythical place of primitive people. Shelton, "Imaginary Southwest."

81. On nineteenth-century Indigenous writers and their strategies, see Wheeler, "Journals and Voices of a Church of England Native Catechist."

82. Penner, "Ojibwe Renaissance," 85.

83. Buick, *Child of the Fire*, 102.

84. See, e.g., Callahan, *Wynema*; Apess, *Son of the Forest*; Alexander, *From the Deep Woods to Civilization*.

85. Buick, *Child of the Fire*, 4.

86. Phillips, *Trading Identities*, 10.

87. Buick, *Child of the Fire*, 4.

88. *Handbook of Rome* (1867), xlii.

89. For more on Lewis's life in Rome, see Bell, "Reconstructing Edmonia Lewis's Roman Life."

90. Nelson notes that Lewis received aid from her colleague and fellow sculptress Harriet Hosmer to set up in Canova's studio. Another colleague, Anne Whitney, also visited Lewis while at Canova's former studio. See Nelson, *Color of Stone*, 196. Regarding Canova himself, his studio was a transnational site for artists, collectors, and travelers who came to Rome: "Canova, was, on the one hand, a cosmopolitan artist who moved easily between individuals and groups, and, on the other, an esteemed citizen and internationally recognized representative of the papal States, one deeply entrenched in its shifting political identity." Ferando, "Truly Transnational?,"104.

91. *Handbook of Rome* (1867), xlii.

92. *Handbook of Rome* (1875), 50. This time, Lewis's address appears as 8A, Piazza di S. Nicola da Tolentino.

93. Buick, *Child of the Fire*, 78.

94. On Lewis's degree of social freedom, see Buick, *Child of the Fire*, 65.

95. Nelson, *Color of Stone*, 17.

96. Anne Whitney, letter to Adele Manning, August 9, 1864, quoted in Nelson, *Color of Stone*, 27.

97. Together the couple published a literary magazine called the *Literary Voyageur*, a compilation of poetry and short stories. Although Henry Rowe Schoolcraft receives the most credit for his long *Narrative Journal of Travels through the Northwest Regions of the*

United States . . . in the Year 1820 (1821), acknowledgment should also be given to his wife, as she provided a direct point of access to Ojibwe legends, myths, epistemologies, and language.

98. For example, Norwegian sculptor Jacob Fjelde was commissioned to create a sculpture of Hiawatha and Minnehaha, first made in plaster and later cast in bronze, for the Minnesota Building at the 1893 World's Columbian Exposition in Chicago.

99. "Personal" (1879).

100. Schweitzer, "Introduction," 2–3.

101. West had a collection of Indigenous material culture. King, "Woodlands Artifacts from the Studio of Benjamin West." While I have not found any official evidence of Lewis's collection, the archive for Lewis remains incomplete and fragmented, and this possibility merits further study and reflection.

102. Dabakis, *Sisterhood of Sculptors*, 2.

103. Lewis made a copy of Michelangelo's Moses figure, complete with horns, which is in San Pietro in Vincoli, Rome. Michelangelo cultivated a rough, gritty image as a worker with marble, working directly with the material, like Lewis. See "Moses (After Michelangelo)," Smithsonian American Art Museum, https://americanart.si.edu/artwork/moses-after-michelangelo-14628.

104. Kirsten Buick discusses the culture around creating Greek-looking Indigenous women. Buick, "Ideal Works of Edmonia Lewis," 12.

105. Nelson, "White Marble."

106. Dabakis, *Sisterhood of Sculptors*, 203. On the Haitian-French artist and a neoclassical precursor of Lewis, see Grigsby, "Revolutionary Sons."

107. Nelson, *Color of Stone*, 129. See also "Facing the Other: Charles Cordier (1827–1905), Ethnographic Sculptor," Musée d'Orsay, accessed August 19, 2023, https://www.musee-orsay.fr/en/whats-on/exhibitions/facing-other-charles-cordier-1827-1905-ethnographic-sculptor.

108. For a discussion of the *carte de visite* made in Chicago, see Shaw, *Portraits of a People*. For the photograph, see "2010.68: Edmonia Lewis (1845–1907), Photographs," Harvard Art Museums, accessed August 19, 2023, https://harvardartmuseums.org/art/201876.

109. Bonfigli, *Guide to the Studios in Rome*, published in 1860, lists Pettrich as follows: "Pettrich Ferdinand (of Dresden) sculptor. Inquire his address at Mr. Spthöver's German library in piazza di Spagna," 91. Lewis operated several studios throughout her career in Rome, including near Piazza del Popolo and Piazza Barberini, with her final studio at via Venti Settembre. Pettrich's studio, like Lewis's was centrally located in Rome in the 1860s at Piazza Ricci and then Piazza dell'Orso. Both studios were within walking distance of each other. For more about the studios please see Bell, "Reconstructing Edmonia Lewis's

Roman Life." For more histories about the Café Greco and Indigenous artists, see Bell, "Lakota Dandies in the Eternal City," 149.

110. James, James, and Boyer, *Notable American Women*, 398.

111. Peers, "Almost True," 540.

112. Gerdts, "Marble Savage," 70.

113. Huhndorf, *Going Native*, 31.

114. Huhndorf, *Going Native*, 31.

115. Vizenor, "Aesthetics of Survivance."

116. For a parallel example of debates around ethnicity and art and the limits of these approaches, see Davis, "End of the American Century," 559.

117. Veracini, *Settler Colonialism*, 75.

118. Francis, *Imaginary Indian*, 104. On American nationalism, see Scheckel, *Insistence of the Indian*, 10.

119. Huhndorf, *Going Native*, 52.

120. Calloway, "Treaties and Treaty Making," 547–48.

121. Nelson, "Edmonia Lewis's 'Death of Cleopatra.'" See also Richardson, "Edmonia Lewis' 'The Death of Cleopatra.'" For the sculpture (marble, 160.0 × 79.4 × 116.8 cm), see "The Death of Cleopatra," Smithsonian American Art Museum, https://americanart.si.edu/artwork/death-cleopatra-33878.

122. The Ojibwe Methodist Missionary Peter Jones was also from the Credit River First Nation and led an international life. See Lyons, *World*, 148.

123. Nelson, *Color of Stone*, 175.

124. See, e.g., Thomas Crawford, *Mexican Girl Dying* (marble, 1848), and Erastus Dow Palmer, *Indian Girl, or The Dawn of Christianity* (marble, 1855–56). "Mexican Girl Dying," Metropolitan Museum of Art, accessed August 19, 2023, https://www.metmuseum.org/art/collection/search/10575; "Indian Girl, or The Dawn of Christianity," Metropolitan Museum of Art, accessed August 19, 2023, https://www.metmuseum.org/art/collection/search/11677.

125. Pratt, *American Indians in British Art*, 13–14.

126. See, e.g., Hermon Atkins MacNeil, *The Sun Vow* (bronze, 1899, cast 1919); "The Sun Vow," Metropolitan Museum of Art, accessed August 19, 2023, https://www.metmuseum.org/art/collection/search/11494. See also "Native Perspectives," Metropolitan Museum of Art, accessed August 19, 2023, https://www.metmuseum.org/about-the-met/collection-areas/the-american-wing/native-perspectives.

127. Much important work has been done in the field, including Flint, *Transatlantic Indian*; Fitz, *Visual Representations of Native Americans*; Seth, *Europe's Indians*; Benn, *Mohawks on the Nile*; Wernitznig, *Europe's Indians, Indians in Europe*. See also the fascinating study by Brody, *Impossible Purities*.

128. The exhibition was organized by the Minneapolis Institute of Art; for a description, see "Hearts of Our People: Native Women Artists," Smithsonian American Art Museum, accessed August 19, 2023, https://americanart.si.edu/exhibitions/native-women-artists#. See also Ahlberg Yohe and Greeves, *Hearts of Our People*.

CHAPTER 2. "THE MOST EXHAUSTIVE RECORD OF THE WORLD'S PROGRESS EVER DISPLAYED"

1. Stoler, *Along the Archival Grain*, 256.

2. Former Vatican curator, conversation with the author, April 20, 2016.

3. The Holy Door of the Jubilee Year tradition extends back to the 1200s. The door is opened only during the Jubilee Year and blessed by the pope on its opening. See "Mostra Giubileo," Senato della Repubblica, accessed August 19, 2023, https://antiquorum-habet.senato.it/.

4. Considine, *Vatican Mission Exposition*, 80.

5. "Il 'vernissage' e la visita della stampa," 62. On Mussolini, see Painter, *Mussolini's Rome*.

6. The *Rivista Illustrata* is accessible by request at Propaganda Fide Library Collections, Rome (Vatican Missionary Exhibition Papers). I have also accessed this publication at the Vatican Apostolic Library and in the Special Collections of the Paul Bechtold Library, Catholic Theological Union, Chicago.

7. Stoler, *Along the Archival Grain*, 2.

8. Dreves, *Visit to the Vatican Missionary Exhibition*, 22.

9. "L'insospettata odissea dei trasporti," 30

10. "L'insospettata odissea dei trasporti," 30.

11. Dreves, *Visit to the Vatican Missionary Exhibition*, 4. The Mill Hill Missionaries is an international fellowship with missions across the globe, headquartered in the UK. I came across Father Dreves's account at the Propaganda Fide Library. The Mill Hill Missionaries had an extensive space at the VME, which they called the "St Joseph's Society Mill Hill" stands. The society set up displays relating to their missions in Borneo, India, and Uganda. Father Dreves Papers, Mill Hill Missionaries Archive, Liverpool.

12. Campino, "Vatican Making Ready for Notable Jubilee Year," 30.

13. "Vatican Exhibition Is Taking Shape."

14. Fabian, *Time and the Other*, 35. For an analysis of this issue in relation to the Canadian artists of the Group of Seven, see Jessup and Bagg, *Aboriginal Representation in the Gallery*.

15. "Silent Eloquence" is the term Pius XI used to describe the VME; Pius XI, *Rerum Ecclesiae*.

16. Hutchinson, *Indian Craze*, 100.

17. Hutchinson, *Indian Craze*, 17.

18. Hutchinson, *Indian Craze*, 218.

19. Hutchinson, "Indigeneity and Sovereignty," 23.

20. Hutchinson, "Indigeneity and Sovereignty," 22; Gere, "Art of Survivance," 655. See also chapter 3.

21. Dreves, *Visit to the Vatican Missionary Exhibition*, 6.

22. Hutchinson, *Indian Craze*, 36.

23. Felix, "Vatican Missionary Exposition," 172. I accessed this source at the Irish Capuchin Provincial Archives.

24. For a discussion of hierarchies more broadly within exhibitions, see Phillips, *Trading Identities*, 252.

25. A Yup'ik mask once owned by Surrealist artist Enrico Donati and similar to those included in the VME was on the market in 2011; see "Rare Yup'ik Mask Could Set Record Price," Donald Ellis Gallery, https://www.donaldellisgallery.com/press/a-rare-yupik-mask-sets-record-price-for-native-american-art. Some representative writings from this time include "The Art of the American Indian" (1920) by Walter Pach, "Red Man Ceremonials" (1920) by Marsden Hartley, and *Savage Art* (1929) by Paul Eluard. These are excerpted in Flam and Deutch, *Primitivism and Twentieth-Century Art*.

26. The papal collections of Indigenous belongings from Turtle Island include some artifacts from Cardinal Borgia's collection. The earliest record of materials from the Americas formed part of the collection of the Jesuit Athanius Kircher (1602–80). See the introduction, note 6. In the early modern period of collecting in Europe, the term "Indian" was used as an opaque signifier and was applied often to any material that may have come from India, Africa, or the Americas. By the nineteenth century, however, the term had become less opaque, and missionary usage was more systematic, although ambiguity remains to this day in tracing the histories of material things. See Keating and Markey, "'Indian' Objects in Medici and Austrian-Habsburg Inventories"; Domenici, "Wandering 'Leg of an Indian King.'"

27. Gere, "Art of Survivance," 655. See also Anderson, "World's Fair of 1919," 273.

28. This assessment is based on my extensive survey of the *Rivista Illustrata*. See, in particular, "L'azione missionaria Cattolica nelle 'reservations' indiane degli Stati Uniti," 575. See also Hesse, "Gesuiti e Franciscani tra le 'Pelli-Rosse,'" 726.

29. For a parallel discussion of a sense of reverence in secular art institutions, see Duncan, *Civilizing Rituals*, 7.

30. Hollengreen et al., *Meet Me at the Fair*; Lonetree, *Decolonizing Museums*; Cole, *Captured Heritage*.

31. Medak-Saltzman, "Transnational Indigenous Exchange," 593.

32. Million, "Felt Theory," 54. Million's affective approach also has parallels with Behar, *Vulnerable Observer*.

33. Million, "Felt Theory," 54.

34. The Vatican describes the entire collection of the Ethnological Museum *Anima Mundi* as "gifts" in its official catalog of the museum, as do the museum wall texts. For the catalog, see, for example, Aigner et al., *The Americas,* 12. The home page for the museum mentions "gifts" three times, "Department for the Ethnological Collections *Anima Mundi*," Musei Vaticani, accessed February 10, 2024, https://www.museivaticani.va/content/museivaticani/en/collezioni/reparti/reparto-raccolte-etnologiche.html. Web pages for individual objects also term them gifts; see, for example, the use of "dono" (gift) to describe a clay pipe made by the Lakota Sioux, in "Pipa in catlinite (fornello)", Musei Vaticani, accessed February 10, 2024, https://catalogo.museivaticani.va/index.php/Detail/objects/MV.103307.2.1?lang=en_US . See also chapter 4.

35. This argument is based on my survey and study of the *Rivista Illustrata*, as well as missionary correspondence and archival records, and my discussions with museum personnel.

36. Beard, *Roman Triumph*, 289.

37. Beard, *Roman Triumph*, 289.

38. Abbattista, "Trophying Human 'Otherness,'" 29.

39. "Papa Pio XI inaugura la mostra," 61. See also chapter 3.

40. Duncan, *Civilizing Rituals*, 95.

41. "Pope Inspects Exhibition."

42. Price, *Paris Primitive*, 95–96.

43. Considine, *Vatican Mission Exposition*, 26.

44. Dries, "1925 Vatican Mission Exposition," 122.

45. Mapelli, Aigner, and Fiussello, *Ethnos*, 152.

46. Some of the Inuit cultural belongings are currently viewable online. See "Amuleto," Musei Vaticani, accessed August 28, 2023, https://catalogo.museivaticani.va/index.php/Detail/objects/MV.104474.0.0.

47. "Quantity and Great Variety of Memorabilia," Vatican Missionary Exhibition, 1925, Mill Hill Missionaries Archive, Liverpool.

48. Schmidt was a prodigious author, and an analysis of his theory of primitive monotheism in relation to the ethnological debates in Europe at the time is beyond the scope of this study. Schmidt's racist ideas were allied to those of the Nazis in Germany, but his Catholic beliefs were not, and for this reason he was persecuted by the Nazis in the late 1930s. See Hauschild, "Christians, Jews, and the Other," 749. It is also interesting to note that Raffaele Pettazzoni was crucial in developing the history of religious studies in universities across Italy. He prided himself on being antifascist. In the early 1930s, ethnology as a discipline was beginning to be taught. For example, in 1932–33 a course in ethnology was offered at the University of Rome. After Italy invaded Ethiopia in 1935, it entered the imperial-colonialist phase. From this point on in Italy,

ethnology and anthropology were both taught. On Pettazzoni, see Stausberg, "Raffaele Pettazzoni," 365.

49. Schmidt was also blatantly antisemitic and published writings to that effect. In the words of social anthropologist Thomas Hauschild, "his work aimed at dethroning the Hebrews as the direct predecessors of the Christians." Hauschild, "Christians, Jews, and the Other," 749.

50. Hauschild, "Christians, Jews, and the Other," 749.

51. Bowen, "Missionary Exhibition," 269.

52. It should be noted that the term *Kulturkreis* was later used by the Nazis in their racial eugenics program.

53. Dietrich, "Mission," 114.

54. Kahn, "Mind over Matter," 190.

55. Kahn, "Mind over Matter," 191.

56. On salvage ethnography and anthropology, see, e.g., Stocking, *Ethnographer's Magic*, 119. On collecting in the colonial period, see Corbey, *Tribal Art Traffic*.

57. "Vatican Exhibition Is Taking Shape."

58. "Vatican Exhibition Is Taking Shape."

59. My use here of the term *visual culture* encompasses popular culture items (such as board games, posters, and photographs) and is part of the broader movement within art history to draw attention to the biases of the standard canon of art history, namely that aspect of the discipline that only examines the work of western artists and so-called high art. For more on this issue, see Elkins, *Stories of Art*.

60. Penkowski, *Il Vaticano e Roma Cristiana*, 26.

61. Considine, *Vatican Mission Exposition*, 108.

62. "L'insospettata odissea dei trasporti."

63. Father Delon Papers 1:9, September 1924, Alaskan Jesuit Archives, University Archives and Special Collections, Foley Center Library, Gonzaga University.

64. In fact, the Jesuits at Holy Cross seized and sent in a beautiful collection of Yu'pik masks for the VME that are now on display in *Anima Mundi*. One mask can be seen online; "Maschera rituale 'Amanguak,'" Musei Vaticani, accessed August 28, 2023, https://catalogo.museivaticani.va/index.php/Detail/objects/MV.101596.0.0.

65. Considine, *Vatican Mission Exposition*, 36.

66. Considine, *Vatican Mission Exposition*, 25.

67. Dries, "1925 Vatican Mission Exposition," 122.

68. Considine, *Vatican Mission Exposition*, 69.

69. "Vatican Missionary Exhibition," 163.

70. Considine, *Vatican Mission Exposition*, 98.

71. Kertzer, *Pope and Mussolini*, 83.

72. Bowen, "Missionary Exhibition at the Vatican," 267.

73. "L'azione missionaria Cattolica nelle 'reservations' indiane degli Stati Uniti."

74. Trébaol, "Les Oblats à l'Exposition des Missions," 65. See also the epilogue for more details.

75. Hesse, "Gesuiti e Franciscani tra le 'Pelli-Rosse,'" 736.

76. Gubbels, *L'exposition missionnaire*, 20.

77. See chapter 1 for more details.

78. These vibrant, incredible textiles are now on view in the *Anima Mundi* space as of 2023, after decades hidden in the vaults. There is no online record available. On material culture made by artisans in the Southwest, see Lidchi, "Material Destinies."

79. The treaty document is reproduced in Ricky, *Encyclopedia of Kansas Indians*, 209.

80. Ink and wash on paper, Ferdinand Pettrich Sketchbook 2, Ayer Special Collections, Newberry Library, Chicago.

81. O'Donnell, "Artist in the Garden," 76.

82. O'Donnell, "Artist in the Garden," 76.

83. See McKenney, *History of the Indian Tribes of North America*. On the treaty process year of 1837, see Viola, *Diplomats in Buckskin*, 61. On the importance of portraits, self-fashioning, and Indigenous diplomacy, see Hutchinson, "From Pantheon to Indian Gallery."

84. Pettrich's strategy was sadly widespread. Male artists placed emphasis on Native American male sitters rather than naming female subjects as well. One exception is the depiction of Pocahontas.

85. Itinerant American artist George Cooke made portraits of the Yankton Sioux delegation to Washington in 1837. Lithographic reproductions can be seen in McKenney, *History of the Indian Tribes*, 2:171–72, 205–7, and plates 69 and 77. Like Pettrich, Cooke also made a grand European tour and spent time painting in Rome. He was given work by Charles Bird King, the official portraitist for the US government and the War Department's Indian Gallery, and commissions for Indian portraits. Cooke's paintings can be viewed at "George Esten Cooke," American Gallery, accessed August 19, 2023, https://americangallery.wordpress.com/2009/08/29/george-cooke-1793–1849/.

86. See discussion of some of the Indigenous cultural belongings that were displayed near Pettrich's statues in chapter 4.

87. The painting is called *A Martyr to Charity*. See discussion in Considine, *Vatican Mission Exposition*, 88.

88. This is based on reading the map shown at the beginning of the Hall of the Americas analysis.

89. The Oblates of Mary Immaculate seized an ancestral sun mask of the Kwakwaka'wakw, which was displayed at the VME. See plate 15 and the discussion in chapter 4. The sun mask is visible at this link "Six Ritual Masks," Patrons of the Arts in the Vatican Museums, accessed February 10, 2024, https://www.patronsvaticanmuseums.org/en

/restoration/projects/six-ritual-masks. On the Oblates of Mary Immaculate, see also Blake, "Pastoral Power."

90. Considine, *Vatican Mission Exposition*, 117.

91. Felix, "Vatican Missionary Exposition," 171.

92. Conversation with the author, November 2016.

93. Considine emphasizes this in his account. Considine, *Vatican Mission Exposition*, 67.

94. Streit, *Catholic Missions in Figures and Symbols*.

95. *Calendario atlante delle missioni*, 5.

96. Considine, *Vatican Mission Exposition*, 85.

97. Bowen, "Missionary Exhibition," 268.

98. For an Indigenous performance artist's critique of museum displays and artifacts, see the important work of Luiseño artist James Luna in Gonzalez, *Subject to Display*, 24.

99. Lonetree, *Decolonizing Museums*, 14.

100. Although it is beyond the scope of this study, the Hall of Medicine merits analysis. Other interesting areas to be researched include the construction of the Belgian Congo, the Hall of China, the Street of Baghdad, and the Library, complete with early Jesuit texts and maps made by missionaries.

101. Dreves, *Visit to the Vatican Missionary Exhibition*, 14.

102. Schwarz, "For the Vatican Missionary Exposition." See also chapter 3 for a discussion regarding children's art at the VME.

103. Gubbels, *L'exposition missionnaire*, 20.

104. Mignolo, "Coloniality," 46.

105. Felix, "Vatican Missionary Exposition," 173.

106. Gaudio, *Engraving the Savage*, 156.

107. Gaudio, *Engraving the Savage*, 156.

108. Gaudio, *Engraving the Savage*, 157. See also Penney et al., *Art of the American Indian Frontier*.

109. Perkins, "Timeless Cultures," 349.

110. For a consideration of the notion of time in art history, see Moxey, *Visual Time*; Karlholm and Moxey, *Time in the History of Art*.

111. Hasinoff, *Faith in Objects*, 5. See also Mitchell, "World as Exhibition."

112. Hasinoff, *Faith in Objects*, 42.

113. Hasinoff, *Faith in Objects*, 42.

114. Hasinoff, "Faith in Objects," 107.

115. "Wembley Pageant 'Westward Ho!'"

116. Roberts, "Palestine on Display."

117. Qureshi, *Peoples on Parade*, 2. I return to this issue in chapter 3.

118. King, "Century of Indian Shows."

119. Clendinning, "Exhibiting a Nation," 79. In another event in Britain called the Pageant of Darkness and Light (1909), an Inuit child was rescued from an Inuit shaman by a missionary "hero." See King, "Century of Indian Shows," 40. Pius XI's tagline for the exhibition, *lux in tenebris* (light in the darkness), likely built on this metaphor.

120. Dawn, *National Visions, National Blindness*, 94. For an Indigenous curator's perspective on the history of exhibitions in Canada, see also Hill, "Indian Art in Canada."

121. Dawn, *National Visions, National Blindness*, 95.

122. Dawn, *National Visions, National Blindness*, 26.

123. Phillips, "Aesthetic Primitivism Revisited."

124. Dawn, *National Visions, National Blindness*, 273.

125. For a discussion of Native American surrealists, see Silberman, "Complexity and Contradiction."

126. Rushing, "Marketing the Affinity of the Primitive and the Modern."

127. Berlo, *Early Years of Native American Art History*, 63. See also Mullin, "Patronage of Difference."

128. Brody, *Pueblo Indian Painting*.

129. Berlo, "Art of Indigenous Americans," 2.

130. McMaster, "Tenuous Lines of Descent."

131. Horton and Berlo, "Pueblo Painting," 269.

132. Horton, "Cloudburst in Venice," 70.

133. Horton, "Cloudburst in Venice," 75.

134. "The word 'trophy' has its origins in the ancient Greek term *tropaion*. Early *tropaia* were erected to mark the place where a turning point occurred, usually in a battle. These consisted of captured weapons and armour of the defeated enemy hung from the branch of a tree. In later periods, they were also erected at ceremonial sites such as Olympia and Delphi where more people might see them, and in the Roman period, *tropaia* were also erected in Rome itself." Jacobs, Knowles, and Wingfield, *Trophies, Relics and Curios?*, 11.

135. Hasinoff, "Faith in Objects," 103.

136. Dawn, *National Visions, National Blindness*, 238.

137. Crosby, "Construction of the Imaginary Indian."

CHAPTER 3. "A WINDOW ON THE WORLD" OF COLONIAL UNKNOWING

1. Considine, *Vatican Mission Exposition*, 31. The title of this chapter draws inspiration from Considine's account.

2. Morrison, "America," 273.

3. Considine, *Vatican Mission Exposition*, 137.

4. Mill Hill Missionaries Archive kindly shared this photograph and several others. I hope to discuss the other photographs in the series in future work.

5. Considine, *Vatican Mission Exposition*, 83.

6. Dawn, *National Visions, National Blindness*.

7. Stoler, *Along the Archival Grain*, 23.

8. Vimalassery, Pegues, and Goldstein, "Colonial Unknowing," 1042.

9. Vimalassery, Pegues, and Goldstein, "Colonial Unknowing." See also Tuck and Yang, "Decolonization."

10. Watson, "Modernist Past of Lawrence Paul Yuxweluptun's Landscape Allegories," 63.

11. Considine, *Vatican Mission Exposition*, 120.

12. Corbey, "Ethnographic Showcases, 1870–1930," See also Sánchez-Gómez, "Human Zoos or Ethnic Shows?"; Sánchez-Gómez, "Imperial Faith."

13. "To Show Church Scientific: Pope Pius Plans Exhibit."

14. "To Show Church Scientific: Pope Pius Plans Exhibit."

15. See Pius XI's official missive of 1923, shown in figure 2.11, "Norme circa gli ogetti destinati all'esposizione" (Norms for objects destined for the exposition).

16. "Programme de l'Exposition."

17. Rydell, "Visions of Empire," 52.

18. Rydell, "Visions of Empire," 55.

19. Rydell, "Visions of Empire," 55; Qureshi, *Peoples on Parade*, 2.

20. The Bronx Zoo exhibited Ota Benga, a "pygmy" man, in a cage in the primate section of the zoo in 1906. An African American minister protested his living conditions. Fusco, "Other History of Intercultural Performance," 154.

21. The 1892 Italian American Exposition in Genoa exhibited four Fuegians and three Mapuche, including children and adults, male and female, with the sponsorship of the Catholic Church. Policed by Salesian missionaries, the Fuegians, dressed in skins, stood outside a hut built for them and worked on handicrafts as instructed by the missionaries. This insensitive, primitivizing display epitomized missionary and colonial exhibition attitudes of the time. Historian Luis A. Sánchez-Gómez writes: "Whilst the Protestant churches (British and North American alike) produced representations of indigenous peoples with the greatest frequency and intensity, it was (as far as we know) the (Italian) Catholic Church that had the dubious honor of being the first to display natives at a missionary exhibition, and did so in a clearly savagist and rudimentary fashion, which could even be described as brutal." Sánchez-Gómez, "Human Zoos or Ethnic Shows?," 17. At the VME, the Salesians also had a role to play, competing with other orders for the favor of Pius XI. See "Contributions of the Salesian Missionaries." See also Sánchez-Gómez, "Por la etnología hacia Dios."

22. Fusco, "Other History of Intercultural Performance," 155.

23. Geronimo, and Barrett, *Geronimo*, 45.

24. Kosmider, "Refracting the Imperial Gaze," 318.

25. Benedict, "Rituals of Representation," 45.

26. Trennert, "Fairs, Expositions, and the Changing Image of Southwestern Indians," 146.

27. Kosmider, "Refracting the Imperial Gaze," 317.

28. Fusco, "Other History of Intercultural Performance," 149.

29. Beard, *Roman Triumph*, 31. See also Rooney, *Global Vatican*.

30. Beard, *Roman Triumph*, 32.

31. "Le Suore Missionarie," 63.

32. See also Abbattista and Labanca, "Living Ethnological and Colonial Exhibitions."

33. Considine, *Vatican Mission Exposition*, 81.

34. Considine, *Vatican Mission Exposition*, 123.

35. Mageo, "'Ferocious Is the Centipede.'" See also Thomas, *Entangled Objects*, 165–67.

36. Ames, *Cannibal Tours*, 3.

37. Étienne, "Dioramas."

38. Étienne, "Dioramas." On dioramas, see also Issac, "From Life?"

39. Considine, *Vatican Mission Exposition*, 84.

40. Stoler, *Along the Archival Grain*, 256.

41. Stoler, *Along the Archival Grain*, 2.

42. Rifkin, *When Did Indians Become Straight?*, 47. See also Pasquier, "'Though Their Skin Remains Brown.'"

43. Felix, "Vatican Missionary Exposition," 173.

44. Hasinoff, "Faith in Objects," 101.

45. Giovanni, *L'Esposizione Missionaria Vaticana*, 44. For a better picture of the Gwich'in summer tunic and the baby belt, see Aigner et al., *The Americas*, 62–63. A handwoven basket from First Nations communities, stolen by the Oblates of Mary Immaculate and displayed at the VME, is described in the Vatican Museums' online database as coming from British Columbia; see "Cestino," Musei Vaticani, accessed February 23, 2024, https://catalogo.museivaticani.va/index.php/Detail/objects/MV.104690.0.0?lang=en_US.

46. For the rattle, see "Sonaglio rituale" Musei Vaticani, accessed February 23, 2024, https://catalogo.museivaticani.va/index.php/Detail/objects/MV.107110.0.0.

47. Huhndorf, *Mapping the Americas*, 25.

48. Connelly notes that Europeans used the "primitive" as a construct for understanding and categorizing non-Western cultures: "The [eighteenth-century] debates concerning 'primitive' art gave little attention to specific stylistic traditions but focused instead upon those attributes that Europeans identified (and later assimilated) as *Urformen*, primordial forms of expression, among them the hieroglyph, the grotesque, and the ornamental. This set of ideas remained remarkably constant, so much so that Gauguin and Picasso's conceptions of 'primitive' expression were still firmly rooted within that

framework of ideas nearly two hundred years later." Connelly, *Sleep of Reason*, 5. See also Phillips, "Aesthetic Primitivism Revisited."

49. Haraway, "Teddy Bear Patriarchy," 55.

50. Haraway, "Teddy Bear Patriarchy," 55.

51. Haraway, "Teddy Bear Patriarchy," 57.

52. Historian Scott Manning Stevens notes: "The choice of massive life-size dioramas was strange to many Native viewers who had grown up wishing to escape these preternaturally strange exhibits in which Native History was depicted as though a species of taxidermy." Stevens, "Collectors and Museums," 488. See also Kalshoven, "Magic of the Mannequin."

53. McCarthy, *Exhibiting Māori*, 42.

54. McCarthy, *Exhibiting Māori*, 42.

55. Kirschenblatt-Gimblett, *Destination Culture*. 39.

56. Glass, "Frozen Poses"; Jacknis, "Franz Boas and Photography."

57. Onciul, *Museums, Heritage and Indigenous Voice*, 212.

58. Cree artist Kent Monkman uses dioramas to critique the colonial legacy of residential schools. See, e.g., his exhibition *Shame and Prejudice: A Story of Resilience* which toured Canada from 2017 through 2020; "Shame and Prejudice: A Story of Resilience—by Kent Monkman," Museum of Anthropology, University of British Columbia, accessed January 2, 2024, https://moa.ubc.ca/exhibition/shame-and-prejudice/.

59. Indeed, the Vatican gift shop to this day sells weird colonial Vatican paraphernalia, including a perfume and home fragrance called Ethnos that is meant to capture the scent of Indigenous people. I intend to critique this issue in future work.

60. See chapter 4. See also Gubbels, *L'exposition missionnaire*, 124.

61. Corbey, "Ethnographic Showcases," 358.

62. The religious organization that issued the game is the present-day Pontificia Opera della Infanzia Missionaria.

63. This wording comes from a subtitle located on the top border of the game (my translation). It should be noted that there were significant gender imbalances in the exhibition displays, with more exhibition space being given to priests than nuns, as well as an unequal distribution in the representation of missionary efforts. Sanchez-Gomez, "Por la etnología hacia Dios," 90.

64. Diaz, *Repositioning the Missionary*, 174.

65. Considine, *Vatican Mission Exposition*, 166.

66. Several powerful precursors for the imagery of this game exist in Rome, including Gian Lorenzo Bernini's *Fountain of the Four Rivers* (1651) and Andrea Pozzo's *Allegory of the Four Continents* (1685–94), which express the power of the Catholic Church in the spiritual and material colonization of the Americas and other continents. On the source

of inspiration for Bernini's god symbolizing the Rio de la Plata, see Kaplan, "Italy," 183. See also Sharpe, *Allegories of Empire*.

67. Rothstein and Inouye, "Visual Games," 287.

68. Rothstein and Inouye, "Visual Games," 293.

69. Diaz, *Repositioning the Missionary*, 112.

70. Considine, *Vatican Mission Exposition*, 106.

71. "Vatican Exhibition Is Taking Shape."

72. The instructions read, "Ogni tappa bisogna recitare una Ave Maria con l'invocazione: Vergine Maria pregate per noi e per i poveri fasciutti infedelli" (my translation).

73. Hasinoff, *Faith in Objects*, 82.

74. Although Benito Mussolini suppressed Protestant missionary activity, it is important to remember that Protestants and Catholics had some parallel aims. Contemporary Protestant missionary exhibitions, such as the World in Boston in 1911, were seen as significant rivals in the race to Christianize the world of unbelievers (as discussed in chapter 2). Much closer to the heart of Catholicism, the American Methodist Episcopal Church initiated work in Rome in 1873 and by 1914 had purchased land on Monte Mario, a hillside perch looking down on the Vatican, with hopes of building an international college and establishing a Methodist influence in Rome. The conjoined efforts of the Knights of Columbus and the fascist government led by Mussolini quashed the Methodists' dreams. D'Agostino, *Rome in America*, 171; Kertzer, *Pope and Mussolini*, 130.

75. I came across the game *Viaggi missionari* (Missionary voyages) at the Yale Divinity Library, where it was part of a curated exhibit, *Spreading the Word: A Selection of Missionary Posters, Games, and Ephemera from the Day Missions Collection*, featuring didactic material from the early twentieth century. See "Missionary Ephemera Collection," Yale Divinity Library, accessed August 19, 2023, https://divinity-adhoc.library.yale.edu/Exhibits/MissionaryEphemera.html. I also consulted the two additional games at Yale Divinity Library. See Missionary Ephemera Collection, RG 221, series VI, box OV3, folder 4, Special Collections, Yale Divinity Library.

76. Carmelo di Monza Institute, email communication with the author, March 1, 2017.

77. Luigi Ciompi and Adrian Seville, "Giuoco (Il) del Missionario," Giochi dell'Oca e di percorso, accessed August 19, 2023, http://www.giochidelloca.it/scheda.php?id=340.

78. Coombes, *Reinventing Africa*, 186.

79. As Griffiths comments, "it has long been recognized how important popular tales of imperial heroism and adventure were in shaping the ideologies of Empire in this period. But we also need to recognize how the influential mission presses employed these popular heroic genres to deliver their message, despite the inherent dangers and contradictions they involved for the Christian message of peace and brotherhood." Griffiths, *Mixed Messages*, 52.

80. "The tale of missionary adventure and exemplary heroism was employed to represent many regions of mission endeavor, notably India, the South Seas, and China. But the

long public fascination with the exploration of the so-called Dark Continent from the 1840s onward, the success of a large body of best-selling secular exploration and hunting journals, and the rapid expansion of imperial interests in Africa from the mid-1870s all ensure that Africa was the region most frequently represented in both secular and mission texts by this genre of the heroic, adventurous tale." Griffiths, *Mixed Messages*, 54.

81. Griffiths, *Mixed Messages*, 55.

82. Griffiths, *Mixed Messages*, 55.

83. Griffiths, *Mixed Messages*, 56.

84. Griffiths, *Mixed Messages*, 62.

85. Truth and Reconciliation Commission (Canada) (hereafter TRC), *They Came for the Children*, 15.

86. Veracini, *Settler Colonialism*, 108.

87. Veracini, *Settler Colonialism*, 81.

88. Ravenscroft, "Girl in the Picture," 512.

89. Digmann, "Dear Father."

90. Ames, *Cannibal Tours*, 3.

91. McMaster, "Tenuous Lines of Descent."

92. Paisley, *Lone Protester*, 7.

93. Archuleta, Child, and Lomawaima, *Away from Home*, 32.

94. Woolford notes that few comparative studies have been undertaken of residential and boarding school experiences in Canada and the United States. However, he notes several key differences between the two countries: "A) Canadian residential schools lasted, on average, longer than American residential schools; B) Canadian policies were unrelentingly assimilationist, since no reformist period occurred in Canada as it did in the United States in the 1930s; C) Indigenous parents in Canada had less say regarding to which schools their children were sent; and D) some Canadian religious denominations lobbied vigorously to prevent diminishment of their control over or the closing of boarding schools. The cumulative effect of these differences . . . is that Indigenous children in Canada typically entered boarding schools at an earlier age than their US counterparts, and the Canadian system affected more generations of Indigenous children, in a more brutal form, than was true for most parts of the United States." Woolford, *This Benevolent Experiment*, 6. Woolford's study is a comprehensive survey of the history and impact of residential schools in Canada and the United States. For an important text that surveys the voices of Indigenous activists, poets, and survivors, see Fear-Segal and Rose, *Carlisle Indian Industrial School*.

95. TRC, *They Came for the Children*, 15.

96. TRC, *They Came for the Children*, 15.

97. Dippie, *Vanishing American*, xii.

98. TRC, *They Came for the Children*, 6–10.

99. The exhibition *Witnesses: Art and Canada's Indian Residential Schools* at Belkin Art Gallery, Vancouver, 2013, also presented contemporary Indigenous artists responding to the history of residential schools. See "Witnesses: Art and Canada's Indian Residential Schools," Belkin Art Gallery, University of British Columbia, accessed January 2, 2024, https://belkin.ubc.ca/exhibitions/witnessesart-and-canadas-indian-residential-schools/. There is no parallel process like the Truth and Reconciliation Commission currently in the United States. See also note 94 above.

100. For a discussion of the architecture and placeless-making nature of Indian residential schools, see Carr, "'House of No Spirit.'"

101. TRC, *They Came for the Children*, 17.

102. Aigner et al., *The Americas*, 53.

103. On this history, see the painting *The Scream* (2016) by Cree artist Kent Monkman. "Kent Monkman: History Painting for a Colonized Canada," Canadian Art, accessed August 19, 2023, https://canadianart.ca/features/kent-monkman-critiques-canada-150/.

104. TRC, *They Came for the Children*, 77.

105. Watson, "Modernist Past of Lawrence Paul Yuxweluptun's Landscape Allegories," 63.

106. Digmann, "Dear Father."

107. Phillips, "Aboriginal Modernities," 349.

108. Lentis, *Colonized through Art*, 33.

109. Lentis, *Colonized through Art*, 34.

110. Lentis, *Colonized through Art*, 45.

111. Woolford, *This Benevolent Experiment*, 3.

112. Lentis, *Colonized through Art*, 45. See also Hutchinson, *Indian Craze*, 171.

113. Archuleta, Child, and Lomawaima, *Away from Home*, 89.

114. Archuleta, Child, and Lomawaima, *Away from Home*, 85.

115. Archuleta, Child, and Lomawaima, *Away from Home*, 92.

116. Archuleta, Child, and Lomawaima, *Away from Home*, 96.

117. Lentis, *Colonized through Art*, 221.

118. Lentis, *Colonized through Art*, 222. On the "Indian corner" in a Parisian context, see Burns, *Transnational Frontiers*, 109–14.

119. Woolford, *This Benevolent Experiment*, 203.

120. Archuleta, Child, and Lomawaima, *Away from Home*, 32.

121. Archuleta, Child, and Lomawaima, *Away from Home*, 58.

122. Green and Troutman, "By the Waters of the Minnehaha," 78.

123. Green and Troutman, "By the Waters of the Minnehaha," 78.

124. Considine, *Vatican Mission Exposition*, 57.

125. Woolford, *This Benevolent Experiment*, 9.

126. "Rilievo statistico delle missioni d'america," 824.

127. Cited in King, "Century of Indian Shows," 40.

128. Considine, *Vatican Mission Exposition*, 31.

129. Mauro, *Art of Americanization at the Carlisle Indian School*, 5. See also Sekula, "Body and the Archive."

130. Mauro, *Art of Americanization at the Carlisle Indian School*, 5.

131. Woolford, *This Benevolent Experiment*, 100.

132. Woolford, *This Benevolent Experiment*, 12.

133. "Vatican Missionary Exhibition," 161.

134. This issue is worth exploring in another project. See, e.g., Dirar, "Church-State Relations." See also Sòrgoni, "'Defending the Race'"; Vargaftig, "Les expositions coloniales."

135. Wrightson, "Shattering Glass Boxes," 100.

CHAPTER 4. ETERNAL SOVEREIGNS AND ANCESTRAL ART

1. Librarian at the Propaganda Fide Library, conversation with the author, March 2016.

2. Haas, *Pablo Tac*, 33.

3. Dr. Lisbeth Haas, email communication with the author, May 9, 2016. I also consulted the Cardinal Mezzofanti Archives in Bologna at the Archiginnasio as well as Pablo Tac's drawings, but those fall outside the parameters of this project. On James Luna's important homage and performance honoring Tac's life, see Luna, Smith, and Lowe, *James Luna*.

4. Chicago, and the United States as a whole, is full of statues and other tributary art to Father Marquette. For an extensive list of statuary, stained glass, and other media on Marquette, see Derome, "Les sources iconographiques."

5. Marsden, "Father Marquette."

6. Venturi, "Il Padre Giacomo Marquette ardito esploratore del Mississippi," 698.

7. It is interesting to compare Trentanove's statue of Indigenous leader Chief Oskosh in the Menominee Park, Oshkosh, WI, which Trentanove completed ten years previously. See Giordano, "Italy's Contributions," 2. See also Morozzi, "Gaetano Trentanove."

8. Statues of Marquette abound throughout the United States, especially in Michigan and Wisconsin, along with murals and other commemorative imagery. The VME statue is the only one in Italy, to the best of my knowledge. On the multiple statues and artforms of Father Marquette, see Nelson, *Searching for Marquette*.

9. "Papa Pio XI inaugura la mostra," 59. See also "Manuale del pellegrinaggio: Diocesano missionario, a Roma 4–10 Agosto," 1, Vatican Missionary Exposition Papers, Propaganda Fide Library and Archive Collections, Pontificio Collegio Urbano "De Propaganda Fide," Rome.

10. Lord, "Silent Eloquence."

11. At this point I am leaving out a Sami runic calendar and a Rapa Nui talking tablet, which were in the VME, as these complicate and expand a discussion of Indigenous

material culture beyond the scope of this study. On the talking tablet, see Lauenroth, "Le 'tavolette parlanti' dell'Isola di Pasqua,"220. For the Sami calendar, see "Tavoletta, parte di un raro calendario runico" accessed February 11, 2024, https://catalogo.museivaticani.va/index.php/Detail/objects/MV.107830.8.3?lang=en_US. See also *Annali Lateranensi*, Propaganda Fide Library Collections.

12. Medak-Saltzman, "Transnational Indigenous Exchange," 594. See also Voelker, "Unfixing the Frame"; Dirks, "Colonial Histories," 279.

13. Considine, *Vatican Mission Exposition*, 124.

14. Regarding the "weight" of things, Harrison notes that "in making reference to the weight of things, we mean not only the physical bulk of collections, which occupy vast storage facilities behind the scenes of museums around the world, but also their political and affective weight. The 'affective' weight of things in museums refers to the charismatic or enchanting qualities of objects, their ability to engage the senses, and their ability to act in ways that are both integral to and generative of human behaviour or even in ways that are person-like, in conjunction with or independently of people." Harrison, "Reassembling Ethnographic Museum Collections," 5.

15. Parker, "Constitution," 1. The Iroquois are also known as the Haudenosaunee, and the English term is *Mohawk*, but all these terms are used interchangeably by Haudenosaunee communities today.

16. Veatch, *Canadian Policy*, 91.

17. Rostkowski, "Deskaheh's Shadow," 1.

18. Trevithick, "Conflicting Outlooks." For the text of the booklet, which contains an appeal addressed to the secretary-general of the League of Nations, see https://law.lib.buffalo.edu/pdf/Redmanappeal.pdf.

19. Rickard, "Sovereignty," 51.

20. Belanger, "Six Nations."

21. Belanger, "Six Nations," 29.

22. Belanger, "Six Nations," 30. Yale D. Belanger does not mention the use of wampum in his article.

23. A beautiful example of a Huron-Wendat chief wearing wampum on his delegation trip to London in 1825 is the painting by Edward Chatfield at the McCord Stewart Museum, Montreal. For a print based on the painting, see Lainey, "The Wampum."

24. Becker, "Maniwaki Wampum Group," 121.

25. One example of the resonance of this belt can be found in reproductions of the Vatican wampum belt on wampum blogs online. For a reproduction of the Vatican wampum belt, although it uses negative coloration, so the white and purple are reversed, see Augustine, "Wampum Belt Archive." See also the recorded presentation by Jamie Jacobs, "The Orator's Dilemma: Wampum as Material, Media, and Memory," in the video *Conserving Active Matter: Indigenous Ontologies*, Bard Graduate Center, April 18,

2018, https://www.bgc.bard.edu/research-forum/articles/286/conserving-active-matter-indigenous-ontologies.

26. In a photograph from the 1940s, the belt is shown in the "Eastern Algonquin" section of the Hall of North America. See Giordano, "Italy's Contributions," 2.

27. Although the Vatican Museums describe it as a "gift," did Algonquin and Haudenosaunee communities gift this belonging? The doubt is raised as the belt was used by the Sulpicians in their land takeovers in Tiohtiá:ke Mooniyang (Montreal) and ultimately also as a form of propaganda for the popes. Algonquin knowledge keeper, conversation with the author, September 2023.

28. Becker, "Maniwaki Wampum Group."

29. Pizzorusso, "Roman Ecclesiastical Archives," 22.

30. Thomas, *Manitou and God*, 27.

31. Bushnell, "North American Ethnographical Material."

32. Becker, "Vatican 1831 Wampum Belt." See also Lysyk, "Evidentiary Issues."

33. Aigner et al., *The Americas*, 72–73.

34. Borrows, "Constitutional Law," 24.

35. Bruchac, "Wampum in Museum Collections."

36. Aigner et al., *The Americas*, 77.

37. Aigner et al., *The Americas*, 73.

38. Bruchac, "Notes from the Trail."

39. Rasmussen, *Queequeg's Coffin*, 17.

40. Borrows, "Constitutional Law," 24.

41. Parker, "Constitution," 1.

42. Pizzorusso, "Roman Ecclesiastical Archives," 21.

43. Aigner et al., *The Americas*, 72–73.

44. Morris, "Running the 'Medicine Line.'"

45. Museum curator, correspondence with the author, January–November 2023. For an extended period, the Vatican Ethnological Museum *Anima Mundi* did not respond to requests for the belt to be included in the exhibition *Wampum: Beads of Diplomacy*. In the end, the director of the Vatican Museums, Barbara Jatta, finally responded, and at the very last minute the wampum belt was shipped from Vatican City.

46. Gubbels, *L'exposition missionnaire*, 120–21.

47. Gubbels, *L'exposition missionnaire*, 124.

48. Diocese of Edmunston, "Saint Ann Parish (Tobique First Nation)," March 24, 2022, http://www.diocese-edmundston.ca/fr/zp_tobique_1st_nation.html.

49. The Wabanaki Confederacy is made up of five Algonquin First Nations. An official record of the museum, the *Annali Lateranensi*, states that this item was sent from the Catholic Mission in Toronto to Rome in the mid nineteenth century. The cross, carved in the early nineteenth century, was used in religious processions. This sacred belonging

was part of the Museo Borgiano di Propaganda Fide in Rome and is now on display at the Ethnological Museum *Anima Mundi*. See Maarschalkerweerd, "Plastiche cristiane." The cross is also now visible in the Vatican Museums online database; see "Crocifisso," Musei Vaticani, accessed February 11, 2024, https://catalogo.museivaticani.va/index.php/Detail/objects/MV.101612.0.0. Errors are common in historical records surrounding Indigenous materials, including in the *Rivista Illustrata* and the Vatican Museums online record for this belonging, which emphasizes Catholic conversion.

50. Pritzke, *Native American Encyclopedia*, 456. Anthropologist Christine Reiser analyzes representations of indigeneity in New England from 1910 to the 1930s. She notes how Indigenous Americans used pageantry to craft their identity. Reiser, "Materializing Community."

51. The "crucifix" was listed in AMDG, *Croquis de visite d'exposition*, 16–17.

52. Maarschalkerweerd, "Plastiche cristiane." I came across the record of this Indigenous cross made by a Passamaquoddy artist while at the Propaganda Fide Library and then saw it at the Ethnological Museum *Anima Mundi*. Catholic orders among the Passamaquoddy since the seventeenth century include the Capuchins, Recollects, Spiritans, and Jesuits.

53. Maarschalkerweerd, "Plastiche cristiane," 16.

54. Maarschalkerweerd, "Plastiche cristiane," 16.

55. Kimmerer, *Braiding Sweetgrass*, 363.

56. Kimmerer, *Braiding Sweetgrass*, 363.

57. Porter, *Art of Native American Basketry*, 21.

58. Laforge, "Burl Bowls and Birchbark Baskets."

59. On Passamaquoddy art traditions, see also Lester, *History on Birchbark*, 10.

60. Lester, *History on Birchbark*, 11.

61. Lester, *History on Birchbark*, 92.

62. Coe, King, and Ostrowitz, *Responsive Eye*, 201.

63. Maarschalkerweerd, "Plastiche cristiane," 16.

64. Thomas, *Manitou and God*, 5.

65. Hedden, "Passamaquoddy Shamanism," 319.

66. See Bushnell, "North American Ethnographical Material."

67. Highway and Moss, *Comparing Mythologies*.

68. Pizzorusso, "Roman Ecclesiastical Archives," 24.

69. Former Vatican curator, conversation with the author, November 2016.

70. Former Vatican curator, conversation with the author, November 2016.

71. See discussion also in the introduction and appendix.

72. In future work I hope to write about *Anima Mundi* and analyze some of the other Indigenous cultural belongings therein and my secret visit at a special event.

73. Densmore, *Songs of the Sioux*, 5.

74. Hansen, *Memory and Vision*, 140. On Plains visual culture more broadly, see also Berlo, *Plains Indian Drawings*.

75. Aigner, "Vatican Museums," 95.

76. Amiotte, "Lakota Sun Dance." On the Sun Dance and settler colonialism, see also Kornhauser and Vittoria, *Jules Tavernier*.

77. Phillips, "Aboriginal Modernities," 349.

78. Rydell and Kroes, *Buffalo Bill*, 110.

79. Aigner, "Vatican Museums," 89. See also Friesen and Chladiuk, *Lakota Performers*.

80. Lincoln, "Social Construction of Plains Art," 58.

81. Aigner, "Vatican Museums," 94.

82. "Disegno su tela della Danza del Sole," Musei Vaticani, accessed August 29, 2023, https://catalogo.museivaticani.va/index.php/Detail/objects/MV.107323.0.0.

83. Densmore, *Teton Sioux Music and Culture*, 116.

84. The harvesting of materials is a significant aspect of Indigenous art creation. Conversation with Linda Aguilar, Chumash horsehair basket weaver, New Mexico, September 2019.

85. For a ledger drawing depicting a "medicine vision" by "Henderson Ledger Artist B," see "A Warrior's Vision," Metropolitan Museum of Art, https://www.metmuseum.org/art/collection/search/717549.

86. Amiotte, "Lakota Sun Dance," 88.

87. Berlo, *Plains Indian Drawings*, 221.

88. The term "X-ray style" is found throughout discussions of Aboriginal art of Australia. See Morphy et al., "Aboriginal Australia."

89. Berlo, *Plains Indian Drawings*, 221.

90. Dana Claxton, conversation with the author, June 15, 2017.

91. Powell, "Sacrifice Transformed," 85.

92. Dana Claxton, conversation with the author, June 2017.

93. See, e.g., Berlo, *Plains Indian Drawings*.

94. Estes, *Our History*, 209–12.

95. "All Animal Dreamers, then, were endowed with special powers from those spirit animals who instructed them. The power was to be used and displayed." Powell, "Sacrifice Transformed," 85. Thirty-one drawings by Standing Bear are held at the Buechel Museum, Saint Francis Mission, Rosebud, South Dakota.

96. For the sepia photographic portrait of Luther Standing Bear by Robert Constant, ca. 1905, see "Portrait of Standing Bear," McCracken Research Library at the Buffalo Bill Center of the West, accessed August 19, 2023, http://library.centerofthewest.org/digital/collection/p17097coll1/id/28/rec/5.

97. Standing Bear, *My People the Sioux*, 113.

98. Other warriors who attended, including Sitting Bull, whose vision inspired the largest Sun Dance ceremony in June 1876 in Little Big Horn, Montana, also made ledger drawings of the rite. Mató Nájin Standing Bear's ledger drawing *The Battle of the Little Big Horn* was part of the 2017 Metropolitan Museum of Art exhibition *Native American Masterpieces: The Charles and Valerie Diker Collection*; see https://www.metmuseum.org/art/collection/search/717548.

99. Pearce, *Women and Ledger Art*. See also Bol, "Gender in Art."

100. Cutschall, "Seen and the Unseen," 65.

101. Greci-Green, "German Missionary Participation," 31.

102. Kehoe, *Ghost Dance*, 14.

103. See, for example, the 2013 exhibition *Ghost Dance: Activism. Resistance. Art*, The Image Centre, Toronto, accessed August 19, 2023, https://ryersonimagecentre.ca/exhibition/ghost-dance-activism-resistance-art/. See also Estes, *Our History*.

104. Jutz, "Recollections," 216.

105. Kehoe, *Ghost Dance*, 15.

106. Wilson, *Research Is Ceremony*.

107. DeLucia, "Antiquarian Collecting."

108. Considine, *Vatican Mission Exposition*, 87.

109. Cree is the one of the most prevalent Indigenous languages and is spoken throughout North America. See Whitecalf, *Kinêhiyâwiwininaw nêhiyawêwin*.

110. Aigner et al., *The Americas*, 66.

111. Oberholtzer, "Trading amongst Themselves."

112. McMaster, "Discovering the Levels of Meaning," 115.

113. Brasser, "In Search of Métis Art," 222. See also Bell, "Oscillating Identities."

114. Racette, "Sewing for a Living," 40.

115. Bol, *Art and Tradition of Beadwork*; Njootli et al., *My Auntie*. See also Brandson, "Ziigimineshin Brings Beaders Together."

116. Belcourt et al., *Medicines to Help Us*.

117. Aigner et al., *The Americas*, 65.

118. Racette, "Sewing for a Living," 36.

119. Phillips, *Trading Identities*, 252.

120. Ray, "Beading." See also Prete, "Beadworking."

121. Oberholtzer, "Thorny Identification," 13.

122. McMaster, "Discovering the Levels of Meaning," 116.

123. For more on this network of domestic and international relations, see Racette, "Sewing for a Living," 41.

124. See the website of Walking with Our Sisters, http://walkingwithoursisters.ca/. See also Anderson, Campbell, and Belcourt, *Keetsahnak*.

125. See, e.g., the text panel in figure 4.3.

126. This is based on my analysis of the *Rivista Illustrata*, the main print organ of the VME, and missionary correspondence as well as an analysis of Pius XI's demand for cultural belongings from across the globe "Norme circa gli oggetti destinati all'esposizione (see figure 2.11). See the bibliography for the full list of archives consulted.

Regarding the discussion of stolen cultural belongings, there are many more in the Ethnological Museum *Anima Mundi* that deserve further attention and study. Stolen belongings from around the globe languish in the collections at present. I reference here a few more belongings that deserve attention from Turtle Island. In particular, I want to include the Inuvialuit kayak that was displayed at the VME. See "Kayak and Double Blade Paddle," Patrons of the Arts in the Vatican Museums, accessed August 28, 2023, https://www.patronsvaticanmuseums.org/en/restoration/projects/kayak-and-double-blade-paddle. A collection of sacred masks stolen for the VME is visible here: "Six Ritual Masks," Patrons of the Arts in the Vatican Museums, accessed August 28, 2023, https://www.patronsvaticanmuseums.org/en/restoration/projects/six-ritual-masks. Also of interest is this Sami calendar: "Tavoletta, parte di un raro calendario runico portatile," Musei Vaticani, accessed August 28, 2023, https://catalogo.museivaticani.va/index.php/Detail/objects/MV.107830.8.3.

127. This purposeful amnesia and lack of discussion of the missionary origins and genocidal labors in Indigenous communities is also present in the Vatican catalogs. See for example Aigner et al., *The Americas*.

128. For more about Pius XI's list of demands, see Dontenwill, "Letter to Steering Committee of the VME," December 21, 1925, Archivium Generale O.M.I. Romae, article 2658. For more information on the Indian Act and residential schools, see chapter 3. See also Truth and Reconciliation Commission (Canada), *They Came for the Children*, 15. On stolen cultural belongings and this era of salvage collecting see Cole, *Captured Heritage*. See also Pettipas, *Severing the Ties That Bind*.

129. Webster, "From Colonization to Repatriation," 25.

130. Webster. "From Colonization to Repatriation," 36.

131. Aigner et al., *The Americas*, 52. There is an online record for this mask: "Six Ritual Masks," Patrons of the Arts in the Vatican Museums, accessed August 28, 2023, https://www.patronsvaticanmuseums.org/en/restoration/projects/six-ritual-masks. The mask was visible for more than a year on the Vatican Museums' main website but has since been taken down.

132. Beginning in the 1960s, the Kwakwaka'wakw petitioned the Canadian government and art institutions for the return of their cultural belongings. See "Our Masks Come Home," Living Tradition, U'mista Cultural Centre, accessed August 19, 2023, https://umistapotlatch.ca/nos_masques_come_home-our_masks_come_home-eng.php. For more on repatriation, see Kramer, *Switchbacks*, 87–103. See also Krmpotich, *Force of Family*.

133. Webster, "From Colonization to Repatriation," 36.

134. Indigenous materials and spiritualities were the subject of an exhibition of the work of the late Kwakwaka'wakw Chief Beau Dick held at the Audain Art Gallery, Whistler, BC, in 2020. See Martens, *Beau Dick*, fig. 1.

135. These items were seen by me in a photograph at the Vatican Fototeca archive as well as on visits to the *Anima Mundi* museum, spring 2023. See also Father Delon Papers 1:9, September 1924, Alaskan Jesuit Archives, University Archives and Special Collections, Foley Center Library, Gonzaga University.

136. See Boll and Fazakas, *Maker of Monsters*.

137. On not writing about masks that are danced in ceremony, I am inspired by the work of Tsimshian art historian Mique'l D'Angeli. See D'Angeli, "Dancing Sovereignty."

138. Webster, "From Colonization to Repatriation," 37.

139. Brown, *First Nations*, 6.

140. See "Procedures for Claims for the Return of Cultural Objects," Gardens, Libraries, and Museums, University of Oxford, accessed August 19, 2023, https://www.glam.ox.ac.uk/procedures-for-return-of-cultural-objects-claims. See also Peers, "Ceremonies of Renewal."

141. In the past several years there have been many repatriations between UK museums (Bristol, Exeter, Edinburgh, Glasgow, and Oxford) and Indigenous museums on Turtle Island. The museums are working from the position of a moral imperative to repatriate and forge new healing connections with Indigenous communities. On a global level, there are complex discussions occurring with Belgium, France, Germany, and the Netherlands regarding the repatriation of cultural patrimony to African nations. At the time of writing, France had returned twenty-six artifacts to Benin, treasures stolen during the colonial era. Germany had restituted twenty-two bronzes to Nigeria as of December 2022, an important motion in its broader protocol to return all 1,130 Benin bronzes in German institutions. See Moulson, "Germany, Nigeria Sign Accord." See also Hicks, *Brutish Museums*.

142. On cultural patrimony and public display in Italy, see Milicia, "Simulacra of Eternal Life." On colonial displays in Italy during the fascist period, see Falcucci, "Bringing the Empire."

143. Senier, "Digitizing Indigenous History." See also Schweitzer and Henry, *Afterlives of Indigenous Archives*.

144. Brown, *First Nations*, 29.

145. Stefanovich, "Inuit Leader."

146. Former Vatican curator, conversation with the author, November 2016.

147. Conaty, *We Are Coming Home*, 55.

148. See the important report by the Canadian Museums Association, a response to the Truth and Reconciliation Commission's call to action #67, Canadian Museums Association, "Moved to Action." There is also repatriation linked to land claims and provincial legislation; see the province of Alberta's First Nations Sacred Ceremonial Objects Repatriation Act, December 13, 2016, https://kings-printer.alberta.ca/documents/Acts/F14.pdf. On the Northwest Coast, the Nisga'a petitioned for the return of an ancestral totem pole, stolen by anthropologist Marius Barbeau in 1929. The National Museum of Scotland will return the pole shortly. See Canadian Press, "Scottish Museum." Anthropologist Jennifer Kramer discusses the need for an "Aboriginal conceptual system" for repatriation outside a western ideological framework. Kramer, *Switchbacks*, 89–90. See also Matthews, *Naamiwan's Drum*.

149. Vatican curator, conversation with the author, March 2022.

150. Povinelli, "Woman on the Other Side," 168.

151. Todd and Fraser, "Decolonial Sensibilities."

152. Garvin, "Missionary Exhibition," 150. Accessed at the Palazzola Library and Collections, Rocca di Papa, Italy.

153. Garvin, "Missionary Exhibition," 150.

154. Gubbels, *L'exposition missionnaire*, 120.

155. Nicks, "Dr Oronhyatekha's History Lessons," 482.

156. Conaty, *We Are Coming Home*, 13.

157. Conaty, *We Are Coming Home*, 14.

158. "La chiusura solenne dell'Esposizione Missionaria Vaticana," 71. See also "Ethnological Museum *Anima Mundi*," Musei Vaticani, accessed August 19, 2023, http://www.museivaticani.va/content/museivaticani/en/collezioni/musei/museo-etnologico/museo-etnologico.html.

159. On sovereignty, see Raheja, "Visual Sovereignty," 29; Rickard, "Sovereignty," 51; Lyons, *X-Marks*, 13.

160. Stefanovich, "Inuit Leader."

EPILOGUE. DEUS EX MACHINA

1. Anthony Martin Fernando's journals are now available in digital form. See "A. M. Fernando Notebooks," Australian Institute of Aboriginal and Torres Strait Islander Studies, https://aiatsis.gov.au/collection/featured-collections/am-fernando-notebooks.

2. Paisley, *Lone Protester*, 86.

3. Paisley, *Lone Protester*, 82.

4. More recently the Vatican Museums have made some of these cultural belongings and ancestral figures visible in an online database, currently functioning only in Italian.

See for example "Gruppo di sette cinture (o collane) con pendenti in madreperla," Musei Vaticani, accessed August 19, 2023, https://catalogo.museivaticani.va/index.php/Detail/objects/MV.109993.0.0?lang=it_IT. There are also two boomerangs from the VME listed: "Boomerang dipinto con disegni rituali in ocra rossa e gialla," Musei Vaticani, accessed August 19, 2023, https://catalogo.museivaticani.va/index.php/Detail/objects/MV.110598.0.0. See also Neale, "God Lives in the Dreaming."

5. Paisley, *Lone Protester*, 82. For the eucalyptus bundle, see "Foglio di corteccia di eucalipto, utilizzato probabilmente per ripararsi," Musei Vaticani, accessed February 25, 2024, https://catalogo.museivaticani.va/index.php/Detail/objects/MV.110599.0.0.

6. For the statuette of Rogo, see "Statua del dio Rongo (Rogo)," Musei Vaticani, accessed February 25, 2024, https://catalogo.museivaticani.va/index.php/Detail/objects/MV.100185.0.0.

7. For an example of a whale bone lei, see "Necklace: Lei niho palaoa," Ethnology Database, Bernice Pauahi Bishop Museum, State Museum of Natural and Cultural History, Hawai'i, accessed August 24, 2023, http://data.bishopmuseum.org/ethnologydb/detailed.php?ARTNO=01270.

8. For a model catamaran from Papua New Guinea in the Vatican Museums collection, see "Modellino di catamarano a tre scafi," Musei Vaticani, accessed February 25, 2024, https://catalogo.museivaticani.va/index.php/Detail/objects/MV.125516.0.0.

9. Stoler, *Along the Archival Grain*, 256. I first came across this image in Corbey, *Tribal Art Traffic*, 56–57. The Damiaan Museum, Leuven, Belgium, kindly provided me with the image.

10. Paisley, *Lone Protester*, 84.

11. See discussion in chapter 2.

12. Paisley, *Lone Protester*, 91.

13. Paisley, *Lone Protester*, 87–92.

14. See discussion in chapter 2.

15. Ghirardo, "Architects," 68.

16. Neville, *Mussolini*, 93.

17. Neville, *Mussolini*, 94.

18. Andreotti, "Aesthetics of War," 82. See also Rocco, "Room O."

19. Andreotti, "Aesthetics of War," 85.

20. Ghirardo, "Architects," 69.

21. Honour, *Neo-Classicism*, 15.

22. Neville, *Mussolini*, 124.

23. Beard, *Roman Triumph*, 32.

24. On the relationship between radio and Italian colonial expansion, see Hirsh, "Transmissions of Fascism."

25. Considine, *Vatican Mission Exposition*, 31.

26. While there has been a longstanding interest in Indigenous American culture in Italy, Italians have not appropriated Native people as a symbol of a bygone era to the same degree as Germans. However, for the strange story about the self-appointed Italian "Tuscarora chief" who met Mussolini in 1925, see Giordano, "Anxiety of Discovery."

27. Trébaol, "Les Oblats à l'Exposition des Missions," 65.

28. Negro, *Roma, non basta una vita.*

Bibliography

ARCHIVES, COLLECTIONS, AND LIBRARIES

Alaskan Jesuit Archives, University Archives and Special Collections, Foley Center Library, Gonzaga University, Spokane, WA.

Archivum Generale O.M.I. Romae (Oblates), Rome.

Archivum Romanum Societatis Iesu (Jesuits), Rome.

Cardinal Mezzofanti Archives, Archiginnasio, Bologna, Italy.

Damiaanmuseum, Tremelo, Belgium.

Edward E. Ayer Special Collections, Newberry Library, Chicago.

Irish Capuchin Provincial Archives, Dublin.

Mill Hill Missionaries Archive, Liverpool, UK.

Palazzola Library and Collections, Rocca di Papa, Italy.

Paul Bechtold Library, Catholic Theological Union, Chicago.

Propaganda Fide Library and Archive Collections, Pontificio Collegio Urbano "De Propaganda Fide," Rome.

Societas Verbi Divini (Verbites of the Divine Word Missionaries) Archive, Rome.

Vatican Apostolic Library, Vatican City.

Vatican Fototeca Archive, Vatican City.

Vatican Secret Archive, Vatican City.

Yale Divinity Library, New Haven, CT.

PUBLISHED SOURCES

Abbattista, Guido. "Trophying Human 'Otherness': From Christopher Columbus to Contemporary Ethno-Ecology." *Cromohs* 16 (2011): 19–41.

Abbattista, Guido, and Nicola Labanca. "Living Ethnological and Colonial Exhibitions in Liberal and Fascist Italy." In *Human Zoos: Science and Spectacle in the Age of Colonial Empires*, edited by Pascal Blanchard, Nicolas Bancel, Eric Deroo, and Sandrine Lemaire, 41–52. Liverpool: Liverpool University Press, 2008.

Ahlberg Yohe, Jill, and Teri Greeves. *Hearts of Our People: Native Women Artists*. Minneapolis, MN: Minneapolis Institute of Art, 2019.

Aigner, Katherine. "The Vatican Museums and Native Americans: From Objects to Subjects." In *Tecumseh, Keokuk, Black Hawk: Portrayals of Native Americans in Times of Treaties and Removal*, edited by Iris Edenheiser and Astrid Nielsen, 86–98. Stuttgart: Arnoldsche Art, 2013.

Aigner, Katherine, Nicola Mapelli, Giovanni Bertello, and Antonio Paolucci. *The Americas: Collections from the Vatican Ethnological Museum*. Vatican City: Edizioni Musei Vaticani, 2015.

Alexander, Charles. *From the Deep Woods to Civilization: Chapters in the Autobiography of an Indian*. Lincoln: University of Nebraska Press, 1936.

Amaral, Ana Rita. "Exhibiting Faith against an Imperial Background: Angola and the Spiritans at the Vatican Missionary Exhibition (1925)." *Journal of Religion in Africa* 50, nos. 1–2 (2021): 79–108.

AMDG (Ad Maiorem Dei Gloriam). *Croquis de visite d'exposition recueillis par un des missionnaires exposants, avril 1925*. Rome: Industria Tipografica Romana, 1925.

Ames, Michael M. *Cannibal Tours and Glass Boxes: The Anthropology of Museums*. Vancouver: UBC Press, 1992.

Amiotte, Arthur. "The Lakota Sun Dance: Historical and Contemporary Perspectives." In *Sioux Indian Religion*, edited by Raymond Demallie and Douglas Parks, 75–90. Norman: University of Oklahoma Press, 1988.

Anderson, Christopher J. "The World's Fair of 1919: Ethnographic and Technological Exhibits on Display at the Centenary of American Methodist Missions." *Methodist History* 43 (2005): 273–85.

Anderson, Kim, Maria Campbell, and Christi Belcourt, eds. *Keetsahnak: Our Missing and Murdered Indigenous Sisters*. Edmonton: University of Alberta Press, 2018.

Andreotti, Libero. "The Aesthetics of War: The Exhibition of the Fascist Revolution." *Journal of Architectural Education* 45, no. 2 (1992): 76–86.

Apess, William. *A Son of the Forest: The Experience of William Apes, a Native of the Forest; Comprising a Notice of the Pequod Tribe of Indians*. New York: Printed by G. F. Bunce, 1829.

Archuleta, Margaret L., Brenda J. Child, and K. Tsianina Lomawaima, eds. *Away from Home: American Indian Boarding School Experiences, 1879–2000*. Phoenix, AZ: Heard Museum, 2000.

Augustine, Stephen J. "Wampum Belt Archive." Wampumbear. Accessed July 24, 2023. https://www.wampumbear.com/W_Stephen%20Augustine%20Belt.html.

Baedecker, Karl. *Italy: Handbook for Travellers*. London: Dulau and Co., 1890.

Beard, Mary. *The Roman Triumph*. Cambridge, MA: Harvard University Press, 2009.

Becker, Marshall. "The Maniwaki Wampum Group: A History." *Iroquoia* 2 (2016): 87–128.

Becker, Marshall. "The Vatican 1831 Wampum Belt: A Day of Study at the Vatican Museums." *Newsletter of the Archaeological Society of New Jersey* 224 (2009): 5–6.

Behar, Ruth. *The Vulnerable Observer: Anthropology That Breaks Your Heart*. Boston: Beacon, 1997.

Belanger, Yale D. "The Six Nations of Grand River Territory's Attempts at Renewing International Political Relationships, 1921–1924." *Canadian Foreign Policy* 13, no. 3 (2007): 29–43.

Belcourt, Christi, Rose Richardson, Rita Flamand, and Olive Whitford. *Medicines to Help Us: Traditional Métis Plant Use; Study Prints and Resource Guide*. Saskatoon: Gabriel Dumont Institute, 2007.

Bell, Gloria Jane. "Lakota Dandies in the Eternal City: Indigenous Travelers Chief Iron Tail and Jacob Ištá Ská." In *(Un)Following in Winnetou's Footsteps: Representations of North American Indigeneity in Central Europe*, edited by Sanja Runtić, Jana Marešová, and Klára Kolinská, 149–72. New York: Springer, 2024.

Bell, Gloria Jane. "Oscillating Identities: Re-Presentations of Métis in the Great Lakes Area in the Nineteenth Century." In *Métis in Canada: History, Identity, Law and Politics*, edited by Christopher Adams, Gregg Dahl, and Ian Peach, 3–58. Calgary: University of Alberta Press, 2013.

Bell, Gloria Jane. "Reconstructing Edmonia Lewis's Roman Life: An Exploration of Her Presence in the Eternal City." In *Female Cultural Production in Modern Italy: Literature, Art and Intellectual History*, edited by Sharon Hecker and Catherine Ramsey-Portolano, 281–98. London: Palgrave Macmillan, 2023.

Benedict, Burton. "Rituals of Representation: Ethnic Stereotypes and Colonized Peoples at World's Fairs." In *Fair Representations: World's Fairs and the Modern World*, edited by Robert Rydell and Nancy Gwin, 28–61. Amsterdam: VU University Press, 1994.

Benn, Carl. *Mohawks on the Nile: Natives among the Canadian Voyageurs in Egypt, 1884–1885*. Toronto: Dundurn, 2009.

Berlo, Janet Catherine. "The Art of Indigenous Americans and American Art History: A Century of Exhibitions." *Perspective* 2015, no. 2 (2015). http://perspective.revues.org/6004.

Berlo, Janet Catherine. *The Early Years of Native American Art History: The Politics of Scholarship and Collecting*. Seattle: University of Washington Press, 1992.

Berlo, Janet Catherine, ed. *Plains Indian Drawings 1865–1935: Pages from a Visual History*. New York: Abrams, 1996.

Blackman, Margaret R. "Studio Indians: Cartes de visite of Native People in British Columbia, 1862–1872." *Archivaria* 21 (1985): 68–86.

Blake, Lynn A. "Pastoral Power, Governmentality and Cultures of Order in Nineteenth-Century British Columbia." *Transactions of the Institute of British Geographers* 24, no. 1 (1999): 79–93.

Bohaker, Heidi. "Reading Anishinaabe Identities: Meaning and Metaphor in Nindoodem Pictographs." *Ethnohistory* 57, no. 1 (2010): 11–33.

Bol, Marsha. *The Art and Tradition of Beadwork*. Layton, UT: Gibbs Smith, 2017.

Bol, Marsha. "Gender in Art: A Comparison of Lakota Women's and Men's Art, 1820–1920." PhD diss., University of Michigan, 2005.

Boll, Natalie, and La Tiesha Fazakas, dirs. *Maker of Monsters: The Extraordinary Life of Beau Dick*. Film. 2016.

Bonfigli, F. S. *Guide to the Studios in Rome with Much Supplementary Information*. Rome: Printed by Tipografia Legale, 1860.

Borrows, John. "Constitutional Law from a First Nation Perspective: Self-Government and the Royal Proclamation." *University of British Columbia Law Review* 28 (1994): 1–24.

Bowen, F. J. "The Missionary Exhibition at the Vatican." *New Blackfriars* 6 (May 1925): 266–70.

Bowes, John P. "US Expansion and Its Consequences, 1815–1890." In *The Oxford Handbook of American Indian History*, edited by Frederick Hoxie, 93–110. New York: Oxford University Press, 2016.

Brandson, Ashley. "Ziigimineshin Brings Beaders Together on Treaty 1." CBC News, February 9, 2020. https://www.cbc.ca/news/canada/manitoba/ziigimineshin-beading-symposium-winnipeg-1.5457363.

Brasser, Ted. "In Search of Métis Art." In *The New Peoples: Being and Becoming Métis in North America*, edited by Jacqueline Peterson and Jennifer Brown, 222–30. Winnipeg: University of Manitoba Press, 1985.

Bresciani, SJ, Father. "A Manuscript on the Indian Statues of Chevalier Ferdinand Pettrich, Sculptor." *Art Journal* 7 (1868): 247–48.

Brody, J. J. *Pueblo Indian Painting: Tradition and Modernism in New Mexico, 1900–1930*. Santa Fe, NM: School of American Research Press, 1997.

Brody, Jennifer DeVere. *Impossible Purities: Blackness, Femininity, and Victorian Culture*. Durham, NC: Duke University Press, 1998.

Brown, Alison. *First Nations, Museums, Narrations: Stories of the 1929 Franklin Motor Expedition to the Canadian Prairies*. Vancouver: UBC Press, 2014.

Bruchac, Margaret. "Notes from the Trail." On the Wampum Trail: Restorative Research in North American Museums. Accessed July 24, 2023. https://wampumtrail.wordpress.com/.

Bruchac, Margaret. “Wampum in Museum Collections: Tracking Broken Chains of Custody.” Native American and Indigenous Studies at Penn, October 2, 2014. https://nais.sas.upenn.edu/events/wampum-museum-collections.

Buffalo, Tamara. “Knowing All My Names.” *International Review of African American Art* 17 (2000): 41–44.

Buick, Kirsten P. *Child of the Fire: Mary Edmonia Lewis and the Problem of Art History's Black and Indian Subject*. Durham, NC: Duke University Press, 2010.

Buick, Kirsten P. “The Ideal Works of Edmonia Lewis: Invoking and Inverting Biography.” *American Art* 9, no. 2 (1995): 4–22.

Burns, Emily. *Transnational Frontiers: The American West in France*. Norman: University of Oklahoma Press, 2018.

Bushnell, David. “North American Ethnographical Material in Italian Collections.” *American Anthropologist* 8, no. 2 (1906): 243–55.

Calendario atlante delle missioni. Rome: Propaganda Fide, 1925.

Callahan, S. Alice. *Wynema: A Child of the Forest*. [1891]. Lincoln: University of Nebraska Press, 1997.

Calloway, Collin G. “Treaties and Treaty Making.” In *The Oxford Handbook of American Indian History*, edited by Frederick Hoxie, 539–52. New York: Oxford University Press, 2016.

Campino, Gaultiero. “Vatican Making Ready for Notable Jubilee Year.” *New York Times*, June 8, 1924.

Canadian Museums Association. “Moved to Action: Activating UNDRIP in Canadian Museums.” 2022. https://museums.ca/site/movedtoaction.

Canadian Press. “Scottish Museum Returning Stolen Totem Pole after Visit from Nisga'a Nation.” CBC News, December 1, 2022. https://www.cbc.ca/news/canada/british-columbia/nisgaa-pole-returning-1.6671229.

Carr, Geoffrey Paul. “‘House of No Spirit’: An Architectural History of the Indian Residential School in British Columbia.” PhD diss., University of British Columbia, 2011.

Cavina, Anna Ottani. *Geometries of Silence: Three Approaches to Neoclassical Art*. New York: Columbia University Press, 2004.

“The Chevalier Pettrich's Sculptures.” *The Examiner* (London?). February 13, 1858.

Cikovsky, Nicolai. “The Ravages of the Axe: The Meaning of the Tree Stump in Nineteenth-Century American Art.” *Art Bulletin* 61, no. 4 (1979): 611–26.

Ciregna, Elise Madeleine. “An Example in the Right Direction: Horatio Greenough's Life and Work in Italy.” In *Sculptors, Painters, and Italy: Italian Influence on Nineteenth-Century American Art*, edited by Sirpa Salenius, 19–36. Padua: Il Prato, 2009.

Clendinning, Anne. “Exhibiting a Nation: Canada at the British Empire Exhibition, 1924–1925.” *Histoire Sociale/Social History* 39 (2006): 79–108.

Coe, Ralph T., Jonathan C. H. King, and Judith Ostrowitz. *The Responsive Eye: Ralph T. Coe and the Collecting of American Indian Art*. New York: Metropolitan Museum of Art, 2003.

Cole, Catherine M. *Performance and the Afterlives of Injustice*. Ann Arbor: University of Michigan Press, 2020.

Cole, Douglas. *Captured Heritage: The Scramble for Northwest Coast Artifacts*. Vancouver: UBC Press, 1985.

Conaty, Gerald T. *We Are Coming Home: Repatriation and the Restoration of Blackfoot Cultural Confidence*. Athabasca, AB: Athabasca University Press, 2015.

Connelly, Frances. *Sleep of Reason: Primitivism in Modern European Art and Aesthetics, 1725–1907*. University Park: Pennsylvania State University Press, 1995.

Considine, John Joseph. *The Vatican Mission Exposition: A Window on the World*. New York: Macmillan, 1925.

"Contributions of the Salesian Missionaries of America to the Vatican Missionary Exposition." *L'Osservatore Romano*, August 31, 1925.

Coombes, Annie E. *Reinventing Africa: Museums, Material Culture and Popular Imagination*. New Haven, CT: Yale University Press, 1994.

Corbey, Raymond. "Ethnographic Showcases, 1870–1930." *Cultural Anthropology* 8, no. 3 (1993): 338–69.

Corbey, Raymond. *Tribal Art Traffic: A Chronicle of Taste, Trade and Desire in Colonial and Post-Colonial Times*. Amsterdam: Royal Tropical Institute, 2000.

Crosby, Marcia. "Construction of the Imaginary Indian." In *Vancouver Anthology: The Institutional Politics of Art*, edited by Stan Douglas, 267–91. Vancouver: Talon, 1991.

Cutschall, Colleen. "The Seen and the Unseen Form the Narrative." In *Plains Indian Drawings 1865–1935: Pages from a Visual History*, edited by Janet Berlo, 64–65. New York: Abrams, 1996.

Dabakis, Melissa. *A Sisterhood of Sculptors: American Artists in Nineteenth-Century Rome*. University Park: Pennsylvania State University Press, 2014.

D'Agostino, Peter R. *Rome in America: Transnational Catholic Ideology from the Risorgimento to Fascism*. Chapel Hill: University of North Carolina Press, 2004.

D'Angeli, Mique'l. "Dancing Chiax, Dancing Sovereignty: Performing Protocol in Unceded Territories." *Dance Research Journal* 48, no. 1 (2016): 75–90.

D'Angeli, Mique'l. "Dancing Sovereignty: Protocol and Politics in Northwest Coast First Nations Dance." PhD diss., University of British Columbia, 2015.

Davis, John. "The End of the American Century: Current Scholarship on the Art of the United States." *Art Bulletin* 85, no. 3 (2003): 544–80.

Dawn, Leslie Allan. *National Visions, National Blindness: Canadian Art and Identities in the 1920s*. Vancouver: UBC Press, 2014.

Deloria, Philip Joseph. *Indians in Unexpected Places*. Lawrence: University Press of Kansas, 2004.

DeLucia, Christine. "Antiquarian Collecting and the Transits of Indigenous Material Culture: Rethinking 'Indian Relics' and 'Tribal Histories.'" *Commonplace: The*

Journal of Early American Life 17, no. 2 (2017). http://commonplace.online/article/antiquarian-collecting-and-the-transits-of-indigenous-material-culture/.

Densmore, Frances. *Songs of the Sioux: From the Archive of Folk Song*. Washington, DC: Library of Congress, 1951.

Densmore, Frances. *Teton Sioux Music and Culture*. Lincoln: University of Nebraska Press, 1992.

Derome, Robert. "Les sources iconographiques des portraits fictifs du père jésuite Jacques Marquette." Université du Québec à Montréal. Accessed August 19, 2023. http://rd.uqam.ca/Marquette/.

Derrida, Jacques. *Archive Fever: A Freudian Impression*. Chicago: University of Chicago Press, 1996.

Deskaheh. *The Redman's Appeal for Justice*. N.p., 1923. https://law.lib.buffalo.edu/pdf/Redmanappeal.pdf.

Diaz, Vincente Miguel. *Repositioning the Missionary: Rewriting the Histories of Colonialism, Native Catholicism, and Indigeneity in Guam*. Honolulu: University of Hawai'i Press, 2010.

Dietrich, Stefan. "Mission, Local Culture and the 'Catholic Ethnology' of Pater Schmidt." *Journal of the Anthropological Society of Oxford* 23, no. 2 (1992): 111–25.

Digmann, Florentin. "Dear Father." *Indian Sentinel*, May 23, 1925, 115.

Dippie, Brian W. *The Vanishing American: White Attitudes and US Indian Policy*. Lawrence: University Press of Kansas, 1982.

Dirar, Uoldelul. "Church-State Relations in Colonial Eritrea: Missionaries and the Development of Colonial Strategies (1869–1911)." *Journal of Modern Italian Studies* 8, no. 3 (2003): 391–410.

Dirks, Nicholas. "Colonial Histories and Native Informants: Biography of a Colonial Archive." In *Orientalism and the Postcolonial Predicament: Perspectives on South Asia*, edited by Carol A. Breckenridge and Peter van der Veer, 279–313. Philadelphia: University of Pennsylvania Press, 1993.

Domenici, Davide. "The Wandering 'Leg of an Indian King': The Cultural Biography of a Friction Idiophone now in the Pigorini Museum in Rome, Italy." *Journal de la Société des Américanistes* 102, no. 1 (2016): 79–104.

Dreves, Father. *A Visit to the Vatican Missionary Exhibition*. Rome: Propaganda Fide, 1925.

Dries, Angelyn. "The 1925 Vatican Mission Exposition and the Interface between Catholic Missionary Theory and World Religions." *International Bulletin of Mission Research* 40, no. 2 (2016): 119–32.

Dunbar-Ortiz, Roxanne. *An Indigenous Peoples' History of the United States*, vol. 3. Boston: Beacon, 2014.

Duncan, Carol. *Civilizing Rituals: Inside Public Art Museums*. New York: Routledge, 2005.

Edenheiser, Iris. "Introduction." In *Tecumseh, Keokuk, Black Hawk: Portrayals of Native Americans in Times of Treaties and Removal*, edited by Iris Edenheiser and Astrid Nielsen, 14–25. Stuttgart: Arnoldsche Art, 2013.

Edenheiser, Iris, and Astrid Nielsen, eds. *Tecumseh, Keokuk, Black Hawk: Portrayals of Native Americans in Times of Treaties and Removal*. Stuttgart: Arnoldsche Art, 2013.

"Edmonia Lewis." *Sheffield Independent* (UK), March 5, 1866.

Elkins, James. *Stories of Art*. New York: Routledge, 2002.

Estes, Nick. *Our History Is the Future: Standing Rock versus the Dakota Access Pipeline, and the Long Tradition of Indigenous Resistance*. London: Verso, 2019.

Étienne, Noémie. "Dioramas, Before and After." *Journal 18*, September 2017. http://www.journal18.org/1934.

Fabian, Johannes. *Time and the Other: How Anthropology Makes Its Object*. New York: Columbia University Press, 1983.

Falcucci, Beatrice. "Bringing the Empire to the Provinces: Colonial Museums and Colonial Knowledge in Fascist Italy." *Cahiers François Viète* 3, no. 10 (2021): 113–46.

Fear-Segal, Jacqueline, and Susan D. Rose, eds. *Carlisle Indian Industrial School: Indigenous Histories, Memories, and Reclamations*. Lincoln: University of Nebraska Press, 2016.

Felix, Father. "The Vatican Missionary Exposition." *Father Mathew Record*, June 1925, 171–73.

Ferando, Christina. "Truly Transnational? Sculpture Studios in Rome after the Restoration." In *Rome, Travel, and the Sculpture Capital, c. 1770–1825*, edited by Tomas Macsotay, 95–115. London: Routledge, 2017.

Fitz, Karsten. *Visual Representations of Native Americans: Transnational Contexts and Perspectives*. Heidelberg: Universitätsverlag Winter, 2012.

Fixico, Donald L. "How We Remember Black Hawk of the Sac and Fox." In *Tecumseh, Keokuk, Black Hawk: Portrayals of Native Americans in Times of Treaties and Removal*, edited by Iris Edenheiser and Astrid Nielsen, 139–48. Stuttgart: Arnoldsche Art, 2013.

Flam, Jack, and Miriam Deutch, eds. *Primitivism and Twentieth-Century Art: A Documentary History*. Berkeley: University of California Press, 2003.

Flint, Kate. *The Transatlantic Indian, 1776–1930*. Princeton, NJ: Princeton University Press, 2009.

Foster, Hal. "An Archival Impulse." *October* 110 (2004): 3–22.

Francis, D. *The Imaginary Indian: The Image of the Indian in Canadian Culture*. Vancouver: Arsenal Pulp, 2011.

Freedburg, David. "Warburg's Mask: A Study in Idolatry." In *Anthropologies of Art*, edited by Mariet Westerman, 3–25. Williamstown, MA: Clark Institute, 2005.

Friesen, Steve, and François Chladiuk. *Lakota Performers in Europe: Their Culture and the Artifacts They Left Behind*. Norman: University of Oklahoma Press, 2017.

Fryd, Vivien Green. *Art and Empire: The Politics of Ethnicity in the United States Capitol, 1815–1860*. Athens: Ohio University Press, 2001.

Fryd, Vivien Green. "Two Sculptures for the Capitol: Horatio Greenough's 'Rescue' and Luigi Persico's 'Discovery of America.'" *American Art Journal* 19, no. 2 (1987): 16–39.

Fusco, Coco. "The Other History of Intercultural Performance." *Drama Review* 38 (1994): 143–67.

Garvin, J. "The Missionary Exhibition." *Venerabile*, April 1925, 147–50.

Gaudio, Michael. *Engraving the Savage: The New World and Techniques of Civilization*. Minneapolis: University of Minnesota Press, 2008.

Gell, Alfred. "Vogel's Net: Traps as Artworks and Artworks as Traps." *Journal of Material Culture* 1, no. 1 (1996): 15–38.

Gerdts, William. "The Marble Savage." *Art in America*, July-August 1974, 64–70.

Gere, Anne Ruggles. "An Art of Survivance: Angel DeCora at Carlisle." *American Indian Quarterly* 28, nos. 3–4 (2004): 649–84.

Geronimo, and S. M. Barrett. *Geronimo: His Own Story*. Edited by Frederick Turner. New York: Meridian-Penguin, 1996.

Ghirardo, Diane. "Architects, Exhibitions, and the Politics of Culture in Fascist Italy." *Journal of Architectural Education* 45, no. 2 (1992): 67–75.

Ghosh, Durba, Jeff Sahadeo, Craig Robertson, and Tony Ballantyne. *Archive Stories: Facts, Fictions, and the Writing of History*. Durham, NC: Duke University Press, 2006.

Giordano, Fedora. "The Anxiety of Discovery: The Italian Interest in Native American Studies." *Rivista di Studi Americani* 5 (1994): 81–109.

Giordano, Fedora. "Italy's Contributions to Native American Studies." *European Review of Native American Studies* 4, no. 2 (1990): 1–2.

Giovanni, P. *L'Esposizione Missionaria Vaticana e l'Ordine dei Frati Minori Cappuccini*. Rome: Societa Tip. A. Manuzio, 1925.

Glass, Aaron. "Frozen Poses: Hamat'sa Dioramas, Recursive Representation, and the Making of a Kwakwaka'wakw Icon." In *Photography, Anthropology and History: Expanding the Frame*, edited by Christopher Morton and Elizabeth Edwards, 89–116. Farnham, UK: Ashgate, 2009.

Gonzalez, Jennifer A. *Subject to Display: Reframing Race in Contemporary Installation Art*. Cambridge, MA: MIT Press, 2011.

Greci-Green, Adriana. "German Missionary Participation during the Ghost Dance of 1890." *European Review of Native American Studies* 6, no. 1 (1992): 31–34.

Green, Rayna. "The Tribe Called Wannabee: Playing Indian in America and Europe." *Folklore* 99 (1988): 30–55.

Green, Rayna, and John Troutman, "By the Waters of the Minnehaha: Music and Dance, Pageants and Princesses." In *Away from Home: American Indian Boarding*

School Experiences, 1879–2000, edited by Margaret L. Archuleta, Brenda J. Child, and K. Tsianina Lomawaima, 60–83. Phoenix, AZ: Heard Museum, 2000.

Griffiths, Gareth. *Mixed Messages: Materiality, Textuality, Missions*. London: Palgrave Macmillan, 2005.

Grigsby, Darcy Grimaldi. "Revolutionary Sons, White Fathers, and Creole Difference: Guillaume Guillon-Lethière's 'Oath of the Ancestors' (1822)." *Yale French Studies* 101 (2001): 201–26.

Gubbels, Noël. *L'exposition missionnaire du Vatican et le Musée Missionnaire Ethnographique du Latran, 1925–1927*. Quaracchi (Ad Claras Aquas), Italy: Typographia Collegii S. Bonaventurae, 1928.

Gubernatis, Angelo De, and Ugo Matini. *Dizionario degli artisti italiani viventi, pittori, scultori e architetti*. Florence: Tipi dei successori Le Monnier, 1889.

Gurney, J., and Son. *On the Exhibition, the Dying Te-Cum-Seh, and Other Elegant Pieces of Statuary, by the Celebrated Sculptor, Chevalier Pettrich, of Rome, Pupil of the World-Renowned Thorwaldsen*. New York: Gurney and Son, [ca. 1860].

Haas, Lisbeth. *Pablo Tac: Indigenous Scholar Writing on Luiseño Language and History, c. 1840*. Berkeley: University of California Press, 2011.

Haltman, Kenneth. "Toward Immobility: Pettrich's Ethnographic Sources." In *Tecumseh, Keokuk, Black Hawk: Portrayals of Native Americans in Times of Treaties and Removal*, edited by Iris Edenheiser and Astrid Nielsen, 44–52. Stuttgart: Arnoldsche Art, 2013.

A Handbook of Rome and Its Environs. 8th ed. London: John Murray, 1867.

A Handbook of Rome and Its Environs. 12th ed. London: John Murray, 1875.

Hansen, Emma I. *Memory and Vision: Arts, Cultures, and Lives of Plains Indian People*. Cody, WY: Buffalo Bill Historical Center, 2007.

Haraway, Donna. "Teddy Bear Patriarchy: Taxidermy in the Garden of Eden, New York City, 1908–1936." *Social Text* 11 (1985): 20–64.

Harney, Elizabeth, and Ruth B. Phillips, eds. *Mapping Modernisms: Art, Indigeneity, Colonialism*. Durham, NC: Duke University Press, 2018.

Harrison, Rodney. "Reassembling Ethnographic Museum Collections." In *Reassembling the Collection: Ethnographic Museums and Indigenous Agency*, edited by Rodney Harrison, Sarah Byrne, and Anne Clarke, 3–35. Santa Fe, NM: School for Advanced Research Press, 2013.

Hasinoff, Erin L. "Faith in Objects: American Indian Object Lessons at the World in Boston." In *Archaeologies of Materiality*, edited by Lynn Meskell, 96–125. Oxford: Blackwell, 2005.

Hasinoff, Erin L. *Faith in Objects: American Missionary Expositions in the Early Twentieth Century*. New York: Palgrave Macmillan, 2011.

Hauschild, Thomas. "Christians, Jews, and the Other in German Anthropology." *American Anthropologist* 99, no. 4 (1997): 746–53.

Hedden, Mark. "Passamaquoddy Shamanism and Rock Art in Machias Bay, Maine." In *The Rock Art of Eastern North America: Capturing Images and Insight*, edited by Carol Diaz-Granados and James R. Duncan, 319–43. Tuscaloosa: University of Alabama Press, 2004.

Hesse, Gerolamo. "Gesuiti e Franciscani tra le 'Pelli-Rosse.'" *Rivista Illustrata della Esposizione Missionaria Vaticana*, November 15, 1925, 726–36.

Hicks, Dan. *The Brutish Museums: The Benin Bronzes, Colonial Violence and Cultural Restitution*. London: Pluto, 2020.

Highway, Tomson, and John George Moss. *Comparing Mythologies*. Ottawa: University of Ottawa Press, 2005.

Hill, Tom. "Indian Art in Canada: An Historical Perspective." In *Norval Morrisseau and the Emergence of the Image Makers*, edited by Elizabeth McLuhan and Tom Hill, 11–27. Toronto: Art Gallery of Ontario, 1984.

Hirsh, Jennie. "Transmissions of Fascism: Advertising Architecture through the Ente Radio Rurale Poster Campaign." Lecture, April 12, 2018, Instituto de Investigaciones Estéticas UNAM. https://www.youtube.com/watch?v=VvoMAbLH6YY.

Hollengreen, Laura, Celia Pearce, Rebecca Rouse, and Bobby Schweizer. *Meet Me at the Fair: A World's Fair Reader*. Pittsburgh, PA: ETC Press, 2014.

Honour, Hugh. "Canova's Studio Practice I: The Early Years." *Burlington Magazine*, March 1972, 146–59.

Honour, Hugh. "Canova's Studio Practice II: 1791–1822." *Burlington Magazine*, April 1972, 214–29.

Honour, Hugh. *Neo-Classicism*. London: Penguin, 1979.

Horton, Jessica. *Art for an Undivided Earth*. Durham, NC: Duke University Press, 2017.

Horton, Jessica. "A Cloudburst in Venice." *American Art* 29, no. 1 (2015): 54–81.

Horton, Jessica, and Janet Catherine Berlo. "Pueblo Painting in 1932: Folding Narratives of Native Art into American Art History." In *A Companion to American Art History*, edited by John Davis, Jennifer Greenhill, and Jason LaFountain, 264–80. Chichester, UK: Wiley-Blackwell, 2015.

Huhndorf, Shari M. *Going Native: Indians in the American Cultural Imagination*. Ithaca, NY: Cornell University Press, 2001.

Huhndorf, Shari M. *Mapping the Americas: The Transnational Politics of Contemporary Native Culture*. Ithaca, NY: Cornell University Press, 2009.

Hutchinson, Elizabeth. "From Pantheon to Indian Gallery: Art and Sovereignty on the Early Nineteenth-Century Frontier." *Journal of American Studies* 47, no. 2 (2013): 313–37.

Hutchinson, Elizabeth. *Indian Craze: Primitivism, Modernism, and Transculturation in American Art*. Durham, NC: Duke University Press, 2009.

Hutchinson, Elizabeth. "Indigeneity and Sovereignty: The Work of Two Early Twentieth-Century Native American Art Critics." *Third Text* 14, no. 52 (2000): 21–29.

Igloliorte, Heather, and Carla Taunton. "Continuities between Eras: Indigenous Art Histories." *RACAR: Revue d'art Canadienne/Canadian Art Review* 42, no. 2 (2017): 5–12.

"Il lavoro di sistemazione della mostra." *Rivista Illustrata della Esposizione Missionaria Vaticana*, December 15, 1924, 29–31.

"Il 'vernissage' e la visita della stampa." *Rivista Illustrata della Esposizione Missionaria Vaticana*, December 31, 1924, 62–64.

Issac, Gwyneira. "From Life? Histories and Contemporary Perspectives on Modeling Native American Humankind through Mannequins at the Smithsonian." In *Mannequins in Museums: Power and Resistance on Display*, edited by Bridget R. Cooks and Jennifer J. Wagelie, 28–44. New York: Routledge, 2021.

Jacknis, Ira. "Franz Boas and Photography." *Studies in Visual Communication* 10, no. 1 (1984): 2–60.

Jacobs, Karen, Chantal Knowles, and Chris Wingfield. *Trophies, Relics, and Curios? Missionary Heritage from Africa and the Pacific*. Leiden: Sidestone, 2015.

James, Edward T., Janet Wilson James, and Paul S. Boyer. *Notable American Women, 1607–1950: A Biographical Dictionary*, vol. 3. Cambridge, MA: Radcliffe College, 1971.

Jessup, Lynda, and Shannon Bagg. *On Aboriginal Representation in the Gallery*. Hull, QC: Canadian Museum of Civilization, 2002.

Jutz, Father. "Recollections of an Old Indian Missionary." *Canisius Monthly*, October 1918, 212–18.

Kahn, Alison. "Mind over Matter: A Catholic Ethnology for the Vatican's Ethnographic Collections (1911–1939)." PhD diss., University of Oxford, 2006.

Kalshoven, Petra. "Magic of the Mannequin: A Guided Look through the Dioramas in the Mashantucket Pequot Museum." *Acta Americana* 16 (2008): 5–25.

Kaplan, Paul H. D. "Italy, 1490–1700." In *The Image of the Black in Western Art*, vol. 3: *From the "Age of Discovery" to the Age of Abolition*, part 1: *Artists of the Renaissance and Baroque*, edited by David Bindman and Henry Louis Gates, 93–190. Cambridge, MA: Harvard University Press, 2010.

Karlholm, Dan, and Keith P. F Moxey, eds. *Time in the History of Art: Temporality, Chronology, and Anachrony*. Abingdon, UK: Routledge, 2018.

Keating, Jessica, and Lia Markey. "'Indian' Objects in Medici and Austrian-Habsburg Inventories: A Case-Study of the Sixteenth Century Term." *Journal of the History of Collections* 23, no. 2 (2011): 283–300.

Kehoe, Alice Beck. *The Ghost Dance: Ethnohistory and Revitalization*. Madison: University of Wisconsin Press, 2006.

Kertzer, David I. *The Pope and Mussolini: The Secret History of Pius XI and the Rise of Fascism in Europe*. New York: Random House, 2014.

Kimmerer, Robin Wall. *Braiding Sweetgrass: Indigenous Wisdom, Scientific Knowledge, and the Teachings of Plants*. Minneapolis, MN: Milkweed, 2013.

King, J. C. H. "A Century of Indian Shows: Canada and the United States Exhibitions in London, 1825–1925." *European Review of Native American Studies* 5 (1991): 35–42.

King, J. C. H. "Woodlands Artifacts from the Studio of Benjamin West, 1738–1820." *American Indian Art Magazine*, Winter 1991, 34–47.

Kirschenblatt-Gimblett, Barbara. *Destination Culture: Tourism, Museums, and Heritage.* Berkeley: University of California Press, 1998.

Kornhauser, Elizabeth, and Shannon Vittoria. *Jules Tavernier and the Elem Pomo*. New York: Metropolitan Museum of Art, 2021.

Kort, Pamela, and Max Hollein. *I Like America: Fictions of the Wild West*. Munich: Prestel, 2006.

Kosmider, Alexia. "Refracting the Imperial Gaze onto the Colonizers: Geronimo Poses for the Empire." *American Transcendental Quarterly* 15, no. 4 (2001): 317–32.

Kramer, Jennifer. *Switchbacks: Art, Ownership, and Nuxalk National Identity*. Vancouver: UBC Press, 2006.

Krmpotich, Cara. *The Force of Family: Repatriation, Kinship, and Memory on Haida Gwaii*. Toronto: University of Toronto Press, 2014.

"La chiusura solenne dell'Esposizione Missionaria Vaticana." *Rivista Illustrata della Esposizione Missionaria Vaticana*, January–February 1926, 71–78.

Laforge, Alison. "Burl Bowls and Birchbark Baskets: Decolonizing Indigenous Material Culture in the Native Northeast." MA thesis, Mount Holyoke College, 2016.

Lainey, Jonathan. "The Wampum and the Print: Objects Tied to Nicolas Vincent Tsawenhohi's London Visit, 1824–1825." The Great Lakes Research Alliance, February 21, 2021. https://grasac.artsci.utoronto.ca/?p=1061.

Lauenroth, Grisostomo. "Le 'tavolette parlanti' dell'Isola di Pasqua." *Rivista Illustrata della Esposizione Missionaria Vaticana*, March 15, 1925, 220–21.

"L'azione missionaria Cattolica nelle 'reservations' indiane degli Stati Uniti." *Rivista Illustrata della Esposizione Missionaria Vaticana*, August 31, 1925, 575–76.

[Lemmey, Karen?] Research Notes. Smithsonian American Art Museum, February 2012. https://d3ec1vt3scx7rr.cloudfront.net/files/collections/search/artwork/researchNotes/1916.8.1.pdf.

Lentis, Marinella. *Colonized through Art: American Indian Schools and Art Education, 1889–1915*. Lincoln: University of Nebraska Press, 2017.

"Le Suore Missionarie." *Rivista Illustrata della Esposizione Missionaria Vaticana*, January–February 1926, 43–63.

Lester, Joan A. *History on Birchbark: The Art of Tomah Joseph, Passamaquoddy*. Bar Harbour, ME: Haffenreffer Museum of Anthropology, 1993.

Lidchi, Henrietta. "Material Destinies: Jewelry, Authenticity, and Craft in the American Southwest." *Journal of Modern Craft* 5, no. 1 (2012): 69–92.

Lincoln, Louise. "The Social Construction of Plains Art, 1875–1915." In *Visions of the People: A Pictorial History of Plains Life*, edited by Evan M. Maurer and Louise Lincoln, 47–60. Minneapolis, MN: Minneapolis Institute of Arts, 1992.

"L'insospettata odissea dei trasporti." *Rivista Illustrata della Esposizione Missionaria Vaticana*, December 15, 1924, 30.

Lonetree, Amy. *Decolonizing Museums: Representing Native America in National and Tribal Museums*. Chapel Hill: University of North Carolina Press, 2012.

Lord, Frances. "The Silent Eloquence of Things: The Missionary Collections and Exhibitions of the Society of Jesus in Quebec, 1843–1946." In *Canadian Missionaries, Indigenous Peoples: Representing Religion at Home and Abroad*, edited by Alvyn J. Austin and Jamie S. Scott, 205–34. Toronto: University of Toronto Press, 2005.

Lugli, Aldagisa. "Inquiry as Collection: The Athanius Kircher Museum in Rome." *Res: Anthropology and Aesthetics* 12 (1986): 109–24.

Luna, James, Paul Chaat Smith, and Truman Lowe. *James Luna: Emendatio*. Washington, DC: National Museum of the American Indian, Smithsonian Institution, 2005.

Lyons, Scott Richard. *The World, the Text, and the Indian: Global Dimensions of Native American Literature*. Albany: State University of New York Press, 2017.

Lyons, Scott Richard. *X-Marks: Native Signatures of Assent*. Minneapolis: University of Minnesota Press, 2010.

Lysyk, Stephen P. "Evidentiary Issues: Oral Tradition Evidence." Aboriginal Practice Points, Continuing Legal Education Society of British Columbia, 2006. https://ceaa-acee.gc.ca/050/documents_staticpost/cearref_21799/86129/Evidentiary_issues_oral_tradition_evidence.pdf.

Maarschalkerweerd, Pancrazio. "Plastiche cristiane delle terre di missione nel Pontificio Museo Missionario Etnologico." *Annali Lateranensi* 1 (1937): 16–19.

Mageo, Jeannette. "'Ferocious Is the Centipede': A Study of the Significance of Eating and Speaking in Samoa." *Ethos* 17, no. 4 (1989): 387–427.

Mapelli, Nicola, Katherine Aigner, and Nadia Fiussello. *Ethnos: Vatican Museums Ethnological Collection*. Vatican City: Edizioni Musei Vaticani, 2012.

Marino, Cesare. "A Preview of the Beltrami Collection with a Note on North American Ethnographic Material in Italian Museums." *Council for Museum Anthropology Newsletter* 10, no. 2 (1986): 2–14.

Markey, Lia. *Imagining the Americas in Medici Florence*. University Park: Pennsylvania State University Press, 2017.

Marsden, K. "Father Marquette and the APA: An Incident in American Nativism." *Catholic Historical Review* 46, no. 1 (1960): 1–21.

Martens, Darren J. *Beau Dick: Revolutionary Spirit*. Whistler, BC: Audain Art Museum, 2018.

Matthews, Maureen. *Naamiwan's Drum: The Story of a Contested Repatriation of Anishnaabe Artifacts*. Toronto: University of Toronto Press, 2016.

Mauro, Peter Hayes. *Art of Americanization at the Carlisle Indian School*. Albuquerque: University of New Mexico Press, 2011.

McCarthy, Conal. *Exhibiting Māori: A History of Colonial Cultures on Display*. Oxford: Berg, 2007.

McKenney, Thomas L., and James Hall. *History of the Indian Tribes of North America with Biographical Sketches and Anecdotes of the Principal Chiefs*, 3 vols. Philadelphia: D. Rice and A. N. Hart, 1855.

McMaster, Gerald. "Discovering the Levels of Meaning." In *All Roads Are Good: Native Voices on Life and Cultures*, edited by W. Richard West, 112–21. Washington, DC: Smithsonian Books, 1994.

McMaster, Gerald. "Tenuous Lines of Descent: Indian Arts and Crafts of the Reservation Period." *Canadian Journal of Native Studies* 9, no. 2 (1989): 205–36.

McMaster, Gerald, and Lee-Ann Martin. "Introduction." In *Indigena: Contemporary Native Perspectives*, edited by Gerald McMaster and Lee-Ann Martin, 1–24. Vancouver: Douglas and McIntyre, 1992.

Medak-Saltzman, Danika. "Transnational Indigenous Exchange: Rethinking Global Interactions of Indigenous Peoples at the 1904 St. Louis Exposition." *American Quarterly* 62, no. 3 (2010): 591–615.

Mignolo, Walter. "Coloniality: The Darker Side of Modernity." In *Modernologies: Contemporary Artists Researching Modernity and Modernism*, edited by Sabrine Breitwieser, 39–49. Barcelona: Museu d'Art Contemporani de Barcelona, 2009.

Milicia, Maria Teresa. "Simulacra of Eternal Life: Ostensions, Exhibitions and the Concealment of Human Remains." In *Public Uses of Human Remains and Relics in History*, edited by Silvia Cavicchioli and Luigi Provero, 246–59. London: Routledge, 2019.

Million, Dian. "Felt Theory: An Indigenous Feminist Approach to Affect and History." *Wicazo Sa Review* 24, no. 2 (2009): 53–76.

Mitchell, Timothy. "The World as Exhibition." *Comparative Studies in Society and History* 31 (1989): 217–36.

Mithlo, Nancy. *Knowing Native Arts*. Omaha: University of Nebraska Press, 2020.

Morozzi, Rosanna. "Gaetano Trentanove: Uno scultore tra due continenti." *Atti della Accademia delle Arti del Disegno* (2004): 1000–1016.

Morphy, Howard, Andrée Rosenfeld, Peter Sutton, Ian Keen, Catherine H. Berndt, Ronald M. Berndt, Paul Memmott, Kate Khan, Betty Meehan, Carol Cooper, Luke Taylor, Robert Layton, J. V. S. Megaw, M. Ruth Megaw, and Francesca Cavazzini. "Aboriginal Australia." *Grove Art Online*, 2018. http://www.oxfordartonline.com/groveart/view/10.1093/gao/9781884446054.001.0001/oao-9781884446054-e-7000000140.

Morris, Kate. "Running the 'Medicine Line': Images of the Border in Contemporary Native American Art." *American Indian Quarterly* 35, no. 4 (2011): 549–78.

Morrison, C. Howard. "America." *Ball and the Cross*, July 4, 1925, 273–74.

Moulson, Geir. "Germany, Nigeria Sign Accord for Return of Benin Bronzes." AP News, July 1, 2022. https://apnews.com/article/africa-germany-berlin-13e1a65da1b08644d3c5d5032d24e426.

Moxey, Keith. *Visual Time: The Image in History*. Durham, NC: Duke University Press, 2013.

Mullin, Molly H. "The Patronage of Difference: Making Indian Art 'Art, Not Ethnology.'" *Cultural Anthropology* 7, no. 4 (1992): 395–424.

Nahwegahbow, Alexandra Kahsenni:io. "From Great-Grandmothers to Great-Granddaughters: 'Moving Life' in Baby Carriers and Birchbark Baskets." *RACAR: Revue d'art Canadienne/Canadian Art Review* 42, no. 2 (2017): 100–107.

Neale, Margo. "God Lives in the Dreaming: Aboriginal Treasures in the Vatican." *Artlink* 31, no. 2 (2011): 116–19.

Negro, Silvio. *Roma, non basta una vita*. Vicenza: Neri Pozza, 2014.

Nelson, Charmaine. *The Color of Stone: Sculpting the Black Female Subject in Nineteenth-Century America*. Minneapolis: University of Minnesota Press, 2007.

Nelson, Charmaine. "Edmonia Lewis's 'Death of Cleopatra': White Marble, Black Skin and the Regulation of Race in American Neoclassical Sculpture." In *Local/Global: Women Artists in the Nineteenth Century*, edited by Deborah Cherry and Janice Helland, 223–43. Aldershot, UK: Ashgate, 2006.

Nelson, Charmaine. "White Marble, Black Bodies and the Fear of the Invisible Negro: Signifying Blackness in Mid-Nineteenth-Century Neoclassical Sculpture." *RACAR: Revue d'art Canadienne/Canadian Art Review* 27, nos. 1–2 (2000): 87–101.

Nelson, Melissa. "The Hydromythology of the Anishinaabeg." In *Centering Anishinaabeg Studies: Understanding the World through Stories*, edited by Heidi Kiiwetinepinesiik Stark, Jill Doerfler, and Niigaanwewidam James Sinclair, 213–33. East Lansing: Michigan State University Press, 2013.

Nelson, Ruth. *Searching for Marquette: A Pilgrimage in Art*. Milwaukee, WI: Marquette University Press, 2012.

Nesselrath, Arnold. "Points of View." In *Tecumseh, Keokuk, Black Hawk: Portrayals of Native Americans in Times of Treaties and Removal*, edited by Iris Edenheiser and Astrid Nielsen, 65–79. Stuttgart: Arnoldsche Art, 2013.

Neville, Peter. *Mussolini*. London: Routledge, 2014.

Nicks, Trudy. "Dr Oronhyatekha's History Lessons: Reading Museum Collections as Texts." In *Reading beyond Words: Contexts for Native History*, 2nd ed., edited by Jennifer S. H. Brown and Elizabeth Vibert, 459–90. Toronto: University of Toronto Press, 2003.

Njootli, Jeneen Frei, Kimberly Phillips, Billy-Ray Belcourt, Lee Maracle, and Melissa Frost. *My Auntie Bought All Her Skidoos with Bead Money*. Vancouver: Contemporary Art Gallery, 2018.

Oberholtzer, Cath. "A Thorny Identification: Rosebuds as Symbols of Native Identity." *Journal of American Studies of Turkey* 8 (1998): 13–27.

Oberholtzer, Cath. "Trading amongst Themselves in Nineteenth Century Canada: John Henry Lefroy and His Contacts and Connections." *Journal of Museum Ethnography* 20 (2008): 33–48.

O'Donnell, Kevin. "The Artist in the Garden: George Cooke (1793–1849) and the Ideology of Fine Arts Painting in Antebellum Georgia." In *Crossroads: A Southern Culture Annual*, edited by Ted Olson, 73–97. Macon, GA: Mercer University Press, 2004.

Onciul, Bryony. *Museums, Heritage and Indigenous Voice: Decolonizing Engagement*. London: Routledge, 2015.

Painter, Borden W. *Mussolini's Rome: Rebuilding the Eternal City*. London: Palgrave Macmillan, 2005.

Paisley, Fiona. *The Lone Protester: A. M. Fernando in Australia and Europe*. Canberra: Aboriginal Studies Press, 2012.

"Papa Pio XI inaugura la mostra." *Rivista Illustrata della Esposizione Missionaria Vaticana*, December 31, 1924, 59–61.

Papafava, Francesco. *Vatican: Monumenti, Musei e Gallerie Pontificie*. Vatican City: Gestione Vendita Pubblicazioni, 1989.

Parker, Arthur C. "The Constitution of the Five Nations." *New York State Museum Bulletin* 184 (1916): 7–158.

Pasquier, Michael. "'Though Their Skin Remains Brown, I Hope Their Souls Will Soon Be White': Slavery, French Missionaries, and the Roman Catholic Priesthood in the American South, 1789–1865." *Church History* 77, no. 2 (2008): 337–70.

Pearce, Richard. *Women and Ledger Art: Four Contemporary Native American Artists*. Tucson: University of Arizona Press, 2013.

Peers, Laura. "Almost True: Peter Rindisbacher's Early Images of Rupert's Land, 1821–26." *Art History* 32, no. 3 (2009): 516–44.

Peers, Laura. "'Ceremonies of Renewal': Visits, Relationships, and Healing in the Museum Space." *Museum Worlds* 1, no. 1 (2013): 136–52.

Penkowski, Giuseppe. *Il Vaticano e Roma cristiana*. Vatican City: Libreria Editrice Vaticana, 1975.

Penner, Robert. "The Ojibwe Renaissance: Transnational Evangelicalism and the Making of an Algonquian Intelligentsia, 1812–1867." *American Review of Canadian Studies* 45, no. 1 (2015): 71–92.

Penney, David, Richard A. Pohrt, Milford Chandler, and George Horse Capture. *Art of the American Indian Frontier*. London: Phaidon, 1992.

Perkins, Maureen. "Timeless Cultures: The 'Dreamtime' as Colonial Discourse." *Time and Society* 7, no. 2 (1998): 335–51.

"Personal." *Harper's Bazaar*, June 11, 1870, 371.

"Personal." *Harper's Bazaar*, January 18, 1879, 39.

Pettipas, Katherine. *Severing the Ties That Bind: Government Repression of Indigenous Religious Ceremonies on the Prairies*. Winnipeg: University of Manitoba Press, 2014.

Pettrich, Ferdinand. *Portraits of Distinguished Indians from Several Tribes Who Visited Washington in 1837; also a Faithful Representation of the Indian War Dance, Which Took Place during Their Visit; Drawn on the Spot by Ferdinand Pettrich*. Baltimore: Edward Weber, 1842.

Phillips, Ruth. "Aboriginal Modernities: First Nations Art, c. 1880–1970." In *The Visual Arts in Canada: The Twentieth Century*, edited by Anne Whitelaw, Brian Foss, and Sandra Paikowsky, 349–70. Oxford: Oxford University Press, 2011.

Phillips, Ruth. "Aesthetic Primitivism Revisited: The Global Diaspora of 'Primitive Art' and the Emergence of Indigenous Modernisms." *Journal of Art Historiography* 12 (2015). https://arthistoriography.files.wordpress.com/2015/06/phillips.pdf.

Phillips, Ruth. *Trading Identities: The Souvenir in Native North American Art from the Northeast, 1700–1900*. Seattle: University of Washington Press, 1998.

Picón, Carlos A., and Seán Hemingway, eds. *Pergamon and the Hellenistic Kingdoms of the Ancient World*. Exhibition catalog. New York: Metropolitan Museum of Art, 2016.

Pius XI. *Rerum Ecclesiae: On Catholic Missions*. Papal encyclical, February 8, 1926. Papal Encyclicals Online. https://www.papalencyclicals.net/pius11/p11rerec.htm.

Pizzorusso, Giovanni. "Roman Ecclesiastical Archives and the History of the Native Peoples of Canada." *European Review of American Indian Studies* 4, no. 2 (1990): 21–26.

Pohlandt-McCormick, Helena. "In Good Hands: Researching the 1976 Soweto Uprising in the State Archives of South Africa." In *Archive Stories: Facts, Fictions, and the Writing of History*, edited by Durba Ghosh, Jeff Sahadeo, Craig Robertson, and Tony Ballantyne, 299–324. Durham, NC: Duke University Press, 2006.

"Pope Inspects Exhibition: Views Preparations for Missionary Fair in Vatican Grounds." *New York Times*, February 8, 1924, 5.

Porter, Frank W. *The Art of Native American Basketry: A Living Legacy*. Westport, CT: Greenwood, 1990.

Povinelli, Elizabeth. "The Woman on the Other Side of the Wall: Archiving the Otherwise." *Differences* 22, no. 1 (2001): 146–71.

Powell, Peter J. "Sacrifice Transformed into Victory: Standing Bear Portrays Sitting Bull's Sun Dance and the Final Summer of Lakota Freedom." In *Visions of the People: A Pictorial History of Plains Life*, edited by Evan M. Maurer and Louse Lincoln, 81–108. Minneapolis, MN: Minneapolis Institute of Arts, 1992.

Pratt, Stephanie. *American Indians in British Art, 1700–1840*. Norman: University of Oklahoma Press, 2005.

Prete, Tiffany. "Beadworking as an Indigenous Research Paradigm." *Art/Research International* 4 (2019): 28–57.

Price, Sally. *Paris Primitive: Jacques Chirac's Museum on the Quai Branly*. Chicago: University of Chicago Press, 2007.

Pritzke, Frank. *A Native American Encyclopedia: History, Culture, and Peoples*. Oxford: Oxford University Press, 2001.

"Programme de l'Exposition." *Missions de la Congrégation des Missionnaires Oblats de Marie Immaculée*, June 1923, 480–84.

Prown, Jules David. *Art as Evidence: Writings on Art and Material Culture*. New Haven, CT: Yale University Press, 2001.

Qureshi, Sadiah. *Peoples on Parade: Exhibitions, Empire, and Anthropology in Nineteenth-Century Britain*. Chicago: University of Chicago Press, 2011.

Racette, Sherry Farrell. "Sewing for a Living: The Commodification of Métis Women's Artistic Production." In *Contact Zones: Aboriginal and Settler Women in Canada's Colonial Past*, edited by Katie Pickles and Myra Rutherdale, 17–46. Vancouver: UBC Press, 2005.

Racette, Sherry Farrell, with Alan Corbiere and Crystal Migwans. "Pieces Left along the Trail: Material Culture Histories and Indigenous Studies." In *Sources and Methods in Indigenous Studies*, edited by Chris Andersen and Jean M. O'Brien, 223–29. Abingdon, UK: Routledge, 2016.

Raheja, Michelle H. "Visual Sovereignty." In *Native Studies Keywords*, edited by Stephanie Nohelani Teves, Andrea Smith, and Michelle H. Rahjea, 25–34. Tuscon: University of Arizona Press, 2015.

Rasmussen, Birgit Brander. *Queequeg's Coffin: Indigenous Literacies and Early American Literature*. Durham, NC: Duke University Press, 2012.

Ravenscroft, Alison. "The Girl in the Picture and the Eye of the Beholder: Viet Nam, Whiteness and the Disavowal of Indigeneity." *Continuum: Journal of Media and Cultural Studies* 18 (2004): 509–24.

Ray, Lana. "'Beading Becomes a Part of Your Life': Transforming the Academy through the Use of Beading as a Method of Inquiry." *International Review of Qualitative Research* 9, no. 3 (2016): 363–78.

Reinhardt, Leslie Kaye. "British and Indian Identities in a Picture by Benjamin West." *Eighteenth-Century Studies* 31, no. 3 (1998): 283–305.

Reiser, Christine. "Materializing Community: The Intersections of Pageantry, Material Culture and Indigeneity in Early 20th-Century New England." *Material Culture Review / Revue De La Culture Matérielle* 69 (2009). http://journals.hil.unb.ca/index.php/MCR/article/view/18146.

Richardson, Marilyn. "Edmonia Lewis' 'The Death of Cleopatra.'" *International Review of African American Art* 12, no. 2 (1995): 36–52.

Richardson, Marilyn. "Friends and Colleagues: Edmonia Lewis and Her Italian Circle." In *Sculptors, Painters, and Italy: Italian Influence on Nineteenth-Century American Art*, edited by Sirpa Salenius, 99–110. Padua: Il Prato, 2009.

Rickard, Jolene. "Sovereignty: A Line in the Sand." In *Strong Hearts: Native American Visions and Voices*, edited by Peggy Roalf, 51–60. New York: Aperture, 1995.

Ricky, Donald. *Encyclopedia of Kansas Indians*. Somerset, PA: Northern American Book Distributors, 1998.

Rifkin, Mark. *When Did Indians Become Straight? Kinship, the History of Sexuality, and Native Sovereignty*. New York: Oxford University Press, 2011.

"Rilievo statistico delle missioni d'America." *Rivista Illustrata della Esposizione Missionaria Vaticana*, December 31, 1925, 824–26.

Roberts, Nicholas E. "Palestine on Display: The Palestine Pavilion at the British Empire Exhibition of 1924." *Arab Studies Journal* 15, no. 1 (2007): 70–89.

Rocco, Vanessa. "Room O of the Exhibition of the Fascist Revolution, 1932." In *Public Photographic Spaces: Exhibitions of Propaganda, from* Pressa *to* The Family of Man, *1928–55*, edited by Anna Jiménez Jorquera, 244–55. Barcelona: Museu d'Art Contemporani de Barcelona, 2008.

Rooney, Francis. *The Global Vatican: An Inside Look at the Catholic Church, World Politics, and the Extraordinary Relationship between the United States and the Holy See*. Lanham, MD: Rowman and Littlefield, 2013.

Rostkowski, Joelle. "Deskaheh's Shadow: Indians on the International Scene." *European Review of Native American Studies* 9, no. 2 (1995): 1–4.

Rothstein, Bret L., and Karen M. Inouye. "Visual Games and the Unseeing of Race in the Late Nineteenth Century." *American Quarterly* 68, no. 2 (2016): 287–313.

Rowland, Ingrid. *The Ecstatic Journey: Athanius Kircher in Baroque Rome*. Chicago: University of Chicago Press, 2000.

Rushing, W. Jackson. "Marketing the Affinity of the Primitive and the Modern: René d'Harnoncourt and Indian Art of the United States." In *The Early Years of Native American Art History*, edited by Janet Catherine Berlo, 191–236. Seattle: University of Washington Press, 1992.

Rydell, Robert. "Visions of Empire: International Expositions in Portland and Seattle, 1905–1909." *Pacific Historical Review* 52, no. 1 (1983): 37–65.

Rydell, Robert, and Rob Kroes. *Buffalo Bill in Bologna: The Americanization of the World, 1869–1922*. Chicago: University of Chicago Press, 2005.

Said, Edward S. *Orientalism*. New York: Vintage, 2014.

Salenius, Sirpa. "Introduction." In *Sculptors, Painters, and Italy: Italian Influence on Nineteenth-Century American Art*, edited by Sirpa Salenius, 5–18. Padua: Il Prato, 2009.

Sánchez-Gómez, Luis A. "Human Zoos or Ethnic Shows? Essence and Contingency in Living Ethnological Exhibitions." *Culture and History Digital Journal* 2, no. 2 (2013): e022. https://cultureandhistory.revistas.csic.es/index.php/cultureandhistory/article/view/31/122.

Sánchez-Gómez, Luis A. "Imperial Faith and Catholic Missions in the Grand Exhibitions of the 'Estado Novo.'" *Análise Social* 44 (2009): 671–92.

Sánchez-Gómez, Luis A. "Por la etnología hacia Dios: la exposición Misional Vaticana de 1925." *Revista de Dialectología y Tradiciones Populares* 2 (2007): 63–107.

Sayre, Gordon M. "The Mound Builders and the Imagination of American Antiquity in Jefferson, Bartram, and Chateaubriand." *Early American Literature* 33, no. 3 (1998): 225–49.

Scheckel, Susan. *The Insistence of the Indian: Race and Nationalism in Nineteenth-Century American Culture*. Princeton, NJ: Princeton University Press, 1998.

Schwarz, Augustine. "For the Vatican Missionary Exposition." *Indian Sentinel*, October 1924, 188.

Schweitzer, Ivy. "Introduction: The Afterlives of Indigenous Archives." In *Afterlives of Indigenous Archives: Essays in Honor of the Occom Circle*, edited by Ivy Schweitzer and Gordon Henry, 1–20. Hanover, NH: Dartmouth College Press, 2019.

Schweitzer, Ivy, and Gordon Henry, eds. *Afterlives of Indigenous Archives: Essays in Honor of the Occom Circle*. Hanover, NH: Dartmouth College Press, 2019.

"Seeking Equality Abroad." *New York Times*, December 29, 1878, 5.

Sekula, Allan. "The Body and the Archive." *October* 39 (1986): 3–64.

Senier, Siobhan. "Digitizing Indigenous History: Trends and Challenges." *Journal of Victorian Culture* 19, no. 3 (2014): 396–402.

Seth, Vanita. *Europe's Indians: Producing Racial Difference, 1500–1900*. Durham, NC: Duke University Press, 2010.

Sharpe, Jenny. *Allegories of Empire: The Figure of Woman in the Colonial Text*. Minneapolis: University of Minnesota Press, 1993.

Shaw, Gwendolyn DuBois. *Portraits of a People: Picturing African Americans in the Nineteenth Century*. Seattle: University of Washington Press, 2006.

Shelton, Anthony. "The Imaginary Southwest: Commodity Disavowal in an American Orient." In *Les cultures à l'oeuvre: Rencontres en art*, edited by Michèle Coquet, Brigitte Derlon, and Monique Jeudy-Ballini, 75–96. Paris: Maison des Sciences de l'Homme, 2005.

Silberman, Robert. "Complexity and Contradiction in Native American Surrealism." *Journal of Surrealism and the Americas* 7, no 1 (2013): 108–30.

Smith, Donald B. *Mississauga Portraits: Ojibwe Voices from Nineteenth-Century Canada*. Toronto: University of Toronto Press, 2013.

Sòrgoni, Barbara. "'Defending the Race': The Italian Reinvention of the Hottentot Venus during Fascism." *Journal of Modern Italian Studies* 8, no. 3 (2003): 411–24.

Standing Bear, Luther. *My People the Sioux*. Lincoln: University of Nebraska Press, 1975.

Stausberg, Michael. "Raffaele Pettazzoni and the History of Religions in Fascist Italy, 1928–1938." In *The Study of Religion under the Impact of Fascism*, edited by Horst Junginger, 365–96. Leiden: Brill, 2008.

Stefanovich, Olivia. "Inuit Leader Says Vatican Museums Open to Repatriating Indigenous Artifacts." CBC News, March 30, 2022. https://www.cbc.ca/news/politics/vatican-museums-indigenous-repatriation-1.6402182.

Stehle, R. L. "Ferdinand Pettrich in America." *Pennsylvania History* 33, no. 4 (1966): 389–411.

Stevens, Scott Manning. "Collectors and Museums: From Cabinets of Curiosities to Indigenous Cultural Centers." In *The Oxford Handbook of American Indian History*, edited by Frederick Hoxie, 475–96. New York: Oxford University Press, 2016.

Stocking, George W. *The Ethnographer's Magic and Other Essays in the History of Anthropology*. Madison: University of Wisconsin Press, 1992.

Stoler, Ann Laura. *Along the Archival Grain: Epistemic Anxieties and Colonial Common Sense*. Princeton, NJ: Princeton University Press, 2010.

Streit, Robert. *Catholic Missions in Figures and Symbols: Based on the Vatican Missionary Exhibition*. N.p.: Society for the Propagation of the Faith, 1927.

Sugden, John. *Tecumseh: A Life*. New York: Henry Holt and Company, 1999.

Sugden, John. *Tecumseh's Last Stand*. Norman: University of Oklahoma Press, 1985.

Sweet, James H. "Reimagining the African-Atlantic Archive: Method, Concept, Epistemology, Ontology." *Journal of African History* 55, no. 2 (2014): 147–59.

Tecumseh. "'Father! Listen to Your Children!' September 18, 1813." In *Great Speeches of Native Americans*, edited by Bob Blaisdell, 61–62. Mineola, NY: Dover, 2000.

Testore, Celestino. "L'Evangelizzazione degli Esquimesi intorno alla Baia di Hudson." *Rivista Illustrata della Esposizione Missionaria Vaticana*, June 30, 1925, 433–38.

Thomas, Nicholas. *Entangled Objects: Exchange, Material Culture, and Colonialism in the Pacific*. Cambridge, MA: Harvard University Press, 1991.

Thomas, R. Murray. *Manitou and God: North American Religions and Christian Culture*. Westport, CT: Greenwood, 2007.

Tindall, George Brown, and David E. Shi. *America: A Narrative History*. New York: Norton, 2016.

Todd, Zoe, and Crystal Fraser. "Decolonial Sensibilities: Indigenous Research and Engaging with Archives in Contemporary Colonial Canada." *L'Internationale*, February 15, 2016. https://www.internationaleonline.org/research/decolonising_practices/54_decolonial_sensibilities_indigenous_research_and_engaging_with_archives_in_contemporary_colonial_canada/.

Torre, Paolo Dalla. "Le plastiche a soggetto indigeno nordamericano del Pettrich nel Pontificio Museo Missionario Etnologico." *Annali Lateranensi* 4 (1940): 9–96.

"To Show Church Scientific: Pope Pius Plans Exhibit on This Line for Jubilee Year." *New York Times*, July 24, 1923, 5.

Trébaol, Goalven. "Les Oblats à l'Exposition des Missions." *Missions de la Congrégation des Missionnaires Oblats de Marie Immaculée* (1925): 58–70.

Trennert, Robert A. "Fairs, Expositions, and the Changing Image of Southwestern Indians, 1876–1904." *New Mexico Historical Review* 62 (1987): 127–50.

Trevithick, Scott R. "Conflicting Outlooks: The Background to the 1924 Deposing of the Six Nations Hereditary Council." MA thesis, University of Calgary, 1998.

Truth and Reconciliation Commission (Canada). *They Came for the Children: Canada, Aboriginal Peoples, and Residential Schools*. Truth and Reconciliation Commission, 2012. https://publications.gc.ca/collections/collection_2012/cvrc-trcc/IR4-4-2012-eng.pdf.

Tuck, Eve, and K. Wayne Yang. "Decolonization Is Not a Metaphor." *Tabula Rasa* 38 (2021): 61–111.

Tufts, Elenor. "Edmonia Lewis, Afro-Indian Neo-Classicist." *Art in America*, July-August 1974, 71–72.

Vargaftig, Nadia. "Les expositions coloniales sous Salazar et Mussolini (1930–1940)." *Vingtième Siècle: Revue d'Histoire* 4 (2010): 39–52.

"Vatican Exhibition Is Taking Shape: Pavilions to Cost 6,000,000 Lire." *New York Times*, September 7, 1924.

"The Vatican Missionary Exhibition." *Catholic Historical Review* 11 (1925): 155–73.

Veatch, Richard. *Canadian Policy and the League of Nations, 1919–1939*. Toronto: University of Toronto Press, 1975.

Venturi, Tacchi. "Il Padre Giacomo Marquette ardito esploratore del Mississippi." *Rivista Illustrata della Esposizione Missionaria Vaticana*, October 31, 1925, 698–704.

Veracini, Lorenzo. *Settler Colonialism*. Basingstoke: Palgrave Macmillan, 2010.

Vimalassery, Manu, Juilana Hu Pegues, and Alyosha Goldstein. "Colonial Unknowing and Relations of Study." *Theory and Event* 20, no. 4 (2017): 1042–54.

Viola, Herman J. *Diplomats in Buckskin: A History of Indian Delegations in Washington City*. Revised ed. Norman: University of Oklahoma Press, 1995.

Vizenor, Gerald. "Aesthetics of Survivance: Literary Theory and Practice." In *Survivance: Narratives of Native Presence*, edited by Gerald Vizenor, 1–24. Lincoln: University of Nebraska Press, 2008.

Voelker, Emily L. "Unfixing the Frame: Visualizing Histories of Transcultural Contact, Exchange and Performance in Prince Roland Bonaparte's *Peaux-Rouges* (1884)." *Transatlantica. Revue d'études américaines/American Studies Journal* 2 (2017): 1–26.

Watson, Scott. "The Modernist Past of Lawrence Paul Yuxweluptun's Landscape Allegories." In *Born to Live and Die on Your Colonialist Reservations*, edited by Charlotte

Townsend-Gault, Scott Watson, and Lawrence Paul Yuxweluptun, 61–71. Vancouver: Morris and Helen Belkin Art Gallery, University of British Columbia, 1995.

Weaver, Jace. *Native American Religious Identity: Unforgotten Gods*. Maryknoll, NY: Orbis, 1998.

Webster, Gloria Cranmer. "From Colonization to Repatriation." In *Indigena: Contemporary Native Perspectives*, edited by Gerald McMaster and Lee-Ann Martin, 25–37. Vancouver: Douglas and McIntyre, 1992.

"The Wembley Pageant 'Westward Ho!': An Empire History Object-Lesson." *Times of India*, September 3, 1924, 5.

Wheeler, Winona. "The Journals and Voices of a Church of England Native Catechist: Askenootow (Charles Pratt), 1851–1884." In *Reading beyond Words: Contexts for Native History*, 2nd ed., edited by Jennifer S. H. Brown and Elizabeth Vibert, 304–29. Toronto: University of Toronto Press, 2003.

Wernitznig, Dagmar. *Europe's Indians, Indians in Europe: Europe's Perceptions and Appropriations of Native American Cultures from Pocahontas to the Present*. Lanham, MD: University Press of America, 2007.

Whitecalf, Sarah. *Kinêhiyâwiwininaw nêhiyawêwin = The Cree Language Is Our Identity: The La Ronge Lectures of Sarah Whitecalf*. Winnipeg: University of Manitoba Press, 1993.

Wilson, Shawn. *Research Is Ceremony: Indigenous Research Methods*. Black Point, Nova Scotia: Fernwood, 2008.

Witgen, Michael. "American Indians in World History." In *The Oxford Handbook of American Indian History*, edited by Frederick Hoxie, 591–614. New York: Oxford University Press, 2016.

Woolford, Andrew. *This Benevolent Experiment: Indigenous Boarding Schools, Genocide, and Redress in Canada and the United States*. Lincoln: University of Nebraska Press, 2015.

Wreford, Henry. "A Negro Sculptress." *Athenaeum*, no. 2001, March 3, 1866, 302.

Wrightson, Kelsey Radcliffe. "Shattering Glass Boxes: Museums and Dene Resurgence against the Colonial Politics of Recognition." PhD diss., University of British Columbia, 2016.

Index

Page locators in italics indicate figures; plate (pl.) numbers indicate plates.